UNBUILDING JERUSALEM

STEVEN GOLDSMITH

Unbuilding Jerusalem

APOCALYPSE AND ROMANTIC
REPRESENTATION

Cornell University Press

ITHACA AND LONDON

First published 1993 by Cornell University Press.

International Standard Book Number 0-8014-2717-7 (cloth)
International Standard Book Number 0-8014-9999-2 (paper)
Library of Congress Catalog Card Number 92-27066
Printed in the United States of America
Librarians: Library of Congress cataloging information
appears on the last page of the book.

∞ The paper in this book meets the minimum requirements of the
American National Standard for Information Sciences—Permanence
of Paper for Printed Library Materials, ANSI Z39.48-1984.

To the Friends in Philadelphia, 1981–1986

CONTENTS

ILLUSTRATIONS

PREFACE

In 1985, when I began the work that evolved into this book, the year 2000 seemed reasonably far away, and apocalypse was the last thing on my mind. Investigating religious discourse after Milton in the British Library, I experienced some uncertainty about the vagueness of my topic, but I felt no fin-de-siècle malaise. The amount of time it has taken to finish this book will assure the reader that I did not feel any hint of apocalyptic urgency. Instead, what initially drew me to apocalyptic literature was the sense that these writings, by describing the end of history, articulated a relation between the textual and the historical that has ideologically shaped our understandings of literature. That idea remains the cornerstone of the book. As time passed, however, the greatest appeal of studying apocalypse became the subject's capacity to accommodate whatever mattered to me most. It would be too grandiose to call apocalypse "the story of all things," as Northrop Frye called epic, but it is only honest to say that apocalypse speaks to far more things than I initially anticipated.

In this spirit of inclusiveness, I wish to say a few preliminary words about the central terms of this study: *apocalypse* and *representation*. *Apocalypse* can mean many things: a particular text (the Book of Revelation); a biblical and intertestamental genre that includes many texts; the eschatological events that occur at the end of history; an internal, psychological event usually referred to as a *revelation* or an *epiphany;* and in the most general usage, any catastrophe that seems incommensurable. Although at times I use the word narrowly in a single sense, I am especially interested in the ways in which the various meanings intersect, for at those points of intersection one sees most vividly the relation between formal literary features (defining text and genre) and the actions a book accomplishes or sets out to accomplish in the world. In the constellation of definitions that includes a single book, a genre, and eschatological events, for example, one begins to see that the idea that history can come to an end (the most basic assumption of apocalyptic literature, the assumption upon which its authority rests) was not articulated until there existed textual forms that were themselves considered to be independent of history. In other words, the idea of textual form and the idea of eschatology are mutually implicated; to treat them separately would be to impose artificial limits on discussion. Moreover, the Book of Revelation did not generate this point of intersection between text and eschatology from scratch; John's text is entirely dependent on the prior existence of a genre of sacred texts in the Hebrew canon which had already been made to seem independent of history. Thus text, genre, and eschatology converge in a way that can be examined only by removing each definition of apocalypse from an isolated treatment.

Representation may have even more meanings than *apocalypse*. It can refer broadly to any system of signs by which something absent is made present in another form; it can refer specifically to the relation between a governing body and its constituents. Again, I focus on the points of intersection—where (primarily verbal) forms become identified with certain kinds of action in the world. Although at some moments I use *representation* in an exclusively aesthetic sense and at other times in an exclusively political sense, when I turn to romanticism I am more often concerned with how these meanings converge in unexpected ways, with how an aesthetic practice becomes indistinguishable (or seems to become indistinguishable) from a political practice.

In an uncharacteristically defiant moment, Mary Shelley once declared of *Frankenstein*, "I did not owe the suggestion of one incident, nor scarcely of one train of feeling, to my husband." Contrary to this declaration of independence, I take great pleasure in recognizing that practically every idea in this book I owe in some way to someone. I begin with two people who, over the years, have become my "ideal readers." They might be surprised to hear it, but in the isolation of my office I write with them in mind. Because Marjorie Levinson took my work seriously, I began to do so; there cannot be a more probing and sympathetic reader. Her example, her interest, and her encouragement have been indispensable. I would never have thought it especially conducive to good fortune to be someone who likes to eat a late lunch, but so it was at the National Humanities Center in 1990–1991. My timing consistently put me at the same table as Gordon Teskey, and thus early in our residence began the conversations and friendship that provoked, sustained, and delighted me. I owe Gordon thanks for many more tangible things, but it is the intellectual fellowship I appreciate most.

At Berkeley, I have benefited from the critical acumen of colleagues who read individual chapters and sometimes the entire manuscript: Elizabeth Abel, Carolyn Dinshaw, Catherine Gallagher, David Lloyd, and Morton Paley. I especially thank Mitch Breitwieser and Sue Schweik. Not only did Mitch read the whole book, offering critical insight and encouragement, he also introduced me to *Trouble in Mind* just when I needed it. Sue's warmth and intelligence were the first things I came to know at Berkeley; they have provided undiminished sustenance ever since. I thank Scott Dykstra for his steady assistance in preparing the final manuscript and for his all-around court sense. I also thank Mills College, which opened its beautiful new library just when I no longer had a quiet place to work at home. Yes, that unshaved stranger who came in on nonteaching days and weekends really was writing a book.

I am grateful to Bernhard Kendler at Cornell University Press for being invariably responsible and considerate, and to Teresa Jesionowski for her fine attention in copyediting. I also thank Morris Eaves, whose careful readings of the manuscript made it a better work. A shorter version of Chapter 5 originally appeared in the *Yale Journal of Criticism* 4.1 (1990): 129–73; I thank the editorial board of the journal for its assertive encouragement.

This book would have been impossible to write without the assistance of several grants. A University of California President's Fellowship helped support a yearlong sabbatical leave; a Berkeley campus grant helped support a one-semester leave. The National Endowment for the Humanities provided a summer stipend. I spent a year at the National Humanities Center thanks in part to a fellowship funded by the Delta Delta Delta sorority, and I cannot imagine what this book would look like if I had not done so. The opportunity for unpressured contemplation, the support of the superb staff, and the sheer enjoyment of discussion in a sunny room all contributed to this book in ways impossible to measure. For these things I will always be grateful. In particular, I thank Leon Fink, Helena Goscilo, Shirley Samuels, Mark Seltzer, and Geoffrey Stewart for their valuable responses to my project, and Nan Martin, whose spirited conversation made highway travel a pleasure, even in the morning. I also thank Geoffrey Harpham, whose phone call relieved the dreary February of that year; I won't forget that unobligated act of kindness.

Despite all the support I have received in recent years, I reserve my most enduring gratitude for a debt that goes back further. I have dedicated this book to the friends Cathy and I made in Philadelphia between 1981 and 1986. At that time, Stuart Curran established a standard of scholarly excellence and generosity that has left an indelible mark on my writing and my teaching. Michael Awkward, Victoria Carchidi, Peter

Dorsey, Chris Flint, Celeste Langan, Pidge Molyneaux, Joe Valente, Athena Vrettos, Tom Yingling, and many others created a moment of communal affection and intellectual excitement that I don't expect to see equaled. Many of these friends directly influenced this book by responding to one or more of its parts; all of them have entered into its life. If the spirit of that enabling community could be embodied in one person, it might well take the form of Tom Yingling, with his lively intelligence, his love of language, and his irresistible good nature. Many years ago, he read the earliest draft of what has become Chapters 1 and 2 of this book; his sharp instincts prevailed, and the suggestions he made then (which he might no longer remember) have found their way into the finished work. I also thank Celeste Langan, who, in Philadelphia, in London, and now in Berkeley, has been something like the touchstone of this project. At no point could I have done without her great mind and heart—so much has she given me, my work, and my family.

Both my parents are teachers by profession. Modifying the dedication my father wrote to my mother for his book on the Golem, I first thank them for teaching me that my heritage could withstand difficult questions. Arnold Goldsmith retired in 1992 after nearly four decades of teaching American literature at Wayne State University. As only he can really know, he is the "origin" of this book. The unwavering support Gladys Goldsmith has given me, even when my interests have surprised her, has been a source of continuous pleasure and much needed reassurance. I thank both parents for teaching me the things that matter.

To Cathy it often must have seemed that this study of the end of the world would never end. Eight years, four cities, and two children later, I can only partially relieve the inadequacy of words by thanking her for the judgment, the love, and the heroically unapocalyptic patience that saw me through these years and, more than that, made them the joyful adventure of two friends. Finally, it may seem odd to thank a four-year-old and a one-year-old for their contributions to a book of this sort, but I must admit I have done all my best work since the arrival first of Samuel Palmer Goldsmith and later of Joel Palmer Goldsmith. I cannot explain the correlation.

STEVEN GOLDSMITH

Berkeley, California

Tom Yingling died on July 28, 1992. In the words of the poet we both loved: "There are no stars to-night / But those of memory."

UNBUILDING JERUSALEM

APOCALYPSE WITHOUT CONTENT

> But obviously a lot of people do trust prophecy, or at least find it fascinating. For some, it may be only a religious equivalent to Nostradamus or Jeane Dixon. For others, it can exercise the same attraction as any complex intellectual puzzle. Those immersed in the Bible can enjoy the delights that Marxism or French literary theory offers others.
>
> *New York Times* (February 2, 1991)

Late in the twentieth century, as we hasten toward the end of another Christian millennium, perhaps it is unremarkable that a front-page article in a major American newspaper should associate end-of-the-world prophecy with high academic gamesmanship, casually remarking the entertainment value of playing any Rubik's cube of images. Detached from anything that might be considered "real," referring not to cataclysmic events but to its own intricately enigmatic words, apocalyptic literature can be made a pleasurable refuge from violence, just as a good crossword puzzle offers welcome distraction from the anxieties of front-page news. Appearing two weeks into the televised 1991 air assault against Iraq (formerly Babylon), a *New York Times* article titled "Gulf War Proving Bountiful for Some Prophets of Doom" documented with a distinctly secular curiosity the sudden new life of Armageddon studies in Christian bookstores. With the weight of a war upon them—and with the specter of fundamentalism before them—nonbelieving readers must have been momentarily amused to consider the possibility of an innocuous, purely formal apocalypse, a fascinating game of signs that, rather than representing the end of the world, becomes a mesmerizing end in itself.

It is hard to say whether a newspaper article's offhand, even whimsical, analogy tells more about biblical apocalypse or the aesthetic pleasures of high theory—be it French, Marxist, or otherwise. By crossing the two discourses, however, it manages to hit a certain cultural mark. From the earliest apocalyptic texts of Judeo-Christian Scripture to the experiments with apocalyptic representation by romantic writers, and on to various rhetorical strands within postmodernism itself, the idea of the end of history has often been bound up with the promise of an *aesthetic* space relieved of historical determinants. It is in this sense that one might call "apocalyptic" any locus or activity (textual, cognitive, or metaphysical) in which historical contingency is not supposed to figure significantly, in which, in other words, history is said to have come to an end. And one might go further: the coupling of apocalyptic desire and aesthetic desire in Western culture has often served to deflect our ability to think either of the two terms historically. From the truncated spectrum of prophetic possibilities offered by the *Times* article (deadpan fundamentalism or liberated intellectualism), the option most conspicuously absent has historically had a powerful impact on our world: namely, political apocalypse, or millenarianism. In the tradition unmentioned by the *Times*, apocalyptic representations function neither as self-referential symbolic forms nor as strictly theological truth claims but rather as cultural agents that work within history to promote or suppress social change. By claiming to transcend or to be unconcerned with mere politics, aesthetic apocalypse encourages its own readers to forget the long, often turbulent past of millenarianism and thus manages to subordinate or even to erase its rival tradition. Even in the *Times* article, the subtle process of depoliticizing the apocalypse is evident the moment the reporter equates Marxism and French literary theory, making both the interchangeable analogues of an apocalypse defined by pleasurable formalism, by disengagement from the actual.

The *Times* article symptomatically echoes the pervasive contemporary association between apocalypse and aestheticization (and the accompanying subordination of politics) that has become a set piece of some much-discussed postmodern discourse. If Fredric Jameson is right in considering the "loss of historicity," or "the matter of historical deafness," to be the primary feature of postmodern culture, then the recourse of postmodern writers to the language of formal apocalypse seems appropriate, if not inevitable. In the age of the image, we are told, history and the world have already ended, replaced by the depthlessness, the superficial and eclectic nominalism of so many simulacra. Postmodernism, writes Jameson, involves "a quantum leap in what Walter Benjamin still called the 'aestheticization' of reality," and, with some detotalizing modifications, *apocalypse* remains the privileged term to describe the passage from historical depth to aesthetic surfaces.[1] History lies behind us, but we have not entered the New Jerusalem promised by outworn, "anorexic" teleologies; we instead remain suspended in the fractured space of a perpetual present, the space of excessive, discon-

---

[1] Fredric Jameson, *Postmodernism, or, The Cultural Logic of Late Capitalism* (Durham: Duke University Press, 1991), x–xi.

tinuous, and exhausted signs. In his contribution to a volume aptly titled *Looking Back on the End of the World,* Jean Baudrillard suggests that we now experience apocalypse, the catastrophe of unreality, "in slow motion." Moreover, we can do nothing but watch with fascination the spectacle of continuous anticlimax.

> It is as if the poles of our world were converging, and this merciless short circuit manifests both overproduction *and* the exhaustion of potential energies at the same time. It is no longer a matter of crisis but of disaster, a catastrophe in slow motion.
>
> The real crisis lies in the fact that policies no longer permit this dual political game of hope and metaphorical promise. The pole of reckoning, dénouement, and apocalypse (in the good and bad sense of the word), which we had been able to postpone until the infiniteness of the Day of Judgment, this pole has come infinitely closer, and one could join Canetti in saying that we have already passed it unawares and now find ourselves in the situation of having overextended our own finalities, of having shortcircuited our own perspectives, and of already being in the hereafter, that is, without horizon and without hope. . . .
>
> Nevertheless, do not panic. Everything has already become nuclear, faraway, vaporized. The explosion has already occurred; the bomb is only a metaphor now. What more do you want? Everything has already been wiped off the map. It is useless to dream: the *clash* has gently taken place everywhere.[2]

This passage displays all the flair of a contemporary Jeremiad, but only the flair; detached from political incentive, *apocalypse* has become the choice rhetorical term to describe the flattening and emptying of experience. In this sense, postmodernism literally represents a state of unpredictability, meaning not so much a condition of random chance but of the impossibility of prediction, the impossibility of prophecy in a post-historical culture where events no longer occur. "The year 2000, in a certain way, will not take place," writes Baudrillard. Arriving as the nondescript turning of another calendar page, the millennium will be indistinguishable from the ongoing, narcotic present. And to complete a rewriting of apocalypse that preserves the term's aesthetic affiliation while erasing its capacity to function historically or politically as an agent of change, Baudrillard advocates that we cultivate "reciprocal indifference," an intellectual detachment in which we knowingly regard the

---

[2] Jean Baudrillard, "The Anorexic Ruins," in *Looking Back on the End of the World,* ed. Dietmar Kamper and Christoph Wulf, trans. David Antal (New York: Semiotext(e), 1989), 33–34.

overstimulation of our unmillennial kingdom "without illusion, without bitterness, and without violence."[3]

How, one must wonder, did apocalypse become so acquiescent, forfeiting its combative edge to become "a very modest or mild apocalypse, the merest sea breeze," as Jameson puts it?[4] How did it ever become an intellectual puzzle that exercises attraction? The postmodern apocalypse is not as new as it claims to be, something evident not only in the fact that—like all cranky apocalypses—it complains about the degenerate state of affairs. The postmodern apocalypse belongs to an old habit of privileging aesthetic concerns over history and politics, an old habit of elevating form above content, that links it not only to some aspects of modernism and romanticism but even to tensions within the earliest apocalyptic texts themselves. In this book I set out to ask why it has become so difficult to think of apocalyptic representations historically and why the idea of an apolitical aesthetic has exercised such compelling power over our understandings of apocalyptic literature. More specifically, I ask the following question of certain texts that attempt to aestheticize the apocalypse: What historical functions are served when a text represents the end of history in this way?

In addressing these questions, I have not considered the many sociological and historical studies of millenarianism as an antidote to formal apocalypse, though such studies have strongly influenced my arguments and the history of millenarian movements is always a necessary context. Instead, I investigate here what might be called the obverse side of millenarianism, the political purposes served by the claims of an apocalyptic aesthetic to have transcended politics just as it claims to have transcended history. Adapting Jerome McGann's principle for reading romantic literature, I want to ask what these apocalyptic representations *do* in *saying* what they say.[5] Much of my analysis thus focuses on the internal claims of apocalyptic texts, on the ways in which their formal, generic features themselves function as political vectors, as normative forces at particular moments—even when these formal features are meant to signify a text's transcendence of historical situation altogether. The authority of an apocalyptic text often depends on how effectively it can make its literary form seem separable from, even antithetical to, historical contingencies. My first assumption, then, is that the exagger-

---

[3] Ibid., 39, 42. For a discussion of the role of "indifference" in the new "aesthetic consciousness" of postmodernism, see Klaus R. Scherpe's "Dramatization and Dedramatization of 'The End': The Apocalyptic Consciousness of Modernity and Post-Modernity," *Cultural Critique* 5 (Winter 1986/87): 95–129.

[4] Jameson, *Postmodernism*, xiv.

[5] Jerome McGann, *Social Values and Poetic Acts: The Historical Judgment of Literary Work* (Cambridge: Harvard University Press, 1988), viii.

ated formalism of these texts is an ideological marker, a primary sign of their motivated participation in historical circumstance. Apocalyptic works represent an especially lucid and influential instance of what Jameson has generally called "autonomization," the process by which a generic form, in certain circumstances, becomes differentiated from the social world in which it originates and comes to seem autonomous. "Genre is itself a social institution," writes Jameson. "Far from proving the autonomy of the work of art, therefore, the very existence of generic convention explains how an illusion of autonomy could come into being, for the generic situation formalizes and thus absorbs into the formal structure worldly elements that could otherwise be passed on in the work of art itself, as content." When the genre concerned is apocalypse, with its vested interest in maintaining strict dualisms, reading form is necessarily a way of apprehending historical content. By attending to "the worldliness of form," one can begin to resist the self-authorizing claim of the apocalyptic text to have left the world behind, in ashes—its claim, in other words, to have originated beyond the parameters of worldliness itself.[6]

Paradoxically, the very source of radical millenarianism, the Book of Revelation, is also a primary source of rival claims to postpolitical, post-historical representation. From the latter perspective, John's Apocalypse describes how the end of history and the appearance of an ideal form occur simultaneously, how time stops with the revelation of a utopian architectural space, the New Jerusalem of monumental and perfect symmetry. The tension between the text's millenarian and aesthetic imperatives, a tension between the competing claims to authority of prophecy and canon, plays itself out across subsequent apocalyptic literatures, and perhaps nowhere more so than in the contradictions of romanticism. Most of this book attempts to specify that tension by tracking its manifestations in some particular and widely separated historical circumstances, ranging from biblical contexts to the early nineteenth century. Here, however, I want to attend more generally to the lingering role played by apocalypse in modern criticism and theory. Since the time of romanticism's well-chronicled adventure with apocalyptic themes and forms, a dominant strain of literary and cultural interpretation has tended to reproduce the imperatives of formal apocalypse by minimizing the role of history in its investigations. Such critical practices enact figuratively what the Book of Revelation imagines will occur literally—the displacement of history. Since midcentury *apocalypse* has become a favorite term for hypostatizing a variety of essentially

⁶ Fredric Jameson, "Beyond the Cave," in *Ideologies of Theory* (Minneapolis: University of Minnesota Press, 1988), 2:116.

ahistorical phenomena: literature itself, consciousness, écriture, textualité, Baudrillard's culture of the simulacrum, and so on. One might even say that *apocalypse*, a word that seems irresistibly to attract monumental generalizations, has become a privileged term for the multiple forms of ahistoricity. Before I propose some alternatives to this understanding of apocalypse, with its more or less deliberate nullification of politics, and before I outline the shape of this book, I will begin by briefly considering how apocalypse has become theoretically entangled with the idea of an ahistorical or even antihistorical aesthetic we sometimes still attribute to romanticism.

Toward the end of his essay "On the Sublime" (1793), Friedrich Schiller confronts the problem of history that has silently hovered about his description of the sublime as an apocalyptic experience, as a "revelation" that occurs "suddenly and by a shock" in order to disclose to the spirit "its true destination, and to oblige it to conceive, for one instant at least, the feeling of its liberty."[7] Throughout the essay, Schiller's orientation toward an ideal future has worked to distance a particular past, the French Revolution, which he mentions only in veiled but nearly transparent terms, as when he cautions against those beautiful and inevitably disillusioned minds "aspiring always to find their moral ideal realised in the world of facts" (131–32). Just before discussing history directly, he again critiques a similar type—the one "who has never any other thought than to reform [the world's] defiant disorder and to substitute harmony" (139). For Schiller, the problem with these stock reformers is that by making history their medium, they have also made their ideas vulnerable to contingencies, to the unforeseeable accidents that lead necessarily to compromise and often to outright failure. History, with its ironclad disappointments, is the problem the sublime must resolve. So when Schiller finally makes history an explicit topic of discussion, it is hardly surprising that he has already distanced himself from it significantly, treating not the French Revolution or any other historical event but "history" as an abstraction, a form with only generalized contents. In other words, by the time he can say, "The world, as a historic object, is only the strife of natural forces" (140), he has already demonstrated the intellectual power to abstract oneself out of history, and thus he has already demonstrated the primary function he assigns to the "*aesthetic tendency*" (130) awakened by the sublime. True liberty, in which the spirit achieves an absolute immunity from external constraint and vio-

---

[7] Friedrich Schiller, "On the Sublime," in *Essays Aesthetical and Philosophical*, unacknowledged translation (London: George Bell and Sons, 1879), 136. Further references are to this edition.

lence, or what Harold Bloom will simply call "influence," requires an apocalyptic release from history altogether: "Nature, in being capricious and defying logic, in pulling down great and little, in crushing the noblest works of man, taking centuries to form—nature, by deviating from intellectual laws, proves that you cannot explain nature by nature's laws *themselves*, and this *sight* drives the mind to the world of ideas, to the absolute" (Schiller, 140; second emphasis mine). The way to end the natural history of disappointment, the way to the millennial kingdom of Kantian Ideas, lies through the aesthetic, just as in the quoted passage violent and undirected change has already been made a "sight," a spectacle, an image through which the mind concentrates itself but to which it is no longer subject. "By frequently renewing this exercise of its own activity, the mind controls the sensuous, so that when real misfortune comes, it can treat it as an artificial suffering, and make it a sublime emotion" (141). Suffering ends in the freedom provided by the aesthetic, and that freedom is literally, almost reductively, apocalyptic in that it means *freedom from history.*

In Schiller we can observe the two features of formal apocalypse that in various ways will persist for the next two centuries. First, Schiller's aesthetic represents the power to end the grip of history, to render it negligible; consequently, his version of "apocalypse" makes obsolete and thus displaces the need for political apocalypse. Apocalyptic rhetoric is simply no longer an agent of historical change; in fact, Schiller can proclaim, "Happy he who learns to bear what he cannot change!" (141). Not surprisingly, as various critics have recently emphasized, Schiller's aesthetic represents not only a utopian critique of modern, industrial society but also an ideological accommodation to it.[8] In the form of the aesthetic, apocalypse now represents a space apart from history, a space which makes available in the present the freedom of the Kantian telos. And yet, because it is utterly without historical content, because it is by definition the very opposite of historical particularity, the aesthetic is also an empty space, a merely general form that purchases its peculiar liberty by sacrificing its substance. What Terry Eagleton has called the "sheer suggestive nothingness," "the nirvanic suspension," of Schiller's aesthetic becomes vividly evident the moment we turn our attention from the sublime to the beautiful, or to what the *Aesthetic Education of Man* calls "living form."[9] Only in the aesthetic state, claims Schiller, do we experience infinite human potentiality, because only there are we

[8] Terry Eagleton, *The Ideology of the Aesthetic* (Oxford: Blackwell, 1990), 102–19; David Lloyd, "Arnold, Ferguson, Schiller: Aesthetic Culture and the Politics of Aesthetics," *Cultural Critique* 2 (Winter 1985–86): 161–69; John Brenkman, *Culture and Domination* (Ithaca: Cornell University Press, 1987), 63–68.

[9] Eagleton, *Ideology of the Aesthetic*, 107–8.

relieved of the determinants that reduce us to particular historical beings acting out the special interests required by particular historical
circumstances.

> True, [a man] possesses this humanity *in potentia* before every determinate
> condition into which he can conceivably enter. But he loses it in practice
> with every determinate condition into which he does enter. . . . Every other
> way of exercising its functions endows the psyche with some special apti-
> tude—but only at the cost of some special limitation. . . . Every other state
> into which we can enter refers us back to a preceding one, and requires for
> its termination a subsequent one; the aesthetic alone is a whole in itself,
> since it comprises within itself all the conditions of both its origin and its
> continuance. Here alone do we feel reft out of time, and our human
> nature expresses itself with purity and integrity, as though it had as yet
> suffered no impairment through the intervention of external forces.[10]

Every time we act we exercise only the limited portion of our faculties
required by the demands of transient circumstance; we never transcend
the vagrant life of a fraction. In the aesthetic state, however, we experience whole, uncompromised possibility, a freedom from having to
participate in history. Schiller's aesthetic is primarily an apocalypse of
glorious inaction. "Reft out of time," the self-referential space of the
apocalyptic aesthetic ("a whole in itself") is doomed to a mere formalism,
for its utopian mirage evaporates the instant one *does* anything. In a way
that anticipates a dominant strain of postromantic criticism, the conjoin-
ing of apocalypse and the aesthetic in Schiller's account relegates both to
a kind of spectacular irrelevance, an exhilarating but uneventful existence that has been made incompatible not simply with politics but with
any type of positive agency.

The translation of formal apocalypse into the work of modern criticism is perhaps best exemplified in the work of Northrop Frye, whose
postulation of "a self-contained literary universe" and of an anagogic
reading experience in which "we have moved into the still center of the
order of words" is an epic variation on Schiller's aesthetic.[11] Like Schiller,
Frye saw culture as the means by which autotelic human form detaches
itself from the weight of circumstantial content, shedding all external
and particular determinants to become "a total vision of possibilities"
(127), a perpetual potentiality as capacious and finally as inoperative as

---

[10] Friedrich Schiller, *On the Aesthetic Education of Man*, ed. and trans. Elizabeth M.
Wilkinson and L. A. Willoughby (Oxford: Clarendon, 1967), 147–51.

[11] Northrop Frye, *Anatomy of Criticism* (Princeton: Princeton University Press, 1957),
117–18. Further references are to this edition.

Schiller's. "At the center of liberal education," Frye argued in *Anatomy of Criticism*, "something surely ought to get liberated" (93), suggesting that the "self-contained literary universe" somehow acts as a liberating agent *in history,* but his use of the term *apocalypse* to describe climactic literary achievement makes it clear that culture acts to liberate its participants *from history.*

> In the anagogic phase, literature imitates the total dream of man, and so imitates the thought of a human mind which is at the circumference and not at the center of its reality. . . . Nature is now inside the mind of an infinite man who builds his cities out of the Milky Way. This is not reality, but it is the conceivable or imaginative limit of desire, which is infinite, eternal, and hence apocalyptic. By an apocalypse I mean primarily the imaginative conception of the whole of nature as the content of an infinite and eternal living body which, if not human, is closer to being human than to being inanimate. (119)

Frye's apocalypse reaches a rhapsodic height unmatched except by his favorite poet, Blake, but at the cost of a certain posthistorical inconsequentiality. Scorning vulgar functionalism, Frye has lifted literature so high, making it such an all-encompassing end in itself, that it no longer affects anything outside its own elevated orbit. The drama of apocalypse now refers solely to a condition of mind ("imaginative conception") or text (literature as "total form"), which paradoxically stakes its final importance on its unreality.

Anatomy of Criticism exerted a formidable influence on the next generation of criticism; even in the skeptical revisions that would converge in the Yale school, readers tended to accept that apocalypse meant a human condition of unqualified self-determination, an absolute freedom from circumstance. Geoffrey Hartman, for instance, would use "apocalyptic" to describe Wordsworth's "strong desire to cast out nature and to achieve an unmediated contact with the principle of things."[12] Such critics as Hartman and Harold Bloom distanced themselves from Frye by stressing the poet's inability to realize apocalyptic desires, which remain inescapably temporal and unachieved. In a typical assessment that anticipated his *Anxiety of Influence* series, Bloom exclaimed of the romantic poets, "They failed of their temporal prophecy, but they failed as the Titans did, massive in ruin and more human than their successors."[13] Yet in reevaluating Frye's grand romantic vision, with its

[12] Geoffrey Hartman, *Wordsworth's Poetry, 1787–1814* (New Haven: Yale University Press, 1964; reprint, 1971), xxii.

[13] Harold Bloom, *The Visionary Company* (Garden City: Doubleday, 1961), xv.

emphasis on the cosmic and individual consciousness and very little in between, his successors reproduced the antihistorical bias that structured his understanding of apocalypse.

Lost in this development, then, is the notion that apocalyptic representations have anything to do with the mundane work of politics. In his recent studies of the Bible, Frye has gone to great lengths to make the Book of Revelation itself look apolitical, reading it primarily as an Augustinian allegory of perception and cognition. For Frye, John of Patmos sets his sights higher than persecution, power struggles, and social emancipation, those ephemeral concerns of history to which apocalypse is an antonym. The fantastic events of Revelation describe "the inner meaning or, more accurately, the inner form of everything that is happening now. Man creates what he calls history as a screen to conceal the workings of the apocalypse from himself. . . . What is symbolized as the destruction of the order of nature is the destruction of the way of seeing that order that keeps man confined to the world of time and history as we know them."[14] Because history is only a veil of illusion in this view, genuine apocalypse can have little to do with specific struggles for freedom in local situations. It comes as no surprise, then, that when in *The Great Code* Frye divides Scripture into seven phases of revelation, he assigns "revolution" to the early, premature phase of Exodus, a phase that will be superseded by the inward-turning Christian dispensation. In this account, the escape from Egyptian slavery, and not the Book of Revelation, becomes the origin of millenarianism, and Frye shrewdly demonstrates that the recurrent features of Western revolutionary movements—the use of canon texts, an "us and them" mentality, and so on—all belong to the Hebrew narrative. Only by tactfully omitting that all such features also belong to, and are indeed exaggerated by, Revelation, can Frye make a purely formal apocalypse the culmination of Scripture.

Even as early as *Anatomy of Criticism*, Frye asserted that the self-referential text of apocalypse is all form, without contents, leading him to conclude that "poets are happier as servants of religion than of politics, because the transcendental and apocalyptic perspective of religion comes as a tremendous emancipation of the imaginative mind" (125). One should not, however, judge Frye's relation to politics too hastily or too harshly. *Anatomy of Criticism* appeared in 1957, the same year as Norman Cohn's *Pursuit of the Millennium,* a blistering account of medieval millenarian movements that likened them in their fanaticism and paranoia to the terrors of Nazism and Stalinism. Cohn's hyperbolic image of blind, destructive zeal helped prompt such historians as Eric

---

[14] Northrop Frye, *The Great Code: The Bible and Literature* (New York: Harcourt Brace Jovanovich, 1982), 136.

Hobsbawm, E. P. Thompson, and later, Christopher Hill to reassess the contribution of millenarianism to progressive politics; their successors continue this scholarly work today. Thompson's warning remains forceful and to the point: "What we must not do is confuse pure 'freaks' and fanatical aberrations with the imagery—of Babylon and the Egyptian exile and the Celestial City and the contest with Satan—in which minority groups have articulated their experience and projected their aspirations for hundreds of years."[15] Set in the context of this emerging debate, the utopian dignity of Frye's apocalypse as a vision of accomplished cultural destiny clearly contradicts Cohn's antimillenarian fears, while his respect for folk culture and his emphasis on categories of manual labor make his vision at least partially compatible with Thompson's populism. In other words, *Anatomy of Criticism* retains a touch of the progressive politics that has often been associated with apocalypse, a link that appears, for instance, when Frye, having already critiqued the petty egoism involved in the fixation on literary originality, bravely praises as an alternative the "richness of association an author can gain by the communism of convention" (98). Frye's greatness, Jameson has suggested, "lies in his willingness to raise the issue of community and to draw basic, essentially social, interpretive consequences from the nature of religion as collective representation." As Jameson also remarks, Frye limited himself only by making social function the penultimate phase of literary experience and reserving the euphoria of the anagogic for purely individual revelation.[16]

Yet it is precisely this privileging of individual revelation that has figured so prominently in the treatment of apocalypse by Frye's successors. What in Frye we might describe as an implied politics that stubbornly resists his own antihistorical inclination becomes in his successors an

---

[15] E. P. Thompson, *The Making of the English Working Class* (New York: Penguin, 1963), 54. See also Eric Hobsbawm, *Primitive Rebels* (New York: Norton, 1959), especially, 57–65, and Christopher Hill, *The World Turned Upside Down: Radical Ideas during the English Revolution* (London: Temple Smith, 1972) and *Antichrist in Seventeenth-Century England* (London: Oxford University Press, 1971). Since these early discussions, historians have tried to describe more particularly the contexts of millenarianism, avoiding arguments that would reduce it to expressions of either religious fanaticism or political discontent on the part of the marginalized. Of the many books that make English millenarianism their subject, I mention only a few that have been most influential for my own work: Clarke Garrett, *Respectable Folly: Millenarians and the French Revolution in France and England* (Baltimore: Johns Hopkins University Press, 1975); J. F. C. Harrison, *The Second Coming: Popular Millenarianism, 1780–1850* (New Brunswick: Rutgers University Press, 1979); Bernard Capp, *The Fifth Monarchy Men* (Totawa: Rowman and Littlefield, 1972); Katharine Firth, *The Apocalyptic Tradition in Reformation Britain, 1530–1645* (Oxford: Oxford University Press, 1979).

[16] Fredric Jameson, *The Political Unconscious* (Ithaca: Cornell University Press, 1981), 69–74.

outright dismissal of politics as a matter essentially irrelevant to apocalyptic poetry. In *Blake's Apocalypse,* Bloom can say of a passage in "Night
the Ninth" of the *Four Zoas,* that "the political vision of Blake reaches its
wishful climax and passes away, to be absorbed into the more strenuous
themes of human integration." And Hartman would retrospectively
describe his study of Wordsworth's apocalypse in this way: "What I did,
basically, was to describe Wordsworth's 'consciousness of consciousness.'
Everything else—psychology, epistemology, religious ideas, politics—
was subordinated."[17] Even M. H. Abrams's masterly and encyclopedic
Natural Supernaturalism, the book that set out to restore history and
politics to romantic apocalypse, reworked their erasure. Abrams's striking departure from the Frye legacy was to argue that the apocalyptic
rhetoric of romanticism had a time and a place, that it was "causally
related to the drastic political and social changes of the age." But his
narrative of political disillusionment leading to belief "in an apocalypse
by imagination or cognition" uncritically celebrated romanticism's most
transcendentalist assertions, thereby reintroducing the priorities of formal apocalypse, with its vision of art and mind freed from circumstance
and thus from the necessity of politics.[18] History, it seems, is not as
exacting a determinant as it first appeared to be, and this tendency to
minimize its force still governs Abrams's distrust of political criticism. In
a 1990 article, what he most objects to in the new historicism and more
overtly political approaches to literature is the idea "that history, not the
author, shapes a literary work and forges its meaning." Abrams's self-
determining poet "is free to write a political poem, but also any kind of
nonpolitical poem he or she may choose to write."[19] Politics, like history,
is expendable, something one may or may not choose to engage in while
exercising a freedom that in the tradition of romantic humanism has
become synonymous with the word apocalypse.

And yet, despite its large and resonant claims, the humanist tradition
has hardly monopolized the word. Perhaps the most remarkable thing
about the perseverance of apocalypse as a category of critical or theoretical discourse has been its elasticity, so that many of those who have
sought to go "beyond man and humanism," who have produced indelible critiques of totality, teleology, and universality, remain committed to
an apocalyptic rhetoric, whether implicitly or explicitly. With both deconstruction and postmodernism, apocalypse comes to signify a rup-

[17] Hartman, *Wordsworth's Poetry,* xii. Harold Bloom, *Blake's Apocalypse* (Garden City:
Doubleday, 1963), 268.

[18] M. H. Abrams, *Natural Supernaturalism* (New York: Norton, 1971), 11, 334.

[19] M. H. Abrams, "On Political Readings of *Lyrical Ballads,*" in *Romantic Revolutions,* ed.
Kenneth R. Johnston, Gilbert Chaitin, Karen Hanson, and Herbert Marks (Bloomington:
Indiana University Press, 1990), 321, 332.

ture, a genuine break with the comfortable and often ideologically pernicious idealisms of the intellectual past. I am more concerned here, however, with the continuities of the term, with the perpetual subordination of history that has been a primary blindness of deconstruction's antihumanist insight. In other words, despite the sound and fury of the theory explosion, apocalypse has continued by and large to have little to do with historical specificity and thus has continued to exercise at best a tenuous relation to politics. I have already noted that Bloom and Hartman began their careers by insufficiently problematizing the apocalypse they inherited from Frye, but even at the height of its academic influence, the Yale school relentlessly critiqued apocalyptic transcendentalism only to reproduce an apocalyptic disregard of circumstance, something especially apparent in the way temporality eclipses history in its rhetoric, a displacement that necessarily subordinates political concerns if it raises them at all. As Paul Morrison has recently argued, de Man's later work, "even when it most explicitly addresses questions of ideology and power, makes no concessions to historical specificity."[20] In any case, one reason that Derrida could be so readily assimilated to the Yale romanticists, despite the different political commitments of everyone involved, was that his work obsessively concerned itself, in style and content, with the nature of apocalyptic writing. With apologies to Abrams, one might say that the joining of Derrida and Yale was a marriage made in the Book of Revelation's heaven.

In this foreshortened narrative of the critical and theoretical uses of apocalypse, Derrida occupies a position in the deconstructive genealogy comparable to that which Frye occupies in the humanist line. In Derrida's work an implicit progressive politics coexists uneasily with a highly abstracted analytical practice, enabling some of his followers to reproduce his formalism without adequately addressing its relation to politics. Such elision can take widely diverse forms, from a disregard of politics altogether to exaggerated assumptions about the political consequences of linguistic analysis. While I do not wish to take up fully the strengths and limitations of the politics of deconstruction, which have been argued endlessly, I do want to show that apocalypse remains central to the issue.[21] In Derrida's own work, especially in his important lecture on

[20] Paul Morrison, "Paul de Man: Resistance and Collaboration," *Representations* 32 (Fall 1990): 56.

[21] Among many others, see Michael Ryan, *Marxism and Deconstruction: A Critical Articulation* (Baltimore: Johns Hopkins University Press, 1982); Gayatri Spivak, *In Other Worlds: Essays in Cultural Politics* (New York: Methuen, 1987); Barbara Foley, "The Politics of Deconstruction," in *Rhetoric and Form: Deconstruction at Yale* (Norman: University of Oklahoma Press, 1985), 113–34. One of the most lucid and sensible discussions of this issue appears in Barbara Johnson's essay "Is Writerliness Conservative?" in her *World of Difference* (Baltimore: Johns Hopkins University Press, 1987), 25–31.

"apocalyptic tone" in philosophy, there abides an unresolved tension between what I have been calling political apocalypse and formal apocalypse. For much of this lecture, Derrida attends to the ideological interests masked by apocalyptic discourses; he argues quite explicitly that those who claim to supersede merely historical interests, those who claim already to be on the apocalyptic other side, do so precisely to extend their power over others here and now.

> What effect do these noble, gentile prophets or eloquent visionaries want to produce? In view of what immediate or adjourned benefit? What do they do, what do we do in saying this? To seduce or subjugate whom, intimidate or make whom come? . . . Lucid analysis of these interests or of these calculi should mobilise a very great number and a great diversity of interpretive devices available today.[22]

As one would expect, however, Derrida does not stop with the ideological demystification he considers necessary but insufficient, insufficient because it reproduces the same apocalyptic tricks it sets out to expose. Like all apocalyptic rhetorics, the critique of ideology claims to identify error in order to "unveil" truth. "Shall we thus continue in the best apocalyptic tradition," asks Derrida, "to denounce false apocalypses?" (29). The lecture modulates between a specifically political critique of apocalyptic interests to a more general and more familiar critique of truth and presence, of logocentrism, which Derrida performs by way of reading the Book of Revelation. Somewhat predictably, John's text discloses not the truth-bearing, messianic logos but the priority of writing, of dissemination. "If the apocalypse reveals, it is first of all the revelation of the apocalypse, the self-presentation of the apocalyptic structure of language, of writing, of the experience of presence, in other words of the text or of the mark in general; *that is, of the divisible dispatch for which there is no self-presentation nor assured destination*" (27–28). The Book of Revelation, then, is something like a deconstructive Ur-text, and fully aware of the contradiction in making such a claim, in proposing that John's apocalypse represents "a transcendental condition of all discourse," Derrida can nonetheless ask, Is not the self-disabling structure of the Book of Revelation "the structure of every scene of writing in general?" (27). The self-consciousness of the rhetoric, which leaves its proposal as an unanswerable question, makes plain Derrida's awareness that his analysis, or deconstructive unveiling, of apocalypse is itself inevitably apocalyptic, inevitably invested in general truth claims that must in turn be rigorously deconstructed.

---

[22] Jacques Derrida, "Of an Apocalyptic Tone Recently Adopted in Philosophy," *Oxford Literary Review* 6 (1984): 23. Further references are to this text.

By telegraphing this paradox and by making it a necessary paradox, Derrida anticipates potential dissent, absorbing it into the self-
perpetuating linguistic activity that becomes an endless confirmation of
the argument. Deconstruction, so the saying goes, requires interminable
analysis. But this foolproof mechanism by which resistance gets recuperated in advance remains effective only so long as we accept that the issue
in apocalyptic representations is the competition between truth and
writing, a competition that writing will always win. Derrida goes out of
his way to make us see that his lecture is itself apocalyptic: "I shall speak
then of/in an apocalyptic tone in philosophy," it begins. He fully displays
the way his lecture rehearses the apocalyptic entanglement of truth and
writing, but by calling exaggerated attention to this particular relationship between his lecture and the apocalypse it addresses he obscures or
deflects our ability to see *other* constructions of that relationship. An
alternative account, for instance, might point out that his emphasis on
the hypothetical "scene of writing in general" shares the dehistoricizing
tendency characteristic of formal apocalypse. The ideological critique of
apocalyptic interests presupposes (or at least implies) a particular situation in which those interests operate. But when Derrida toys with the
idea of a "scene of writing in general," no matter how self-consciously, he
drains apocalypse of anything but linguistic contents, distancing the
relationship between representation and historical situation. In this crucial sense, though perhaps only in this sense, Derrida's apocalypse resembles Schiller's aesthetic: the magnitude of what he claims in the
name of apocalypse—that it represents the condition of *all* writing—is
matched only by a certain detachment or vacuity. This disengaged quality becomes apparent as soon as Derrida deviates from the apocalyptic
inaction of Schiller's aesthetic to imply that formal apocalypse, for all its
free-floating weightlessness, does something, and does something radical. "By its very tone, the mixing of voices, genres, and codes, apocalyptic discourse can also, in dislocating destinations, dismantle the
dominant contract or concordat" (29–30). Dismantling occurs almost as
a by-product of the necessities of language ("apocalyptic discourse can
also . . ."). Surely this marks a quantum leap in the empowerment of
"tone," that nonsemantic component of language which, simply by going about its business as usual, produces subversive effects. More to the
point, Derrida folds the millenarian desires of political apocalypse into
the functions of formal apocalypse, into a gravity-free textual politics
without precise historical coordinates. As I argue in greater detail later,
the transformation of matters of power into matters of language, which
is as characteristic of democratic culture generally as it is of deconstruction specifically, is perhaps the most persistent vestige of formal apocalypse in modern critical practices.

Because apocalypse functions as an organizational "horizon" (30) in

Derrida's writings, its influence was extensive even before this lecture, especially in the United States, where, as he observes, "people are always more sensitive to phenomena of prophetism, messianism, eschatology, and apocalypse-here-now" (30). In one sense, then, the impact of apocalypse on contemporary theoretical discourse has been nearly as widespread as that of deconstruction itself, but I confine myself in conclusion to discussing two essays in literary criticism that explicitly make apocalypse their central analytical category. The first essay provides an instance of the historical amnesia that a fascination with formal apocalypse can induce. The second, more in line with the constitutive tensions of Derrida's work, keeps a distant eye on politics, but a politics that is so automatically the by-product of ahistorical linguistic and phenomenological necessities that it becomes unconvincing, a mere political fantasia. In the first, Andrzej Warminski takes up the venerable topic of "Wordsworth's Apocalypses," and while he argues that apocalypse signifies the irreducibly plural, his apocalypse does one thing only: it marks the inevitable revelation that language is "syntax, articulation, nonsignifying jointings or cleavings, a system of meaningless differential markings." The real threat of apocalypse for Wordsworth, he argues, lies not in the exhilarating, transgressive autonomy of consciousness that does violence to nature, but in the fact that language consumes both nature and consciousness, textualizing them totally. Thus Warminski can revise Hartman's long-standing argument while retaining his key terms:

> To take "Apocalypse" as the death *of* Nature is still to take it as natural, as belonging to Nature, Nature's own (dialectical) negation. But to take "Apocalypse" as Nature *read* (figuratively, for example) rather than Nature *dead* (naturally, for example) is to introduce into the world still another death and another Apocalypse, one not based on a naturalistic model, indeed heterogeneous with it. An Apocalypse conceived, as it were, apocalyptically and not naturalistically (or "phenomenologically," i.e., on the model of consciousness)—provisionally we can call it the Apocalypse of Imagination.[23]

Apocalypse uncontaminated by anything other than its own terms, apocalypse apocalyptically conceived, refers neither to mind nor to nature; apocalypse is linguistic and nothing but linguistic. The most remarkable feature of this ingenious argument, however, is the way it fully reproduces the practice of formal apocalypse at the very moment it stakes its

---

[23] Andrzej Warminski, "Missed Crossing: Wordsworth's Apocalypses," *Modern Language Notes* 99 (December 1984): 986, 988.

claim to revisionary importance. Perhaps my point can be made most efficiently by recalling that Frye chose to conclude his discussion of literary apocalypse in *Anatomy of Criticism* by quoting Mallarmé: "Tout, au monde, existe pour aboutir à un livre [All earthly existence must ultimately be contained in a book]."[24] Of course, Frye's utopia of total textualization, of a literary universe in which all things signify, is just the opposite of Warminski's nihilistic apocalypse of "non-signifying jointings and cleavings," but like all pure opposites, like all "dialectical negations," these apocalypses have much in common, primarily, the comprehensive displacement of "the world as historic object" (Schiller's phrase) by the world as language. Mallarmé is as plausible a motto for Warminski as for Frye.

The second example ostensibly takes us out of romanticism and into postmodernism, though it also suggests the strong continuity of the two. Not only does its idea of postmodern apocalypse as a "spasm" of "textual fractures, explosions, catastrophes" resemble what Warminski sees in Wordsworth, but its discourse also curiously returns us to both Baudrillard and Schiller, the bookends of my discussion. In an essay on Ashbery, Derrida, and Blanchot, Herman Rapaport characterizes postmodernism according to its "apocalyptic tone" and thereby reconfigures some by-now-familiar terms.[25] Using Ashbery as a representative case, Rapaport suggests that the postmodern writer or artist does not

> make cataclysm or disaster climactic or apocalyptic in the sense we usually have of the word. He takes catastrophe as something pervasive and banal, so ubiquitous and monotonous, that we live this end of man to the end each day, exist against the backdrop of a deathwork or *thanatopraxie* whose style we have become. . . . [T]he disaster is . . . tediously inhabited as a style of life whose oppression lacks a certain density or weight, whose oppression is even luminous and inviting, an enveloping disaster in whose end we are eternally suspended. (390)

This passage is particularly instructive for the way it crosses the topoi of different apocalyptic discourses. So, for instance, with the change of a word or two, it might recall Schiller, whose apocalyptic aesthetic was also an immanent end, an eternal suspension luminous and inviting precisely to the extent it was weightlessly free of content. On the other hand, as with Baudrillard's catastrophe in slow motion, Rapaport's apocalypse represents a disaster, a tedious disaster, in that the insubstantiality, the

---

[24] Frye, *Anatomy of Criticism*, 122.

[25] Herman Rapaport, "Deconstructing Apocalyptic Rhetoric: Ashbery, Derrida, Blanchot," *Criticism* 27 (Fall 1985): 389. Further references are to this text.

nothingness, of the aesthetic has leaked into the whole of experience. Schiller's aesthetic constituted a realm of apocalyptic freedom because it "alone," uniquely among human activities, released us from the density of history. Here history itself has become impossible, and there is no release from the depthless existence of the aesthetic or the linguistic. Apocalypse now refers to an unending "style of life," a life in which everything but style has ended.

And yet, despite this reversal, what remains constant is the idea that apocalypse without content, formal apocalypse, might signify a rapturous freedom; stubbornly persistent is the idea that apocalypse simply means a liberation from historical determinants.

> What has happened? The "I" has achieved what Emmanuel Levinas calls a difficult liberty, a break in participation with the life-world as world. We are on the brink of infinitude, since in the negativity of non-participation the difference between selfhood and otherness is given up, and intelligibility too gives way to a certain madness or disequilibrium. Whatever holds the life world together is by means of a difficult freedom unhinged and the subject vertiginously swept into an abysm or catastrophe of relations where no word serves to reobjectify or systematize what has been unloosened.... [Apocalyptic] tone is part of a plural which cannot be unified or centered or institutionalized, however much postmodernism and deconstruction will operate as recuperative code words to the vulgar for such purposes. (392)

For all its condescension to the uninitiated, for all the self-congratulation regarding the difficulty of the experience it espouses, doesn't this passage look back on a world that has ended all too easily? Without putting up much resistance, the "life world" yields rather quickly to the rhetoric of an apocalyptic dissolution that in fact rehearses the most conventional routines of the aesthetic. To define "difficult liberty" as the "negativity of non-participation" is to take a page straight out of Schiller's book, while layering it with Levinas or Nietzsche. The significant difference is that while Schiller substituted a formal apocalypse of inaction for the revolutionary politics he felt had failed, Rapaport suggests, however vaguely, that formal apocalypse can do the work of politics, unhinging the powers that hold the life world together and defeating the designs of some unspecified process of institutional coercion. Schiller said, "Happy he who learns to bear what he cannot change"; Rapaport's postmodernism makes no such concession to its own ineffectual unreality. Perhaps the only thing worse than a joining of apocalypse and aesthetic form that minimizes the significance of history and politics is one that assumes it can do the work of politics automatically, without historical attachments.

All too often in the tradition of formal apocalypse, in building the various New Jerusalems of criticism and theory, only those constructions that subordinate history have commanded serious attention.

In this book I discuss some of the political consequences that have followed from the relation between apocalypse and aesthetic forms, a relation connate with the biblical origins of the genre. Although the topic of apocalypse has traditionally provoked encyclopedic, often heroic, efforts, I have by no means tried to be exhaustive. I range freely among discourses, from biblical and romantic literature to contemporary theory of different sorts, but the range is not comprehensive. I do not, for instance, fully address millenarian movements of any period, and even my discussion of romanticism is limited to a set of problems centered on the apocalyptic representations of three authors, William Blake, Percy Bysshe Shelley, and Mary Shelley. Moreover, while my topic is the politics of apocalyptic representations, I have attended primarily to conservative tendencies, to the way in which images of the end of history have, sometimes inadvertently, aided those who wish to preserve their authority by resisting social change.

In one way or another, a formalist aesthetic enters into the claims apocalyptic texts have made to a normative authority independent of historical situation. Thus Part I, "Building Jerusalem," considers how conservative ideology and an idea of ahistorical literary form became mutually constitutive in both biblical apocalypse and its exegesis. One aim of this section is to reverse the nearly somnambulant tendency of some literary criticism, especially some romantic criticism, to assume that apocalypse, if it is considered political at all, always implies radical millenarianism. By looking first at the development of apocalypse as a biblical genre and then at a type of modern exegesis (Renaissance and beyond) that foregrounds the "literary" qualities of the Book of Revelation, I try to show how formal apocalypse actually evolved as a means of suppressing social conflict and, more specifically, of containing millenarianism. Far from being automatically or inevitably radical, apocalypse in some circumstances can serve to legitimate and stabilize a given social order, particularly by minimizing the significance of historical conflict within it. By no means do I wish to deny the radical heritage of Western apocalypse. As early as the second century, the Montanist movement prompted Christian women to leave their husbands because they believed that the New Jerusalem was about to descend upon a small town in Asia Minor; within a generation or two of John's letter to the seven churches, the Apocalypse already served the function of social disruption it sometimes continues to serve today. I wish rather to explain how the Book of Revelation, for all its political dynamite, could settle

into the canon of New Testament texts, which was organized and promulgated by the early Roman church in large part to silence the rival
claims to authority advanced by such dissenting groups as the Montanists. This functional contradiction, I believe, is internal to and constitutive of John's Apocalypse. The Book of Revelation is already the product
of a tension between prophecy and canon that goes back to the Hebrew
Scriptures, and even in that ancient material, the power of canon to
suppress prophecy is bound up with the emergence of a formalist aesthetic. This originary and tacit political function of aesthetic forms has
had a remarkable staying power in the literary uses of apocalypse. So,
for instance, literary-minded exegesis of Revelation has tended to reproduce the political priorities of canon, something one sees especially
clearly in the modern readings that set out to make Revelation put an
end to its own millenarian legacy.

My first two chapters, then, are on the Book of Revelation, its production and its reception. In order to describe the canonical work of apocalypse, Chapter 1 develops in some detail a reading of Revelation that I
will indicate only briefly here but will return to throughout the book. If
one considers the Book of Revelation not simply as an act of resistance to
Roman authority but as an act of community formation in line with the
incipient institutionalization of the church, it becomes evident that the
text functions to create and even to impose the universal and metaphysical consensus in Christ that it claims to transcribe. Perhaps this ideological work is implied by any canon. But in the Apocalypse that eventually
came to mark the closure of Judeo-Christian Scripture, the West's first
self-described canon, this ideological activity is especially vivid and consequential. The Book of Revelation describes the violent end of history
that results in the New Jerusalem, with its transcendental harmonies
that are at once formal (architectural) and social; at the same time, this
narrative, primarily in the form of a linguistic allegory, describes the end
of historical differences, as if the vanishing of difference were itself a
necessary and inevitable component of social redemption and liberation. John's Apocalypse tells the story of a military victory that is also a
linguistic victory; the forces of Christ, the Logos whom Austin Farrer
once called "the warrior Word," triumph as they destroy the Whore of
Babylon, a figure also inscribed with a linguistic valence—namely, the
inheritance of fallen language derived from the Tower of Babel. Babylon is, among other things, the preapocalyptic condition of "peoples,
and multitudes, and nations, and tongues"; she represents the unwieldy
multiplicity of voices, the stubborn persistence of difference in history,
society, and language, which must be terminated in order to legitimate
the unified image a new social order claims for itself. One function of
this allegory is to allow John to speak in history as if he already occupied

the space beyond history, to arbitrate conflicts from the hindsight of their preordained resolution. John looks back on the end of the world, in other words, to secure a particular authority in that world. The full force of this maneuver becomes clear only when one understands that the Book of Revelation represented but one voice among several competing for authority within the early Christian communities.

By "Building Jerusalem," then, I mean to signify one of the political uses of apocalypse: the attempt to arrogate power by speaking in/of a voice that originates outside history. In focusing on this political strategy, I want to call attention to a feature of apocalyptic representations that has demonstrated a remarkable and sometimes subtle capacity to reproduce itself. To return for a moment to Northrop Frye, for instance, the chapter of *Anatomy of Criticism* that is itself an apocalyptic narrative on the destiny of literature begins by recognizing a variety of competing critical approaches and types of literary meaning, but it does so only to propose its own capacity to master this plurality. "Once we have admitted the principle of polysemous meaning, we can either stop with a purely relative and pluralistic position, or we can go on to consider the possibility that there is a finite number of valid critical methods, and that they can all be contained in a single theory" (72). Not surprisingly, we eventually learn that the "self-contained literary universe" of the anagogic phase is "a universe in which everything is potentially identical with everything else" (124), a New Jerusalem of "total metaphor" (136). The canonical work of apocalypse persists in imagining the end of history to be the end of historical differences. In a passage that I will refer to often in the chapters that follow, Luce Irigaray suggests that the ideal of an apocalyptic Logos that can master a field of differences and reduce them to identity has become a general feature of patriarchal discourse:

> Now, this domination of the philosophic logos stems in large part from its power *to reduce all others to the economy of the Same.* The teleologically constructive project it takes on is always also a project of diversion, deflection, reduction of the other in the Same. And, in its greatest generality perhaps, from its power to *eradicate the difference between the sexes* in systems that are self-representative of a "masculine subject."[26]

Irigaray's argument can be applied to apocalyptic works as widely separated as the Book of Revelation and *Anatomy of Criticism*. In the former, John represents the termination of linguistic differences through the

[26] Luce Irigaray, *This Sex Which Is Not One* [1977], trans. Catherine Porter (Ithaca: Cornell University Press, 1985), 74.

erasure of a female character, the Whore of Babylon, in a symbolic act that likely reflects a conflict in the early Christian communities regarding the status of women; in the latter, Frye imagines apocalypse as the containment of the world within a "single infinite body," a Blakean "man who builds his cities out of the Milky Way." That this is literally a generic "man" only confirms the point: as a single body, no matter how much it infinitely contains, "he" can have but one sex, and in this androcentric image the logos demonstrates "its power to eradicate the difference between the sexes in [a system] that [is] self-representative of a 'masculine subject.'" Even when apocalyptic texts speak the inviting language of inclusiveness, they often practice the exclusion that has been the traditional prerogative of canon.

Somewhere between formal apocalypse in the biblical lineage and formal apocalypse in recent criticism and theory lies romanticism, the cultural moment that gave the West its modern version of the aesthetic. Abrams argued that despite its relation to an age of revolutions, romantic writers mainly affirmed an unbroken tradition: their "mission was to assure the continuance of civilization by reinterpreting to their drastically altered condition the enduring humane values."[27] I do not believe this is entirely the case. In the second part of this book, I have grouped my discussions of Blake, Percy Shelley, and Mary Shelley under the heading "Unbuilding Jerusalem" in order to suggest that, in different ways and to different degrees, their representations of the end of history resisted the temptation to speak with the authority that comes from positioning oneself outside history. In these three chapters I focus on ways in which some romantic writers emphasized the historical embeddedness of literary discourse; in each chapter I address a particular issue that makes problematic the claims of formal apocalypse: representation in Blake, politics in Percy Shelley, and gender in Mary Shelley. As I suggested earlier, this list is not meant to be exhaustive; rather, it is meant to open a reconsideration of romantic apocalypse that might be extended to other problems and to other authors. I have not included a discussion of Wordsworth, for instance, though this book would have been impossible without the recent work on Wordsworth's strategies of historical displacement.[28] Despite all the attention the topic has generated over the past thirty years, I hope that my arguments will indicate, if only by extension and if only in the light of such recent criticism, that the book on Wordsworth's apocalypse has not yet been closed.

[27] Abrams, *Natural Supernaturalism*, 430–31.

[28] I am thinking especially of Marjorie Levinson's *Wordsworth's Great Period Poems* (Cambridge: Cambridge University Press, 1986).

If "Unbuilding Jerusalem" is meant to indicate some types of resistance to formal apocalypse within romantic literature, the phrase
itself says nothing of the successes or failures of that resistance. Scholars
have long recognized that the millenarian rhetoric of the American and
French revolutions bears a crucial relation to the romantic fixation on
apocalypse, although the precise nature of that relation is sometimes
disputed. Romanticism emerged at a time when political events allowed
a break with the traditions of formal apocalypse that had been so powerful during the eighteenth century; especially in the early 1790s, the
French Revolution provoked interpreters of prophecy to subordinate
the claims of aesthetic formalism to a concern with immediate history, so
that the Book of Revelation and the daily newspapers glossed one another as "signs of the times." At the same time, however, the millenarianism that politicized apocalypse and shaped romanticism took a particular form, *democratic* revolution. The relation between apocalypse and
democratic politics is central in assessing romanticism's resistance to
formal apocalypse. Therefore, in my discussion of apocalypse and representation, I write as much about Tom Paine as about Blake. In one
sense, modern democratic politics clearly opposes itself to the practice of
formal apocalypse I am calling "Building Jerusalem": by dispersing
power across multiple and potentially conflicting social voices through
political representation, modern democracy makes resistance to the
Logos, to the apocalyptic unity that would suppress differences, an
inviolable principle of government. The poststructuralist critique of
logocentrism and its accompanying valorization of difference are themselves deeply implicated in the modern democratic culture that fosters
them and that took shape at the same time as romanticism, something
that might well help to explain deconstruction's disproportionate concentration on romantic texts. There is, however, another side to the
democratic millenarianism that informs romantic apocalypse. With its
emphasis on representation as the means of resisting coercive power,
democratic culture tends to treat matters of social conflict and empowerment as if they were indistinguishable from matters of linguistic conflict
and empowerment. By privileging language so fully, democratic politics
threatens to introduce a new, more subtle formalism that in practice
might serve the oldest conservative function of formal apocalypse: the
containment of millenarianism, or in secular terms, the containment of
disruptive actions that are based on conviction. Romantic apocalypse of
the kind I discuss here is not so much a response to "the failure" of the
French Revolution, the turn from history and politics that some have
argued, as it is a manifestation of "the success" of the democratic politics
that, for better or worse, have structured Western societies for two

centuries. One purpose of the "Unbuilding Jerusalem" portion of this book, then, is to suggest the staying power of formal apocalypse in those discourses that make an agenda of resisting it.

Kant once argued that what comes after history is unthinkable for historical beings. In "The End of All Things," he confirmed the teleological faith that is so important to his *Critique of Judgment,* but he also urged readers to think of eschatology in terms of its usefulness now, its effect on actual behavior: "These Ideas are to be regarded . . . in a practical sense. . . . [W]e are required to contemplate them on behalf of the moral principles which pertain to the ultimate purpose of all things."[29] In the five chapters of this book I consider the "practical sense" of the end of history. That is, I read specific eschatological representations according to their ideological content. I read apocalyptic texts as if they were political arguments called for, if not required, by circumstances, even and especially when they assert their unconcern with politics or when they display a particular political argument that, deliberately or not, does not fully coincide with their political practice.

Perhaps it is impossible to "unbuild Jerusalem"; perhaps it is impossible to resist formal apocalypse. If in its broadest sense that latter term means the displacement of history that occurs whenever historical phenomena are represented, then it describes all acts of criticism and interpretation. I realize that one cannot resist formal apocalypse simply by chanting the word "history" or by immersing oneself in the density of historical detail. Even historicism, after all, is not automatically immune to charges of formalism. "Once we insulated ourselves from reality in universalisms and totalisms," writes Alan Liu. "Now we wrap ourselves in detailed layers of context as thick and multiform as cotton."[30] But if deconstructive theory has often involved what one might call a politics without history, perhaps a greater danger lies in a history without politics, the peculiar indulgence of "postoppositionalism." For that reason, these essays are not so much descriptions of historical representations as they are arguments about them. Politics is never something past.

[29] Immanuel Kant, "The End of All Things," trans. Robert E. Anchor, in *On History,* ed. Lewis White Beck (New York: Bobbs-Merrill, 1963), 76.

[30] Alan Liu, "Local Transcendence: Cultural Criticism, Postmodernism, and the Romanticism of Detail," *Representations* 32 (Fall 1990): 98–99.

PART I

Building Jerusalem

CHAPTER ONE

HISTORY ENDS IN A BOOK: BIBLICAL APOCALYPSE AND THE SUPPRESSION OF DIFFERENCE

From Prophecy to Apocalypse

Almost everything I want to say about biblical apocalypse emerges from the following instance of textual revision. In the Hebrew book that bears his name, only once is Jeremiah seen writing his own oracles: by means of his messenger, Seraiah, he sends to the Jews in captivity a letter prophesying the destruction of Babylon. Oddly enough, Jeremiah speaks these oracles before he commits them to writing; the long condemnation of Israel's archenemy begins with the familiar prophetic formula, "Thus says the Lord," and only after Yahweh speaks through his prophet, only after the oracles have been performed, are we told that "Jeremiah wrote in a book all the evil that should come upon Babylon" (51:1, 60).[1] But even in this scene of speech become writing, speech gets the last word. Jeremiah has specific instructions for Seraiah regarding the reading of his letter to the exiles: "When you finish reading this book, bind a stone to it, and cast it into the midst of the Euphrates, and say, 'Thus shall Babylon sink, to rise no more, because of the evil that I am bringing upon her'" (51:63–64). These are Jeremiah's last recorded words, and ironically they ask that the very book of his own writing be drowned, that words attributed to Yahweh himself not be preserved for future consideration but be used (and used up) immediately as a momentary and functional sign, like speech itself. As the book goes down, so goes Babylon; in the transiency of the gesture lies Yahweh's message, which addresses this situation and no other. Centuries later, Jeremiah's

---

[1] Unless otherwise indicated, citations of the Bible are from the Revised Standard Version.

symbolic act, now preserved in a text he never wrote, struck another would-be prophet with peculiar force. John of Patmos borrowed almost the entire image for Revelation's account of the fall of the Whore of Babylon: "Then a mighty angel took up a stone like a great millstone and threw it into the sea, saying, 'So shall Babylon the great city be thrown down with violence, and shall be found no more'" (18:21). Of course, what's missing here is what's most important: by the time John writes the apocalypse that becomes the model for all others, the idea of a permanent and authoritative book has become indispensable to a vision of final retribution and salvation. Following Jeremiah, John submerges the stone, but departing from him, he saves the book.

This revisionary episode suggests one of many distinctions between prophecy in the Hebrew Scriptures and apocalypse as it evolved out of prophecy into a variety of Jewish and Christian literatures.[2] Apocalypse is a "bookish" phenomenon, not just in that books feature prominently within the visions themselves, but also in the fact that apocalyptic revelation often comes indirectly through a book.[3] Classical prophecy is typically (though not invariably) spoken; the word passes from Yahweh to the prophet without mediation (sometimes he physically places the words into the prophet's mouth, as in Jeremiah 1:9), and the result of such inspiration is speech rather than text. At the minimum, this difference reflects the fact that authors of apocalypses wrote only after a body of canonical Scripture was already in place; not only were they accountable to the tradition and authority represented by that canon— in other words, the *content* of the canon—they also produced their visions within a culture that was increasingly associating such tradition and authority with the literary *form* of the book. Apocalypse developed as it did in part because it had an idea and a formal technics of the book that classical prophecy never had.[4] This distinction is constitutive, not

---

[2] In arguing that apocalypse evolves out of prophecy, I am following the lead of Paul Hanson in *The Dawn of Apocalyptic* (Philadelphia: Fortress, 1975). Hanson rejects the notion that apocalypse is so antithetical to Hebrew prophecy that it must instead have its source in Wisdom literature and in dualistic tendencies that entered Hebrew thought through the Exile. For a judicious assessment of the multiple sources that contributed to the development of apocalyptic literature, see Michael A. Knibb, "Prophecy and the Emergence of the Jewish Apocalypses," in *Israel's Prophetic Tradition*, ed. Richard Coggins, Anthony Phillips, and Michael Knibb (Cambridge: Cambridge University Press, 1982), especially 165–76.

[3] Bernard McGinn characterizes apocalypse according to "the 'bookish' nature of the revealed message." "Early Apocalypticism: The Ongoing Debate," in *The Apocalypse in English Renaissance Thought and Literature*, ed. C. A. Patrides and Joseph Wittreich (Ithaca: Cornell University Press, 1984), 5.

[4] When I speak of a "formal technics of the book," I refer more to the writing practices aimed at producing an appearance of literary coherence and integrity than to matters of

simply incidental or circumstantial; apocalypse is not merely written prophecy. The most significant change introduced by apocalyptic eschatology, the idea that history is something that can and must come to an end, is inseparable from the literary form of the book that accompanies and perhaps even enables it. A classical prophet such as Jeremiah can imagine dramatic historical change, the very day of Yahweh when the wicked will be punished amid universal and terrifying destruction, but he cannot imagine the end of history. After predicting imminent doom, Jeremiah, with his flair for symbolic action, buys land in Israel; he remains invested in the world, for the world will end with neither destruction nor salvation. It is only with apocalypse that history ends, that all those melting mountains and precipitant stars are imagined to be literal, that a new (genuinely new, not merely restorative) order descends from the heavens in the form of the New Jerusalem. Given this altered understanding of history, my initial question is this: How and why is the representation of the end of history bound up with the emergence of the book as an authoritative, cultural force? More specifically: Is an idea of the book as a structure that transcends history necessary to imagine history as something capable of ending? At the conclusion of his apocalypse, an angel orders Daniel to "shut up the words, and seal the book, until the time of the end" (12:4). In the most surprisingly literal way, the author imagines the opening of the book and the ending of history to be simultaneous, something we see repeated in Revelation with John's book sealed with seven seals. How is it that history ends with the opening of a book?

---

physical production. Late in the evolution from prophecy to apocalypse there did occur a transformation in book technology, as the individual scroll of late Jewish Scripture gave way to the codex of the second century c.e., an innovation that allowed more material to be collected and thus made it easier to transmit the gospels as an "anthology," as a single book composed of discrete parts. The codex may well have assisted the process of canon formation, for it allowed sacred texts to be presented in authorized combinations and sequences. One might be tempted, then, on the basis of the relationship between power and book technology, to set up a dialectic between "scroll" and "book," as W. J. T. Mitchell has done in discussing William Blake: "In the context of Romantic textual ideology, the book is the symbol of modern rationalist writing and the cultural economy of mechanical reproduction, while the scroll is the emblem of ancient revealed wisdom, imagination, and the cultural economy of hand-crafted, individually expressive artifacts. . . . The book represents writing as *law:* it is usually associated with patriarchal figures like Urizen and Jehovah. . . . The scroll represents writing as *prophecy:* it is associated with youthful figures of energy, imagination, and rebellion." "Visible Language: Blake's Wond'rous Art of Writing," in *Romanticism and Contemporary Criticism,* ed. Morris Eaves and Michael Fischer (Ithaca: Cornell University Press, 1986), 64–65. Mitchell's categories may well reflect Blake's iconography, but, as we will see, they hold little historical validity, for just as the modern book replaced the codex and the codex replaced the scroll, so the scroll already functioned to replace (and contain) the oral practice of prophecy by means of the superior technology of writing.

Speech, Writing, and the Idea of History

Between prophecy and apocalypse falls canonization, the largely un-documented process by which a collection of binding sacred texts (first the Pentateuch and later the Book of the Prophets) emerged sometime between the exile in Babylon (early sixth century) and the beginning of the second century B.C.E. On one side of this murky divide are the practices of such classical prophets as Elijah, Isaiah, and Amos; on the other side emerges the first fully apocalyptic book, the Book of Daniel, which describes how its hero reads Jeremiah for insight into his own predicament. Scholars generally explain the differences between proph-ecy and apocalypse (as well as the obvious continuities) by outlining the contours of the circumstances to which they variously responded. Among the many such contextual elements, however, is one surprisingly neglected: the fact that writers of apocalypses had books to read. Canon-ization, itself a protracted historical event of the greatest significance, had not only literary and theological consequences but, as we will see, social and ideological consequences as well. In this chapter I address the complicated enmeshing of these consequences. But before I turn to the processes by which prophecy evolved into apocalypse, perhaps it would be helpful, even at the risk of schematization, to outline briefly the two modes.

The most fundamental distinctions between prophecy and apoc-alypse follow upon their markedly different understandings of his-tory. For the prophet of the Hebrew Scriptures, history is the medium through which Yahweh realizes his will, as is evident in verses as late as these from 2 Isaiah:

> For as the rain and the snow come down from heaven,
> and return not thither but water the earth,
> making it bring forth and sprout,
> giving seed to the sower and bread to the eater,
> so shall my word be that goes forth from my mouth;
> it shall not return to me empty,
> but it shall accomplish that which I purpose,
> and prosper in the thing for which I sent it.
>
> (55:10–11)

Paradoxically, the very God who defies material embodiment, whose transcendence is so severe that he cannot be represented by an image, acts decisively through the material world.[5] Yahweh's presence within

---

[5] "Historical events were not to be denigrated as a threat to the eternal order wherein rested man's hope for salvation, but to be studied and recorded as the context within which

history defined every significant aspect of the prophetic office. For one thing, it sanctioned, or even required, the prophet's participation in political events, whether that meant Isaiah advising Hezekiah to reject a proposed alliance between Israel and Egypt or Elijah challenging the social injustices of Ahab and Jezebel. For another, it accounts for the strong ethical imperative characteristic of these works, since to further the cause of justice is to act as God's agent in the world. The first chapter of Isaiah puts the matter plainly: "Cease to do evil, learn to do good; seek justice, correct oppression; defend the fatherless, plead for the widow" (1:16–17). Classical prophecy inevitably conveys the message that historical action matters, so much so that even communal salvation on the grand scale depends on the local actions of individuals. History proceeds by means of a provisional if/then relation that binds the community's activities to the activities of God: as Yahweh says through Isaiah, "if you pour yourself out for the hungry and satisfy the desire of the afflicted, then shall your light rise in the darkness and your gloom be as the noonday" (58:10). Such a relation, one must realize, presupposes that the prophet addresses a sovereign nation; he asks a free people to exercise their power by acknowledging and correcting their social failings. Classical prophecy takes shape, then, before the fall of Jerusalem and the Babylonian exile.[6] History is always divinely motivated, but never predetermined; it has form, undergirded at every moment by the word of Yahweh, but the subtext is alterable. Thus history is implicitly endless, and while the climax of a particular drama (even that of the exile) may require an eschatological rhetoric, prophecy typically defines the furthest extent of redemption as a return to life as normal: "They shall build houses and inhabit them; they shall plant vineyards and eat their fruit" (Isaiah 65:21).

The identifying mark of apocalypse, on the other hand, is the author's belief that history has been so usurped by evil forces that it cannot possibly function as the medium of divine activity. "And there shall be a time of trouble, such as never has been since there was a nation till that time; but at that time your people shall be delivered" (Dan. 12:1). With this prediction of an unprecedented crisis, Daniel initiates a nearly universal convention of the genre. Apocalyptic redemption occurs as an act of divine intervention that breaks in on the corruption of history from elsewhere; in fact, redemption can only be imagined as the abrupt end of history brought about by a thoroughly transcendental agent, a

---

and through which the cosmic deity Yahweh was active on behalf of his nation." Hanson, *The Dawn of Apocalyptic*, 18.

[6] Tony Stoneburner makes this point in "Notes on Prophecy and Apocalypse in a Time of Anarchy and Revolution: A Trying Out," in *Literature in Revolution*, ed. George Abbott White and Charles Newman (New York: Holt, Rinehart, and Winston, 1972), 265.

messiah who introduces a new and otherworldly order typically distinguished by its atemporality. As a rule of thumb, this wishing away of history reflects extraordinary and seemingly insurmountable historical pressures. Apocalyptic eschatology, according to Paul Hanson, takes its earliest form during the exile, when prophets and disciples adjust their original message to suit an enslaved community dispossessed of political power.[7] Many of the explicitly eschatological passages found in the prophetic books are probably late additions meant to temper earlier visions of doom with promises of hope. Thus the text most relentless in its social criticism of Israel, the Book of Amos, ends with Yahweh proclaiming: "Behold, the days are coming . . . when . . . the mountains shall drip sweet wine, and all the hills shall flow with it. I will restore the fortunes of my people Israel, and they shall rebuild the ruined cities and inhabit them" (9:13–14). A composite and deeply contradictory text, Amos clearly addresses several historical moments, at least one of which is pre- and another postexilic.

The discrediting of history and the subsequent turn to mythical visions of cosmic redemption tend to occur only when an apocalyptic writer perceives no viable means of self-determination for the community. Amid the general persecution under Antiochus IV Epiphanes, the author of Daniel warns against those calling for rebellion: "In those times many shall rise against the king of the south; and the men of violence among your own people shall lift themselves up in order to fulfil the vision; but they shall fail" (11:14). As the book's first dream indicates, the oppressor-kingdom can be felled only by "a stone . . . cut out by no human hand" (2:34). Daniel belongs to a debate among second-century Jews regarding the proper response to an immediate crisis, and this debate in turn foregrounds conflicting assumptions about the nature of history. An angel can say to Daniel, "Blessed is he who waits" (12:12), because the author sees history as a terminal structure governed by an immutable, providential design, in which the crisis and its resolution are equally inevitable. In this schema, the visionary can do little more than wait and nervously calculate the arrival time of the end. That's why Daniel, an observer of eschatological events to come rather than a participant in them, can shut up his book until the end of time. The classical prophet prophesies because he can influence the course of history; technically, it makes no difference whether a Daniel or a John even experiences his visions, since the end will arrive on schedule with or without him. Of course, this is to exaggerate the passivity bound up with apocalypse. Elisabeth Schüssler Fiorenza and Adela Collins have argued, for instance, that Revelation's call to passive resistance implicitly

[7] See Hanson, *The Dawn of Apocalyptic*, especially 12–31.

operates in the same if/then pattern as prophecy, with martyrdom functioning as the catalyst necessary to bring on the messianic victory.[8] At the
very least, when Revelation asks its audience to abide by Christian faith
despite the near certainty of persecution, it demands a decision of
enormous significance for historical lives as well as metaphysical souls.
And yet, neither can the difference between prophetic history and apocalyptic history be ignored when John adds toward the end of his text,
"Let the evildoer still do evil, and the filthy still be filthy, and the righ-
teous still do right, and the holy still be holy" (22:11). Social action, while
it may bear on the individual's fate, has no bearing on history as a whole,
which advances toward its prescripted conclusion regardless of all contingencies. Of all the contradictions that make up the Book of Revelation, perhaps none has had more lasting impact on its readers than its
mixed signals regarding the efficacy of historical action.

I want to turn now from these broadly stroked thematic issues to what
will at first seem a more superficial distinction between prophecy and
apocalypse, the simple fact that apocalyptic texts, for all of their noto-
rious symbolic extravagances, read like books. That is, they generally
exhibit the rudimentary and normative signs of formal organization we
typically expect from objects that call themselves books—for instance,
that the words placed between a beginning and an end will more or less
form a continuous whole. While this may seem a ludicrously basic re-
quirement, it is one not obviously met by classical prophecy. By 1794,
already echoing century-old arguments, Tom Paine wrote of Isaiah:
"Whoever will take the trouble of reading the book ascribed to Isaiah will
find it one of the most wild and disorderly compositions ever put together."[9] With its "prose run mad" (Paine apparently had not read
Bishop Lowth), with its fits and starts and internal fragmentation, its
thematic and structural and stylistic incongruities, the Book of Isaiah
seemed to violate the generic expectations aroused by its title. Paine had
no such problem with the Book of Daniel, which he concluded was
written by a single author as Isaiah was not.[10] What many eighteenth-
century exegetes first recognized has long since become commonplace
in biblical scholarship, that the prophetic books took the form they now
have only through a long process of assemblage and redaction that
remains almost entirely unavailable to us. Most scholars today agree
that we cannot distinguish with any certainty the original sayings of a

---

[8] Adela Yarbro Collins, "The Political Perspective of the Revelation to John," *Journal of
Biblical Literature* 96/2 (1977): 241–56. Elisabeth Schüssler Fiorenza often makes this
argument, but see especially "Visionary Rhetoric and Social-Political Situation," chap. 7 of
The Book of Revelation: Justice and Judgment (Philadelphia: Fortress, 1985), 181–203.

[9] Thomas Paine, *Age of Reason* (New York: Prometheus Books, 1984), 122.

[10] Ibid., 138.

prophet from material added and shaped by later editors, though there tends to be little consensus on how modern readers should respond to this situation.[11] Crude as he could often be in his reading of Scripture, Paine at least understood with some clarity that the matter was political as well as theological or literary:

> When the Church Mythologists established their system, they collected all the writings they could find, and managed them as they pleased. It is a matter altogether of uncertainty to us whether such of the writings as now appear under the name of the Old and New Testament are in the same state in which those collectors say they found them, or whether they added, altered, abridged, or dressed them up. . . . Who the people were that did all this, we know nothing of; they called themselves by the general name of the Church, and this is all we know of the matter.[12]

Implicit in Paine's polemical argument is his belief that the biblical redactors understood perfectly well that textual structure and style are ideological forces. Formal coherence of even a superficial sort bears its own authority. Thus Paine called attention to as many contradictions as he could find in the biblical books, hoping to demonstrate that the word of God is in fact the composite word of men advancing a variety of interests.[13] He needed, in other words, to show that biblical books are not books of the coherent, unitary kind his readers took for granted, and he had much better success with the prophecies of Isaiah than he had with the apocalyptic text of Daniel.

The reasons for this are now obvious: Isaiah includes material produced and assembled over the course of at least three centuries, while Daniel is the work of a single historical moment, a book modeled on the example of other books, although it certainly combines new materials

[11] A. S. Van Der Woude, for instance, remarks, "Should one maintain the methodological postulate that not the inauthenticity of the utterances in a prophetic book but the authenticity has to be proved . . . , then it must be feared that hardly any text can with confidence be attributed to a prophet and consequently the bulk of the content of a prophetic book can only be ascribed to the process of redaction." "Three Classical Prophets: Amos, Hosea, and Micah," in *Israel's Prophetic Tradition,* 42–43.

[12] Paine, *Age of Reason,* 18.

[13] Jerome McGann has recently made the same point, suggesting that the historical inscription of various interests within Scripture makes the Bible particularly instructive: "No Word has ever been more textualized than the Word of God, none is more surrounded by, and immersed in, human words. . . . Reading the Bible, therefore, one may observe—in socially and historically particularized contexts—the struggle by which a 'permanent' and transcendental meaning is deployed: the drama—set down monumentally and as a form of domination—of the conflicts of various human interests." *Social Values and Poetic Acts* (Cambridge: Harvard University Press, 1988), 57.

with traditional sources.[14] But the differences run deeper. Amid the confusion that is the Book of Isaiah, the contradiction that frames all others is that between form and content. The prophet's words come to us in a shape no prophet would have provided them. There are occasional biblical examples of a classical prophet commanded to write (some of which might be subsequent additions meant to validate the assemblage of the book), but in no case do we see a prophet recording his sayings with the idea of preserving them for a future audience. Prophecy is almost exclusively an oral phenomenon, a historically committed response to immediate and specific circumstances. Gerald Bruns describes it well: "The most important point, however, is that the prophetic word is always addressed to the situation in which it is uttered, that is, to the moment at hand; it is not a traditional idea, intended as part of a permanent record. It does not bind the future but only addresses the present. . . . The prophetic word has something unwritable about it."[15] With its fixation on the historical present, prophecy generates a linguistic practice generally incompatible with the durability of text. And when redactors pieced together into a book the sayings of this "unwritable" word, the result was something like "prose run mad." Jeremiah's letter to the Babylonian exiles, then, is both the exception—a prophet writing— and the norm: it privileges speech over writing, insisting that writing serve a momentary function that conforms to the impermanence of speech. In Jeremiah's only other textual adventure, he dictates directly to his scribe, Baruch, but this too is entirely a matter of expediency: having been jailed as an agitator, Jeremiah has no other way to address the people of Israel.

If a gradually assembled, makeshift book fits awkwardly the prophetic practices it records, just the opposite is true of apocalypse, in which an idea of history and the book as coherent verbal form mutually sustain one another. By the time of the Book of Daniel, textual construction has become so skillful that one wonders how the book's pseudonymity was ever believed; even a first glance reveals that this text could not have been contemporary with the words of Isaiah or even Jeremiah,

---

[14] I do not mean to ignore the complexities of Daniel's composition, the fact that it comes to us in two languages, Hebrew and Aramaic, something still not fully explained, and that it involves the weaving together of new and inherited materials. My point is that, regardless of the composite nature of the traditional sources incorporated into the text, the various materials of the Book of Daniel seem to have been put together by a single author in a single act of composition. See Shemaryahu Talmon's entry on Daniel in *The Literary Guide to the Bible*, ed. Frank Kermode and Robert Alter (Cambridge: Harvard University Press, 1987), 343–56, for a brief account of interpretive controversies still unresolved.

[15] Gerald Bruns, "Canon and Power in the Hebrew Scriptures," in *Canons*, ed. Robert von Hallberg (Chicago: University of Chicago Press, 1983), 73.

which perhaps helps to explain why Jews placed Daniel not with the Prophets but in the miscellaneous collection of Writings. The author of Daniel simply knew how to construct a book, building into his neatly contained work an impressive and total symmetry. The first six chapters of Daniel amount to six self-contained short stories describing Yahweh's miraculous ability to deliver those exiles who suffer for him; the last six amount to six self-contained visions describing events preceding the end of history. In fact, all twelve chapters tell the same tale—one of worldly persecution yielding to divine intervention and salvation—so that the very book which imagines the end of history represents itself as a re- markably static structure. Full of stories, Daniel is on the whole a book that does not move, an essentially spatial form founded on a fundamen- tal, definitive repetition. This is not to say that the book lacks develop- ment; each story involves its own narrative movement of crisis and resolution, as does each vision, and the whole book moves from local manifestations of Yahweh's power in the first half to visions of global victory in the second. Yet every one of these instances of temporal or narrative or historical development is contained by the idea that de- velopment, that change itself, ultimately comes to an end. There is finally only one change that matters, that represented by the movement from the first to the second half of the book, from narrative to vision, from participation in historical events to the observation of history's terminal event.

The force of this static dimension in Daniel requires further explana- tion. The stories of the first half, such as Daniel's rescue from the lions' den or his colleagues' from the fiery furnace, all encourage hope in God's power to liberate, but they serve a contradictory function as well. Strung along in a repetitive series, one following the other, they suggest that while any instance of suffering may be relieved and any abuse of power undercut, the history of suffering and power is itself endless; if redemption follows suffering, suffering also follows redemption, ad infinitum. The only genuine change, then, occurs at the beginning of chapter 7, when Daniel "had a dream and visions of his head" (7:1). Not only do these dreams remove Daniel from the course of actual history and place him in a purely visionary space, they also set the individual and potentially endless experiences of suffering within the context of a master, providential narrative that achieves a final, universal closure, a last judgment that ends suffering altogether simply by ending history. Thus the symmetry of the book is anything but ornamental: the em- phatic repetitions that serve to contain development, to reduce it to one stark, absolute pattern, and finally to eliminate it altogether in a vision of temporality brought to an end, have as their analogue the book defined by spatial form rather than narrative movement, the book whose structure already seems immune to time, an allegory in language of that which is about to be eschatologically accomplished. Merely to open the book (sealed until the end of time) suggests that one has already joined the apocalyptic event, that one has crossed over to a spatial order differentiated from history.

The implicit relation here between form (the book) and content (the end of history) only becomes explicit with the Book of Revelation, which drew on many Jewish texts but Daniel particularly. Most biblical scholars today acknowledge that Revelation, odd and excessive as it may be, is a unified composition probably written by a single author, and many agree that repetition of some sort provides the structural basis for that unity.[16] In this regard, however, Revelation does two things that Daniel does not; it self-consciously refers to its own closure and permanence as a verbal form, and, in the most overt and startling way, it makes these qualities inseparable from its vision of the end of history. Three verses from the book's conclusion, John makes the following declaration: "I warn every one who hears the words of the prophecy of this book: if any one adds to them, God will add to him the plagues described in this book, and if any one takes away from the words of the book of this prophecy, God will take away his share in the tree of life and in the holy city, which are described in this book" (22:18–19). In this remarkable admonition, apocalypse, the book, has been made coextensive with apocalypse, the event; the two are woven together as a single fabric. According to John, the visionary text can take this verbal form and no other; to alter it would be to alter both providential history and the millennial kingdom, to redistribute their prescripted contents. By staking out such an exemption from change, the book claims already to lie on the other side of historical process; it claims to occupy a final, utopian space analogous to that of the New Jerusalem itself, which, no longer subject to the rising and setting of sun and moon, knows only the single, unvarying light of the Lamb. A sense of commanding, inviolable permanence is as integral to the book of apocalypse as a commitment to immediacy was to the speech of prophecy. How did we get from Isaiah and Jeremiah to Daniel and Revelation?

[16] McGinn suggests there is "a consensus among the most recent interpreters that the Apocalypse is a unity . . . and there is some agreement that the notion of recapitulation, i.e., the repetition of the same series of events from different perspectives, enables us to solve most of the difficulties and problems of the structure." "Early Apocalypticism," 22. Schüssler Fiorenza provides a powerful account of the text's unity in "The Composition and Structure of Revelation," in *The Book of Revelation: Justice and Judgment*, 159–80. The most recent of such criticism can be found in Leonard Thompson's *The Book of Revelation: Apocalypse and Empire* (Oxford: Oxford University Press, 1990), the entire second section of which is given over to a detailed reading of Revelation's literary unity.

Book Building

Although the process by which the biblical books came about remains a mystery, some preliminary answers to the question of the development from the classical prophets to the later apocalyptic writings may be found in the Book of Ezekiel, which seems to be a transitional text between speech and writing. Despite unresolved questions about the book's redaction, one thing is clear: Ezekiel depends on the existence of sacred Scripture in a way 1 Isaiah and Jeremiah do not, as is evident in the memorable (and influential) description of the prophet's commission by Yahweh: "And when I looked, behold, a hand was stretched out to me, and, lo, a written scroll was in it; and he spread it before me; and it had writing on the front and on the back, and there were written on it words of lamentation and mourning and woe. And he said to me, 'Son of man, eat what is offered to you; eat this scroll, and go, speak to the house of Israel' " (2:9–3:1). Ezekiel was a prophet born into a priestly, Zadokite family, and a passage like this one reinforces the conclusions initially advanced by Wellhausen and modified recently by Joseph Blenkinsopp, that Ezekiel is a "link between pre-exilic prophecy and post-exilic cultic theology."[17] If indeed the passage points toward the destiny of prophecy, its eventual subsumption within textual forms, it should also be observed that this result is far from certain here. Yes, the source of Ezekiel's inspiration is an already established book that exercises authority over him, but the episode also imagines the book to be soluble, digestible, an artifact that apparently has no absolute autonomy but rather gives way to that historically immersed activity which is so often critical of priestly institutions, namely, prophetic speech. This element of textual impermanence quickly becomes obvious when one considers John's use of the same scene in Revelation, which he has to reconfigure in much the way he did Jeremiah's letter to the exiles. In what is essentially a tribute to Hebrew prophecy, and Ezekiel in particular, John describes how an angel first commands him to eat the "little scroll" he holds in his hand (10:2) and then explains, "You must again prophesy about many peoples and nations and tongues and kings" (10:11). Here, the rewriting of Ezekiel is strictly a matter of resetting the original material: John can include a consumable book only because Revelation has a book to spare, only because it involves two books, one of which is prior and inviolable. Indeed, the episode of the little scroll occurs *within* the framework of the larger book sealed with seven seals, the book in which verbal matter can neither be created nor destroyed; the episode thus confirms the contain-

[17] Joseph Blenkinsopp, *Prophecy and Canon* (Notre Dame: University of Notre Dame Press, 1977), 55.

ment of speech within writing, prophecy within apocalypse. John under-scores this point by transferring the salient features of Ezekiel's scroll (written on the front and on the back) to his preserved book, while leaving the eaten book so nondescript, so featureless, that its only adjec-tive ("small") accurately reflects its diminished status.

Given that the authority of writing over speech is hardly so certain in the pivotal scene of Ezekiel's calling, one must still account for the final form of the prophet's book, which may not quite rival Daniel in struc-tural coherence, but which convinced readers well into this century that the book had a single, inspired author. In 1783, Thomas Howes could confidently turn to Ezekiel to resist the Enlightenment assault upon prophecy: "The whole appears throughout to be arranged with so much order, obvious connexion and oratorical argumentation, that we may as well suppose the words, writ on a Sybill's leaves and scattered by the winds, capable of falling by mere accident into sufficient order to form an epic poem."[18] Modern form-text criticism has demonstrated that the book did involve substantial redaction, but the question remains: why were redactors more successful with Ezekiel, arranging its forty-eight chapters in symmetrical halves that respectively emphasized judgment and salvation, than they were with Isaiah and Jeremiah? Not only is Ezekiel more consistent in its theology, it also reveals, as R. E. Clements recently put it, "a remarkable element of planned literary structure," an aesthetic form which he asserts could not have originated with the prophet himself.[19] One possibility seems to be that Ezekiel's prophetic practice already involved something we might call canon consciousness, by which I mean not so much the detectable influence of already fixed texts as participation in the very ideas and beliefs that anticipated, even promoted, the development of canon as the center of Jewish national life. Brevard Childs has put the case persuasively: "Ezekiel's original historical role was shaped by forces closely related to those which have been characterized as canonical. The effect of this joining of influences has been that there has emerged the strongest continuity between the original oracles and the final canonical shape." Such continuity would help to explain not only the coherence of the final book but the problem scholars have had trying to fit Ezekiel into the classical prophetic para-digm, with its emphasis on immediate historical engagement and its disregard of preservation. Informed by a "radical theocentric orienta-tion," an emphasis on the absolute transcendence of Yahweh that aligns

---

[18] Thomas Howes, *Critical Observations on Books Ancient and Modern* (London: B. White, 1783), 210–11.

[19] R. E. Clements, "The Ezekiel Tradition: Prophecy in a Time of Crisis," in *Israel's Prophetic Tradition*, ed. Coggins, Phillips, and Knibb, 127.

the prophet with the priesthood, "Ezekiel's message never takes on the particularity of the usual prophetic activity in which specific issues and groups are addressed in invective and threat."[20] Already partially unmoored from the markers of circumstance, Ezekiel's more literary and myth-colored words were well-suited to the permanence of text.

Drawing on Childs, to whom I will return momentarily, I want to push this largely speculative argument a step further. Biblical scholars generally concede that the first phase of canonization reached its completion in the priestly redaction that, during the exile (and Ezekiel's ministry), and then across the sixth and fifth centuries, brought about the Pentateuch substantially as we know it.[21] While the priestly school probably had a final hand in influencing the shape of Torah, we still have only a vague understanding of P, even to the extent that it represents ancient material or postexilic redaction of inherited sources. Moreover, while P bears a close thematic and stylistic relation to sections of Ezekiel, we don't know the historical nature of that relation, whether the priestly school partially consisted of Ezekiel's disciples or whether the prophet and the school drew on a shared tradition that predates both, just to mention two options. In our context, these intractable complications remind us that we cannot define any causal relation between Ezekiel's prophecy, which is moving in a direction compatible with canon, and the first consolidation, and closure, of a body of canonical texts (the five books). Recognizing that they may best be imagined as intersecting movements within the development of Israel's canon consciousness, I want to isolate one shared feature of Ezekiel and the priestly Pentateuch that not only enhanced the authority of canon but would become constitutive of the bookish nature of apocalypse.

Among the various concerns that characterize P, one finds the representation of sacred space as that which can be minutely, precisely measured, that which is signified by a severe geometry. Whether this preoccupation with mathematical design is ancient or postexilic (or both), it helps provide unity to the final form of the Pentateuch, shaping the whole into a single, continuous book. Evident especially in the construction of the ark and the tabernacle in Exodus (chaps. 35–40), this emphasis on numerological rigor suggests that a space occupied by Yahweh's presence, by the Shekinah, must be defined atemporally, erected upon abstract principles undisturbed by time. The ark is built by inspired craftsmen to Yahweh's own specifications, and its exhaustive

[20] Brevard Childs, *Introduction to the Old Testament as Scripture* (London: SCM, 1979), 361–62. Clements also seeks to explain the literary coherence of Ezekiel on the basis of a continuity between the prophet and his priestly redactors. "The Ezekiel Tradition," 120.

[21] Robert Alter refers to the documentary hypothesis as "a periodically challenged consensus." *The Literary Guide to the Bible*, ed. Kermode and Alter, 24.

formalism reflects the belief that, although this structure is built of worldly materials, its blueprint exists as an idea in God. In order to become consonant with its divine origin, the physical space of the ark must be completely transfigured, marked off by an immaterial border that radically removes its contents from things that change. The burden of this transfiguration belongs to numbers, or more accurately, to the fetishization of quantities. The persistent attention to sacred space, then, coincides with one of P's more general concerns, what Blenkinsopp calls "the attempt to overcome time . . . in a thoroughgoing and systematic way."[22] It would be difficult to miss the political advantages bound up with this spatial orientation: amid the uncertainty of the exile and the subsequent return to Israel, the priestly writers enhanced the authority of the official cult by grounding its institutions in transcendental designs prescribed by Yahweh himself and realized under the heroic leadership of Moses.[23] More important for my immediate purposes, P had the effect of associating a sacred book ("the law") with the idea of an atemporal, architectural space. After all, in the ark, at the center of the tabernacle's sacred space, is a text, the tablets of the decalogue. Contiguous with the Shekinah itself, sacred writing requires the containment of a timeless, spatial order, the essence of which has everything to do with numbers and nothing to do with historical flux.

I do not mean to suggest that the priestly redactors of the Pentateuch self-consciously conceptualized their texts in terms of a spatial form removed from and antithetical to history; I merely wish to point out that at an early stage of canonization the representation of sacred text and the representation of sacred space were mutually implicated. Indeed, we know so little about the historical identity of these author-editors that it is nearly impossible to speculate on their working idea of the book—or rather, it would be impossible were it not for the fact that their very self-effacement, their stunning success in removing from the biblical texts the signs of their own involvement, is in itself revealing. "Basic to the canonical process," Childs has argued, "is that those responsible for the actual editing of the text did their best to obscure their own identity. Thus the actual process by which the text was reworked lies in almost total obscurity."[24] This seemingly indisputable premise, with its damaging implications for traditional form-text criticism, does suggest one

[22] Blenkinsopp, *Prophecy and Canon*, 73–74.

[23] Blenkinsopp offers the fullest account of this argument in his chapter, "The Priestly Work," in *Prophecy and Canon*, 54–79. Similar claims appear throughout the first two chapters of Ellis Rivkin's *The Shaping of Jewish History* (New York: Scribner's, 1971), where he discusses ways in which the priests tried "to ground their claims in the remote past," especially in the revelation at Sinai (15).

[24] Childs, *Introduction to the Old Testament as Scripture*, 78.

vitally significant thing we can say with certainty about the biblical redactors, priestly or other: *they understood their texts to be independent of the circumstances of their production.* The self-erasure practiced religiously by these authors is our most concrete instance of the erasure of historical specificity necessary to produce canon, necessary to produce books that could speak permanently to history but had their origin and essence elsewhere.

Through canonization the book begins to be understood as something other than historical circumstance, a notion that played an especially crucial role in reshaping prophecy as it passed into written forms. Although his polemical conclusions are often debatable, Childs again provides the best description of prophecy become canon: "The growth of Israel's canon consciousness can be clearly detected when the words of a prophet which were directed to a specific group in a particular historical situation were recognized as having an authority apart from their original use, and were preserved for their own integrity (cf. Isa. 8.16f.). The heart of the canonical process lay in transmitting and ordering the authoritative tradition in a form which was compatible to function as scripture for a generation which had not participated in the original events of revelation."[25] Thus, by diminishing the historical markers which situated the work of actual, living prophets, editors could eventually collapse the oracles of three centuries into a single mythical identity, Isaiah. The second part of Isaiah almost certainly spoke to a specific group of Babylonian exiles, but "even though the message was once addressed to real people in a particular historical situation . . . the canonical editors of this tradition employed the material in such a way as to eliminate almost entirely those concrete features and to subordinate the original message to a new role within the canon."[26] In short, the biblical redactors imagined their books to consist of words at least one step removed from any particular historical dimension, something that in turn implicitly privileged a new, spatially oriented textual formalism. Not only were the books immune to future change (assuming a final form in the canon), they became places from which historical embeddedness could be written out of consideration.

In Ezekiel, a transitional text between spoken and written prophecy, all these various strands are evident, though the logic that links them is not necessarily self-conscious at this stage of textual production. These strands are best thought of as contiguous until the Book of Revelation (even more so than Daniel) gathers them together into the single weave of apocalypse. As mentioned, Ezekiel already subordinates concrete

---

[25] Ibid., 60.
[26] Ibid., 325.

historical detail to his more visionary, theocentric concerns, something that probably allowed for the relatively easy passage of his oracles into book form. Moreover, with its overarching symmetry, the canonical book is clearly, deliberately, organized on spatial principles.[27] Most important to the book's representation of its own form, however, is the fact that it achieves closure only through a vision of monumental and ideal architecture, a vision of the restored temple that reproduces the obsessive mathematical stylization of P. Escorted by a mysterious bronze figure, Ezekiel witnesses the minute measuring of the temple and its accoutrements, down to the last doorjamb, an activity that binds the visionary temple to the original ark and tabernacle in Exodus. Despite the destruction of the first temple, despite all historical misfortunes, the text seems to say, the dwelling place of the Shekinah has remained unchanged in its mathematical, immaterial essence. It makes no difference in this context whether the last eight chapters of Ezekiel are based on an original vision of the prophet himself or whether they represent a subsequent attempt to legitimate the priesthood as restored Israel's rightful authority. The point here is that in this instance of prophecy's modulation into writing three things converge: oracles to some extent already dehistoricized; an austere, closural vision of sacred space, timeless in its monumental, geometric order; and a book organized with considerable success on such spatial principles as symmetry. With this configuration taking shape in the relatively early stages of canonization, the ground is prepared for apocalypse, where the end of history will become inseparable from a literary formalism, where (in both meanings of the phrase) history will end in a book.

To see the Book of Revelation as the culmination of this development from prophecy to apocalypse asks that we first read the book literally. John tells the story of the end of history and the foundation of an ideal space, the New Jerusalem. The telos of time is space.[28] Thus the fun-

---

[27] See H. Van Dyke Parunak, "The Literary Architecture of Ezekiel's Marot Elohim," *Journal of Biblical Literature* 99 (1980), which emphasizes the text's many symmetrical devices in order to demonstrate "the intricacy and the skill with which the final redaction of the material . . . has been carried out" (62).

[28] We thus need to qualify the valuable generic definition John Collins put forward to help clarify debate among biblical scholars: " 'Apocalypse' is a genre of revelatory literature with a narrative framework, in which a revelation is mediated by an otherworldly being to a human recipient, disclosing a transcendent reality which is both temporal, insofar as it envisages eschatological salvation, and spatial insofar as it involves another, supernatural world." "Introduction: Towards the Morphology of a Genre," in *Apocalypse: The Morphology of a Genre, Semeia* 14 (1979): 9. This definition helpfully allows one term to cover both the "vertical" and "horizontal" leanings of apocalyptic literature (ascensions to heaven and visions of events leading to the end of time), but it elides the fact that in many apocalypses, and especially in Revelation, the temporal and the spatial exist in a particular and hierarchical relation: one irreversibly eclipses the other.

damental theological question of Revelation—how will the community of believers pass from history to God?—is framed within a narrative whereby the spatial eclipses the temporal. Granted, W. J. T. Mitchell is right when he argues that time and space cannot be thought without one another, and that the most persistent obstacle to an adequate study of spatial form in literature is the belief that "literary works achieve 'spatiality' only by denying temporality."[29] But in the most literal way, Revelation constructs that very obstacle, perhaps in its most abiding Western form. The transformation of prophecy into apocalypse is complete when Revelation merges its own linguistic order with the sacred space of the New Jerusalem and makes both sites, verbal and architectural, antithetical to history, something we have already glimpsed in John's final injunction against tampering with the text.

At the end of Revelation, history and text achieve closure simultaneously. Consider history first. Immediately following the Last Judgment, that irreversible divide between old and new, chapter 21 begins:

> Then I saw a new heaven and a new earth; for the first heaven and the first earth had passed away, and the sea was no more. And I saw the holy city, new Jerusalem, coming down out of heaven from God, prepared as a bride adorned for her husband; and I heard a great voice from the throne saying, "Behold, the dwelling of God is with men. He will dwell with them, and they shall be his people, and God himself will be with them; he will wipe away every tear from their eyes, and death shall be no more, neither shall there be mourning nor crying nor pain any more, for the former things have passed away." (21:1–4)

In this moment of radical discontinuity, what makes familiar things new—like heaven, earth, Jerusalem, patriarchal relations, and so on—is the presence of God and the absence of time; former things, if they are not eliminated altogether like the sea, assume their final, unchanging, sacred form and thus become new. If history is time with content, then the New Jerusalem is content without time. As in Ezekiel, and Exodus before it, Revelation systematically foregrounds the absence of time by emphasizing the spatial dimensions of its foursquare city: "And he who talked to me had a measuring rod of gold to measure the city and its gates and walls" (21:15). John borrows this measuring rod straight from

---

[29] W. J. T. Mitchell, "Spatial Form in Literature: Toward a General Theory," *Critical Inquiry* 6 (Spring 1980): 542. Mitchell's argument seems to me impeccable when it is kept at the phenomenological level of time and space, but when one considers instead the relationship between space and history, a different set of questions arises. Most significant to me is this: How does the foregrounding of spatial form influence a text's representation of history?

Ezekiel, acknowledging the vision's debts, but he also makes clear that the heavenly city supersedes Ezekiel's temple, not merely in scope but in that the Shekinah returns to dwell with "men" *permanently*. The New Jerusalem realizes, makes literal, what had always been implied by the meticulous measurements and numerical fixations of those sacred spaces that anticipated it: the only architecture commensurate with God's presence is that which lies on the other side of history, that which is altogether ideal. Writing not long after the destruction of the second temple, John knew the inadequacy of building a sacred space within history. The temple signified a coexistence of the sacred and the profane, as if one could exist within the other, separated merely by a stone wall. For a second time, events proved that a wall would collapse under pressure. Only with the decisive end of history does sacred space achieve its destiny, become permanent and total, extending its mathematical lineaments beyond a single, contained structure to an entire built environment. The New Jerusalem has and needs no temple.

At the same moment in which history gives way to a city, the Book of Revelation achieves its own dramatic spatialization. Assessing some typical structuralist assumptions regarding narrative closure, Geoffrey Harpham provides an unexpected gloss on Revelation: "The horizontal [element of narrative], which is doubled in the reading act, can be formed, but cannot form itself; this responsibility falls to the vertical axis, a principle of atemporality, abstraction, and rationality that emerges most forcefully at the end when the reader gathers the narrative into 'spatial form' in a kind of 'memorial synthesis' or last judgment."[30] The end unveils the narrative's spatial organization, which, like providential design itself, has been obscurely operative all along. Harpham's final pun on the apocalypse, poking fun at structuralist metaphysics, is not gratuitous. Although there are many ways to read John's prophecy, Revelation *invites* a structuralist, or at least formalist, reading in which the text's closure creates a supremely coherent, aesthetic whole, a form that can be visualized spatially. John's warning neither to add to nor subtract from the text, with its invocation of an ideal verbal form, has for centuries proven as hypnotic as it is intimidating. I know of no other text more consistently diagramed by its commentators, either literally (analysis accompanied by charts, tables, schematic drawings) or figuratively (analysis in a distinctly spatial vocabulary). In its most modest form, this impulse appears when a reader considers the text circular because it begins and ends with epistolary conventions. On the grand scale, it can take the form of a wholesale architecturalization

[30] Geoffrey Harpham, *The Ascetic Imperative in Culture and Criticism* (Chicago: University of Chicago Press, 1987), 75–76.

of the text, whereby the book gets figured as a magnificent building one must enter (typically a temple) or as a well-guarded space to be unlocked hermeneutically, a motif common in the eighteenth century and not uncommon even today.[31] More often, the spatialization of Revelation occurs in the countless works of criticism that emphasize the text's intricate synchronic structure, the formal unity and wholeness that result from its manipulation of symbols (especially numbers) and narrative devices—in short, its impressive closure. In a chapter called "The Linguistic Unity of the Book of Revelation," Leonard Thompson tells us, "The language of Revelation is so intertwined that it cannot be easily dissected. The threads crisscross in different ways, sometimes tracing a path forward, sometimes backward, sometimes intertwining through overlays of metaphoric simultaneity."[32] These "simultaneity" readings seem to me entirely faithful to the text's display of literary sophistication, even if they do not tell the whole story. My point is simply that Revelation calls attention to its aesthetic self-containment; it invites, among other things, recognition of its status as a brilliantly crafted linguistic space, and that invitation has been, for good reason, difficult to resist.

By the time John wrote the Book of Revelation, with a well-established scriptural canon already in place, textual formalism had come to signify authority. Without this context, it would be impossible to grasp the force of the text's defensive insistence on its own integrity: any transgression of its form (adding or subtracting) will be punished according to its content (denial of access to the utopian, posthistorical pleasures described). To alter the text is to be denied citizenship in the New Jerusalem. John clearly anticipated resistance to his vision and hoped to overwhelm that resistance. By having its form as well as its content converge on the New Jerusalem, Revelation claims for itself an extraordinary privilege. The latent equivalence between sacred space and sacred text, which we saw in Ezekiel and the priestly redactors of the Pentateuch, gets realized and perfected the moment John can extend the very signs of sacred space, those precise measurements and quantifications, across the entire structure of his book as its most significant principle of formal organization. Revelation includes two explicit acts of measurement: John's use of the rod to measure the temple in chapter 10, which in turn anticipates the angel's measuring of the New Jerusalem in chapter 21. This motif alone sets the entire text squarely within the biblical tradition of sacred space. But more significantly, Revelation is a book built obsessively, relentlessly, on numbers, mainly, but not exclusively, the famous number seven. Read

---

[31] Some of these formalist strategies for reading Revelation and their ideological implications are considered in Chapter 2.

[32] Thompson, *The Book of Revelation: Apocalypse and Empire*, 52.

strictly within the rather narrow concerns of literary form, these numbers are important more for their general, formal significance than for any specific symbolic function (the fact, for instance, that seven is the day of the sabbath). Within the context of canon, they signify the text's participation in a wholly spatial order where time does not factor. Repeated across the Apocalypse as both a narrative pattern (seven seals, seven trumpets, seven vials) and a feature of various elements related to those patterns (seven churches, seven stars, seven heads), seven is the measure of Revelation's sacred space. It provides the text with a blueprint, just as twelve does for the gates and foundations of the New Jerusalem. It indicates something like Harpham's "principle of atemporality, abstraction, and rationality that emerges most forcefully at the end"; only here, the end does its closural work in a way that has never been rivaled: in the figurative form of a city, the end offers the book an image of itself as measurable, sacred space.

Although the Greek word *canon* was not used to describe Christian Scripture until 350 C.E., we should remember that its earliest and most common usage was that of a builder's measuring rod or plumb line, like that used by Ezekiel's bronze man or John's engineering-minded angel.[33] Applied later to sacred books, *canon* metaphorically stood for a reliable standard against which other texts could be measured, but sedimented within that figure is a more literal identification: textual and architectural construction, two things that share the common denominator of spatial orientation. Book and building each have their essential geometry, that shape mathematically defined which can be no other. A millennium and a half later, the Renaissance architect Alberti could define a standard for beauty in much the same terms John had used to describe his inviolable order of words: "A harmony of all the parts in whatsoever subject it appears, fitted together with such proportion and connection, that nothing could be added, diminished, or altered but for the worse."[34] Neither add nor subtract—or put at risk the utopian order of "proportion and connection," the canon of ideal measurement that must remain permanently fixed. By the end of the first century, John could move freely between linguistic and architectural utopian spaces. In the letter to the Philadelphians, which includes Revelation's first reference to the New Jerusalem, Christ says, "'He who conquers, I will make him a pillar in the temple of my God; never shall he go out of it,

[33] Bruce Metzger provides a brief but thorough account of the word *canon* in *The Canon of the New Testament: Its Origin, Development, and Significance* (Oxford: Clarendon, 1987), 289–93.

[34] Colin Rowe quotes Alberti in *The Mathematics of the Ideal Villa and Other Essays* (Cambridge: MIT Press, 1976), 217. Rowe suggests that "a particular Utopia can be subjected to neither alteration, addition, nor subtraction" (213).

and I will write on him the name of my God and the name of the city of my God, the new Jerusalem which comes down from my God out of heaven, and my own new name'" (3:12). The Messiah encourages his faithful by promising them translation out of history and into an alternative order that is at once, without differentiation, architectural and linguistic. To become a pillar of a sacred space is also to be written upon, to become the text of a new language. In Revelation, it becomes impossible to determine whether language is a figure for architecture or architecture a figure for language; both signify that transfigured condition one imagines as the end of history.

When the descent of the New Jerusalem brings Revelation to a close, two things are so deeply implicated they might be said to enable each other: a vision of the end of history, those events soon to be accomplished, and a book in which that end is already accomplished, a linguistic space outside history. One imagines the other. In *The Sense of an Ending*, Frank Kermode argues that apocalypse has preserved its grip on Western consciousness by modulating from literal, imminent forms (like Revelation) to figurative, immanent forms, a modulation first perfected by Augustine. Faced with the inevitable failures of prediction, visionary writers eventually relocated apocalypse to consciousness where it could occur in the present, in mental events like epiphany. While this narrative is certainly accurate, it is also true that Revelation anticipates the decisive shift by striking its own balance between imminence and immanence: the end is already present in the form of the book.

If the end of history and the formation of the book are not merely coincidental, then apocalypse, which M. H. Abrams claims gave the West its idea of history, also contributed in no small measure to the West's idea of the book.[35] More to the point, it helped set the two in opposition, helped create the tradition whereby the book came to be conceived as a space into which history did not significantly enter, a space, in other words, where history came to an end. For good reason, it should seem surprising to see in any apocalypse, and especially in the Book of Revelation, the imagining of an ahistorical verbal order, and my discussion thus far has been deliberately one-dimensional. Has any book more deeply engaged history, either in its original opposition to Rome or in its later reception, when readers, uncertain how to act, pored over its pages for

[35] As M. H. Abrams states in "Apocalypse: Theme and Variations," "The prototype of the Western concept that history has an intelligible and end-determined order, whether fideistic or naturalistic, is the scheme of the course of earthly affairs from genesis to apocalypse which is underwritten by a sacred text." In *The Apocalypse in English Renaissance Thought and Literature*, ed. Patrides and Wittreich, 344. The idea is played out much more fully, of course, in M. H. Abrams, *Natural Supernaturalism* (New York: Norton, 1971).

signs of their own immediate and crisis-ridden times? Probably not. And indeed, my interest lies not simply in the way that Revelation's literary form and its vision of the end of history are mutually constitutive but also in the ideological work performed by that formalism.

As always, the question is this: What historical functions are served when an author represents the end of history? The complicated answer begins with recognition that the end of history can serve a variety of purposes, only one of which is reflected in the activist millenarian tradition Revelation helped to produce. Attention to the radicalism of millenarian movements has been so dominant in historical studies that a concentration on Revelation's formalist investments must seem narrowly literary at best, fully misguided at worst. And this would be true if Revelation consistently produced a politically charged response, which it did not. The image of the end of history may invoke a crisis that invites participation in historical conflict, but it can also serve to represent an immanent order and authority that lie beyond history and therefore mark the definitive limit of historical conflict, the line beyond which dispute cannot pass. As I argue in the following section, Revelation yokes the transcendence of history with the suppression of dissent, a combination that helps to explain how a controversial book could become not only a canonical book but the very guardian of canonical authority, the book capable of permanently closing the two-testament canon that had evolved over a period of at least seven hundred years.

Seeking to correct the exclusively millenarian picture of medieval apocalypse created by Norman Cohn in his influential *Pursuit of the Millennium,* Bernard McGinn has written, "This approach is almost totally blind to those manifestations of apocalyptic traditions that were intended to *support* the institutions of medieval Christianity rather than to serve as a critique, either mild or violent. . . . Beliefs about the coming age . . . were as important for social continuity as they were for social change. Better understood as forms of political rhetoric rather than as pre-political phenomena, they were as often designed to maintain the political, social, and economic order as to overthrow it."[36] In this book, I investigate the politics of apocalypse that promotes institutional order. I am more concerned with Revelation the canonical text than with the radical sermon preached against Roman authority on behalf of a persecuted, minority sect. But even this formulation is deceiving, as it suggests the existence of two texts when there is only a single, deeply contradictory text. Revelation did not enter the New Testament canon— or more accurately, provide the canon with its powerful closure—be-

---

[36] Bernard McGinn, *Visions of the End: Apocalyptic Traditions in the Middle Ages* (New York: Columbia University Press, 1979), 29–30.

cause church fathers misread it for their own purposes. The canonical text and the radical sermon coexist side by side *within* Revelation. Until now I have talked about canonization as the process that allowed an idea of the book and a vision of the end of history to converge; now I want to talk about the ideological work performed by that convergence.

The Canonical Work of Revelation

According to Brevard Childs, the story of canon in the Hebrew Scriptures is the story of a community's movement away from "sociological and historical differences" to "identity"—identity defined on a literary plane where those differences do not obtain.

> Increasingly the original sociological and historical differences within the nation of Israel—Northern and Southern Kingdom, pro- and anti-monarchical parties, apocalyptic versus theocratic circles—were lost, and a religious community emerged which found its identity in terms of sacred scripture. Israel defined itself in terms of a book! The canon formed the decisive *Sitz im Leben* for the Jewish community's life, thus blurring the sociological evidence most sought after by the modern historian. When critical exegesis is made to rest on the recovery of these very sociological distinctions which have been obscured, it runs directly in the face of the canon's intention.[37]

In Childs's terms, this narrative possesses a certain inevitability, coupled with an odd passivity: differences were lost, identity was found, a nation emerged. Yet how are we to respond to this disappearance of history into Scripture? How does one read a book that has effaced the circumstances of its own production and thus claimed for itself a space outside of historical difference, as if the community it represents were, in its essence, monolithic and unchanging? To attempt the excavation of buried circumstance is indeed to violate the canon's intentions, but to accept the erasure of history, and to read the text for its own literary and theological integrity, as Childs would have us do, is to submit to the canon's intentions, to allow the canon an uninterrogated exercise of power.

Power is at issue: although it has succeeded in subordinating historical specificity to a presentation of higher concerns, the canon itself

---

[37] Childs, *Introduction to the Old Testament as Scripture*, 78.

played a central role in the power struggles of ancient Judaism and early Christianity. Far from representing a universal or timeless voice, the canon speaks for those specific parties who were able to secure their social and theological authority against the rival claims of others. In concluding his study of New Testament canon formation, Bruce Metzger respectfully defers to the conclusion of one of his mentors: "It is the simple truth to say that the New Testament books became canonical because no one could stop them doing so."[38] While ostensibly an argument for canonization by aesthetic or theological merit ("these books were so good they inevitably earned their proper place"), this sentence bears another, related meaning: good books become canonical when their proponents are sufficiently powerful to withstand the dissent of those who oppose them, even if any original resistance is eventually written out of the record, as if it never existed. Moreover, by effacing its origin in past conflict, the canon lays claim to a noncontingent authority that binds future readers as well, regardless of their circumstances. It acts, in other words, to contain conflict *perpetually*.[39]

Oddly enough, the canonization of Hebrew prophecy accomplished two apparently contradictory things: it preserved prophecy for all time in the form of sacred texts, and it put an end to prophecy as a living phenomenon. Why should the establishment of canon as the dominant feature of postexilic Israel coincide with the decease of prophecy, and what does this coincidence indicate about the power concerns of canon? In the Hebrew Scriptures, prophecy and canon hardly seem incompatible, let alone antagonistic: the Book of the Prophets followed the canonization of the Pentateuch, and the Pentateuch itself provides a central

[38] This sentence, quoted from one William Barclay, appears on page 286 of Metzger, *The Canon of the New Testament*.

[39] In what follows, my argument is very much influenced by John Brenkman's recent critique of Hans-Georg Gadamer. Gadamer's idea of tradition as a force in history that is at the same time free of the mere specificities of circumstance lies close to Childs's work on canon: "The real meaning of a text, as it speaks to the interpreter, does not depend on the contingencies of the author and whom he originally wrote for." *Truth and Method* (New York: Seabury Press, 1975), 263. As Brenkman demonstrates so effectively, this construction of tradition as "a kind of timeless present" (*Truth and Method*, 256) bears, as it denies, a set of ideological consequences. "These methods obliterate the traces of the work's historical imbeddedness in a society, cast its contemporaneous power as the sign of art's absolute autonomy vis-à-vis society, and thus construe the artwork's claim to universal validity as its achievement of meanings whose continuity over time transcends the discontinuities of societal change." In opposition to this approach, Brenkman formulates a series of questions that might be productively put to the relation between Revelation and canon: "How does an artwork bear within its formal and communicative structures the traces of its inherence in a set of social relations and practices? How at the same time does it effect a break with its context, and how do this break *and* that context become readable in the course of aesthetic-hermeneutical experience?" John Brenkman, *Culture and Domination* (Ithaca: Cornell University Press, 1987), 34.

place for prophecy in the figure of Moses. Yet some scholars, most vigorously Blenkinsopp, have observed in the relationship between spoken prophecy and written canon a version of the tension Max Weber believed constitutive of ancient Judaism itself—that between charismatic leadership and institutional government.[40] Bruns is most direct in his summary statement: "The thesis here is that canonization is the priestly appropriation of prophetic authority by means of the superior forces of writing and textuality; or, in other words, writing was a way of getting rid of prophecy."[41] By privileging spontaneous, individual inspiration (embodied in the immediacy of speech), prophecy represented an unpredictable source of authority, one that lay outside the jurisdiction of the temple cult. One effect of canonization was to stabilize the priesthood's theocratic power vis-à-vis prophecy by fixing the source of that power in permanent, binding texts no longer open to alteration, no longer open to new revelation. It should come as no surprise that the first phase of canonization involved the consolidation of Torah, literally written "law," a set of texts centered on Moses' receiving the tablets at Sinai. Even the representation of Moses reinforces the subordination of prophecy that canonization entailed; in the text of priestly redactors, Moses fulfills his role as archetypal prophet by delivering the law to the people, by receiving the only divine revelation Israel would ever need, the fulfillment of its destiny as a chosen nation. Deuteronomy, which claims to record the final speeches of Moses, closes Torah with a definitive image of the prophet: in a series of extended, detailed monologues, Moses expounds the law to the people about to enter the promised land. The written prophet becomes a spokesman for the written law.

Along these lines, perhaps Blenkinsopp's most impressive insight involves the way canon established its supremacy through a cumulative process of containment. "Clerical scribalism," he suggests, "met the prophetic claim not by confrontation but by assimilation and redefinition, seeking to bring prophecy within its own institutional grid."[42] This notion helps explain, for instance, how there came to be a Book of the Prophets that functioned as a supplement to Torah. The need for such an addition implies some early dissatisfaction with Torah, a sense that it was somehow incomplete. According to a leading sociological reconstruction, that of Otto Plöger, the primary conflict within the weak and bewildered postexilic community was between theocratic and eschatological factions. In securing power upon their return from Babylon, the

---

[40] For Max Weber's description of the tension between the state and the "nomadic ideal" promoted by the prophets, see *Ancient Judaism* (New York: Free Press, 1952), 100–117.

[41] Bruns, "Canon and Power in the Hebrew Scriptures," 77.

[42] Blenkinsopp, *Prophecy and Canon*, 8.

Zadokite priests sought to represent the rebuilding of the temple and the restoration of life under Mosaic law as Israel's accomplished destiny, the very telos of its national hopes. Those groups excluded from social power, however, looked instead to the eschatological visions produced during the exile, visions of a glorious redemption which from their perspective did not seem to match the unideal conditions of Second Temple life. With these circles emphasizing more and more an apocalyptic reading of prophecy, a reading strikingly different from that provided by Deuteronomy, the Book of the Prophets emerged as a countervoice expressing the longing for an alternative social order beyond that prescribed by the law.[43] And yet, this expansion of the canon has all the makings of a battle won and a war lost, precisely because the struggle occurs entirely on the canon's own terrain—writing.

The Book of the Prophets ironically signaled the decisive end of prophecy in ancient Israel. With permanent access to the classical sayings of pre-exilic heroes, there was little need for new revelations; it is hard to imagine how a would-be prophet could compete with the visions or teachings of Isaiah, especially amid the canon's persistent warnings about false prophets. In this way, prophecy came to be seen as an activity that belonged to a distant, richly mythologized past, one that reached its apex long ago in Moses (whom no other prophet could rival) and which had a secondary wave of activity before and during the exile. As the prophetic books took hold in the Second Temple period, actual prophecy dwindled in prestige and finally disappeared. In the long view of the emergence of ancient Judaism, prophecy had been successfully assimilated into the written domain of canon and had become an integral part of its institutional authority.

I dwell on these arguments at some length because they form a necessary prelude to any discussion of the complicated social functions of the Book of Revelation. If in the development of Judeo-Christian Scripture prophecy and canon are to some extent deeply antithetical forces, then where do we situate apocalypse, which evolves not simply out of prophecy, but out of canonized prophecy, prophecy already reworked in written forms that bear an institutional inscription?[44] No one can doubt the explosive threat that occurs when apocalypse adopts the

---

[43] As Otto Plöger puts it, "The gradual preparation of a prophetic canon as a supplement to the *Torah* is to be regarded as a telling appeal to maintain the Law without surrendering the expectation of a millennium." *Theocracy and Eschatology*, trans. S. Rudman (Oxford: Blackwell, 1968), 24.

[44] "Apocalypse is the child of prophecy, but prophecy which had already been taken over and transformed by priests and scribes. The writers of apocalypses claimed access to revelation not by virtue of direct communication from God, as did the classical prophets, but by access to the true meaning of prophetic texts." Blenkinsopp, *Prophecy and Canon*, 138.

most subversive feature of prophecy, its absolute faith in ongoing, non-institutional, individual inspiration, its testimony to the fact that anyone, regardless of official position, can experience revelation. The inherent volatility of the genre surely helps to explain why only two apocalypses entered the two-testament canon when so many more were written. Consider, for instance, this preface to the late and relatively conservative Apocalypse of Paul, which purports to explain how the text of so famous an author happened to be only recently discovered:

> In the consulate of Theodosius Augustus the Younger and of Cynegius a certain respected man was living in Tarsus in the house which had once belonged to St. Paul; during the night an angel appeared to him and gave him a revelation telling him to break up the foundations of the house and to make public what he found. But he thought this was a delusion.
> However the angel came the third time and scourged him and compelled him to break up the foundations. And when he had dug he discovered a marble box which was inscribed on the sides; in it was the revelation of Saint Paul and the shoes in which he used to walk when he was teaching the word of God.[45]

While this preface obviously bids to legitimate the text that follows, it also, probably inadvertently, sends another signal: it suggests what happens when "a certain respected man" experiences a private revelation on the order of apocalypse. Immediately, such vision prompts an act of destruction, as if by its very nature the vision were incompatible with any establishment built on stable foundations. One remembers the orders Yahweh gave to Jeremiah: "to pluck up and to break down, to destroy and to overthrow, to build and to plant" (1:10). With its debt to prophetic ecstasy and spontaneity, apocalypse prompts one to leave behind the inauthentic security of the house: the respected man of Tarsus breaks up the floor to find not only Paul's words but his shoes. Apparently, apocalypse requires an itinerant prophet outside institutional stability and vigilance.

The strongest case for regarding the Book of Revelation as prophecy has been put forward by Elisabeth Schüssler Fiorenza. In her readings, John hardly concerns himself with constructing literary masterpieces and otherworldly visions; he writes instead to a Christian community in crisis, demanding an immediate response of the sort expected by the Hebrew prophets when they addressed the people of Jerusalem. His book consists of "visionary rhetoric," with the emphasis squarely on

---

[45] Apocalypse of Paul, trans. R. McL. Wilson, in *New Testament Apocrypha*, ed. Wilhelm Schneemelcher (Philadelphia: Fortress, 1965), 2:759.

rhetoric; he urgently needs to persuade. In fact, John's book is no book at all, but rather a letter, an epistolary sermon designed for a specific occasion, and Schüssler Fiorenza is right to deride those commentators who isolate the literary integrity of the apocalyptic vision from its setting within the epistolary framework. Revelation is not so much bookish as it is overtly political. Thus she states unequivocally: "Literary activity constitutes only a difference in degree but does not destroy the prophetic character of apocalyptic works," and "[Revelation's] main objective is not the reinterpretation of the Hebrew Scriptures nor the calculation of the end time events, but the prophetic communication of the revelation (i.e. *apokalypsis Iesou Christou*) to the seven communities in Asia Minor."[46] Finally, while almost all apocalyptic literature is pseudonymous, John unabashedly writes in his own name; at the very least, this indicates that prophecy as individual, private revelation outside institutional routines maintains significant force in the early Christian communities. Apparently, canon and the apocalyptic writings that emerged in its wake do not necessarily or universally spell the death of prophecy.

I find these arguments for the most part persuasive, and had Revelation been shut out of the New Testament like every other independent Christian apocalypse I would find them sufficient. But Revelation did enter the New Testament, and by defining that testament's closure this work of prophecy paradoxically put an end to individual and authoritative revelation; it eventually did for the central church what the Book of the Prophets did for Second Temple Judaism. We know the various factors that made this canonization controversial: McGinn cites the book's lurid symbolism and its dangerous chiliasm, as well as the uncompromising nature of its anti-Roman stance that must have worried early Christians even before Constantine's conversion. Moreover, the patristic church remained deeply and generally suspicious of all apocalyptic writings because of the popularity experienced by millenarian splinter groups like the Montanists. What we don't know with comparable certainty is why, given these circumstances, Revelation could ultimately enter the canon as its final chapter. Two pages after outlining the controversies blocking Revelation's easy acceptance, McGinn can state, "there is no denying that it is the most powerful apocalyptic work ever written," as if that put an end to such questions.[47] It would seem that Revelation became a canonical book simply because no one could stop it doing so.

In what follows, I shift attention away from Revelation as prophecy, not to deny that aspect of the text, but to focus instead on its antithetical function as canon, as that which contains and finally eliminates proph-

[46] Schüssler Fiorenza, *The Book of Revelation: Justice and Judgment,* 140.
[47] McGinn, *Visions of the End,* 14.

ecy. Both aspects, I believe, are internal to John's vision of the end of history. In the preceding section, I emphasized the closure secured by John's last-second injunction against tampering with the text. This command, linked to the stiffest penalties for disobedience, has its precedent oddly enough in Deuteronomy, the book which centuries earlier might have represented "an official countertext to prophecy."[48] In Deuteronomy, Moses sometimes glosses his exposition of the law with comments like these: "Everything that I command you you shall be careful to do; you shall not add to it or take from it" (12:32), or, "If you are not careful to do all the words of this law which are written in this book, that you may fear this glorious and awful name, the Lord your God, then the Lord will bring on you and your offspring extraordinary afflictions, afflictions severe and lasting, and sicknesses grievous and lasting" (28:58– 59). The formula forbidding addition to and subtraction from a text has its origin in ancient Near Eastern law codes, and Deuteronomy's use of the formula helps to confirm the image of Moses as servant to the law.[49] Probably the first book to take on official canonical status within the priestly cult, Deuteronomy began the process of defining revelation in terms of written law, the process that eventually eliminated prophetic activity from the accepted practices of the Jewish community. No one could be surprised at the extent to which John draws upon the Book of the Prophets, but what has Revelation to do with Deuteronomy?

Language beyond History

The Book of Revelation describes the sublime rupture that occurs when time becomes space, when history meets its final antithesis in both a heavenly city and a book. At the same time, the Book of Revelation describes a fundamental change in the nature of language. The interdependence of these two narratives is the necessary foundation of Revelation's authority, since the representation of the end of history must in a convincing way seem already to participate in a language beyond history. In order to have a decisive impact, the words of the book must seem to have their origin not in any ongoing, circumstantial debate about how to act and what to do, but in that space already outside of mere contingency, that end-space where historical conflict will have been definitively resolved. Revelation can command such authority because it claims to speak from the end with perfect hindsight; it therefore requires a language commensurate with its vision.

[48] Bruns, "Canon and Power in the Hebrew Scriptures," 79.
[49] See Blenkinsopp, *Prophecy and Canon,* 24.

The first time Revelation achieves an eschatological climax—that is, the first time one of its many sequences advances from a penultimate six to a closural seven—the odd result is the text's quietest moment: "When the Lamb opened the seventh seal, there was silence in heaven for about half an hour" (8:1). Although this passage is surprising, it is not unprecedented in apocalyptic literature. The fourth book of Ezra, an intertestamental work probably written not long before Revelation, describes an interlude between the temporary millennial kingdom and the definitive Last Judgment: "And the world shall be turned back to primeval silence for seven days, as it was at the first beginnings; so that no one shall be left. And after seven days the world, which is not yet awake, shall be roused, and that which is corruptible shall perish" (7:30–32).[50] Silence can mark the narrative pivot in apocalyptic literature because on either side of the gulf between the historical and the posthistorical lie irreconcilable uses of language; like anything else belonging to the corruptions of history, language must be reduced to zero before it can be re-created as something altogether new. Revelation frequently stresses that the proximity of the redeemed to God will be reflected in their possession of new words: they will hold a white stone inscribed with God's unspeakable name; they will have that name written on their foreheads; they will sing ritual hymns as yet unknown. This change in language brought about by the end of history is no auxiliary matter, no mere side effect of the general transformation, for the only human activity left after history ends is a distinctly linguistic one—the worship of God in prayer and song. John describes the physical features of the New Jerusalem in some detail. He also informs his audience of the human experiences—tears, pain, suffering, death—that will no longer trouble their transfigured lives, but when he turns to a positive description of just what the redeemed will *do* there, he provides only this: "his servants shall worship [God]; they shall see his face, and his name shall be on their foreheads" (22:3–4). The result of apocalyptic liberation is a space where the redeemed can praise God ceaselessly, invariably.

By itself, this sparse passage would frustrate any effort to imagine the nature of language in the New Jerusalem, but throughout Revelation, John so often reproduces a single model of proper worship that by the time one reaches the text's concluding vision his linguistic ideal has become entirely clear, as has his idea of preapocalyptic linguistic failure. Samuel Hopkins, in his 1794 *Treatise on the Millennium,* was not merely indulging an overheated imagination when he suggested that the inhabitants of the New Jerusalem would speak a universal language, one "with

[50] *The Old Testament Pseudepigrapha,* ed. James Charlesworth (Garden City: Doubleday, 1983), 1:537–38.

less ambiguity and danger of being misunderstood than could be done before."[51] Put schematically, Revelation's linguistic model is as follows: informed by history, language consists of a jarring plurality, of social division and conflict; transfigured beyond history, language is marked by spontaneous consensus and uniformity, by the utter absence of hierarchical distinctions on the one hand and of deviation on the other. John typically represents the passage from the former to the latter as the moment in which a heterogeneous multitude discovers a single voice in praising God: "After this I looked, and behold, a great multitude which no man could number, from every nation, from all tribes and peoples and tongues, standing before the throne and before the Lamb, clothed in white robes, with palm branches in their hands, and crying out with a loud voice, 'Salvation belongs to our God who sits upon the throne, and to the Lamb!'" (7:9–10); "After this I heard what seemed to be the mighty voice of a great multitude in heaven, crying, 'Hallelujah! Salvation and glory and power belong to our God'" (19:1). In these instances of liturgical celebration, the polyglot of history—which Revelation frequently calls to attention with the formula "peoples and multitudes and nations and tongues"—is instantaneously transfigured into a postapocalyptic social and linguistic identity. These scenes of univocalization recur with regularity across the text, and always they involve either figures already around the throne of God (the four living creatures, the twenty-four elders, the angels) or the redeemed themselves, as if the very sign of holiness, of inclusion in the heavenly space, consists in one's ability to speak precisely the same words as others. Additionally, as Leonard Thompson points out, such scenes often occur at the climax of a particular eschatological drama, creating the impression that the fulfillment of providential history, its very telos, lies in the unification of a community in prayer, in the distilling of social polyphony to the purity of one ritual voice.[52]

What I am describing here in Revelation as the transfiguration of language from the polyphonic to the monological is so common in apocalyptic literature that one might consider it a definitive convention of the genre. Most often the convention is centered on the Kiddusha, a set of prayers celebrating divine holiness that is sung by worshipers surrounding the throne of God (*kiddush*, holy).[53] As in the Apocalypse of

[51] Samuel Hopkins, *Treatise on the Millennium* (Edinburgh: John Ogle, 1794), 92.

[52] See Thompson, "Unity through the Language of Worship," in his *The Book of Revelation: Apocalypse and Empire*, 53–73.

[53] In the actual Jewish liturgy of the first-century synagogue, some variant of the Kiddusha would have been part of the Shemonah Esreh, the eighteen benedictions that, along with the Shemah, represent the oldest established forms of prayer in Judaism. See Allan Bouley, *From Freedom to Formula: The Evolution of the Eucharistic Prayer from Oral Improvisation to Written Texts* (Washington: Catholic University of America Press, 1981), 23–24.

Abraham, it is thus linked to the tradition of merkabah mysticism: "I saw under the fire a throne of fire and the many-eyed ones round about, reciting the song, under the throne four fiery living creatures, singing. . . . And I heard the voice of their sanctification like the voice of a single man" (18:3, 14).[54] A classical source of the convention lies in Isaiah's vision of the divine throne, which exegetes traditionally considered the moment of the prophet's calling. In his ecstasy, Isaiah witnesses the angels singing, "Holy, holy, holy is the Lord of hosts; the whole earth is full of his glory," a revelation of the highest function of words, which immediately prompts the prophet to recognize his own linguistic degradation: "I am a man of unclean lips." An angel then touches a burning coal to Isaiah's mouth, enacting the ritual purification necessary for Isaiah to enter a new order of inspired speech, to enter, in other words, upon his prophetic ministry (6:3–9).

Nearly one thousand years later, an anonymous Christian author developed this brief scene of transcendence into a popular apocalypse, the Ascension of Isaiah, also emphasizing the linguistic transformation that occurs as one moves away from the world and nearer to the spirit of God. In each of the early spheres to which Isaiah ascends on his journey to the seventh heaven, he sees angels arranged on either side of an unoccupied throne, with those on the left positioned lower than those on the right. The left angels thus form a link to the heaven below them, the right to that above them, and this steady rise in stature is accompanied by a steady improvement in worship: "for those on the right possessed a greater glory, and they all praised with one voice . . . ; and likewise those on the left sang praises after them, but their voice was not such as the voice of those on the right, nor their praise like their praise" (7:15). The very division of angels into ranks suggests the distance between the lower heavens and God; as Isaiah ascends, these differentiations disappear along with all others. The sixth heaven has no throne at all and hence only "right" angels—"all had one appearance and their song of praise was the same" (8:16)—and in the seventh heaven, Isaiah hears all the voices below rising to a single concentrated point, "all directed to the glorious One" (10:2) who is the origin and end of linguistic identity.[55] The entire apocalypse, then, is organized by an inexorable upward movement from difference to likeness, from division to unity, from imperfect discourse to Logos. In Revelation, John doubles this movement, incorporating it into both his vertical ascent to heaven and his horizontal account of history's progression toward the appointed end. His initial merkabah vision begins with the four living creatures not only singing the Kiddusha in customary unison but also placing it within

[54] *Old Testament Pseudepigrapha*, ed. Charlesworth, 1:698.
[55] *New Testament Apocrypha*, ed. Schneemelcher, 2:653–59.

a distinctly eschatological rhetoric: "Holy, holy, holy, is the Lord God Almighty, who was and is and is to come!" (4:8). The unity of God in heaven is also the unity that frames history below, that structures history as a narrative closed on either side by the self-identical alpha and omega.

Because the making of many voices into one is represented as an inexorable process, these linguistic transfigurations suggest not only a powerful egalitarian motive, a desire to eliminate rank and distinction of any kind, but also an element of coercion, one that is sometimes quite explicit in the apocalyptic literature. After all, the ideal of ritual worship without deviation is as much an image of institutional discipline as it is one of utopian social harmony.[56] These works always associate dissent or even simple variation, difference itself, with that which is to be transcended; they sometimes represent it as punishable. One of the most elaborate texts in the merkabah tradition, 3 Enoch, a book dating to the fifth or sixth century C.E., discusses in vivid detail the consequences of irregular worship in the seventh heaven:

> Whenever [the angels] do not recite the 'Holy' according to its proper order, devouring fire goes out from the little finger of the Holy One, blessed be he. It falls on their ranks, and splits into 496,000 myriads of parts corresponding to the four camps of the ministering angels, and devours them at a stroke, as it is written,
>
> > A fire precedes him as he goes,
> > devouring all enemies around him.
>
> Then the Holy One, blessed be he, opens his mouth, and, with one word, creates new ones like them to take their place. Each of them stands in song before his throne of glory and recites 'Holy,' as it is written,
>
> > Every morning they are renewed;
> > great is his faithfulness.
>
> (40:3–4)[57]

In the late Christian apocalyptic literature, the disciplinary consequences of transcendence through linguistic unity become apparent when ascensions to heaven get coupled with descents into hell. Both the

---

[56] Occasionally, these scenes of liturgical harmony become quite transparent, and one can observe the immediate problems of congregational discipline that form part of their motivation. In the Apocalypse of Paul, when Paul observes an elaborate Kiddusha performed incessantly by the redeemed in the City of God, he questions his accompanying angel about many things, ending with the following inquiry: Does "someone who is doting or very old sin" by not participating in the ritual hymn? The angel replies, "No, but whoever is able, and does not join in the singing, you know that he is a despiser of the word. And it would be proud and discreditable that he should not bless the Lord God his maker." Ecclesiastical case closed. *New Testament Apocrypha*, ed. Schneemelcher, 2:779.

[57] *Old Testament Pseudepigrapha*, ed. Charlesworth, 1:291–92.

Apocalypse of Peter and the Apocalypse of Paul, for instance, represent the redeemed as those who can praise God "with one voice," but they spend far more time detailing the torments of various verbal offenders, torments which are almost always directed at the organs of speech: deviants gnaw their tongues; blasphemers are strung up by them; liars "have their lips cut off and fire enters into their mouths"; a hypocritical church reader has his lips and tongue lacerated by "a great blazing razor."[58] In Paul's vision, just as the center of the City of God consists of a holy congregation singing "Hallelujah!" so the ultimate punishment of hell is to be written out of God's lexicon altogether, to have one's linguistic identity annihilated: "If some one is sent into this well of the abyss and it is sealed above him, reference is never made to him before the Father and the Son and the Holy Spirit and the holy angels." The author reserves this place for heretics.[59]

In these late apocalypses, which so obviously relish the gruesome fate of a group's internal enemies, the intimidation that forms the underside of linguistic transcendence and communal identity becomes fully visible. The shared words of glory and triumph, articulated in ritual speech and song, also bear a brute, terrifying, silencing force. Although hell plays no significant role in the Book of Revelation, something like the disciplinary power of its linguistic vision does enter into the book's most fundamental mythical axis, the holy war between Christ and the anti-Christian powers. John's Messiah is a warrior, but he is also the Word, the Logos; he defeats his enemies solely by means of a word-weapon: "from his mouth issued a sharp two-edged sword" (1:16). When Christ appears late in the text as the captain of a sacred army, John reports that he is called "The Word of God" and "From his mouth issues a sharp sword with which to smite the nations" (19:13–15). On the other hand, the last antagonist introduced to the Book of Revelation, the final obstacle to the triumphant end of history, is the Whore of Babylon, a complex figure who signifies many evils—the Roman cult of emperor worship most specifically, but also more generally the confusion of tongues, the punishment incurred by the fallen descendants of Adam for building the Tower of Babel. As I will suggest momentarily, Babel is a trope sedimented deeply within John's representation of the Whore of Babylon, but here let me simply point out the broad allegory that emerges consistently and powerfully across Revelation: history ends and the New Jerusalem begins when the forces of the Logos annihilate the multi-

[58] *New Testament Apocrypha*, ed. Schneemelcher, 2:676, 781.

[59] Ibid., 2:786. An angel explains to Paul that those sealed in the pit without language are they "who have not confessed that Christ came in the flesh and that the Virgin Mary bore him, and who say that the bread of the Eucharist and the cup of blessing are not the body and blood of Christ" (786).

plicity of tongues, when the Word can reverse the fall by restoring the prelapsarian linguistic unity that existed before Babel.[60]

The Whore of Babylon is a nearly indecipherable figure, dangerously so; the text itself must produce an angel-interpreter to read her properly, that is, to fix her meaning finally. She enters Revelation almost as an afterthought—following the destruction wrought by the seventh vial, suddenly "God remembered great Babylon, to make her drain the cup of the fury of his wrath" (16:19)—yet she receives the text's most vitriolic punishment: "they will make her desolate and naked, and devour her flesh and burn her up with fire" (17:16). Although she seems generally to duplicate the symbolic function of the other beasts (all are bound up with Roman oppression and the Imperial Cult), readers have often followed the text in singling her out for a retribution incommensurate with her role, as when the Renaissance exegete Thomas Brightman expressed his desire to "see this impudent harlot at length slit in the nostrils, stripped of her garments and tires, besmeared with dirt and rotten eggs, and at last burnt up and consumed with fire."[61] While an undisguised misogyny accounts for much of the virulent rhetoric here, what concerns me most is the way misogyny is bound to an attack on a certain idea of fallen language. From John's very first description, Babylon becomes a linguistic inversion or parody of the community to be redeemed, the members of which will be inscribed by the holy Word; "Upon her forehead was a name written, Mystery, Babylon the Great" (King James, 17:5). "Mystery" designates Babylon as a figure of indeterminacy, one who threatens the apocalyptic movement toward total linguistic consensus with unreadability, with the danger of proliferating unregulated meanings. Her punishment therefore becomes inevitable: she must be stripped naked, unveiled in the original sense of the word *apocalypse,* and given a determinate meaning that allows the text both to dismiss her and to advance toward its vision of a community centered on the Logos.

[60] In the account that follows, I have deliberately resisted the temptation to link the Logos of Revelation with that introduced in the first line of the fourth gospel. The relationship between the two Johns—whether they were the same person (generally discredited), whether they belonged to the same school, whether they represent different traditions altogether and are thus unconnected in any way—has no bearing on my argument. Even had the first line of John's gospel never been written, one would not hesitate to refer to Revelation's Christ as the Logos. Not only is he explicitly designated by that title (19:13), but the text also consistently foregrounds the Messiah's linguistic agency—primarily, but not exclusively, by reference to the sword issuing from his mouth. Whatever he thought about beginnings, John of Patmos seemed convinced that "in the eschaton will be the Word."

[61] Quoted by Bernard Capp in "The Political Dimension of Apocalyptic Thought," in *The Apocalypse in English Renaissance Thought and Literature,* ed. Patrides and Wittreich, 93.

Through Babylon, Revelation stages its own authority to contain meaning and to silence alternative readings, but its linguistic vision does not end with a minor lesson in power hermeneutics. Following the designation of Babylon as Mystery, in a scene that for later commentators came to signify Revelation's capacity for autointerpretation, an angel explains to John that the harlot's seven-headed beast refers to seven hills and seven kings. Babylon, it turns out, is no mystery at all; she is simply Rome. The angel, however, complicates matters by adding to his explanation: "The waters that you saw, where the harlot is seated, are peoples and multitudes and nations and tongues" (17:15). Beyond any one-to-one historical identification with the empire, Babylon takes on more general significance; the angel associates her with the condition of preapocalyptic heterogeneity itself, the plurality of tongues and identities that signals the grip of circumstance, the earthly contingencies that must be transcended to effect a radical break with history. To eliminate Babylon is to liberate the multitudes from what the text represents as the tyranny of multiplicity and difference. And this is the work of the Logos. The punishment I quoted above (stripped, devoured, burned) occurs when the beast turns its horns upon its own rider, but this action takes place strictly through the messianic agency: "for God has put it into their hearts to carry out his purpose by being of one mind and giving over their royal power to the beast, *until the words of God shall be fulfilled*" (17:17; my emphasis). At an apocalyptic stroke, the Word of God destroys Babylon and ends the sovereignty of Babel. Not surprisingly, the heavenly songs celebrating the demise of Babylon yield immediately to a Kiddusha, another vision of multitudes translated into a single voice: "After this I heard what seemed to be the mighty voice of a great multitude in heaven, crying, 'Hallelujah! Salvation and glory and power belong to our God'" (19:1).

It is worth pausing a moment to consider the embedding of Babel within the figure of Babylon, a resonance to which later millenarian traditions would remain alive, as in this anonymous seventeenth-century lyric: "The Whore that rides in us abides, / A strong beast is within. . . . / Alas, we may, most of us, say / We're stones of Babel's tower."[62] This association runs deep into prophecy's past and far into its future, but in John's representation there can be no simple collapsing of Babel and Babylon. Whether he strategically reconstructs the relation or simply perpetuates what had become an established motif of the Judeo-Christian lineage would, of course, be difficult to determine. Throughout the Bible, representations of Babylon subtly but consistently incor-

---

[62] Christopher Hill cites this poem from New England, 1661, in *Antichrist in Seventeenth-Century England* (London: Oxford, 1971), 144.

porate the legend of Babel; when John's book eventually entered the canon, its figurative use of Babylon helped to confirm the unity of the two testaments, rendering them a single self-referential whole from Genesis to Apocalypse.[63]

The Hebrew story of the great tower probably had its origins in the twelfth century B.C.E., but it assumed importance of another kind six hundred years later with the Babylonian exile, when the redactors of the Pentateuch began the final consolidation of ancient source material that included Genesis.[64] From the perspective of the captivity, the tale shifted emphasis, becoming not so much an etiology of linguistic diversity as an account of God's miraculous ability to overturn the designs of those whose earthly power seems unlimited. In a clever exercise of folk etymology, the Genesis passage offers an alternative interpretation of the word *Babel,* which in Akkadian meant "Gate of God," but in Hebrew punned upon *balal*—"to confuse." Although the builders saw themselves erecting a structure that would lift them to heaven and make them the rivals of God, the Hebrew story contends that all along they were subject to God's will, who when he saw fit, put an end to their ambition by introducing the confusion of tongues. The legend, in other words, demonstrated Yahweh's unique mastery over human events. This aspect of the tale became especially significant when Nebuchadnezzar set captive Jews to work restoring the magnificent buildings of Babylon that had been destroyed a century earlier by Sennacherib, buildings that included among them the original Tower of Babel. Biblical archaeologists today agree that the Genesis tower was most likely the largest of the Babylonian ziggurats or terrace-temples, Etemenanki, which dated at least to the first great Babylonian rule under Hammurabi (eighteenth century B.C.E.). When Nebuchadnezzar employed slave labor to restore the former empire's glory, the Jews must have been painfully reminded of one of their oldest stories. Thus, in an oracle predicting the eventual fall of Babylon, Isaiah taunts his enemies by alluding to Genesis: "You said in your heart, 'I will ascend to heaven; above the stars of God I will set my throne on high'" (14:13), and in the passage that immediately precedes this one he describes the imminent Babylonian defeat as a sudden act of Yahweh that annihilates the enemy's linguistic capacities,

[63] In the preface to *Babylon and the Bible* (Grand Rapids: Baker Book House, 1969), John Larue suggests, "The influence of Babylon is woven throughout the biblical narrative from Genesis to Revelation, first related to the linguistic divisiveness of mankind, then historically dramatized as an enemy of the Kingdom of Judah, finally appearing as a symbol of anti-God powers."

[64] For an account of the Genesis tale and its ancient variants, see Robert Graves and Raphael Patai, *Hebrew Myths: The Book of Genesis* (New York: McGraw-Hill, 1964), 125–29. For a historical account of Babylon and its representation in the Hebrew Scriptures, see Larue, *Babylon and the Bible.*

reducing the splendid city to ruins inhabited by inarticulate beasts: "But wild beasts will lie down there, and its houses will be full of howling creatures; there ostriches will dwell, and there satyrs will dance. Hyenas will cry in its towers, and jackals in the pleasant palaces; its time is close at hand and its days will not be prolonged" (13:21–22).[65]

The association of Babel and Babylon enters Hebrew prophecy through the belief that God may punish his enemies at any moment; as one might expect, it takes on even greater force in the apocalyptic literature, where messianic deliverance involves a release from the multiplicity of tongues. Although the Book of Daniel belongs to the second century, its author takes full advantage of the text's exilic setting: Babylon is not only the city of persecution where Jews await redemption, but a site of stunning linguistic confusion. Revelation's favorite formula, "peoples and tribes and tongues and nations," comes directly from Daniel; the only two apocalyptic books in the Bible are also the only two to employ this phrase, which they each repeat about half a dozen times.[66] In both cases, attention to bewildering heterogeneity would accurately reflect the melange of cultures to be found in the cosmopolitan and slave-importing center of a world empire. For Daniel, however, this bit of historical realism also bears a symbolic lesson in hope. Nothing more immediately dramatizes the continuing influence of divine will than the fact that proud Babylon, as it rebuilds the "Gates of God," already contains within its walls the very signs of its previous punishment. "Babel" is still "balal." Across the tales that make up the first half of the book, this state of linguistic confusion comes to define the city's insurmountable limitations: Babylon is the place where interpretation of the true word has become impossible. Whether it is a matter of reading dreams or the writing on the wall, the ineptitude of the Babylonian sages always creates a necessary contrast to Daniel's right understanding of signs. Indeed, it is Daniel's divinely inspired interpretive skills, his ability to transcend linguistic confusion, that consistently saves his life, foreshadowing the general salvation ahead in history. A right relation to God and language is literally redemptive.

And a wrong relation ultimately means an apocalyptic fall. Chapter 4, in which Daniel interprets Nebuchadnezzar's dream of a tree which "grew and became strong, so that its top reached to heaven, and it was visible to the end of the whole earth" (4:20), reintroduces the Tower of Babel theme in order to demonstrate God's continuing power over an-

---

[65] According to *The Interpreter's One-Volume Commentary on the Bible*, ed. Charles M. Laymon (Nashville: Abingdon, 1971), this passage from 1 Isaiah (chapter 14) derives from "the period of the exile in Babylon," when "there is the prospect of a release from servitude when Babylon falls" (341).

[66] Daniel 3:4, 3:7, 4:1, 5:19, 6:25, 7:14; Revelation 7:9, 10:11, 11:9, 13:7, 17:15.

tagonists who deem themselves omnipotent. The king's subsequent fit of insanity, in which God suddenly reduces him to an inarticulate beast of burden, shows that while Babylon has already fallen from the prelapsarian harmony of the Adamic language, it will be made to fall further and finally: "At the end of twelve months he was walking on the roof of the royal palace of Babylon, and the king said, 'Is not this great Babylon, which I have built by my mighty power as a royal residence, and for the glory of my majesty?' While the words were still in the king's mouth, there fell a voice from heaven, 'O King Nebuchadnezzar, to you it is spoken: The kingdom has departed from you, and you shall be driven from among men, and your dwelling shall be with the beasts of the field'" (4:29–32). Presaging God's apocalyptic victory over Israel's earthly enemies, Nebuchadnezzar tumbles from his self-created heights when he literally has his words taken out of his mouth. This adaptation of the Tower of Babel to a fully eschatological schema is even more pronounced in Jubilees, a Hebrew text contemporary with Daniel. As part of a history of the world through Moses, a history informed by apocalyptic longings, the author recounts the story of Babel from Yahweh's perspective, making a few significant additions: "Behold, the people are one and they have begun working. Now nothing will escape them. Behold, let us go down and let us mix up their tongues so each one will not hear another's word, and they will be scattered into cities and nations, and, therefore, *one counsel will not reside with them until the day of judgment*" (10:22; my emphasis). Daniel only implied that apocalypse would entail the delivery from Babel/Babylon; in Jubilees, Yahweh states unequivocally that eschatological redemption will involve a return of the originary linguistic unity, the "one counsel" lost with Eden.[67]

With the Whore of Babylon, this revisionary appropriation of the

---

[67] *Old Testament Pseudepigrapha*, ed. Charlesworth, 2:77. In a later apocalypse of the intertestamental period, 3 Baruch, the Tower of Babel again plays a central role. After assuring an angel that he will neither add to nor subtract from the visions he is about to observe, Baruch ascends to five of the levels of heaven. Oddly enough, in the first two, he sees repeated before him the drama of the tower; he watches the builders and is told, "And the Lord God appeared to them and confused their languages" (3:6). Since the third level advances him toward "the glory of God," it seems that the author has chosen the Babel episode as his single representation of fallen humanity's distance from the divine. The text breaks off before Baruch approaches God's throne, so we have no way of knowing whether the confusion of tongues would have formed the fit counterpart to a univocal Kiddusha. One other point is worth mentioning: Baruch describes how the builders of the tower "forced men and a multitude of women to make bricks" (3:5). Although the editor, H. E. Gaylord, Jr., suggests that this refers to the slave labor in Egypt, and it might, it certainly refers as well to the slave labor under Nebuchadnezzar. Baruch was supposed to have been Jeremiah's scribe, and the book is thus set pseudonymously in the sixth century, B.C.E., the time of the exile. *Old Testament Pseudepigrapha*, ed. Charlesworth, 1:664.

Babel legend reaches a violent conclusion. To understand the full force of John's representation, however, I need to reintroduce a consideration of misogyny, which was conspicuously absent from my sketch above. The vision of Babylon as an adulteress, "the mistress of kingdoms" as 2 Isaiah puts it (47:5), is nearly as old as the city's association with linguistic multiplicity, but I know of no author before John whose symbolism systematically unites these two traditional motifs. In Revelation, the desire to free a community from the fallen history of social and linguistic differences is explicitly tied to a fear of sexual difference: through the Whore of Babylon, John represents the multiplicity of tongues as a particularly feminine evil. Because apocalypse occurs as the triumph of the Logos over Babylon, the text only achieves its closure when the deep threat of the feminine can be properly contained by a male champion.[68] In this eschatological narrative, the insatiable Whore of Babylon, "drunk with the wine of her fornications," is not only unveiled and consumed with fire, a punishment already laden with implications of hermeneutical and sexual dominance, but she is finally rewritten by the Logos as Jerusalem, the faithful bride in white linen. After the fall of Babylon, this mythical reconstruction of the feminine first appears in the monological chorus of a Kiddusha: "Then I heard what seemed to be the voice of a great multitude . . . crying, 'Hallelujah! For the Lord our God the Almighty reigns. Let us rejoice and exult and give him the glory, for the marriage of the Lamb has come, and his Bride has made herself ready'" (19:6–7). The linguistic transformation of the many made one is accompanied here by the invocation of patriarchal marriage law; it is as if the purity of the Word beyond history depended on the regulation of female sexuality.

The appearance of the bride Jerusalem is only the climax of John's consistent antifeminism in Revelation. Even before Babylon enters the text to become the focal point of its fierce, patriarchal energies, the logic that twists together language and sexuality is already evident in a pivotal Kiddusha scene. Chapter 14 begins with a description of the redeemed community, and, as elsewhere, this passage emphasizes that community's unique linguistic power: "They sing a new song before the throne and before the four living creatures and before the elders. No one could learn that song except the hundred and forty-four thousand who had

---

[68] Revelation is thus a monumental instance of the textual strategy Patricia Parker dubs "*Ecrasez la femme*," or "the narrative topos of overcoming a female enchantress or obstacle en route to completion and ending." *Literary Fat Ladies: Rhetoric, Gender, Property* (London: Methuen, 1987), 11. Parker considers the Whore of Babylon to be one of the earliest instances of a "literary fat lady"—a feminine construction "used as a figure for the space and time of language, discourse, and history before a Master's apocalyptic return" (9). See also p. 12.

been redeemed from the earth" (14:3). In this case, however, John adds to the familiar merkabah scene a description of the congregation's salient features: "It is these *who have not defiled themselves with women,* for they are chaste; it is these who follow the Lamb wherever he goes; these have been redeemed from mankind as first fruits for God and the Lamb, and *in their mouth no lie was found,* for they are spotless" (14:4–5; my emphasis). Male chastity and linguistic purity are the equally necessary components of an innocence worthy of redemption.[69] Although these hundred and forty-four thousand have been saved prior to the Last Judgment, there is little reason to believe that those redeemed later will differ significantly in kind. God's "first fruits," the proto-inhabitants of the New Jerusalem, form a priesthood of Christian ascetic males, those who can already learn the language of a postapocalyptic Kiddusha because they have remained free from women, because their continence has already made them independent of what Blake would call "generation."[70] Ironically, it seems that the text's "feminine" ideal, the New

---

[69] An early second-century text, The Testaments of the Twelve Patriarchs, is filled with a similar association of male linguistic and sexual purity. Most of the patriarchs confess having fallen into a variety of feminine temptations, but the Testament of Issachar, who claims not to have committed a single sin, provides an effective parallel to John's vision of the redeemed priesthood:

> I have not had intercourse with any woman other than my wife,
>   nor was I promiscuous by lustful look,
> I did not drink wine to the point of losing self-control.
> I was not passionately eager for any desirable possession of my neighbor.
> There was no deceit in my heart;
>   no lie passed through my lips.
>   (7:2–4, in *Old Testament Pseudepigrapha,* ed. Charlesworth, 1:804.)

[70] John offers sexual renunciation here as the privileged symbol among the living of an already achieved eschatological salvation. The "first fruits" have thus severed their ties with the world and bound themselves exclusively to God in a way that will be possible for the community at large only with the coming of Christ. This ascetic ideal, however, is not necessarily incompatible with the marriage symbol that organizes John's subsequent representation of the New Jerusalem. As Peter Brown has argued extensively, many Christian communities (and Jewish communities before them) praised the continence of a few exemplary members without requiring the same of the householders who by and large made up the congregation; on the contrary, sexual renunciation among church leaders often coincided with teachings that valued marriage and procreation, which, after all, were the only means of securing the community. "Powerful though its breath might be, the Spirit respected the domestic structures without which Christianity would have found it impossible to survive" (79). Sexual renunciation sometimes became a force powerfully disruptive of social norms, but it could also be contained and made compatible with ongoing social structures. As Brown shows in his discussion of Hermas, who wrote only one generation after John, a prophet could depend on continence as a sign of legitimacy without disturbing the conservative values generally maintained by a congregation. Brown compellingly demonstrates how complex and contradictory the issue of asceticism was in

Jerusalem, will house a perfect patriarchal order, perfect because perfectly *homo*geneous.[71] Before this new male order can triumph, however, the Whore of Babylon, in every way the antithesis of male asceticism, must be purged.

According to Patricia Parker, there is a well-established Western convention that binds a representation of women's promiscuity to one of female linguistic excess and aberration. In the Judeo-Christian tradition, harlotry thus refers not only literally to illicit sexual practices but also figuratively to a punishable abuse of signs, the worship of idols. In fact, the latter reference was never merely figurative, for the Gentile rituals that early Jews and Christians considered idolatrous often included the worship of fertility goddesses and typically involved the practice of sacred prostitution. The Babylonian ziggurats, for instance, which the exiled Jews helped to rebuild, housed goddess cults that regularly employed ritual prostitutes.[72] As late as the exile and after, there were Jewish men and women worshiping asherim, or female idols, as Jeremiah's invective against the members of a Jewish colony in Egypt indicates (44:15–19). Redactors of the prophet's canonical book apparently found it advantageous to preserve this reprimand for the entire Israelite community.[73] Long after ancient Judaism had officially for-

---

the early church, how much its meaning depended on the very particular circumstances in which it was pursued. *The Body and Society: Men, Women, and Sexual Renunciation in Early Christianity* (New York: Columbia University Press, 1988).

[71] Schüssler Fiorenza argues the opposite: "To assume that either the heavenly or the eschatological followers of the Lamb are a class of exclusively male ascetics seems to be unfounded in the overall context of the book." *The Book of Revelation: Justice and Judgment*, 190. Unfortunately, I see in the overall context of the book no evidence of sexual egalitarianism and a great deal of evidence for the opposite. I can only surmise that Schüssler Fiorenza's deep commitment to the revolutionary potential of Revelation informs her apologetics.

[72] J. B. Segal points out that in Babylon "women formed a part of the regular staff of the great temples" as they had not in Jerusalem and that "perhaps their most important function was to serve as sacred prostitutes at the great seasonal festivals." J. B. Segal, "The Jewish Attitude towards Women," *Journal of Jewish Studies* 30 (1979): 125. Like Segal, Merlin Stone suggests that a Babylonian priestess would not only experience no social stigma, but would also be to some extent empowered, allowed, for instance, to own her own land and to distribute her own property. See Merlin Stone, *When God Was a Woman* (New York: Harcourt Brace Jovanovich, 1976), 156.

[73] In *The Creation of Patriarchy* (Oxford: Oxford University Press, 1986), Gerda Lerner describes the persistence of goddess cults and their sexual rites in a variety of ancient Middle Eastern cultures moving toward patriarchy (see 141–60). Lerner also stresses the role that Jewish monotheism played in perfecting a patriarchal social order that required the elimination of goddess worship. It is in Hebrew prophecy that one first finds Yahwism coupled with a violent intolerance of other gods (166), as well as the rhetoric that figures Israel in the dichotomous terms of faithful wife or fallen harlot. Lerner suggests that this powerful movement, which worked its way into the center of Jewish faith through canonization, had a tremendous impact on the formation of power in actual social insti-

bidden such activities, ritual prostitution remained relatively common among Gentiles well into the Christian era, and it was practiced in Asia Minor, where John preached.[74] Whether or not John meant to target such rituals in his representation of the Whore of Babylon remains unclear, for he may simply have drawn upon the symbolic resonance of harlotry to condemn any participation in the Roman Imperial Cult. In either case, he does not hesitate to associate Babylon with a female pagan sexuality that is hyperbolic and grotesque. She is the harlot "with whom the kings of the earth have committed fornication, and with the wine of whose fornication the dwellers on earth have become drunk" (17:2). She is seduction itself, luring those who should remain faithful to God into an adulterous betrayal indicated by *both* linguistic *and* sexual straying.

By constructing Babylon as the stereotypical idolatrous harlot, John exploits a fearful, deeply rooted association of polytheism and female sexuality. From this perspective, the patriarchal prerogatives of his uni-vocal Kiddusha become increasingly clear; at stake is the nature of both proper worship itself and the community capable of such worship. As with the hundred and forty-four thousand "first fruits" of redemption, the monotheistic male God requires unity in prayer, a unity symbolized by the coalescence of a congregation into a single male voice. In the redeemed community, polyvocity is as rigorously excluded as idolatry itself, for each is the image of the other. In at least one ancient variant, even the original confusion of tongues at Babel was a punishment for idolatry.[75] The fall into the polyvocal and the fall into the polytheistic occur simultaneously; together they register the failure of Noah's de-scendants to make good on the opportunity afforded by the flood, a second chance to sustain a unified human origin.[76] In the biblical tradi-

---

tutions. "The prolonged ideological struggle of the Hebrew tribes against the worship of Canaanite deities and especially the persistence of a cult of the fertility-goddess Asherah must have hardened the emphasis on male cultic leadership and the tendency toward mysogyny, which fully emerged only in the post-exilic period" (178).

[74] This is no place to take up vexed arguments about the relationship between priestly Judaism and patriarchy, which, as Susannah Heschel recently argues, can take an anti-Semitic cast when ancient Judaism gets blamed for *inventing* patriarchy. While the anti-feminism of ancient Judaism is both real and lasting, there is no evidence that patriarchy originated with monotheism and little evidence that women generally experienced greater social equality in early goddess-worshiping societies than they did among Jews. See Susannah Heschel, "Anti-Judaism in Christian Feminist Theology," *Tikkun* 5 (May/June 1990): especially 25–27.

[75] Nimrod, who built the tower to war against God and so avenge the loss of his ancestors in the flood, forced his enemies to worship idols of wood and stone. See Graves and Patai, *Hebrew Myths*, 126.

[76] Von Rad considered the tower episode in Genesis to be the last event of primeval history, the last in the series of movements away from Yahweh. The impact of the passage,

tion, then, the multiplicity of tongues, the actual practices of idolatry, and unchecked female sexuality merge within a single symbolic matrix. Given the textual heritage that John attends to as fully as any other early Christian writer, one might say that the Whore of Babylon was a nearly inevitable construction.

In the West, as Abrams has exhaustively demonstrated, the desire for a teleological movement from the many to the one is so deeply en-grained that it has often seemed second nature. This particular under-standing of history, however, is not universal, not even within apoc-alyptic thought. According to the anthropologist Pierre Clastres, the millenarian prophets of the Tupi-Guarani Indians believed their final redemption would consist of a radical departure from the fallen "one" to the utopian "not-one," and thus Clastres can put an important question to the West: *"What conditions must obtain in order to conceive of the One as the Good?"*[77] In what might be a partial answer to that question, Irigaray suggests that teleologies of the one have always been bound up with patriarchal programs: "Now, this domination of the philosophic logos stems in large part from its power to *reduce all others to the economy of the Same.* The telologically constructive project it takes on is always also a project of diversion, deflection, reduction of the other in the Same. And, in its greatest generality perhaps, from its power to *eradicate the difference between the sexes* in systems that are self-representative of a 'masculine subject.' "[78] Guided by the convergence of monotheism and patriarchal interests, Revelation's Logos-driven, providential movement toward one language, one community, one God, demands the construction and subsequent elimination of a Babylon. The scope of that severe dualism which John focuses on the antagonism between Logos and Babylon is not, however, limited to a vicious antifeminism, though that is its pri-mary (or in Irigaray's terms, most general) symptom. On one side of the apocalyptic sword lie history, linguistic and theological plurality, and deviant female sexuality; on the other lie a sacred, monotheistic space,

---

he argues, depends entirely on what follows it, the beginning of sacred history, the selection by Yahweh of Abraham, who becomes the first patriarch of a new monotheism. See *Genesis: A Commentary,* trans. John H. Marks (Philadelphia: Fortress, 1972), 147–55.

[77] Pierre Clastres, *Society against the State,* trans. Robert Hurley, Abe Stein (New York: Zone, 1987), 217. Clastres argues that the popular millenarian movement of the Tupi-Guarani prophets, who called themselves "the last men," was a rejection of European influences pushing the tribal society toward the unity ideal of a state: "Tupi-Guarani prophetism is the heroic attempt of a primitive society to put an end to unhappiness by means of a radical refusal of the One, as the universal essence of the State" (217). See also his essay, "Of the One without the Many," where he shows that the Tupi-Guarani "Land without Evil" is imagined to be a land of the "not-one" (172–73).

[78] Luce Irigaray, *This Sex Which Is Not One,* trans. Catherine Porter (Ithaca: Cornell University Press, 1985), 74.

the containment and even the erasure of female sexuality, and, perhaps most important, the disappearance altogether of the means for express-ing dissent. The point, then, is not simply that Revelation indulges a misogyny that one could find in innumerable ancient texts, but that by programmatically imagining a world rid of the *feminine* it imagines as its more general social ideal a community rid of *all* differences. When Revelation speaks from that apocalyptic place beyond history, it imag-ines for itself a voice with extraordinary social power, a voice that im-poses its vision upon the present by claiming to speak from a future site beyond conflict, beyond difference, beyond change.[79]

The Silencing of Jezebel

History ends in a book; the multiplicity of tongues ends in a single voice of worship. Revelation could not coordinate this double axis with-out the example of canon already in place, without the belief that the words of a sacred text have their origin not in conflictual social circum-stances but in the divine unity that transcends history. When Revelation binds this belief to a totalizing eschatological vision, it offers something like a cosmological allegory of the canonization process: it describes how the destiny of historical differences is to disappear in words, how "peo-ples and nations and multitudes and tongues" achieve their end in the communal identity defined by a book. To say this, however, to argue that well before the Book of Revelation achieved its privileged canonical

[79] Given Revelation's program of containing and finally eliminating difference through the agency of the Logos, it is not surprising that some recent feminist theology has turned to a poststructuralist understanding of discourse as an alternative model for the Word. Rebecca S. Chopp sets out to reconstruct, through "a theological semiotics," "the pro-claimed Word as the perfectly open sign that funds multiplicity and otherness in and through feminist discourse" (7). Women, she argues, "may not so much balance or equalize the hierarchy as change its monotheistic ordering of the 'one' as opposed to the 'other' into a multiplicity, allowing differences and connections instead of constantly guaranteeing identities and oppositions." *The Power to Speak: Feminism, Language, God* (New York: Cross-road, 1989), 2. This project implicitly demands an acceptance of Babel as the necessary and healthy condition of language. Similarly, although without any appeal to semiotics, Schüssler Fiorenza rejects the idea of revelation as archetype, an unchanging, timeless pattern, in favor of revelation as prototype, a pattern open to the possibility of its own transformation. It is sometimes difficult to see how this strong feminist stance accords with her ongoing inclination to champion Revelation: "A feminist theological hermeneutics having as its canon the liberation of women from oppressive patriarchal texts, structures, institutions, and values maintains that . . . only those traditions and texts that critically break through patriarchal culture and 'plausibility structures' have the theological author-ity of revelation. The 'advocacy stance' of liberation theologies cannot accord revelatory authority to any oppressive and destructive biblical text or tradition." *In Memory of Her: A Feminist Theological Reconstruction of Christian Origins* (New York: Crossroad, 1983), 33. See note 71 above.

status it already bore the inscription of canon, is in no way to explain the text's social functions. We still need to ask what historical purposes this representation of the end of history served, and to do so we need to consider, so far as this is possible, the contexts of its production, even though the text itself claims a source in the purely noncircumstantial, the genuinely timeless.

Twice in Revelation, John is chastised for bowing in reverence before an angel, who informs him that no hierarchy can exist among believers: "I am a fellow servant with you and your brethren who hold the testimony of Jesus. Worship God" (19:10). The Kiddusha itself is integral to this egalitarian desire; everyone surrounding God, regardless of previous social rank, now sings the same words of the same song. No vestige of privilege remains in the New Jerusalem. But John's egalitarianism is perhaps too insistent; its self-conscious display helps to offset, and even mask, the inherently hierarchical transmission of the revelation, the fact that the Logos singles him out for the vision and thus elevates the one who writes above the many who must listen. Clearly, John enhances the authority of his words when he purports merely to record the contents of a seven-sealed book authored by the Logos itself, a book which then goes on to dramatize the very omnipotence of that Logos, its miraculous ability to end all opposition through an irresistible linguistic agency.[80] But why should his "rhetorical situation" require such a simultaneous flaunting of egalitarianism and individual verbal prestige?

Almost all contextual studies have followed Revelation's own lead in stressing the conflict between Domitian's Rome and the marginalized Christian churches of Asia Minor, and there can be no doubt that John's appeal to the all-conquering power of the Logos is an attempt to encourage Christian resolve in the face of persecution, to create a unified front of nonviolent resistance based on faith and hope. At the same time, however, there is another, less obvious, context in which Revelation functions as a text of binding authority. During the Roman crisis, John was not the only teacher instructing the young, and as yet undefined, Christian communities. Revelation seems to have appeared as part of a debate among Christians themselves regarding the proper conduct of the faithful living under an intolerant empire. As his own introductory letters to the churches make perfectly explicit, John had rivals. The first

---

[80] Derrida has effectively outlined the process of demystification necessary to undermine the basis of John's authority, the claim that his writing and the voice of Christ are identical. In Derrida's reading, Revelation amounts to a series of "sendings" in which the links of transmission proliferate beyond control, making the whole a parody of mediation disguising itself as unmediated vision. The "one" voice disintegrates into an unregulated plurality, and Derrida can say, "as soon as one no longer knows who speaks or who writes, the text becomes apocalyptic." Jacques Derrida, "Of an Apocalyptic Tone Recently Adopted in Philosophy," *Oxford Literary Review* 6 (1984): 27.

time the Word/sword threatens military action in Revelation, it is aimed at neither Babylon nor the beast: in only the second chapter, Christ announces through John, "I will come to you soon and war against them with the sword of my mouth" (2:16). "You" refers to the Christians of Pergamum, "them" to alternative church leaders there, John's competitors for that congregation. When Revelation claims to speak in the very voice of the Logos that ends history it engages in a distinctly political act of intimidation. The end of Babylon on the vast cosmological plane of apocalypse would seem to have a more concrete social coordinate in the desire to silence some specific internal adversaries. The Logos may wield its sword against Rome, but as a "two-edged sword" that weapon cuts more than one way.

"It must be asked," states Schüssler Fiorenza in her pathbreaking feminist history of early Christianity, "whether it is legitimate to speak of Christianity in the singular or whether we have to speak of Christianities or Christian communities. Whether or not these early Christian groups were 'church,' denomination, established sects, sectarian movements, or charismatic sects—and which groups were what—needs to be explored much more carefully."[81] The idea that the church had its origins in social and theological unity is largely the product of canon, and one of the canonical appeals of the Book of Revelation, I would argue, is its symbolic legitimation of a transcendental unity of faith that denies the validity of existing conflict.[82] Revelation not only formed the logical narrative closure of the two-testament canon, binding the whole into a seemingly organic literary unit from beginning to end; it also helped manufacture a powerful mythic image of church identity at a time when differences among Christians were as readily apparent as similarities. Well before the institutional acceleration of the second and third centuries, the earliest Christian communities probably resembled Babel more than Logos, and, quite the contrary to John's ideal of the monological Kiddusha, their social constitution involved a substantial degree of heterogeneity and theological diversity. When Paul tried to convince the Christians of Corinth that conflict is necessary to separate true believers from pretenders, he allowed us to glimpse the reality of dispute: "For, in the first place, when you assemble as a church, I hear that there are divisions among you; and I partly believe it, for there must be

[81] Schüssler Fiorenza, *In Memory of Her*, 78.

[82] Brenkman's critique of Gadamer is once again pertinent. By arguing that tradition is that which has been liberated from the merely circumstantial past, Gadamer in turn can "mute the unsettled, unsettling dialogue among the conflicting self-interpretations of the present and thus . . . position the constructed tradition as the univocal source of legitimate meanings and values for our own era. The monologue of tradition can thus eclipse the dialogical plurality of contemporary culture." *Culture and Domination*, 39. In other words, a text claiming to be free of historical differences *requires* the suppression of differences and conflict among its audience.

factions among you in order that those who are genuine among you may be recognized" (1 Cor. 11:18–19). Regarding Asia Minor the historical record is thin, but we know from Revelation itself that John also addressed a divided community. At the very moment John represents the power of the Logos over difference, he makes us aware that a variety of voices influenced the Asia Minor churches: the Nicolaitans, those "who hold the teaching of Balaam" (2:14), and especially "the woman Jezebel, who calls herself a prophetess" (2:20). Given the vehemence with which John attacks the latter, her authority, as Schüssler Fiorenza suggests, "seems to have at least equaled that of John whom, in turn, she might have perceived as a false prophet."[83]

From the perspective of this "second" context, the context of tension within the churches, Revelation's rhetorical function takes on an added burden. Is it not possible, after all, that the failings John observes in the historical churches—their lack of discipline and consensus, their straying from the rules of faith and service as he prescribes them—prompt the content of his vision, which is supposed to have originated beyond history? The rupture between chapters 3 and 4, when the epistles to the churches end and the apocalyptic vision proper begins, is especially instructive here. This radical *structural* discontinuity—John suddenly leaves the historical world for a purely visionary space ("At once I was in the Spirit, and lo, a throne stood in heaven" [4:2])—registers a significant *polemical* continuity: the elaborate Kiddusha the prophet describes in heaven, which introduces the recurring theme of the many made one, serves to reprimand the churches for dissension, or more accurately, for their willingness to entertain beliefs and practices other than those John advocates in the name of the Logos. Nowhere does Revelation more fully exhibit the totalizing consensus demanded by the Logos than in this merkabah scene juxtaposed against the discordant Babel of the churches. Chapters 4 and 5 represent a single Kiddusha that builds in scope until the Lamb comes forward to open the sealed book, a climactic event that inspires the four living creatures and the twenty-four elders to join in a "new song":

> Worthy art thou to take the scroll and to open its seals,
> for thou wast slain and by thy blood didst ransom men for God
> from every tribe and tongue and people and nation,
> and hast made them a kingdom and priests to our God.
>
> (5:9–10)

The first scene in heaven establishes what will become the familiar burden of the Kiddusha: salvation consists in one's removal by divine

---

[83] Schüssler Fiorenza, *In Memory of Her*, 55.

agency from the multiplicity of historical identities and tongues to a single kingdom concentrated upon the single God. In the King James translation, the nature of this transformation is even more pronounced: the crucifixion lifts the faithful "to God" and "out of every kindred, and tongue, and people, and nation." At this point in chapter 5, the expansive power of the Kiddusha becomes irresistible, and the entire sentient universe must be drawn into the ritual benediction, must be made to sing in one voice:

> Then I looked, and I heard around the throne and the living creatures and the elders the voice of many angels, numbering myriads of myriads and thousands of thousands, saying with a loud voice, 'Worthy is the Lamb who was slain, to receive power and wealth and wisdom and might and honor and glory and blessing!' And I heard every creature in heaven and on earth and under the earth and in the sea, and all therein, saying, 'To him who sits upon the throne and to the Lamb be blessing and honor and glory and might for ever and ever!' (5:11–13)

The apocalyptic vision begins, then, by exhaustively demonstrating the liturgical practice that will eventually be the only human activity in the posthistorical New Jerusalem. There, at the end of the text, Jerusalem will form the fit antithesis to Babylon; here the Kiddusha performs the same function in relation to the churches, especially Thyatira, harboring its own miniature Babylon, "Jezebel." One cannot overestimate the importance of the Kiddusha to Revelation's structural and polemical unity. Without exaggeration, John Gager can state that "to an extent shared by no other primitive Christian document, the book's language, content, and structure is thoroughly liturgical; at one level it is little more than a compilation of prayers, benedictions, and hymns."[84] John's introductory verses indicate that he intended Revelation to be read aloud by Christian leaders to their congregations. Thus the textual repetition of a paradisal, Babel-reversing liturgy was not simply a wishful, utopian expression, a mythical representation projected onto the space above and beyond history. Rather, the Kiddusha was meant to be implemented immediately in actual church practice, signifying not just the imminent end of history but also the social and theological harmony demanded in the present.

The debate in which John and Jezebel took up opposite sides itself involved the nature of proper worship, and more particularly, the interpretation of idolatry. The very fact that John calls his rival "Jezebel"

---

[84] John Gager, *Kingdom and Community: The Social World of Early Christianity* (Englewood Cliffs, N.J.: Prentice-Hall, 1975), 56.

suggests this; Ahab's queen had infamously raised the worship of the Canaanite fertility goddess Asherah to official cult status in ancient Israel.[85] By combining the dangers of the feminine, the foreign, and the idolatrous, the Jezebel of 1 Kings points straight to the Whore of Babylon. In the actual letter to the church of Thyatira itself, which (like all seven letters) transcribes the voice of the Logos, John goes even further in associating his immediate doctrinal adversary with the great Harlot that will come to dominate his apocalyptic vision.

> 'I know your works, your love and faith and service and patient endurance, and that your latter works exceed the first. But I have this against you, that you tolerate the woman Jezebel, who calls herself a prophetess and is teaching and beguiling my servants to practice immorality and to eat food sacrificed to idols. I gave her time to repent, but she refuses to repent of her immorality. Behold, I will throw her on a sickbed, and those who commit adultery with her I will throw into great tribulation, unless they repent of her doings; and I will strike her children dead.' (Rev. 2:19–23)

We will probably never know whether Jezebel actually promoted or participated in sexual rites or whether John simply uses "immorality" and "adultery" in the age-old, inflammatory way; regardless, before the apocalypse proper even begins, he has already exploited the cultural nexus that binds linguistic abuse (false teaching, false worship) with female sexual deviance, and, moreover, he makes them both severely, preternaturally punishable. In a display of disciplinary force, John demands that Thyatira cast out the teachings of Jezebel. The sublime allegory of Logos and Babylon that follows this admonition thus functions not exclusively as Christian encouragement in the face of Roman persecution but also as a cautionary tale aimed at dissenters.

The differences that John imagines will disappear as history ends were significant in the late first-century setting of Asia Minor. Most obviously at issue was the degree to which Christians could accommodate themselves to the Imperial Cult, the compulsory emperor worship that Roman authorities adapted to local civic and religious festivals. More generally, the theological question took this form: Could Christians "eat food sacrificed to idols," that is, eat the meat that had been used in cultic rituals, without participating in idolatry? Indeed, some Christians who refused to worship the "image of the beast" in this way were persecuted, but not all of them assumed John's extreme antipathy

---

[85] Elijah's confrontation at Mount Carmel with "the four hundred and fifty prophets of Baal and the four hundred prophets of Asherah, who eat at Jezebel's table" is described in 1 Kings 18:19.

to assimilation of any kind.[86] Disagreement in the Asia Minor communities arose in part because the Imperial Cult affected church members differently depending on, among other things, their class positions. Many disenfranchised Christians would have confronted the issue rarely, perhaps only at the great imperial festivals when meat was sacrificed at public altars and distributed to the entire city. On the other hand, wealthier church members who regularly purchased meat in the market and others who associated professionally with the larger non-Christian community faced more of a day-to-day dilemma. A skilled laborer, for instance, might have to attend private guild meetings where sacrificial meat would be served. Thus Paul, a tent-maker who had to defend his participation in the trade against those who believed he should rely entirely on faith for his sustenance, also tended to minimize the significance of eating consecrated meat. When he addressed a similar difficulty in Corinth, Paul argued, "as to the eating of food offered to idols, we know that 'an idol has no real existence,' and that 'there is no God but one.'" As long as one possesses this knowledge, participation in a meaningless practice makes little difference: "Food will not commend us to God. We are no worse off if we do not eat, and no better off if we do" (1 Cor. 8:4, 8). As Gerd Theissen has argued so effectively in his sociological analysis of first-century Corinth, debate among early Christians regarding idolatrous practices reflects the persistence of social divisions that did not evaporate simply because community members shared a faith in Christ.[87] I quote Paul on the eating of sacrificial meat to suggest that John's opponents in Asia Minor had considerable authority on their side. Moreover, no one can quote Jezebel, who, despite her substantial following, was successfully silenced from the Christian record.

[86] In *Rituals and Power: The Roman Imperial Cult in Asia Minor* (Cambridge: Cambridge University Press, 1984), S. R. F. Price suggests that sacrifice to the emperor was usually linked with sacrifice to local pagan gods; the record indicates that Christians were rarely required to sacrifice to the emperor alone. Thus persecution was more the result of Christians rejecting the entire system of sacrifice than of compulsory emperor worship per se (220–22).

[87] Gerd Theissen, *The Social Setting of Pauline Christianity*, trans. John H. Schütz (Philadelphia: Fortress, 1982). See especially pp. 121–43. In another invaluable book, Colin Hemer assesses the historical evidence for similar debates in Asia Minor. He concludes that both the Nicolaitans and Jezebel encouraged liberal practices that allowed Christians a greater range of social and economic accommodations with the non-Christian community. In Thyatira, a city with a widely heterogeneous population that had developed various forms of religious syncretism, "the particular problem seems to have been the guild-feasts, as the occasions when the Christian may have been particularly pressed by the need to conform to his environment." Colin Hemer, *The Letters to the Seven Churches in Asia in their Local Setting* (Sheffield: JSOT Press, 1986), 120. Hemer generally provides a richly detailed account of the historical setting of John's introductory epistles.

We know of the early Christian rift regarding the eating of sacrificial meat, a rift which extended to larger questions about class and assimilation. Almost as certain is another late first-century debate that also addressed a set of internal differences, this one concerning gender. John's invocation of harlotry in his sharp attack on Jezebel, aside from bearing on the issue of idolatry, may well reflect a more generally misogynist campaign at a time when local church organization was unregulated and therefore open to a variety of charismatic influences, including that of inspired women. Schüssler Fiorenza has demonstrated convincingly that the paucity of New Testament information regarding the participation of women in the early churches tells us more about "the androcentric traditioning and redaction of the early Christian authors" than it does about historical realities.[88] Figures energetically attacked like Jezebel—or other leading women simply mentioned in the New Testament narratives without elaboration—hint at the prominence some women enjoyed, but they come to us through layers of patriarchal mediation constructed to minimize their importance. By equating a historical woman with heresy and by projecting the mythical anti-Christian powers onto a monumental figure of feminine evil, John not only intimidated the women within the range of his immediate ministry but he also promoted the more general silencing that occurred through the process of New Testament canonization.

With the gradual patriarchalization of the church in the second and third centuries, as Elizabeth Clark suggests, the ecclesiastical leadership of women was erected as "one of the boundary markers . . . to separate orthodoxy from heterodoxy." But already as early as 100 C.E., Christian texts roughly contemporary with Revelation (circa 95 C.E.), texts that later became canonical, were openly advocating the silencing of women.[89] It is even possible that one of the early forms of this conflict underlies John's labeling of Jezebel as a false prophet, since it involved the very question of women's ability to receive divine revelation. Churches endorsing greater sexual equality often traced their authority to Mary Magdalene's vision of the resurrected Christ, which they believed to be the first such vision. Mary appears to have had apostolic authority in some communities as late as the fourth century. Other

---

[88] "The androcentric selection and transmission of early Christian traditions have manufactured the historical marginality of women, but they are not a reflection of the historical reality of women's leadership and participation in the early Christian movement." Schüssler Fiorenza, *In Memory of Her*, 52, 49.

[89] Elizabeth A. Clark, "Patrons, Not Priests: Gender and Power in Late Ancient Christianity," *Gender and History* 2(3): 254. Clark refers to a text roughly contemporary with Revelation, 1 Timothy 2:12: "I permit no woman to teach or to have authority over men; she is to keep silent."

churches emphasized instead Christ's appearance to Peter, thus marginalizing and even deliberately discrediting Mary's claim to priority. At stake, of course, was not so much a theological dilemma as an ecclesiastical struggle: would women be ordained as the church rather quickly advanced toward centralization?[90] John's menacing representation of Jezebel and Babylon as harlots leading the faithful astray, serving false gods with catastrophic consequences, would have made Revelation increasingly attractive in those patriarchal circles that steadily established the church's dominant institutional form.

What I am suggesting is that Revelation's spectacular afterlife, an afterlife it could have only because readers in emerging positions of power saw in the text some value that transcended its original circumstances, came about in part because the text evolved out of and continued to serve the ideological purposes of canon. It provided the inspirational image of a unified church community defined on a plane where historical differences were effaced, and through the heavenly Kiddusha, it did so in mythological terms transparently linked to immediate problems of standardizing church service and liturgy.[91] More important, though this one must say with some caution, Revelation probably continued to exercise its influence over dissent as it passed into patristic hands. We know, for instance, that in the second half of the second century a millenarian movement broke out that seemed to embody the full threat of individual, charismatic prophecy to the institutional authority of the church. Led by Montanus, who spoke in tongues and claimed in his trances to transmit the words of the Logos, the popular "new prophecy" established its church at Pepuza in Asia Minor, where its followers expected the New Jerusalem to appear momentarily. Even when these eschatological expectations failed, the movement continued to spread, persisting in some Mediterranean communities into the sixth century. The movement, moreover, collected its leaders' oracles in writings which seem to have had a ritual status comparable to sacred Scripture, a circumstance that helped pressure the church into defining its canon, into declaring that perfect corpus of inspiration that can neither be added to nor subtracted from. The question remains, then:

---

[90] For the debate regarding Mary Magdalene and Peter, see Schüssler Fiorenza, *In Memory of Her*, 51–54, and more generally, Elaine Pagels, *The Gnostic Gospels* (New York: Vintage, 1979), 3–27 and 48–69, especially 64–65.

[91] In the Jewish synagogue liturgy, which would have been an important matrix from which the liturgical aspects of Revelation emerged, the fixing of normative prayer forms began only in the latter half of the first century, following the destruction of the temple. This process was gradual, but was already underway when John wrote Revelation. See Bouley, *From Freedom to Formula*, 18–19.

Why, amid the general distrust of apocalyptic literature stirred by Montanism, could Revelation continue to hold a privileged place for central church authority?[92]

There are many possible answers here, the full range of which must include the aesthetic and spiritual power the text possessed for its early audience and, in a different key, the fact that most readers believed it to have been authored by the John of the fourth gospel, thus providing the text with apostolic authority. But such speculations must also include the political edge that John's antifeminist vision of an apocalyptic patriarchal order might have wielded against the new prophecy of Asia Minor. After all, Montanus shared his authority with two women, Priscilla and Maximilla, both of whom left their husbands after being taken by the spirit; the movement seems to have advocated in principle the dissolution of marriages. Although canonization has left us next to no firsthand material from the Montanists, one of the few oracles generally considered authentic suggests how thoroughly this egalitarian apocalyptic movement ran counter to the patriarchal vision of John: "In the form of a woman, says she, arrayed in shining garments, came Christ to me and set wisdom upon me and revealed to me that this place [Pepuza] is holy and that Jerusalem will come down hither from heaven."[93] Not only is a woman capable of receiving revelation in this anonymous oracle, but the Logos itself is of indeterminate gender, suggesting that the very origin of divine vision cannot be reduced to an exclusionary principle of unitary identity.[94] The Montanist Logos is capable of sexual difference. The new message attracted women both in leadership and membership, and curiously enough, it thrived in Thyatira, where three-

[92] "In the Great Church there developed a certain mistrust of all recent writings of a prophetical nature. Not only did such a feeling tend to discredit several apocalypses that may have been, in various parts of the Church, on their way to establishing themselves, but also; as was mentioned earlier, even the Apocalypse of John was sometimes brought under a cloud of suspicion because of its usefulness in supporting the 'new prophecy.'" Metzger, *The Canon of the New Testament*, 104. I am also drawing on the discussion of Montanism in Elaine C. Huber, *Women and the Authority of Inspiration: A Reexamination of Two Prophetic Movements from a Contemporary Feminist Perspective* (Lanham, Md.: University Press of America, 1985), chapter 2, and the general discussion of early Christian women in Elizabeth A. Clark's "Devil's Gateway and Bride of Christ: Women in the Early Christian World," in *Ascetic Piety and Women's Faith: Essays on Late Ancient Christianity* (Lewiston, N.Y.: Edwin Mellen, 1986), 23–60.

[93] *New Testament Apocrypha*, ed. Schneemelcher, 2:687.

[94] This is not to say that Montanism rejected either monism or monotheism; on the contrary, one oracles states: "Christ has a single nature, a single energy both before the flesh and with the flesh, in order that he does not become different by doing actions dissimilar and different." Huber, *Women and the Authority of Inspiration*, 220. The coexistence of these two oracles seems to suggest that the idea of God as the One was capable of accommodating differences.

quarters of a century earlier Jezebel's teachings held sway, an influence that perhaps continued for generations.[95]

At a more advanced stage of institutionalized misogyny than John's attack on Jezebel, the central church considered exorcizing the demonic spirit from Priscilla and Maximilla, although no record indicates a similar proposal regarding Montanus. In fact, the gatherings of bishops in Asia Minor to formulate an initial response to Montanism may well represent the first such synods in church history; the earliest, anonymous source cited by Eusebius in *Ecclesiastical History* states that "when the faithful throughout Asia had met frequently and at many places in Asia for this purpose, and on examination of the new-fangled teachings had pronounced them profane, and rejected the heresy, these persons were thus expelled from the Church and shut off from its communion."[96] In declaring such "heresies," along with those of Marcion and the various gnostic sects, the central church took powerful strides toward defining and consolidating its institutional and patriarchal identity. As Gager puts it, "If the church had not encountered heretics, it would have created them."[97] And when the church countered dissent with the gradual formation of its own official canon, Revelation, despite all the controversies surrounding it, not only survived the cut but eventually established itself as a text of extraordinary canonical privilege, the one that could most effectively indicate closure in every sense of the term—historical, aesthetic, and scriptural.

John wrote the Book of Revelation on the cusp between an internally diverse religious movement and its subsequent consolidation as an institution. His vision of the end of history at once preserves the antinomian impulse of prophecy and the antithetical, stabilizing imperatives of "official" prophecy, canonical prophecy. The extent to which Revelation is consonant with the canonical interests of the emerging church is indeed remarkable. John's antifeminism provides our best glimpse into

---

[95] See Schüssler Fiorenza, *In Memory of Her*, 55.

[96] Eusebius, *The Ecclesiastical History and the Martyrs of Palestine*, 2 vols., trans. H. J. Lawler and J. E. Oulton (London: SPCK, 1954), 1:160 (16.10). Elaine C. Huber assesses the evidence that the response to Montanism may have inspired the first church synods in *Women and the Authority of Inspiration*, 56–57.

[97] Gager, *Kingdom and Community*, 79. Oddly enough, it seems that Montanist beliefs did not in any obvious way contradict the teachings of the gospels; in fact, the early accusations of heresy do not involve issues of doctrinal error. This continuity between Montanism and the central church suggests that one must look elsewhere for the conflict's source: perhaps to the place of women in the new prophecy, perhaps to the fact that as Montanism grew in popularity, it established its own organization for collecting funds and paying wages to its preachers, creating an infrastructure in no way dependent on that formed simultaneously by the central church. See Huber, *Women and the Authority of Inspiration*, 36–40.

this consonance, since it demonstrates most explicitly how the text's largest eschatological dramas are bound up with immediate agendas of internal intimidation and exclusion. But John's antifeminism opens onto more general strategies of suppressing difference, strategies that get built into the impressive textual formalism that I discussed in the first part of this chapter. In the second and third centuries, the process of canonization would extend the boundaries of that seemingly ahistorical or posthistorical formalism and so perpetuate the text's power to silence. Not long after Revelation appeared, Irenaeus justified his privileging of four gospels by appealing to the authority of both nature (four corners of the earth, four winds) and John's Apocalypse (the four living creatures around the throne of God).[98] In other words, for Irenaeus an intertextual relation with Revelation served to legitimate his selection of sacred narratives, an argument prompted historically by the proliferation of gospels among early Christian groups on the one hand and on the other by Marcion's heretical refusal to recognize any gospel other than Luke's. Beginning with the Gospels and ending with Revelation, Irenaeus's incipient New Testament could form a self-referential literary unit, an idea carried out in the iconographic tradition that associates each of the four gospel authors with one of the animal faces described by John.

Irenaeus certainly stretches Revelation here, but his interpretation remains consistent with the text's self-representation, and it is therefore instructive. Positioning itself as the heir to and fulfillment of previous canonical books, the most allusive text in the Bible foregrounds its power to draw other, select writings into the monumental closure and aesthetic unity it projects for itself. Indeed, the image of a single, continuous testimony gets built into the symbolism of the New Jerusalem itself, which, as I argued earlier, represents not only the sacred space beyond history but the text's own timeless, architectural structure. Just before measuring the city, John describes the gates and foundations that belong to its walls: "It had a great, high wall, with twelve gates, and at the gates twelve angels, and on the gates the names of the twelve tribes of the sons of Israel were inscribed; on the east three gates, on the north three gates, on the south three gates, and on the west three gates. And the wall of the city had twelve foundations, and on them the twelve names of the twelve

---

[98] "As is the activity of the Son of God, such is the form of the living creatures; and as is the form of the living creatures, such is also the character of the Gospel. For the living creatures were quadriform, and the gospel and the activity of the Lord is fourfold. . . . Since this is the case, they are foolish and uninstructed, even audacious, who destroy the pattern of the gospel, and present either more or less than four forms of the gospel." Irenaeus, *Against Heresies*, ed. and trans. Edward Rochie Hardy, in *Early Christian Fathers*, ed. and trans. Cyril C. Richardson (Philadelphia: Westminster Press, 1953), 1:383.

apostles of the Lamb" (21:12–14). The symmetry of the New Jerusalem is a symmetry of Jewish and Christian: the spatial formalism that sets Revelation outside history extends to the tradition which precedes it, those sacred books which now share in a literary trajectory that has Revelation as its end.[99] Through an apocalyptic vision the Old and New Testaments could be imagined as a single book, one as capacious as the New Jerusalem and one as equally immune to time.

This magnificent apocalyptic formalism, with its vision of history ending in a transcendental literary structure, had ideological work to do. It would be a mistake to leave Revelation with its own linkage of the New Jerusalem and an all-encompassing two-testament canon. We know that the canon is not all-encompassing, that many voices were aggressively excluded from it. The canon was formed, one might say, in order to exclude them. Even the Christian belief that the Old and New Testaments form a single, continuous tradition had to emerge from a circumstance of theological dispute, which in turn reflected a struggle for power over the early Christian communities. Many of the texts Irenaeus sought to exclude by forging a symbolic unity between the four gospels and Revelation were gnostic gospels, and one of the most troubling of gnostic heresies was the denial that the Hebrew Scriptures and the new inspired writings formed an essential unity. Marcion, who was perhaps the first to designate his own Christian canon, blatantly rejected the sanctity of the Hebrew Scriptures. Not only, then, did the early church have to determine which texts it considered sacred, it also had to defend the status of the Hebrew Bible, the very ground of canon.[100] For us, the terms of this reconstructed dispute remain sketchy. But the canonical Book of Revelation, with its vision of one architectural corpus spanning Hebrew and Christian Scripture, a city-book founded in the place beyond history, stands as a permanent reminder that a once significant historical difference ended in a timeless literary unity.

[99] Thus Irenaeus sees Revelation as the fulfillment of a single, unvarying line of prophecy: "John therefore predicted precisely the first resurrection of the just, and [their] inheritance of the earth in the Kingdom, and the prophets prophesied about this in agreement with each other." *Against Heresies*, in *Early Christian Fathers*, 397.

[100] As Pagels demonstrates, this dispute was linked to the patristic defense of traditional monotheism against gnostic modifications, which in turn reflected a struggle over ecclesiastical authority in the earliest stages of the church's institutionalization. "Specifically, by the latter part of the second century, when the orthodox insisted upon 'one God,' they simultaneously validated the system of governance in which the church is ruled by 'one bishop.' Gnostic modification of monotheism was taken—and perhaps intended—as an attack upon that system. For when gnostic and orthodox Christians discussed the nature of God, they were at the same time debating the issue of *spiritual authority*." *Gnostic Gospels*, 34.

CHAPTER TWO

APOCALYPSE DISARMED

The Prophetical Scriptures are holy, harmless, and without fault . . .
— Anonymous, "The Life of the Reverend and
Most Learned Joseph Mede" (1677)

From this short delineation and explication given of the book in its several chapters, it will strike every one on slightest perusal, that the book is composed with transcendent art, and that the parts of it are so admirably adapted and adjusted together, and the connexion and dependency of them each upon other so exact and regular, that it fills the measures of perfection, which are described by Aristotle for an Epic Poem or Tragedy.
— W. Cooke, *The Revelations Translated* (1789)

If we are trying to comprehend this book, we must abandon the conception of an ensemble of tumultuous, explosive visions, of cataclysms and disorder at the end of the world. It is clear that even the use of this word itself exposes the usual error: apocalypse, understood as an aggregate of frightful disasters. This is all that has been retained. During bombardments we speak of an apocalypse of iron and fire. Of course, the meaning "revelation" has been totally forgotten. *Apocalyptic* means the same as frightful visions. . . . The popular meaning shows clearly what we are always tempted to retain and to forget. But objectively the content of the Apocalypse is not the former.
— Jacques Ellul, *Apocalypse* (1975)

The Book of Revelation is a violent book. Despite the ambiguities and contradictions that make it notoriously resistant to interpretation, this violence is evident even upon a cursory reading. Landscapes disintegrate, seas turn to blood; the collective sign of the enemy, the Whore of Babylon, is stripped, burned, and eaten. Imagining the total victory that results from a military battle between irreconcilable antagonists, John directs our attention to the loser's fate without flinching. "Then I saw an angel standing in the sun, and with a loud voice he called to all the birds that fly in mid-heaven, 'Come, gather for the great supper of God, to eat the flesh of kings, the flesh of captains, the flesh of mighty men, the flesh of horses and their riders, and the flesh of all men, both free and slave, both small and great'" (19:17–18). That this is equal opportunity carnage does nothing to lessen the scene's vindictive, primitive brutality. Nor does the fact that the vultures' supper forms a neat structural antithesis to "the marriage supper of the Lamb" (19:9), which is introduced earlier in the same chapter. For all of its attention to systematic symbolism, to a formidable literary logic, the Book of Revelation never strays far from a palpable, visceral violence. One simply knows not to be caught on the wrong side of its dangerous God. Under what extraordinary circumstances, then, might a reader come to see the apocalyptic text as the very antithesis of impending, violent change, indeed, even as a model of order, harmony, stability?

In one instance, where we can begin by way of introduction, the circumstance was World War II. Austin Farrer wrote his brilliant, beautiful, hopelessly antiquated book, *Rebirth of Images*, between 1941 and 1948, and it reads like a litany of the interpretive strategies that will occupy this chapter, strategies that train the analytical eye to read Revelation as literature. The idiosyncratic heir of an exegetical tradition going back at least to the early seventeenth century, Farrer believed Revelation was a lyric poem and John an inspired poet; these assumptions allowed him to bypass the book's graphic violence in order to refocus attention on its aesthetic composition, to withdraw into the "delicate web" of text and find there "an intricately planned paradise, which we can make the home of our thoughts for a while, and explore from end to end."[1] In Farrer's hands, Revelation becomes a metaphysical trapdoor out of history and violence, its textual form—"the literary miracle of the Apocalypse" (307)—opening the escape, painstakingly constructing the verbal exit through which we can pass but history cannot. With the disciplined myopia of a relentless literary critic, Farrer creates out of Revelation a self-contained verbal gem, one which is best explained by reference to archetypal symbols, intertextual relations within Scripture, mathematical formulae, and the mystical dimensions of Solomon's Temple as described in the Hebrew Bible. Not surprisingly, his formalist tour de force moves inexorably toward a systematic spatialization of the text, so that the whole of Revelation can ultimately be distilled to the geometry of a "Sacred Diagram," literally a "pull-out analysis of the Apocalypse" (35) that on a single sheet visualizes the text's imagery patterns according to the rhythms of the Jewish Festal calendar (fig. 1). With an earnest, charming absurdity, Farrer insists that John himself used the diagram or one much like it; how else could such an intricate literary work have been realized? In the end, the foursquare

---

[1] Austin Farrer, *A Rebirth of Images: The Making of St John's Apocalypse* (Westminster: Dacre Press, 1949), 18. Further citations are to this text.

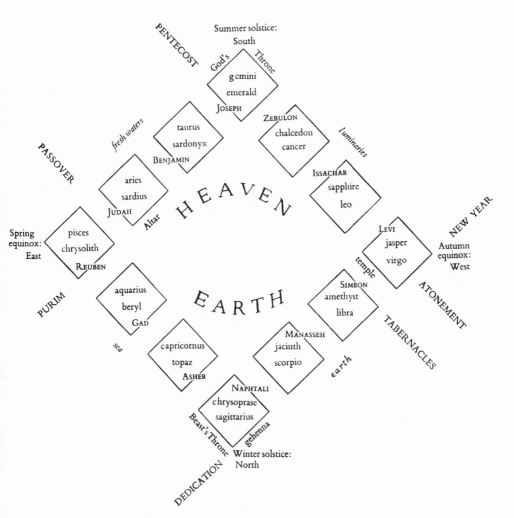

Figure 1. The Sacred Diagram, from Austin Farrer, *A Rebirth of Images* (Gloucester, Mass.: Peter Smith Publisher, Inc., 1970).

symbolic map displaces the text and becomes indistinguishable from the foursquare New Jerusalem itself; in a way much like that I described in the previous chapter, time miraculously has been converted into space. Apocalypse, the end of history, already exists in the measured form of a book: "As the mind passed over and over it," he writes of his Ouija-board-like diagram, "the several stages of ascent were built up, the depth and breadth of the divine Kingdom were made full, until the World to

Come burst on the seer's vision."[2] With London and his own Cambridge under constant threat of bombardment, and later with disclosures of the Holocaust to ponder, Farrer persisted in perhaps the most sustained and fiercely hermetic close reading ever given John's Apocalypse.

History, however, does not easily disappear, and it threatens the edges of this formal analysis from two directions. First, there is the irritating matter of chapter 17, where John identifies the Whore of Babylon with Rome and thus seems to anchor his prophecy within particular circumstances. In this single detail, John indelibly makes history intrinsic to the text, and as Farrer states early on of his totalizing interpretation, "every detail will bear examination" (18). Faced with this problem, Farrer's uneasy response is to recognize the impression left by John's circumstances, but then to trivialize it, to make it secondary to, even separable from, the *real* apocalypse. The Antichrist is "written out of scripture and principle rather than out of contemporary history" (296); it is "worked out on the plane of symbolism" (294). The particular applications and predictions thus seem embarrassing, "a trifle arbitrary" (291), and Farrer, reading his own needs into John, suggests that we might ignore the particulars without doing any real injustice to the text: "We, presumably, are unlikely to feel that the particular prediction as such was part of divine revelation; Providence has not permitted it to become a clear part of the inspired text, and we might even wonder how firmly St John himself was attached to it" (295). In predicting the downfall of Rome, John halfheartedly followed prophetic conventions that have little to do with the essence of his vision.[3] Farrer's strategy is thus convenient but costly. By opening such a fissure *within* the text between history and metaphysics, between the arbitrary and the necessary, he inadvertently contradicts the one principle upon which his entire poetic analysis depends, that Revelation "is a single and living unity from end to end" (6).

The filtering of historical impurities, however, serves a necessary function on Farrer's second historical front, a function which helps explain why he risks the blatant contradiction discussed. Having trivialized the role of history in the origins of the Apocalypse, making it a mere footnote dwarfed by the grandeur of the text's literary architecture, he can now turn to his own more daunting circumstances. Scattered infrequently but conspicuously across *Rebirth of Images* are brief, oddly casual references to contemporary horrors: literary analysis is

---

[2] Ibid., 307. According to Farrer, "The diagram represents the final object of St John's vision, the Kingdom of Heaven," so that the prophet actually began to compose already holding "the form of what he aspired to see, final blessedness" (307).

[3] As Farrer says early on, "Prophecy, no doubt, often had a particular and quite practical address, but it was distinguished from mere exhortation by *ultimate* dependence on the pressure of supernatural mysteries within the mind" (ibid., 16; my emphasis).

likened to military maneuvers, Patmos to a concentration camp, the relation between Hitler and Goebbels to that between Antichrist and the false prophet.[4] The effect is just the opposite of what one would expect. The Apocalypse does nothing so vulgar as to predict World War II; it puts World War II in perspective; it provides a vast nonviolent mindscape from which the most unthinkable terrors of history shrink to insignificance, to mere glosses on an aesthetic reality so magnificent it makes them all but disappear. Hitler and Goebbels are simply convenient analogies to help us see the power of a literary truth. Farrer acknowledges them to conjure them away; but in doing so, in providing these mere traces of the situation in which he writes, the whole motivating force of his project becomes visible. Farrer needs Revelation to be a sacred space into which one can retreat, needs to imagine literary form as the antonym of violence, and in at least one poignant passage, history seems to intrude upon his analysis inadvertently, without his careful staging of its insignificance. Describing the advances and setbacks his reading entails, he reverts to the architectural trope that so epitomizes his method: the Apocalypse "bears the promise of formal consistency, of a continuous grand architecture spanning the whole book, into which all the visionary detail is to be fitted. Yet, as we advance, it does not appear to us that the promise is fulfilled. The lines of the schematic architecture elude us, and the work seems in danger of disintegrating into a mere pile of visions and oracles. Then architectural elements reappear . . ." (36). In the image of a building reduced to rubbish one just glimpses the literal fury of aerial devastation Farrer works so hard to banish from sight, and one begins to understand his desire to reconstitute architectural space on the literary plane of apocalypse.

A Rebirth of Images is an extreme example of a type of reading of Revelation which has persisted across the modern period, even (and perhaps especially) under circumstances considerably less extreme. I earlier called this type of reading a tradition, but it lacks the consistency this term implies; it is more like a cluster of strategies from which a commentator might draw, strategies used to distance the literary form of Revelation from historical engagement and thus from any implication of violence. With these strategies, asking readers to see the Apocalypse as a "text" often means asking that they turn away from something else, that they cultivate a careful, selective blindness. Robert Alter, coeditor of *The Literary Guide to the Bible,* once described what it would mean to read the Bible seriously as literature: "By serious literary analysis I mean the manifold varieties of minutely discriminating attention to the artful use of language, to the shifting play of ideas, conventions, tone, sound,

---

[4] Ibid., 5, 24, 286.

imagery, narrative viewpoint, compositional units, and much else; the kind of disciplined attention, in other words, which through a whole spectrum of critical approaches has illuminated, for example, the poetry of Dante, the plays of Shakespeare, the novels of Tolstoy."[5] To read Revelation as literature, with all the disciplined, minutely discriminating attention that involves, has largely been to engage in an ideology of diversion. It requires practice in the art of deflection. I want to suggest in this chapter that the emergence, or perhaps I should say creation, of Revelation as an object of formal literary analysis occurs in part as a concerted effort to occlude the book's relation to violence—that is, both its own graphic depiction of acts of violence and its long historical association with violent, revolutionary movements.

In Farrer's case, this optical illusion involves a relatively simple escapism. The cases that will concern me here are ideologically less innocent. Whereas Farrer responds to immediate and extraordinary violence, the authors whose works I will consider tend to deploy arguments like his in order to preempt "perceived" threats of violence, in order to secure the already existing peace of an established social order. The programmatic effort to read violence out of Revelation can sometimes mask a desire to limit the book's capacity to articulate or promote conflict of any sort. With form and violence set in inverse proportions, distinctly "literary" conceptions of the Apocalypse—by which I mean considerations of textual properties apart from their historical embeddedness and social consequence—emerge in the modern period in order to silence, diffuse, deflect, or otherwise contain the book's volatility, an operation made all the more persuasive by its claim to be grounded in the readily visible, concrete evidence of the text itself. Even Farrer could insist that his reading escaped "the suspicion of phantasy," or subjective bias, because it attended so closely to the indisputable words on the page.[6] To render Revelation harmless all one need do is read the book attentively, concentrating on its intricate symbolic harmonies until all else fades around that single, mesmerizing focal point. "To Scripture then we must go,"

---

[5] Robert Alter, "A Literary Approach to the Bible," *Commentary*, December 1975, 70. Regina M. Schwartz quotes this article in her introduction to *The Book and the Text: The Bible and Literary Theory* (Oxford: Basil Blackwell, 1990) and goes on to question its underlying assumptions for pedagogy and criticism: " 'The Bible as Literature' is a course title fraught with dangers: it suggests that we know what literature is, what the Bible is, and with all these confident formulations behind us, we can now make them analogous, or even equate them, as the case may be. To construct a poetics of the Bible, as we would for Shakespeare, Dante or Tolstoy, is valuable; but there can be no poetics that does not have ideological implications" (12).

[6] "The study can be exact, it can escape from the suspicion of phantasy." Farrer, *Rebirth of Images*, 18–19.

says eighteenth-century Anglican Bishop Richard Hurd, "for all the information we would have concerning the use and intent of prophecy: and the text, *to look no farther,* will clearly reveal the great secret to us."[7] Later in the same sermon, Hurd, who wrote extensively on literature and aesthetics, suggests that the entire "system" of prophecy, considered not as an amalgam of isolated visions but as a single self-referential text, "concentered into one point, shall form a strong light, and strike the sense very powerfully" (48). To see prophecy in this clear Newtonian light is also to be blinded by its aesthetic power, and the aggressiveness of Hurd's rhetoric suggests his significant political stake in steering the reading of prophecy this way. Not all the figures I will examine in this chapter share Hurd's curious scientism, but each shares his urgent desire to posit literary form, textual artifice itself, as an antidote to the political disturbances they believe Revelation has been distorted into endorsing.

In this chapter, then, I extend the argument of Chapter 1: I suggest how literary form, so integral to the text's original canonical function, continues to serve that function in some varieties of modern interpretation. We will see how "literary" readings tend to follow Revelation's own lead, marking the apocalyptic text as a space into which history does not significantly enter and thus, paradoxically, enlarging the text's authority over historical differences. These readings can take strikingly different shapes in different contexts, but some general contours remain stubbornly persistent, something I hope to demonstrate by looking at three authors from three centuries. The first two authors belong explicitly to a single trajectory of influence. In 1627 Joseph Mede wrote his *Clavis Apocalyptica,* the impact of which, according to Joseph Anthony Wittreich, "marks all subsequent commentary up to the present day."[8] Richard Hurd published the first Warburton lectures on prophecy in 1772; in them, he spends nearly as much time celebrating "the sublime Genius" Mede and the critical method he championed as he does interpreting Revelation itself (122). The times and the needs change over a century and a half, but Mede's text-centered reading of apocalypse remains remarkably serviceable. Finally, in what is almost a coda, I will turn to Leonard Thompson's *The Book of Revelation: Apocalypse and Empire,* published by Oxford in 1990, to see if any ideological vestige of Mede remains in the most recent scholarly study of Revelation, a book that would know his influence only in the most distant and indirect fashion.

[7] Richard Hurd, *An Introduction to the Study of the Prophecies concerning the Christian Church,* 4th ed. (T. Cadell: London, 1776), 27. Further citations are to this edition.

[8] Joseph Anthony Wittreich, Jr., *Visionary Poetics: Milton's Tradition and His Legacy* (San Marino: Huntington Library, 1979), 38.

Joseph Mede: Apocalypse and the Citizen-Reader

We start with a contradiction. On 18 April 1642, four years after the author's death, the House of Commons ordered the printing of Joseph Mede's *Key of the Revelation*, which had been recently translated from the Latin by Richard More, a member of Parliament. Thus began the wide dissemination of a scholarly tract that had originally been circulated only privately, and thus began Mede's association with radical Puritan politics. We often assume an automatic link between millenarianism and revolutionary imperatives, and indeed, Mede's *Key* did provide such radicals as the Fifth Monarchy Men with two influential arguments. While many others dated Revelation's millennial period in the past, beginning with Constantine's conversion and the linking of church and empire, Mede placed it in the future, as a condition still to be achieved. More important, he took the millennium literally, assuming Christ would rule a terrestrial kingdom, a political state, and not, as Augustine had interpreted it, a spiritual one. As the interest in prophecy increased in the 1640s, so did Mede's authority, and eventually he became a posthumous contributor to the English Revolution.[9]

In 1677 the fourth edition of *The Works of Joseph Mede* appeared in an exquisite, enormous volume, "Printed by Roger Norton, for Richard Royster, Bookseller to His Most Sacred Majesty." At dead center of the tome, book 3 reprinted Mede's famous analysis of Revelation, but in Latin. And in one of the two lengthy biographical essays that introduce the elaborate publication, an anonymous author declares that Mede "was a true Son of Peace, and lived a life of Obedience to the Laws of the Realm, and of Conformity to the Discipline of the Church: He *feared* both *the Lord and King, and meddled not with them that were given to change.*"[10] Thirty-five years after the translation of *Clavis Apocalyptica*, twenty-eight after the execution of Charles I, Mede had become a Restoration hero.

Scholars of English millenarianism have recently begun to see that of the two posthumous Medes, the Restoration version is closer to the

[9] Bernard Capp notes that the new freedom of the press in the 1640s brought the publication or translation of several books on prophecy, including ones by Brightman, Alsted, and Mede. The most crucial development, however, in the Puritan radicalization of prophecy occurred when preachers took up these scholarly works and made their arguments available to a much wider audience. See Bernard Capp, *The Fifth Monarchy Men: A Study in Seventeenth-Century English Millenarianism* (Totowa: Rowman and Littlefield, 1972), 36–37.

[10] "The Life of the Reverend and Most Learned Joseph Mede, B.D." in *The Works of Joseph Mede, B.D., in Five Books*, 4th ed. (London: Richard Royster, 1677), xii. Further citations are to this text.

original.[11] Anything but a firebrand, Mede remained quietly within the university and the church, writing learned, apologetic sermons with such titles as "Churches, That is, Appropriate Places for Christian Worship" and "The Reverence of God's House," sermons that, almost with a touch of Counter-Reformation nostalgia, sought to defend the propriety of uniform public worship and official ceremony.[12] In his reading of Revelation, Mede was strictly antipapist, which, by 1627 in England, is to say traditional; without adding anything strikingly new, he simply produced the most persuasive interpretation of the Roman Antichrist to date, thus providing, as Michael Murrin puts it, "a long range service for Protestant polemic." Even more than the Puritans' brief appropriation of his treatise, Murrin suggests, it is "Mede's conservativism [that] helps to explain his influence. Scholars recently have stressed Mede's millenarianism and its effect during the Revolution. . . . Just as important, however, was his justification of the standard reading of Revelation," a standard reading that served a Restoration call to obedience as well as it did a Puritan call to arms.[13] But Mede's justification of a standard, politically malleable line does not in itself explain his stunning appeal to establishment Anglicans, an appeal that remained unbroken for the

[11] See, for instance, *The Apocalyptic Tradition in Reformation Britain, 1530–1645* (Oxford: Oxford University Press, 1979), where Katharine Firth states that Mede "was interested neither in the active promotion of political or ecclesiastical change nor in reaching the great mass of the English people with his ideas" (214); or Bernard Capp's "The Political Dimension of Apocalyptic Thought," in *The Apocalypse in English Renaissance Thought and Literature,* ed. C. A. Patrides and Joseph Wittreich (Ithaca: Cornell University Press, 1984), which puts the paradox plainly: "After his death [Mede's] writings inspired first the revolutionaries and then the leaders of the Anglican establishment. His ideas were borrowed for the manifesto of the bloody Fifth Monarchist rising of 1661, and yet were also warmly admired by Sancroft and his circle (whose approach was certainly far closer to Mede's own)" (117–18).

[12] In these two sermons, Mede goes to great lengths to demonstrate the validity of organized, centralized church service, at one point arguing that, even though God is everywhere, his presence is superconcentrated in churches because more of his angels reside there. The sermons make evident Mede's worry that the Reformation threatens to introduce rampant religious individualism. If God demands only an inward obedience of conscience, Mede asks, does this mean there is no place for public form and ritual? "If this reasoning were admitted, a man might upon the same ground absent himself from coming to Church upon the dayes and times appointed, or come thither but now and then, alledging the indisposition of his heart to joine with the Church in her publicke worship at other times; Or if he came thither, act a mute, when others sing and praise God, to be altogether silent, and not open his mouth, nor to say Amen, when others doe. For all these are externall services. . . . But who would not thinke this to be very absurd?" "The Reverence of God's House," in *Works,* 68. One can hear the univocal Kiddusha of apocalypse pressing upon this exhortation.

[13] Michael Murrin, "Revelation and Two Seventeenth-Century Commentators," in *The Apocalypse in English Thought and Literature,* ed. Patrides and Wittreich, 138–39. Murrin's discussion of Mede is subtle and illuminating, generally one of the best available.

next hundred and fifty years; rather, it was *how* he demonstrated this widely accepted interpretation, and what happened to the Book of Revelation in the process, that secured his success. Clarke Garrett has argued that Mede's remarkable staying power derived from his capacity to relate Revelation to contemporary events.[14] While this is undeniably true and important, it is also the case that Mede's study survived others of the same sort because it provided a way *to regulate the application of Revelation to history.* Mede struck a deep chord with subsequent readers by discovering an effective means of limiting the range of apocalyptic interpretation, and that means was to see Revelation first as an intricately patterned, self-referential aesthetic object, to see it, in other words, as a literary text.

Given the "new spirit of millenarianism" that built across early sixteenth-century England toward the Revolution, the initial question one must ask of Mede is this: Why did his major hermeneutical innovation—his "discovery" that Revelation was a text organized by intrinsic structural relations that he called "synchronisms"—take the form it did?[15] To move toward an answer is to see that Mede was a paradoxical product of the Reformation, at once an example of inner-light Protestantism and of a reaction against the diffusion of authority it implied. Christopher Hill has shown that by the revolutionary decades, the spirit of charismatic revelation had spread to such extent in England that one recognizes "what was almost a new profession—the prophet, whether as interpreter of the stars, or of traditional popular myths, or of the Bible."[16] In a verse from Numbers, which Blake would later quote as an epigraph to *Milton,* Moses had exclaimed, "Would that all the Lord's people were prophets" (11:29), and within Puritan polemics, any faithful reader of Scripture was indeed capable of receiving the spirit directly, that is, independent of institutional mediation. Individual exegesis could thus become the conduit of a new prophecy, and it is easy to see Mede in terms of this development. In the *Key of the Revelation,* after all, he appeals directly to the Father and the Son to guide him—"Open the eyes of thy servant, and direct his hand and minde"—and as I will argue, he boldly makes his insight into the text's structure analogous to John's original reception of the divine vision, so that the unfolding of his interpretation mimes the opening of the book sealed with seven seals.[17]

---

[14] Clarke Garrett, *Respectable Folly: Millenarians and the French Revolution in France and England* (Baltimore: Johns Hopkins University Press, 1975), 125–26.

[15] Firth, *Apocalyptic Tradition,* 204.

[16] Christopher Hill, *The World Turned Upside Down: Radical Ideas during the English Revolution* (London: Temple Smith, 1972), 73.

[17] Joseph Mede, *The Key of the Revelation,* trans. Richard More (London, 1643), 2. Further citations are to this text.

Readers rarely failed to appreciate the author's affinity with his subject, and the apotheosis of Mede was under way shortly after his death: the preface to the 1642 translation referred to the "blessing of God upon his labors";[18] his most enthusiastic admirer, John Worthington, called him "The Revealer or Interpreter of hidden Things" and likened him to another Joseph, the biblical reader of dreams;[19] even the more sober biographer of 1677 describes how God, having selected Mede for "a great Blessing to the world," delivered him from smallpox at age ten (i).

All of this, however, is apt to provide the misleading impression that Mede simply rode the turbulent wave of millenarianism that characterized his age. Instead, I want to argue, he sought to stem the tide, and herein lies the secret of his long-term success. If Mede was a prophet, he was a distinctly canonical prophet, and the special authority he claimed for his criticism depended on its power to beat back rivals, the many mere pretenders to inspired exegesis. The Reformation had endowed individual subjectivity with a powerful and unsettling legitimacy, creating both a "Nation of Prophets" (as Hill titles his chapter) and a threat to traditional social hierarchy, but Mede wondered how one might continue to distinguish "divine authority" from what he called "meere humane conjectures" (27), especially when it came to the dangerous matter of apocalypse.[20] Apparently, he was as troubled as he was enabled by the spread of prophecy. His compelling solution was to posit a ground of interpretation outside interpretation, outside all subjectivity; the ground he proposed was simply the apocalyptic text itself, the timeless words on the page purged of the interested, dogmatic overlays that had made Revelation the battleground of conflicting factions. When Mede looked at the text itself, he saw such an intricate verbal network that its sophisticated formal relations made ludicrous any self-interested attempt to isolate a particular passage for historical application; because it had an inviolable *aesthetic* integrity, the book could not be treated piecemeal at the reader's *political* whim. By calling attention to the book's complicated, metaphysical form, which exists independent of merely temporal acts of interpretation and therefore governs all such acts a priori, Mede developed a new set of rules for reading Revelation. "By the characters of Synchronisms," he asserted, "is every interpretation to be tryed as it were by a square and plumb-rule" (27). Mede's *Key*, in other words, sought to reproduce Revelation as "canon"; it claimed to measure the text's intrinsic architecture, providing the ahistorical geom-

[18] The preface, by one Dr Twisse, is not paginated.

[19] John Worthington, "General Preface" to *The Works of Joseph Mede*. The "General Preface" is not paginated.

[20] Hill, *The World Turned Upside Down*, 70.

etry by which any alternative argument might be judged and silenced; it was "a Touch-stone for the finding out of the true interpretation, and *disproving of the false*" (1; my emphasis). By the time Isaac Newton could say of the study of prophecy that Mede "layed the foundation and I have built upon it," it was the elevation of the text's authority above that of presumptuous modern readers which had become a privileged axiom.[21] Newton chided the folly of interpreters who recklessly apply Revelation to contemporary and future events, "as if God designed to make them prophets."[22] There is no new prophecy; all one can do, all one need do, is study the fulfillment of ancient prophecies in past events, so that God's "own Providence, and not the Interpreters, be then manifested to the world" (251). Ironically, Mede, who made claims to charisma, articulated the very principles of criticism that enabled an emphatic curtailment of charisma.

On the title page of his commentary, an epigraph from Revelation indicates the fundamental problem facing Mede: "Blessed is he that readeth, (that is, interpreteth) and they that heare, (him that interpreteth) the words of this Prophesie, and keep those that are written therein" (1:3). Revelation imposes contradictory requirements on its readers: on the one hand, it seems to invite interpretation; on the other, in the final admonition so central to the text's canonical function, it threatens to punish anyone who dares add to a book already perfect in its form. To interpret a text without in some way adding to it is clearly an impossible task, as the parenthetical insertions in the epigraph demonstrate most literally. Given this predicament, Mede needed to create the illusion of reading without interpreting, to make it seem that his act of exegesis was in fact a simple act of empirical observation, albeit aided by a touch of divine grace that accounts for his rare disinterestedness. Revelation has to be considered "according to the letter only" (*Key*, 27), "without supposal of any Interpretation whatsoever."[23] This severe freedom from assumptions, this inspired and scientific neutrality, allows Mede to privilege his arguments, which are "firmly demonstrated out of the very characters of the visions inserted by the Spirit of God of set purpose" (*Key*, 1). It also provoked him to worry obsessively about the intrusion of his own subjectivity; according to a letter cited by Worthington, "it was his daily Desire and Prayer to God that he might not be led away with delusions." The effect of Mede's rigorous textual attention is to make Revelation take on all the dense integrity of a freestanding

---

[21] Isaac Newton, as quoted in Wittreich, *Visionary Poetics*, 38.

[22] Isaac Newton, *Observations on the Prophecies of Daniel, and the Apocalypse of St. John* (London: Darby and Brown, 1733), 251. Further citations are to this text.

[23] The second quotation can be found in Firth, *Apocalyptic Tradition*, 218.

object, or better yet, to make it look like a self-regulating system of signs and meanings that repels foreign influences. Sealed in an aura of self-definition, Revelation needs no readers because it reads itself. The way for the reader to transcend detrimental bias is to enter Revelation through its own process of autointerpretation, chapter 17, the angel's instruction to John regarding the Whore of Babylon. Amid the text's bewildering images, here is "a most plaine interpretation" (108), one conveniently initiated by divine agency so that "an entrance be opened, as it were a door to the rest otherwise inaccessible" (28). To put it simply, chapter 17 opens Revelation from the inside. Even on such sure ground, however, Mede relies on a sleight of hand, since this foundation of all intrinsic meaning is itself susceptible to an indeterminacy that might reopen the very need for human interpretation it promises to close. While he accepts that Babylon refers allegorically to Rome, as the angel plainly states, he dismisses the possibility that in this symbolically excessive text "Rome" itself might refer allegorically to something else: "For what strangeness should this be, or more truely madnesse of an interpreter?" (108). Mede just glimpses the vertigo of infinite regress that Paul de Man would eventually consider definitive of allegory, but as I argued in Chapter 1, Revelation constructs this site of indeterminacy in order to stage its own power to control the proliferation of meaning.[24] Babylon's punishment is to be stripped naked, to have her "Mystery" laid bare. Mede works the same ground to roughly the same ideological effect, fixing the textual point upon which he can build an "objective" criticism. A century later, such Anglican officials as Bishop Thomas Newton will continue to return to this site, heralding chapter 17 as "the best key to the Revelation, the best clue to direct and conduct us thro' this intricate labyrinth."[25]

Once inside Revelation, once one functions solely on its terms rather than one's own, one can begin to map the textual interior. Mede promoted his *Key* according to such cartographical metaphors, calling it "an Apocalyptic compasse," "a station or watch-tower [from which] thou mayest take the scantling of the rest of the Revelation" (28), "a sure

[24] In "The Rhetoric of Temporality," Paul de Man argues that "it remains necessary, if there is to be allegory, that the allegorical sign refer to another sign that precedes it." Thus allegory invokes a "pure anteriority." *Blindness and Insight* (Minneapolis: University of Minnesota Press, 1983), 207.

[25] Thomas Newton, *Dissertations on the Prophecies, Which Have Remarkably Been Fulfilled, and at This Time Are Fulfilling in the World* (London: Tonson and Draper, 1754), 3:283. Another midcentury commentator, Bishop Robert Clayton, considers chapter 17 "to have been inserted by the Angel as a Key to the whole." The motif is commonplace. *A Dissertation on Prophecy, Wherein the Coherence and Connexion of the Prophecies in both the Old and New Testament are fully considered: Together with an Explanation of the Revelation of St. John* (London, 1749), v of the preface and 134.

guide" through the textual "Labyrinth" (1). This pervasive spatial rhetoric is not gratuitous; it lies at the very foundation of his ambitious
critical system, the synchronisms which he and others considered his
most important achievement. The mistake of earlier commentators was
to assume that John's visions occur textually in the same sequence in
which they will be fulfilled historically, one event after another. Mede
sought to demonstrate instead that Revelation doubles and triples back
on itself, that the same event might be represented several times by a
number of scattered symbolic episodes. Synchronism 1, for instance,
reveals that the woman's trial in the wilderness, the revival of the seven-
headed beast, the Gentiles overrunning the Temple's outer court, and
the witnesses prophesying in sackcloth all reconfigure the same event.
As Twisse puts it in his preface to the *Key*, the synchronisms draw
together "the homogeniall parts of the text." Although this innovation
did remarkably little to alter received interpretation, it did present a
powerful new image of Revelation; it suggested that the text is organized
primarily by an interior, nonlinear, spatial logic, that it represents, in
other words, an order already antithetical to that of temporality. Mede
had fashioned Revelation into an autonomous verbal world, re-creating
through an aesthetic formalism the power of apocalypse suddenly and
dramatically to subordinate historical sequence to the metaphysical
forces that transcend it. In the *Key of the Revelation*, this eschatological
drama occurs with the unveiling of a sacred diagram, a blueprint of
literary architecture every bit as intricate as the one Farrer would use
centuries later to transcend World War II. Placed between pages 26 and
27, folded into four small squares, is the key of Mede's title (fig. 2), a
wholesale spatialization of the text that invites one, with all the force of a
supernatural vision, to comprehend the apocalypse all at once, as if one
could bypass the temporal process of reading. To unfold the diagram is
to unseal the Lamb's book of visions all over again, to see Revelation
itself instantly laid bare, and, like John before him, Mede can stand back
in awe and say "behold!"

> Moreover Reader; behold here is the order, and course of all the proph-
> ecies in Revelation, according to the things therein to be done in this figure
> drawne before thine eye, to be viewed at once; which I have framed by the
> exact rule of the synchronisms already demonstrated for mine own, and (if
> thou please) for thy use, Lord open the eyes of the understanding of either
> of us, that we may behold his marvellous workes. Amen. (26–27)

The dazzling effect of this gesture is that Mede's criticism seems merely
to reproduce the reality of the text, to repeat the revelation, while it in
fact creates something not at all evident to the untrained reader's eye.

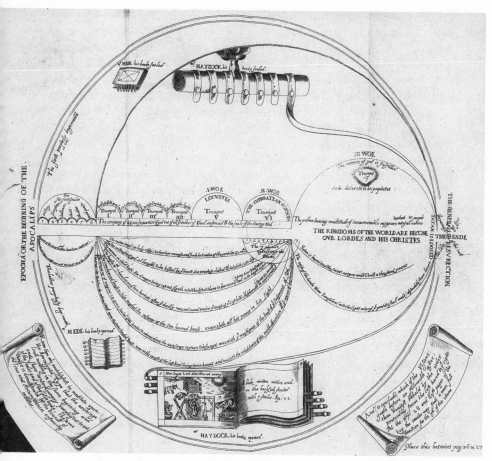

Figure 2. A Diagram of Revelation, from Joseph Mede, *The Key of the Revelation* (1642), bet. 26–27. RB 146819. Reproduced by permission of The Huntington Library, San Marino, California.

Seen with this literary x-ray vision, Revelation suddenly becomes a harmonious, mathematical order, a serenely drafted, all-encompassing circle. Paradoxically, interpretation seems to have disappeared into the text itself at the very moment it substitutes its own formalist construction for the text.[26]

[26] Mede is neither the first nor the last to make critical insight into the Book of Revelation analogous to divine revelation itself. Perhaps the most famous instance is that of Joachim of Fiore, who on Easter Eve broke through with his hermeneutical struggle with the text: "About the middle of the night's silence, as I think, the hour when it is thought that our lion of the tribe of Judah rose from the dead, as I was meditating, suddenly something of the fullness of this book and of the entire agreement of the Old and New Testaments

Farrer believed that his Sacred Diagram would "save the reader from ever getting lost in St John's text" (35). In different circumstances, Mede envisioned a similar grid that would keep wayward readers on the proper interpretive path.

> For truely, he that will endeavour with successe to find out the meaning of the Apocalyptique visions, must first of all place the course, and connexion of them one with another according to things done, being thoroughly searched out by the foresaid characters and notes, and demonstrated, by intrinsicall arguments as the basis, and foundation of every solid, and true interpretation. Therefore (which we see are to be done amisse by very many) the order it self is not to be conformed to every aptness of interpretation, according to the will of the interpreter; but according to the Idea of this chronicall order framed before hand. . . . For without such foundation, thou shalt scarce draw any thing out of the Revelation, that will soundly assure the interpretation and application therof, and which resteth upon divine authority, but upon begged principles, and meere humane conjectures, on the contrary side, this being admitted for a foundation, when as now the pales of time and order, shall not suffer the application to rove at randome, and according to pleasure. (27–28)

Mede himself went on to make historical applications; one might even say he roved at random, arguing (and thereby causing embarrassment to his future admirers) that Revelation's fourth vial referred, among other things, to King Gustav of Sweden. But Mede's admiring readers also recognized that a mistake in specific application did little damage to the general system; if anything it confirmed the need to focus attention on the reliable textual harmonies rather than risk the folly of too particular a discussion of actual events. Moreover, Mede established a lasting principle by asserting the priority of structural analysis over historical analysis in reading the Apocalypse. Historical reference remained important, but it was now subordinated to an aesthetic principle of self-referentiality. After Mede, a reader had to conform to Revelation's well-ordered form *before* entering into the inevitably subjective adventure of political speculation, and this erected significant obstacles to the freedom of interpretation. The *Key of the Revelation* was written nearly a generation before the revolution that killed an English king, but its

---

was perceived by a clarity of understanding in my mind's eye." In *Visions of the End: Apocalyptic Traditions in the Middle Ages,* ed. Bernard McGinn (New York: Columbia, 1979), 130. Nearly eight hundred years later, Farrer uses something of the same rhetoric to describe the illumination that results from his Sacred Diagram: "Before we proceed any further, a great light breaks upon us here" (*Rebirth of Images,* 221), an image he repeats five pages later.

countermillenarian lesson of containment was not lost on those who survived the violence of civil war and wished to avoid a recurrence.

Toward the end of Katharine Firth's study of English millenarianism, which generally extends only to 1645, the author glances forward to argue that "after the Restoration it became even more difficult for the admirers of the method and interpretation of Joseph Mede to quell fears that such an interpretation led only to revolution."[27] The nature and persistence of Mede's influence suggest otherwise. The 1677 edition of Mede's *Works*, for instance, is a virtual manual of the uses of apocalypse for the Restoration establishment. Defending Mede against mistaken charges of chiliasm, the extended introductory essays recommend his commentary as just the right cure for the disastrous millenarian excesses of the past. Seen through the aesthetic lens of the *Key of the Revelation*, apocalypse did not have to be shunned by polite society as something intrinsically dangerous; rather it could be vindicated, wrested out of the hands of Puritans and back into those of church and state apologists where it belonged. Following Mede's example, a "studious enquiry and diligent search" into prophecy becomes something of a Christian civic obligation (xiii). Not only does a close reading demonstrate on uncontestable principles "that S. John's Apocalypse contains nothing that may in the least encourage to disobedience or disorder," it also arms one against the dissenting opinion of those who read it otherwise. By appealing to the letter of the text, one can, as the same anonymous author states, "put to silence those men of Noise and Confidence rather than of Reason and Judgement" (xiii). Given these objectives, it is hardly surprising that the system of synchronisms commands the greatest prestige, for it represents a textual measure seemingly separated from the temporal interests of *all* readers, enabling one to distinguish between legitimate and subjective, potentially noxious interpretations. Thus Worthington could confidently dismiss any commentary departing from Mede's synchronic key as "a pile of private fantasies, slight conceits and weak conjectures."

Beyond their usefulness in identifying and policing dissent, the synchronisms offer a further appeal that moves closer to an ideology of "literary" apocalypse: existing prior to all interpretation as part of the textual order, they promise to produce a certain kind of reader. In the movement generated by Mede, the term that best describes this reader is rational, but a more pertinent description would be "apolitical." In order

[27] Firth goes on to say, "In vain Worthington attempted to disentangle the thought of Joseph Mede from his reputation as a prophet of the Revolution" (*Apocalyptic Tradition*, 245). Mede's criticism, however, not only survived but thrived among eighteenth-century commentators, making Worthington's project more successful than he himself could have imagined.

to see the real Apocalypse, the formal Apocalypse, one must enter the text without convictions, without an agenda; one must enter already disarmed of self-interest and purpose. One must begin, in other words, to see oneself as an essentially ahistorical subject whose real interests exist apart from the dynamics of conflict and change. In the 1677 edition, the model for such a reader is Mede himself, "free from all Partiality," exemplary in "the cool and calm temper of his spirit," remarkable for "a singular Sedateness and Sobriety of spirit, and a due regard to Authority" (Worthington). One could go on. What is striking, however, is not so much the way these eulogies transform Mede into a unique specimen of virtue, a man in whom the turbulence of history had already miraculously ended, but how they expect these characteristics to be disseminated by means of his writings. Mede requires a mimetic reader: "And whosoever would read the Author with most profit and judgment, must read him also with a free, impassionate and unprejudiced spirit" (Worthington). To Mede's Restoration champions, the quiet Cambridge scholar had discovered what amounted to a system of self-replicating analogical unity. Mede's temperament, the textual form of the Apocalypse, the subjectivity of the reader, and even the nature of the millennium itself—all come to look alike in their shared structural stability. "As our Author himself was a man of a cool Spirit, so likewise is his Notion and Representation of the Millennium cool and calm and moderate, not ministering to Faction and Sedition" (xii). And each analogical sphere survives by its capacity to cast out whatever would disturb it. As the millennium will have no place for "men of embitter'd passions and a destroying Spirit" (xii), so the text has a canonical form that excludes deviant readings, so Mede purges himself of the prejudices that implicate people in violence—and so readers must make themselves into like microcosms of order and stability.

It would seem that the synchronisms draw more than merely the parts of the apocalyptic text into "homogeniall" interdependence. They do nothing less than envision the necessary relations of a harmonious social order. At the origin of the chain of equivalences is the text of Revelation, or I should say, the image of Revelation as a text. Mede's blueprint claims to reproduce the text, but at the same time it diagrams a type of subjectivity (spatial, reasonable, ahistorical) that rests comfortably within a social framework resembling, in turn, nothing so much as the inviolable text. The final link, then, is the complicity between textual and political order. The Apocalypse, says his anonymous biographer, contains no incentive for violence or sedition, "but on the contrary represents Christian Kings and Princes (those that are Defenders of the Holy Apostolic Faith) under a fair Character, as friends to the Holy and Beloved City, the New Jerusalem" (xiii). And by following Mede,

Worthington suggests, "we should be the better enabled to vindicate the Prophecies from the corrupt Glosses which unlearned and unstable Souls (ill-willers also to the stability and peace of Christian States and Kingdoms) would force upon them." Worthington's parentheses speak volumes, making parallel the need to secure both the Christian kingdom and the apocalyptic text against transgression. To do violence unto Revelation by forcing millenarian glosses upon it is tantamount to a crime against the state. With this analogy comes an unstated corollary: to read Revelation through Mede's synchronisms, to see it as an intricately harmonized literary text, is to practice good citizenship.

Richard Hurd: Apocalypse and the Eighteenth-Century Anglican State

When Isaac Newton interpreted the books of Daniel and Revelation with the supreme confidence he brought to all his intellectual work, he did not hesitate to correct Mede's *Key of the Revelation,* pointing out that his predecessor had missed a synchronism, the one identifying the sounding of the trumpets with the emptying of the vials. In doing so, he secured for future readers the authority of Mede's system, which might be finessed in its details but remained fundamentally unchallenged. Mede's attention to what he called "the singular workmanship of the Revelation," to its astonishing formal coherence, was particularly important to Newton.[28] It confirmed his sense that of all the books in the Bible only the authority of Daniel and Revelation was absolutely reliable. Other scriptural texts were either composite redactions or late, sometimes corrupt, additions; these two recorded revelation directly and thus preciously contained the most certain foundation of Christianity.[29] "The authority of the Prophets is divine," he would write, "and comprehends the sum of religion" (14). In support of this view, Newton believed that Daniel and Revelation were literally one prophecy, that Daniel had sealed the very book John later sees opened, and this meant that divine

[28] Joseph Mede, *Key of the Revelation,* 29.

[29] Newton had a strong sense of the Bible's state of redaction. On the one hand, he believed no Old Testament texts were written down until the talmudic days of Ezra. Even Daniel was a composite book, with only the second half, the six visionary chapters, clearly attributable to the prophet himself. On the other hand, Newton's Arianism led him to believe that Revelation was the earliest of the New Testament books, making suspect all subsequent texts that introduced corrupt, Trinitarian doctrines.

agency played an unusually assertive role in preserving the eschatological visions, in guaranteeing the integrity of their written form. According to Richard Popkin, an unpublished note written by Newton on the
back of an envelope explains how "God was so concerned that John get
the text right that he sent Jesus . . . to watch over John as he wrote down
the prophecies."[30]

Mede's structuralist scrutiny made easier the claim that Revelation
was the real thing, a text of transcendent art, but Newton engaged in
little formal analysis of his own, taking that groundwork for granted. He
did, however, couple Mede's understanding of the book with an image
that would characterize prophecy for the next century. In one of his
most influential arguments, Newton demonstrated the importance of
the ancient Jewish Temple in John's visionary symbolism, and with this
context in mind he likened the seven-sealed book to Moses' "prophetic
book of the Law laid up on the right side of the Ark" (261). Within
Revelation's own symbolic logic, then, prophecy becomes associated
with Torah, and indeed, Newton's general understanding of prophecy
was strictly Deuteronomic. Not only is the prophet a servant of the law,
ideally represented by Moses, but once genuine prophecy enters a sanctioned, written form, new revelation is no longer necessary:

> In the infancy of the nation of Israel, when God had given them a Law, and
> made a covenant with them to be their God if they would keep his com-
> mandments, he sent the Prophets to reclaim them, as often as they re-
> volted to the worship of other Gods: and upon their returning to him, they
> sometimes renewed the covenant which they had broken. These Prophets
> he continued to send until the days of Ezra: but after their Prophecies
> were read in the Synagogues, those prophecies were thought sufficient.
> For if the people would not hear Moses and the old Prophets, they would
> hear no new ones, no not *tho they should rise from the dead.* At length when a
> new truth was to be preached to the Gentiles, namely, that Jesus was the
> Christ, God sent new Prophets and Teachers; but after their writings were
> also received and read in the Synagogues of the Christians, Prophecy
> ceased a second time. (13)

And ceased for good, as his sharp attack on the pretensions of contemporary interpreter-prophets tries to make clear. Newton shrewdly perceived the antithetical rhythms of canon and spontaneous revelation,
positing an alliance between canonical prophecy and law that was not so

---

[30] Richard Popkin, "Newton as a Bible Scholar," in *Essays on the Context, Nature, and
Influence of Isaac Newton's Theology,* by James E. Force and Richard H. Popkin (Dordrecht:
Kluwer Academic Publishers, 1990), 109.

much reiterated by subsequent eighteenth-century interpreters as it was realized concretely. When Richard Hurd delivered the first Warburton lectures on prophecy in 1772 and recognized Mede and Newton as "our ablest writers," "two incomparable men" (111), he spoke to the legal establishment of Lincoln's Inn Chapel. In fact, Warburton's endowment stipulated that the preacher at Lincoln's Inn should always receive the first offer of the five-hundred-pound salary, though he arranged for his close friend Hurd to receive the initial four-year appointment. The endowment also required that the lectures be published, assuring a wider audience, and when Hurd's volume appeared, it began with a dedication to the trustees, Sir John Eardley Wilmot and Lord Mansfield, Chief Justice of England, who four years earlier on the Court of King's Bench had famously sentenced John Wilkes to a one-thousand-pound fine and twenty-two months in prison. Perhaps no study of prophecy had ever so proudly advertised its legal connections.

In his grand overview of eighteenth-century English society, Roy Porter remarks wryly that "religion in Georgian England rubber-stamped social, power and property relations, generally ingrained already."[31] The mutually beneficial partnership between prophecy and law seems to confirm this generalization, though prophecy served a particular, and particularly significant, role in establishing and maintaining the legitimacy of the Georgian state, a role that helps to explain why Enlightenment bishops never relinquished the study of Revelation, despite its association with the dangers of radical millenarianism and civil war.[32] In bringing about a dynastic shift, the Revolution settlement of 1688 relied on a new language of political contract and secular law that seemed to loosen the hold of divine-right ideology on which the Restoration had so heavily depended. But as J. C. D. Clarke has shown, the Hanover line managed to retain much of the religious authority of its Stuart predecessor by transforming claims of divine right by birth into those of divine right by Providence. If the introduction of a new lineage marked a dramatic break with tradition, it was at least a break

---

[31] Roy Porter, *English Society in the Eighteenth Century* (London: Penguin, 1982), 199.

[32] Paul Korshin's excellent article, "Queuing and Waiting: the Apocalypse in England, 1660–1750," in *The Apocalypse in English Renaissance Thought and Literature*, ed. Patrides and Wittreich, charts the changes in millennialism that followed upon the Revolution, but he tends to underestimate the significance of prophecy to the Anglican establishment: "Orthodox Anglican churchmen were involved in millenarian thought—indeed, the pursuit of the Millennium in the age of reason is by no means limited to the contributions of Dissenters or Puritans—but their involvement slowly declined after the onset of the eighteenth century" (240). Later he adds, "Perhaps one of the greatest paradoxes of the Millennium in the early Enlightenment is that, as the notion of the apocalypse diminishes in immediacy for the established church, it grows in importance for minority religions and in popular literature" (260).

guided and smoothed by the will of God. Divine right by Providence, Clarke suggests, is no less "supernatural" than the former, and it involves "almost identical implications for the proper behavior of subjects. Humility, reverence, submission and obedience to social superiors continued to be the message of the pulpit."[33] In this light, Porter's metaphor of the rubber stamp is somewhat too dismissive of Georgian religion, which played a more active role in ideologically sustaining a remarkably resilient church-state establishment, one that managed to resist political challenge right up to the 1832 reform bill. As late as the 1790s, the notion of divine right by Providence, the belief that God had directed the people in the choice of their new king, was marshaled against those republicans who sought to draw specious analogies between 1789 and 1688. "The act of the people," wrote Samuel Horsley in a sermon commemorating "the Anniversary of the Martyrdom of Charles I," "is only the means which Providence employs to advance the new sovereign to his station: the obligation to obedience proceeds secondarily only from the act of man, but primarily from the will of God."[34] For well over a century, providence remained a foundational concept of the state's self-representation, and it is in this context that one begins to understand the Anglican investment in prophecy.[35]

[33] J. C. D. Clarke, *English Society, 1688–1832: Ideology, Social Structure, and Political Practice during the Ancien Régime* (Cambridge: Cambridge University Press, 1985), 126. Clarke's massive study is a valuable but self-congratulatory exercise in revisionist history, taking most of its pleasure from pricking the bubbles inflated by historians concerned with the period's progressive politics. He sets out to undermine "the Whig interpretation" that has ruled the study of English history, an interpretation that sees the period as the prelude to modern democratic, capitalist society, and thus overemphasizes the forces of change during a time of surprisingly resilient stability. In opposition to this tendency, he considers his book "an appreciation of the unity of the English ancien régime as a thing-in-itself, not an anticipation of industrial society" (4). Clarke is at his best in characterizing the establishment's self-representations and in restoring a sense of the staying power of its hegemony, which, as he points out again and again, resisted progressive challenges for nearly a century and a half. He tends, however, to hear mainly the dialogue between the establishment and itself, and only by ignoring so many of the period's other voices, does he manage to make the establishment's self-image look like history itself.

[34] *The Theological Works of Samuel Horsley* (London: Longman, Brown, Green, and Longmans, 1845), 2:234. As Clarke argues, in terms that apply to Burke as well as to Horsley, "It becomes clear that the conservative case was not suddenly contrived in response to a radical challenge after 1789. Nor did it then return to the doctrine of divine right: it had never left it." *English Society, 1688–1832*, 200.

[35] In "'Virtue, Religion and Government': the Anglican Uses of Providence," John Spurr shows that this ideological function of Providence was already well established during the Restoration, which saw "a deliberate attempt to wrest providentialism away from the puritans." This ideological function involved a dual project that the church continued into the next century: "proclaiming the providential rule of the world against atheists and sinners . . . [and] warning against the misreading and abuse of providences." In *The Politics of Religion in Restoration England*, ed. Tim Harris, Paul Seaward, Mark Goldie (Oxford: Blackwell, 1990), 33.

Newton himself did much to authorize a study of prophecy that primarily set out to demonstrate how "the world is governed by Providence" (251). Despite his Arianism, despite his unwillingness to subscribe to the Thirty-nine Articles, Newton appealed to all political sides precisely because he envisioned a permanently hierarchical cosmos in which God reigned supreme over all activity, providentially directing the motion of everything from inert atoms to human history. The study of prophecy in no way contradicted the general program of his physics, and both served the needs of a state whose clergy, like Bishop Robert Clayton, read Revelation as proof that God "governs the World, and doth whatsoever pleaseth him both in Heaven and Earth."[36] Newton's *Observations* appeared posthumously in 1733, a year after Pope's *Essay on Man*, the poem that William Warburton celebrated by claiming "all Complaints against Providence are at an end."[37] A generation later, having benefited from Warburton's generosity ("my dear Lord . . . you have made me rich"), Richard Hurd demonstrated how well he had learned the century's lesson on prophecy.[38] His final lecture on the uses of his study appealed to "the secret aid of divine providence"; just as Pope and Warburton set out to vindicate the ways of God to men, so Hurd could conclude: "Thus, the reasonable expectations of men are answered; and the honour of God's government abundantly vindicated" (207–8).[39] God's government presumably refers to his providential ac-

---

[36] Clayton, *A Dissertation on Prophecy*, 29. The best essay on the intersection of Newton's various interests with his ideas on prophecy is James E. Force's "Newton's God of Dominion: The Unity of Newton's Theological, Scientific, and Political Thought," in his *Essays on the Context, Nature, and Influence of Isaac Newton's Theology*, 75–102. Force shows how Newton's Arianism, which heretically posited God the Father as the sole and supreme master of the cosmos, touched all aspects of his thought, and won him the support of any party vested in a theory of hierarchy. Thus, nothing less than a royal dispensation in 1675 exempted him from subscription and allowed him to retain his chair in mathematics at Cambridge, while after 1688, he received regular assistance from the Whig establishment in the form of appointments at the Mint. On the latter front, James R. Jacob and Margaret C. Jacob have argued that the new science initiated by Newton and Boyle provided "powerful ideological support" to "the Whig version of the constitution." The Newtonian Enlightenment was hardly meant to foster deism and critique traditional values; rather, it "was intended by its participants as a vast holding action against materialism and its concomitant republicanism, against what is best described as the Radical Enlightenment." "The Anglican Origins of Modern Science: The Metaphysical Foundations of the Whig Constitution," *Isis* 71 (1980): 251, 265.

[37] Alexander Pope, *An Essay on Man*, with notes by William Warburton (London: Knapton, 1745), 14.

[38] In William Warburton, *Letters from a Late Eminent Prelate to One of His Friends* (New York: Sargeant, 1809), 315.

[39] In the first section of the first book of *The Divine Legation of Moses Demonstrated* (reprint, New York: Garland, 1978), William Warburton describes himself as one who would attempt "to vindicate the Ways of God to Man" (1:5), following Pope's lead in the *Essay on Man* more than Milton's in *Paradise Lost*.

tivity, not the English state whose chief legal representative Hurd so conspicuously acknowledged in his dedication.

None of this evidence should be seriously surprising; aside from suggesting a more prominent role for official versions of prophecy in the period, it rests comfortably within the standard portrait of eighteenth-century Anglicanism. To understand the function of "literary" apocalypse, however, we need to consider a narrative usually constructed against this conservative backdrop. According to this narrative, two developments in the eighteenth century run counter to the official line on prophecy, thus sustaining and transforming the subversive potential of apocalyptic Scripture: first, a strain of popular millenarianism that is sporadic but persistent and, second, an ongoing scholarly investigation into the rhetorical form of prophecy that enables a progressive subculture to read the Bible as literature and even to appropriate it as the basis of new, potentially heterodox, literary forms. The attention to the Bible as literature begins to pry the text out of the Anglican theological matrix in which it served a nearly transparent ideological function. Especially with regard to William Blake, studies of this development have become something of a subspecies of romantic criticism, demonstrating in full detail how the romantic association between poetry and prophecy, an association which seems to politicize both poetry and prophecy, has an eighteenth-century genealogy that looks back to Mede and inevitably passes through Robert Lowth's *Lectures on the Sacred Poetry of the Hebrews*. Typical of such arguments is John Drury's statement that Blake "transgressed orthodox bounds by making honest indignation and poetic genius the divine inspirations of the Bible: a lesson which he had learned from the Bishop of London, Robert Lowth."[40] In summarizing the influences that led Blake to his apocalyptic aesthetic, Leslie Tannenbaum offers a more complete picture:

> This constellation of ideas about the pictorial nature of prophetic language, much of which was derived from older traditions, would have been available to Blake mainly through the several editions of the works of Daubuz, Lowth, Fénelon, Jones, Warburton, and Hurd that were published in the eighteenth century, as well as through the citation of those works by other biblical commentators and literary critics. From these ideas Blake would have discovered either the impetus or the theoretical sanction for his decision to cast his prophecies into a form that combines both words and pictures.[41]

[40] John Drury, "Introductory Essay," in *Critics of the Bible, 1724–1873* (Cambridge: Cambridge University Press, 1989), 7.

[41] Leslie Tannenbaum, *Biblical Tradition in Blake's Early Prophecies* (Princeton: Princeton University Press, 1982), 60–61.

The same chapter begins by reminding us that it was Mede who had "introduced the idea that the book with the seven seals contained pictures rather than words."[42] I have no argument with this type of intellectual lineage, which responsibly outlines the stream of biblical scholarship that fed into romanticism. I do, however, want to consider an assumption that this approach occasionally seems to imply, namely, that the "aesthetic" dimension of apocalypse is necessarily linked to an oppositional politics. In this version, while prophecy may be ideologically "distorted" for a variety of purposes, the apocalyptic text *as text* lies unambiguously on the progressive side of conflict, promoting almost by necessity a contestatory vision of change. When Revelation is read properly, its literary form becomes an *inherently* revolutionary agent that escapes and even subverts the distorting, conservative strategies that would turn apocalypse into state propaganda. Joseph Anthony Wittreich, who has figured so importantly in the study of apocalypse and English literature, puts it directly: "A model like the Book of Revelation suggests that form is a means to an end" and that that end is "to effect liberation."[43] More narrowly, Tannenbaum suggests that through the traditions of eighteenth-century scholarship Blake discovered in the biblical text "a principle of inner coherence that served the poet-prophet's need to protest against the moral, religious, and political abuses of his time."[44]

In studies of apocalypse and literature, it is this semiautomatic tendency to assume that apocalyptic literary form coincides with the needs of social protest that calls for reconsideration. This is not to say that Blake or any other writer in the Miltonic tradition was incapable of manipulating that form to such ends; it is merely to call attention to both the magnitude of the task and its vulnerability to recuperation, even when a poet seems to revise the idea of form dramatically. In the matter of prophecy, the "literary" was by no means there for radical picking, awaiting its inevitable conscription into the opposition cause. Quite the contrary, by the time Blake inherited and reworked an understanding of Revelation as a uniquely powerful text, the aestheticization of prophecy and apocalypse had rather effectively served the interests of state apologists.

To begin with, the threat eighteenth-century biblical literary criticism posed to public authority, while real, is sometimes exaggerated. If

[42] Ibid., 55.

[43] Wittreich, *Visionary Poetics*, 44. A page earlier, Wittreich states, "Structure, then, is an agent in the process that culminates in our seeing all things anew, this process finding its completion in the moment when an audience, casting off the garments of orthodoxy, dons the new ones woven by the prophet."

[44] Tannenbaum, *Biblical Tradition*, 35.

Lowth's discovery of verse parallelism in the Hebrew Scriptures encouraged readers to see the Bible as a historically produced document that could be read like other forms of poetry, thus diminishing its special authority, he also provided the tools of formal contemplation by which it could be safely returned to a privileged aesthetic space outside historical change.[45] The Bible began to enter a new stage of canonization, one that would eventually allow Matthew Arnold to say, "most of what now passes with us for religion and philosophy will be replaced by poetry."[46] Lowth himself never considered a literary treatment of prophecy to be at odds with his strictly establishment politics; roughly halfway between the original publication of his lectures and their translation into English, he reasserted in a sermon the most traditional party platform, including a hint of divine right by Providence: "That civil government cannot subsist without regard to the will of God, or, in other words, without the sanctions of religion, is manifest in the universal experience and practice of mankind. . . . Human laws can never inforce an obedience adequate to their purpose, unless it be grafted upon a prior principle of obedience to the laws of God."[47] One finds similar positions articulated by other contributors to the distinctly literary understanding of prophecy. Warburton's *Divine Legation of Moses* exerted a lasting influence by comparing figurative language in the biblical prophecies to Egyptian hieroglyphics, but the book's main purpose was to function as a sequel to his earlier, more widely read *Alliance between Church and State*, the treatise from which Lowth likely derived his reactionary argument. If Blake or other romantic writers read the *Divine Legation* for clues to the nature of prophetic language, they would also have encountered an extended summary of the earlier work in which Warburton argues repeatedly that a state religion enforced by law is "the universal Voice of Nature," so essential to "securing the Obedience of the People" that no society ever existed without one. On the actual mechanics of ideology, the book is similarly and stunningly blunt: religion serves power "by bestowing additional Reverence and Veneration on the Person of the Civil Magistrate, and on the Laws of the State."[48] In defending the contemporary

[45] Stephen Prickett, in one of the best books on biblical scholarship and romantic literature, writes of Lowth, "Thus alongside the rediscovery of the Bible within a historical context runs a no less important rediscovery of the Bible as *poetry*. The debate over the Bible opened up by Lowth is as much aesthetic as historical." *Words and The Word: Language, Poetics and Biblical Interpretation* (Cambridge: Cambridge University Press, 1986), 112.

[46] Matthew Arnold, "The Study of Poetry," in *Essays in Criticism* (London: Macmillan, 1888), 3.

[47] Robert Lowth, *A Sermon Preached before the Lords: on January 30, 1767* (London, 1767), 7.

[48] Warburton, *Divine Legation of Moses*, 232, 243. Warburton surveyed the history of civilization to find that the natural arrangement of society looked remarkably like that of

Whig establishment, Warburton assigned a position of special importance to the "System of Prophecy," with its proof of divine providence. "I am confident that nothing but the light which will arise from thence can support Christianity in its present circumstances," he wrote in a letter to Hurd, twenty years before he took matters into his own wealthy hands and endowed a lecture.[49]

Given this side of the eighteenth-century genealogy of prophecy and literature, Richard Hurd was the perfect, perhaps inevitable, choice to initiate Warburton's lecture series. On the one hand, Hurd's politics smoothed the steady professional advancement that eventually made him a bishop. By 1776 he would be invited to deliver a Fast Day sermon to the House of Lords, and he would use the occasion to suggest that the colonial rebellion was merely a symptom of widespread disobedience at home. Politics in England had degenerated into "noise and clamour and violence," reflecting more generally "a contempt of all that wears the face of authority." As one might expect, Hurd ended by calling for a "readiness to submit ourselves to the authority of Government in all those just measures, which it may see fit to take in the present emergency."[50] On the other hand, Hurd's most abiding loves were aesthetics and criticism; it has sometimes been argued that his writings on poetry anticipate the transition from neoclassicism to romanticism.[51] In his "Dissertation on the Idea of Universal Poetry," for instance, he occasionally sounds like a distant cousin of Coleridge, especially in the opposition he constructs between utilitarian practices and poetic pleasure: "In all other kinds of literary composition, pleasure is subordinate to use; in poetry only, pleasure is the end, to which use itself . . . must submit."[52]

---

his England—a church-state establishment that tolerated religious dissenters so long as they stayed out of government, or what Roy Porter calls "religious freedom with strings" (187). "In a Word, an Established Religion and a Test Law is the universal Voice of Nature. The most barbarous Nations have employed it to civilize their Manners; and the Politest knew no other Way to prevent their Return to Barbarity and Confusion." Thus Warburton's *Alliance* was "written with no other View than to furnish every Lover of his Country with Reasonable Principles, to oppose the destructive Fancies of the Enemies of our present happy Establishment: Not to reform the fundamental Constitutions of the State; but to shew they needed no Reformation." *Divine Legation,* 1:258–63.

[49] Warburton, *Letters from a Late Eminent Prelate* (January 30, 1749), 24.

[50] Richard Hurd, "A Sermon, preached before the House of Lords," in *The Works of Richard Hurd* (1811; reprint, Hildesheim: Georg Olms Verlag, 1969), 8:13, 15.

[51] Stephen Curry surveys the history of response to Hurd's criticism, which was respected in his own time, ignored in the early nineteenth century, but revived later by some scholars, such as Wellek, who considered him a preromantic defending the literature of the imagination against neoclassicism. Curry himself holds no such illusions, demonstrating Hurd's dependence on Augustan assumptions and stating flatly, "Hurd's lack of importance to later writers is uncontestable." "Richard Hurd's Genre Criticism," *Texas Studies in Language and Literature* 8 (1966): 207–8.

[52] Richard Hurd, "Dissertation on the Idea of Universal Poetry," in *Works,* 2:3.

Before I return specifically to prophecy, it is worth pausing a moment here, since a tendency to aestheticize his object of study will direct the entire course of Hurd's lectures, though there the resulting pleasure will be of a particular kind—that which accompanies awe.

Across a variety of contexts, Hurd's aesthetic seems to fulfill a recurring function. At first, his proposal of an autotelic pleasure seems to place poetry outside the domain of pragmatic reason, recognizing in it a space uniquely exempt from the cramped routines of the ordinary. Throughout the "Dissertation," poetry is synonymous with "the vast, the incredible," the "restless and the aspiring," and, of course, the "sublime."[53] In fact, however, Hurd uses poetry to just an opposite effect, to curb the dangers of pleasure and the senses, bringing them back into the stable orbit of a thoroughly rationalized order. Terry Eagleton has argued that the aesthetic developed as a conceptual category in the eighteenth century in order to produce "an entirely new kind of human subject," one which would experience the abstract dictates of the bourgeois social order through the immediacy of the individual body. "The aesthetic is in this sense no more than a name for the political unconscious," he writes; "it is simply the way social harmony registers itself on our senses, imprints itself on our sensibilities. The beautiful is just political order lived out on the body, the way it strikes the eye and stirs the heart."[54] To experience Hurd's poetic pleasure involves no indulgence of deviant desires; on the contrary, it is to domesticate what only seems "extravagant," to make individual pleasure consonant with the prerogatives of a social order. "True taste," he writes toward the end of his essay, "requires chaste, severe, and simple pleasures; and true genius will only be concerned in administering such."[55] This process of reclaiming the potential deviancy of pleasure is especially visible in Hurd's most lasting contribution to criticism, his *Letters on Chivalry and Romance*. Remarkable for its time, the book sets out to revive interest in the "Gothic" aesthetic of Spenser and Tasso, vindicating it from the abuses of narrow neoclassical standards. Hurd goes so far as to elevate romance above ancient epic, since its peculiar pleasures result from a superstitious fabric "more sublime, more terrible, more alarming."[56] Here again, however, an aesthetics of the sublime is not a means of embracing the irregular but of colonizing it. The ideological agenda appears on the first page, with a quotation: "Nature once known, no prodigies remain."[57] Gothic monsters need cause no fear; the unnatural is so in appearance only. All

[53] Ibid., 8–9.
[54] Terry Eagleton, *The Ideology of the Aesthetic* (Oxford: Blackwell, 1990), 19, 37.
[55] Hurd, "Dissertation," 10, 20–21.
[56] Richard Hurd, *Letters on Chivalry and Romance*, in *Works*, 4:290.
[57] Ibid., 237.

things, even and especially prodigies, belong squarely to the reasonable-
ness of nature; anything can be systematized, that is, anything can be
shown to participate in a formal structural whole, a necessary relation of
parts.[58] *The Faerie Queene* looks "barbarous" not because it operates
without rules, but because critics apply inappropriate rules. If you read
according to the Gothic model, suddenly "you find it regular" and safe
for consumption. "This, it is true, is not the classic Unity, which consists
in the representation of one entire action: but it is an Unity of another
sort, an unity resulting from the respect which a number of related
actions have to one common purpose. In other words, it is an unity of
design, and not of action."[59] In Hurd's hands, aesthetic form becomes a
remarkably pliable category, one capable of demonstrating that nothing
lies beyond the naturalizing power of unity, that every entity is organized
from within by an identifiable principle of formal coherence.[60]

Can there be any question, then, why Hurd felt such an affinity for
Joseph Mede that he made him the guiding light of his lectures on
prophecy? In the study of apocalypse, Mede had already done Hurd's
aesthetic work for him, taking the text most notoriously resistant to
interpretation, a text famous for its inexplicable monsters, and showing
that it in fact possessed all the cogent regularity of a geometric figure.
Hardly disturbing, Revelation is more an exemplary model of Hurd's
favorite phenomenon, a systematicity internally generated.[61] The *Key of
the Revelation* proved conclusively that John's apocalyptic text was organized by intrinsic aesthetic principles, "carried on in its own proper
form" (116), as Hurd would say in a phrase reminiscent of his remarks
on *The Faerie Queene*. And just as Hurd urged neoclassical critics to
abandon their predispositions in order to see Spenser's poem according
to its own autogenic rules, so Mede had revealed that the primary error
misleading readers of Revelation was their tendency to impose private

[58] Samuel Johnson poked fun at Hurd's obsessive systematicity: "It has been a fashion
to wear scarlet breaches; these men would tell you, that according to causes and effects, no
other wear could at that time have been chosen." Quoted in John Butt, *The Mid-Eighteenth
Century*, vol. 8 of *The Oxford History of English Literature* (Oxford: Clarendon, 1979), 27.

[59] Hurd, *Letters on Chivalry and Romance*, 297, 301.

[60] "Let others explain away these *wonders*, so offensive to certain philosophical critics,"
Hurd writes of the irrational elements of romance. He goes on, however, to indicate why
they remain inoffensive to him: "They are welcome to me *in their own proper form*, and with
all the extravagance commonly *imputed* to them." *Letters on Chivalry and Romance*, 321; my
emphasis.

[61] Hurd likened the "system of revelation" to the "system of nature," both of which
operated according to self-generative principles; thus he could transfer the argument by
design into the sphere of prophecy: "Wise men collect, from what they see done in the
system of nature, so far as they are able to collect it, the intentions of its author. They will
conclude, in like manner, from what they find delivered in the system of revelation, what
the views and purposes of the revealer were." *Introduction to the Study of the Prophecies*, 25.

interests on the self-definition of the text. "Laying aside, then, all hypotheses whatsoever," Hurd writes of his mentor, "he sate down to the book itself, and resolved to know nothing more of it, than what the frame and texture of its composition might clearly reveal to him" (127). Oddly enough, Hurd's initial account of Revelation gradually modulates into a biographical sketch of Mede, one that rehearses in miniature all the salient points of the 1677 *Works:* his exceptional learning, his nearly supernatural disinterestedness, his humility, his freedom from the influence of faction, and perhaps most important, his "cool, deliberate, and severe" psyche (124), the traits of which sound strikingly similar to those Hurd earlier used to describe aesthetic pleasure, "chaste, severe, and simple." Most remarkable, however, is the way Mede and his critical system come to displace Revelation altogether in Hurd's lecture, where, for all his praise of Mede's systematic attention to the text itself, Hurd himself never quotes a single passage. The discussion of methodology becomes a way to avoid reading the book. The lecture begins with Hurd stating outright that his concerns are "the STYLE and the METHOD" of Revelation, not its "subject" (112). It ends by justifying his refusal to apply Mede's system, which he has summarized so fully: "Interpreters, I think, have generally been too much in haste to apply these prophecies, before they have sufficiently prepared the way for their application" (139). Form remains a preemptive strike against the dangerous temptations of history, or more specifically, of millenarianism.

By the time Hurd eulogized Mede as a "sublime genius," the image of Revelation promoted by the *Key of the Revelation* was firmly in place. Even when commentaries disputed Mede, they still sought to ground interpretation as he had, in some variant of the internal key, still safely within the authority of the text's self-interpretation. Beyond that, the persistent metaphors of "keys" and "doors" and "maps" suggest that the most powerful conceptualization of Revelation remained a rigorously spatial one; before it can be put to any other use, John's apocalyptic text is a self-standing, ahistorical space that one must unlock, enter, and negotiate. Johann Albrecht Bengel, who read Mede, likened Revelation to "a great and elegant, magnificent and sacred Temple" and went on to explain that "this very regularly disposed System brings its own Key along with it; having, tho' uncommonly difficult in its Subject, a singularly easy Method, being provided with Variety of Partitions, Pauses, Forms of Expression, and such helps to an analysis of it."[62] Formal and structural designs modeled on the synchronisms, which seemed inseparable from the textual artifact itself, remained the most common keys to unlock Revelation from within. But of such eighteenth-century writers, it was

[62] Johann Albrecht Bengel, *Bengelius's Introduction to His Explication of the Apocalypse,* trans. John Robertson (London: Syall and Withy, 1757), 133, 65–66.

Hurd who most fully articulated the built-in political advantage this type of formalism supplied the establishment. In a way deeply congruent with Mede's original program to set limits on prophecy, he saw that while the synchronic "key" might open up this difficult text, it could also lock out undesirable interpretations:

> The knowledge of this order is a great restraint on the fancy of an exposi-tor; who is now not at liberty to apply the prophecies to events of any time, to which they appear to suit, but to events falling only within that time, to which they belong in the course of this pre-determined method. And if to this restriction, which is of itself considerable, we add *another*, which arises from the necessity of applying, not one, but many prophecies (which are thus shown to synchronize with each other), to the *same* time, we can hardly conceive how an interpretation should keep clear of these impedi-ments, and make its way through so many interfering checks, unless it be the true one. Just as when a Lock, (to take the author's allusion) is com-posed of many and intricate wards, the *Key,* that turns easily within them, and opens the Lock, can only be that which properly belongs to it. (130–31)

Revelation is a textual space protected by the security system of its own closure. Hurd's rhetoric of restraints, restrictions, impediments, and checks, his detailed, almost loving metaphor of the lock and key, make nearly literal what Mede and his Restoration followers had always im-plied, that in the reading of Revelation, literary form is constructed not simply as a means of diverting attention away from historical application but as a means of political intimidation, a means of excluding alternative voices. At the same time that Hurd's language likens Revelation to a piece of jealously guarded property, it also invokes a law-and-order apparatus capable of enforcing property rights. To apply the text to history prematurely or recklessly, or worse, to read in it an endorsement of millenarian conflict, is to enact unacceptable violence upon the verbal order; the punishment for textual misappropriation is to have one's interpretive liberty restrained. Access to the text, moreover, is granted only to those who comply with the requirements of a preestablished aesthetic harmony, checking any propensity to criminal activity at the door. "The whole Book of Revelation being thus resolvable into a par-ticular and determinate order . . . no exposition of this book [can be accepted] that does not refer every single prophecy to its true place in the system, and provide that *no violence be done* to any other prophecies which synchronize with it" (131–32; my emphasis). Revelation has be-come the guardian of an already established peace that is at once literary and social, the former creating the ideological image of the latter.

In the preceding chapter, I argued that political intimidation and formal closure emerge simultaneously in Revelation, at the moment John threatens with supernatural punishment anyone who alters the text. After the fixing of the scriptural canon, that stern warning carried even wider authority, as it closed not merely an isolated text but a corpus of sacred texts. By "fenc[ing] round the last written word from God," as an anonymous author of 1787 states, it endowed all of Scripture with the same aesthetic power of a protected, exclusionary space able to ward off the encroachment of history's illegitimate interpretations.[63] In a commentary published in 1770, while Hurd was still writing his lectures, William Dodd reiterated a common gloss upon Revelation 22:18–19: "With what sacred observance should these books be guarded which contain a message of such infinite importance! Of what dreadful curses are they worthy, who presume to add to what is already perfect, or to take away from that, which is in every part divine."[64] Revelation, especially after Mede's innovations, provided the precise textual model needed to make convincing what the Latitudinarian Bishop Edward Stillingfleet, writing at the turn of the century, considered an internal proof of the Bible's authority, "the agreeableness of the parts of Scripture to each other, which are not to be found in mere human writings."[65] Hurd's concern was more modest, addressing one aspect of Scripture rather than the whole, but in his lectures one can observe clearly how the principles Mede established for reading Revelation could be expanded at will, drawing more and more of the biblical word into an aesthetic circuit. Hurd simply read all the prophets as Mede had read John, embarking on a sweeping project of aestheticization that fashioned prophecy into a single, self-referential text, a total prophetic "system" or "oeconomy" (44). If, for instance, the primary danger in interpreting Revelation is the intrusion of subjective interests on the text, could not the same be said of all of prophecy? On the first page of the first lecture, and with a particularly revealing passive construction, Hurd discloses the extent of his debt to Mede: "The argument from prophecy, in the support of Christian revelation, would be thought more conclusive, at least would be more distinctly apprehended, if men could be kept from mixing their own prejudices and preconceptions with it." What will keep men from doing so, at least hegemonically if not by naked force, is the strict establishment of a set of objective, internal textual relations that allow prophecy "to be its own interpreter" (25). Indeed, in Hurd's argu-

[63] Anonymous, *The Revelation of St. John. Considered as Alluding to Certain Services of the Jewish Temple* (London: Printed for the author, 1787), 358.

[64] William Dodd in fact quotes Dr. Doddridge in his *Commentary on the Books of the Old and New Testament* (London: R. Davis, L. Davis, T. Carnan, and F. Newbery, 1770), no pagination.

[65] Edward Stillingfleet, *Origines Sacrae* (Oxford: Oxford University Press, 1836), 2:234.

ment, prophecy as a whole mirrors Mede's vision of its most exemplary part:

> You see, every thing here is of a piece: all the parts of this dispensation are astonishingly great, and perfectly harmonize with each other. . . . The argument from prophecy is not to be formed from the consideration of single prophecies, but from all the prophecies taken together, and considered as making one system; in which, from the mutual dependence and connection of the parts, preceding prophecies prepare and illustrate those which follow, and these, again, reflect light on the foregoing; just as in any philosophical system, that which shows the solidity of it is the harmony and correspondence of the whole; not the application of it in particular circumstances. (45–47)

By means of its dazzling intertextuality, prophecy forms a "representation at once so sublime and consistent" (46), "something so astonishingly vast" that, considered through the powerful lens of the aesthetic, it must inevitably "strike an awe into the hearts of all men" (201).

At the time of Hurd's appointment at Lincoln's Inn Chapel, millenarianism posed no immediate threat to the social order. And yet, the antimillenarian strategies Hurd adopted from Mede cannot be considered an unmotivated rehearsal of the establishment's century-old self-image, a mere pat on the back of its ideological stability. Hurd apparently felt some pressure to "strike an awe" into his audience, or better yet, to reassure his audience's faith in the establishment's power to strike awe into others. Although he had no Puritan prophets to contend with, the ambitious preacher still faced the specter of their highly visible descendants, the full variety of dissenters and "fanatics." Even as he wrote to Warburton to accept the position, Hurd already understood that Mede should be his "example in every thing," and he hinted at why this mentor would be especially apt for the occasion: "I think I may promise not to disgrace your Institution by any extravagancies at setting out; and this caution, on such a subject, and in such times, may not be without its merit."[66] With its memorable legacy of social disruption, prophecy continued to represent a reservoir of potential volatility, but in the summer of 1768, even without an explicit millenarian challenge, the discussion of prophecy seems to have called for a particular delicacy, a cautious and persuasive reaffirmation of its place within the respectable concerns of the Anglican state. The general contours of this circumstance are not difficult to perceive. Historians have long recognized that the 1760s and 1770s witnessed a sharp increase in English oppositional

---

[66] Warburton, *Letters from a Late Eminent Prelate* (July 18, 1768), 310, 311.

politics. "The first two decades of George III's reign," according to John Brewer's litany, "saw the successful formation of an extraparliamentary association in the SSBR [Society of Supporters of the Bill of Rights], the public advocacy both in print and in Parliament of householder suffrage, the publication on both sides of the Atlantic of the iconoclastic works of William Moore and Tom Paine, the synthesizing of the radical heritage in James Burgh's much-admired *Political Disquisitions,* and the warm support of dissenters and commonwealthmen such as Richard Price and Joseph Priestley for the American cause." Brewer accepts as historically accurate what Hurd himself would argue polemically to the Lords in his 1776 Fast Day sermon, that "the colonial crisis of the 1760s and 1770s was but the English crisis writ large."[67]

Over the four years in which the Warburton lectures were first conceived, endowed, and finally brought to publication, however, the most conspicuous sign of public insubordination was not the American disturbance across an ocean but the decade-long popular unrest centered on the career of John Wilkes. From the publication of the infamous *North Briton* 45 in 1763 to the month and a half of sporadic London rioting that followed Wilkes's election to Parliament in 1768, events that culminated in the Massacre of St. George's Fields, and on through the extraordinary petitions (sixty thousand or so) of 1769–70 that dramatically challenged Parliament's decision to deny him the seat he had won, the slogan "Wilkes and Liberty" was a ceaseless reminder that just beyond the state's self-image lay a threatening turbulence. In 1771, with Hurd still at work on his lectures and with Wilkes yet again at the center of controversy, this time over the freedom of the press to report on Parliamentary debate, Hurd delivered a sermon that conjured images of civil war, choosing as his text James's question, "From whence come wars and fighting among you?"

> Ask the people, at large, and under whatever denomination, what occasions their contempt of authority, their disobedience to magistrates, their transgressions of law, their cabals and tumults, their hatred, defamation, and persecution of each other; and clarity herself, for the most part, can dictate no other reply for them to this question, than that they are excited to all these excesses by *the lust of riot* and misrule, or, of, what they call, LIBERTY.[68]

The thunderous final capitals leave little doubt that Hurd writes against the backdrop of Wilkes's stubborn influence, a force of civil disruption

[67] John Brewer, "English Radicalism in the Age of George III," in *Three British Revolutions: 1641, 1688, 1776,* ed. J. G. A. Pocock (Princeton: Princeton University Press, 1980), 342, 361.

[68] Hurd, *Works,* 6:103.

that, for Hurd, posed no less a threat than Puritan "excesses" did in the previous century.

Curiously, attention to Wilkes had always run parallel to the early development of the Warburton lectures. On March 31, 1768, just after rioters smashed windows and held London streets in celebration of Wilkes's election victory three days earlier, Warburton wrote to Hurd to discuss "the proper title of the Lecture" and other plans for its institution. The same letter begins, however, with Warburton's thoughts on the current situation, and one begins to see how the lectures, which would affirm the alliance between prophecy and law, in fact originated out of a profound anxiety about lawlessness: "Public matters seem to be grown desperate, and Government is dissolving apace. I always thought Wilkes possessed by a diabolical spirit; but now a legion of them have possessed the people. . . . Either they have lost all sense of right and wrong, or have no power to make a separation between them, and assign to each its place. Things are now come to a crisis."[69] Indeed, Warburton had personal reasons to think Wilkes diabolical; the two had been entangled from the very beginning of Wilkes's emergence into notoriety. In 1763, after being unable to prosecute Wilkes successfully for printing the *North Briton* 45, the government tried again, this time with a blasphemous and libelous poem Wilkes had not yet published, but which they were able to secure from one of his printers, probably by bribery or intimidation. The poem in question was called *An Essay on Woman;* not only did it savagely parody Pope's *Essay on Man,* of which Warburton had produced the standard edition with notes, but it claimed to be authored by none other than Warburton himself. In order to avoid conviction, Wilkes eventually fled to France, but only after the Earl of Sandwich had read the poem aloud to the House of Lords, an event which created not only the scandal the government needed to swing opinion against Wilkes, but also, presumably inadvertently, a public embarrassment for Warburton.

Of course, the Wilkes affair, especially as its ramifications were felt throughout the decade, amounted to more than a matter of personal antagonism for Warburton, that "enemy of all heresy," as he has been called.[70] The threat extended beyond an individual's political charisma, especially as Wilkes's array of followers seemed to represent a new social alliance that might draw middle and lower orders into common cause. "It was, in fact, one of the most significant of Wilkes's achievements," writes George Rudé, "that he was able to tap the loyalties and political energies of such varying and distinctive social groups as City merchants,

---

[69] Warburton, *Letters from a Late Eminent Prelate,* 306.

[70] S. C. Carpenter, *Eighteenth-Century Church and People* (London: John Murray, 1959), 147. Carpenter also states that it was Warburton "who coined the epigram 'Orthodoxy is my doxy. Heterodoxy is the other man's doxy'" (147).

the 'middling' and lesser freeholders of Middlesex, and the small crafts-men, petty traders and wage-earners of the capital."[71] Rudé himself points out that no real coalition developed among these groups, each of which to a varying extent identified with Wilkes in pursuit of its own interests. Middle-class political unrest about issues of parliamentary representation occurred at the same time as a series of high-profile labor disputes, but such movements "were virtually independent and unre-lated." Still, to establishment eyes confronted by the immediacy of wide-spread and sometimes violent opposition, the independence of political and economic protest was not always apparent.[72] Moreover, by 1772 the nearly continuous unrest from below was joined by the internal dissent of the Feathers Tavern petition, in which a contingent of Cambridge divines publicly urged an end to subscription for Anglican clergy. Hurd's successor as Warburton lecturer, Samuel Hallifax, vigorously fought the establishment battle on both fronts, warning against the degeneration of liberty into licentiousness and attacking those Socinian-leaning clergy-men who broke rank from within.[73] His appointment merely confirmed the already political function of the Lincoln's Inn lectures. Prophecy had become a central means for the Warburton circle to fend off what its leader called "the madness of the times, whether shewn in the ravings of impiety or fanaticism."[74] In 1772, as Hurd's lectures were published and as Hallifax, a former Regius Chair of Civil Law at Cambridge, assumed the post, the time was right for the Anglican state to reassert publicly that formidable self-representation that had kept it essentially intact since 1688 and that would substantially resist future challenges for another sixty years. For that act of reaffirmation, Hurd followed Mede in focusing attention on the literary form of prophecy, hoping that this "strong light" would "strike the sense very powerfully." In a series of lectures from state clergy to the representatives of state law, he re-created, through the sublime aesthetic harmony of the apocalyptic text, the very image of an inviolable social order positioned beyond the threat of historical change.

Given the trajectory that originates with Joseph Mede and reaches something of a climax with Richard Hurd four years before the Ameri-

[71] George Rudé, *Wilkes and Liberty* (Oxford: Clarendon, 1961), 183–84. A detailed analysis of the events involving Wilkes and his followers can be found in this still-definitive treatment of the topic.

[72] Rudé, *Wilkes and Liberty,* 104. Rudé quotes the Duke of Grafton, who wrote in his *Autobiography* of the uprisings of 1768: "Artisans of almost every denomination . . . combined for an advance of wages, and their discontents, and disobedience to the laws led them to join often, in numbers, those mobs which the consequence of the elections for Middlesex frequently produced" (90–91).

[73] See Clarke's portrait of Hallifax (*English Society, 1688–1832,* 228–30).

[74] Warburton, *Letters from a Late Eminent Prelate* (July 3, 1771), 343.

can Revolution and seventeen before the French, how should we situate the romantic involvement with apocalypse, an involvement which is first and foremost "literary"? To begin with, it would be easy to argue that the millenarian revival of the early 1790s restored an oppositional politics of apocalypse that the aesthetic approach had deliberately sought to bar. From numerous pamphlets with revolutionary sympathies to Joseph Priestley's Fast Day sermons of 1793 and 1794 to the spectacular phenomenon of Richard Brothers, the interest in apocalypse encouraged an immediate application of Scripture to contemporary political events. To read Revelation was to read *The Signs of the Times*, as the title of James Bicheno's popular pamphlet indicated. In 1793 Bicheno took his risky stand in favor of the French Republic because "circumstances led him to conjecture, that the beast which John saw coming up out of the earth, was *Louis the Fourteenth*, or the French Tyranny perfected by him, and supported by his successors." After the Revolution, the key to Revelation no longer lay within the text.[75] These readings, at which I merely hint here, reopened Revelation to the purposes of immediate historical and political conflict, but most important in this context, they did so by blatantly bypassing the aesthetic claims of the text or, more accurately, the claims made for the text by those fixated on issues of form, which in the Mede-Hurd approach was meant to command an authority independent of the merely temporal circumstances in which the text was read. This is not to say that "literary" apocalypse and "political" apocalypse are by nature mutually exclusive practices; it is to suggest that the real tensions between them did not simply evaporate in the early, formative years of romanticism when poets attempted to develop new types of apocalyptic representation; and after 1795, as romantic writers extended their literary experiment with apocalyptic themes and forms beyond the initial revolutionary phase, those tensions were, if anything, exacerbated. Even as ideas of apocalyptic form changed, sometimes drastically, so long as these changes continued to privilege aesthetic form, the political volatility of apocalypse remained vulnerable to circumscription.[76]

[75] James Bicheno, *The Signs of the Times*, 4th ed. (London: Printed for the author, 1794), iv. Bicheno could claim that immediate history provided the key "by which the mazes of these wonderful visions . . . may be traced with precision" (iv).

[76] Take for instance Tannenbaum's description of the changes wrought by Blake upon prophetic form: "The subordination of the general to the particular, with a reliance upon internal coherence among the parts rather than upon an externally imposed order, was precisely the principle that Blake, like many of his contemporaries, found to be operating in the Bible. . . . In the prophetic books of the Bible, the same principle works on a larger scale; particular units are combined to form whole books that are connected through the internal coherence of their parts" (*Biblical Tradition*, 25–26). I hope to have shown at the very least that the idea of internally coherent form built on textual particulars is as important to the Mede-Hurd idea of apocalypse as it is to romanticism, so that this revision

We need to question, then, the tendency to see apocalyptic aesthetics, especially as it evolved out of the seventeenth and eighteenth centuries, as the natural companion of progressive, or even millenarian, political desires. Poetic projects of the 1790s and beyond remained susceptible to the pressure that the "literary" had exerted since the origins of apocalypse, susceptible, that is, to the cultural power of aesthetic form to contain, deflect, and discredit historical differences and conflict. Even when the language of apocalyptic aesthetics merges with a secular idea of historical process and change, as M. H. Abrams has so comprehensively charted, one can still see romanticism operating within the terms and objectives of canonical prophecy. In a passage that invokes Blakean contraries and post-Kantian dialectic, Abrams describes the modern version of apocalypse, the dynamic interaction of polar opposites, as "a ceaseless movement toward a consummation which is *the annulment, or else the stable equilibrium, of all oppositions.*"[77] This description subtly preserves an ideological function that from the beginnings of apocalyptic writing has steered its literary investments. In the remainder of this book, my primary task is to address the extent to which some romantic writers perceived and resisted the power of the apocalyptic aesthetic to neutralize opposition, that is, if they did at all. Before I turn to romanticism, however, I want to take one last look at the legacy of Mede and Hurd in the form of a contemporary permutation, a work of scholarship which suggests just how powerfully attention to literary apocalypse can still serve the prerogatives of conservative ideology.

Leonard Thompson: Apocalypse and the Citizen-Reader (II)

At first glance, Leonard Thompson's richly argued and massively researched study *The Book of Revelation: Apocalypse and Empire* seems the least likely candidate for a modern *Key of the Revelation*. It might even

---

is not as dramatic as it at first appears. A much more extreme version of Blake's aesthetic revisionism, especially in regard to *The Book of Urizen*, has been argued by McGann, who sees Blake, under the influence of Alexander Geddes's controversial theories of Scripture, deliberately developing indeterminate texts that call into question their own ideological grounds of authority. *Social Values and Poetic Acts*, 152–72. In the next chapter, I take up the politics of Blake's Enlightenment investment in indeterminacy and critique.

[77] M. H. Abrams, "Apocalypse: Theme and Variations," in *The Apocalypse in English Renaissance Thought and Literature*, ed. Patrides and Wittreich, 346.

seem just the opposite. Working from a postformalist perspective that seems to leave the autonomous literary object far behind, Thompson sees a text considerably wider and more porous than the one Mede saw, a cultural text thoroughly mediated by its particular and intricate historical transactions. For Thompson, "the whole of the book is moored in the specific social context of first-century, Asian, urban Christianity," and because of this deep historicity, the book requires a reader who can manage a variety of focuses simultaneously.[78] Even while restricting himself to the circumstances in which the book originally appeared, Thompson envisions a daunting task of montage: "I seek a framework for integrating literary, conceptual, and social aspects of apocalyptic so that the language, religious sensibilities, and social political experience of the writer, readers, and hearers of the Book of Revelation can be seen as aspects or dimensions of an order of wholeness" (34). So much for "Revelation considered according to the letter only," as Mede once put it. *The Book of Revelation* goes further; on its opening page it lays to rest the myth so necessary to Mede's formalist authority, the myth that distinguishes subjective, motivated readings from neutral, scientific, text-centered interpretation. Given the subjective basis of all knowledge, the scholar cannot differ in kind from the millenarian. "Nor do scholars necessarily participate in a 'more objective manner' than millenarians," Thompson writes. "The persona of disinterested, cool, objective observation sometimes slips, and then passions and commitments become visible to everyone. We all have our axes to grind" (1). Indeed, in the case of "cool, deliberate, and severe" Mede, the claim to read Revelation without interests actually served to grind his axe a bit sharper. With an acutely modern self-consciousness, Thompson immediately sets aside any pretense to objectivity, though as I will argue, his appeal to an inherent relativism will ultimately be marshaled to the same ends as Mede's scientism; both serve to regulate the reading of Revelation, and more specifically, to restrain the very millenarianism Thompson gestures toward so tolerantly in his introduction.

Because it assiduously challenges some of biblical scholarship's most widely accepted notions, Thompson's *The Book of Revelation* is sure to be controversial. My concern with this work, however, has less to do with the merits of its conclusions than with the function of its arguments. Why these arguments now? What enables Thompson to make them? What consequences do they in turn anticipate? And finally, what do they say about an ongoing tension between aesthetic form and historical conflict in the study of apocalypse? Thompson's most startling argument

[78] Leonard Thompson, *The Book of Revelation: Apocalypse and Empire* (Oxford: Oxford University Press, 1990), 6. Further citations are to this text.

asserts that Revelation is not the response to persecution, alienation, and crisis we almost invariably assume it to be; rather, the book arises out of conditions of relative social stability and security. In fact, John draws on the literary genre of apocalypse in order to rattle the complacency of early Christians; he writes in order to force a perception of crisis on his audience, to make Christians feel a spiritual urgency generally lacking in lives all too comfortable with the cultural order of Rome. Revelation, to put it simply, is a wake-up call; it has to construct the conflict with the Roman Antichrist because in the social world of Asia Minor at the end of the first century no such conflict exists. Accordingly, Thompson can make this incendiary text look surprisingly casual: "The Book of Revelation arises from normal processes of adaptation to ordinary human conditions" (199). As one might imagine, such a sharp revision of received understanding demands a substantial burden of proof, and Thompson locates his evidence both internally, in the literary form of Revelation itself, and externally, in the historical documentation for the period. In the latter case, oddly enough, the strategy is not to introduce new sources but to introduce ambiguity into the old ones relentlessly. Thus, for instance, the Emperor Domitian may not have been as tyrannical as we generally believe because our primary sources for his reign, Pliny, Tacitus, and Suetonius, all had political motives for exaggerating his evil ways. In a minor but equally characteristic example, the author goes to great lengths to argue that the phrasing of Revelation 1:9 is ambiguous; it could just as easily signify that John willingly went to Patmos to study and to preach as that he was banished into exile there. By the accretion of such details, Thompson creates at least the possibility that the early Christians of Asia Minor lived in relative harmony with their neighbors. I leave this conclusion for the historians to debate. Given the stalemate between evidence for conflict and for harmony, my question is why Thompson systematically favors the latter, other than simply to indulge in revisionist sparring. To answer that question, one has to consider Thompson's other source of evidence, the Book of Revelation itself, and the role that aesthetic form plays in his reading of it.

One of the most frequently acknowledged premises of *The Book of Revelation* is that text and context are inseparable, mutually constitutive, but it becomes apparent early on that aesthetic considerations retain an unspoken primacy, framing and directing most of the book's ideas. Even Thompson's antiformalist belief that literature, history, and society are "all part of one dynamic cultural system" (8), that they constitute "an order of wholeness" (34), betrays an unexamined organicism of parts and whole that structures each phase of his argument. In other words, before he looks at a single piece of evidence, historical or textual, he deploys an aesthetic model of culture and knowledge that is already predisposed against conflict. The deep appeal of the aesthetic surfaces throughout the book, and nowhere more so than in its general organization. Like Farrer before him, and Hurd before that, Thompson writes in twelve chapters, conspicuously likening his study to traditional epic arrangement. Shifting genres but retaining the literary "feel," he then divides the chapters into three sections—"The Script," on the text of Revelation; "The Stage," on the setting of first-century Asia Minor; "The Play," on the performance of Revelation in its context. While this metaphor aptly serves the project's interdisciplinary purpose, it also suggests the extent to which an idea of "literature" has shaped the whole investigation. Beyond that, the divisions themselves indicate a willingness to separate out those elements of text and context that in theory were to be inextricable. Thompson says he does so merely "for analytic purposes" (7), and after all, any argument must unfold piecemeal, in one sequence or another. But this particular sequence has a history; it enables him to do what Mede and Hurd did before him, that is, to treat Revelation as a self-referential verbal form *before* turning to history. What Thompson sees when he considers Revelation formally, I would argue, has a direct bearing on what he does and does not see in the historical record; moreover, the literary text he sees looks remarkably like the one Mede and Hurd envisioned.

In his finely detailed section "The Linguistic Unity of the Book of Revelation," Thompson does not draw a single diagram, at least not literally. So pervasive is the spatial orientation of his criticism that he does not have to. The structuralist ambitions that prevail here rework some of the oldest hermeneutical desires involved in apocalyptic exegesis, desires that go back even as far as John's reading of the Hebrew Scriptures. "I seek to map out the seer's world comprehensively" (76), Thompson states rather boldly, and each of the analytical categories he applies to Revelation bears out this totalizing and topographical construction of text and criticism.[79] The first and most dominant such category is "the spatial metaphor *boundary*," the term he uses to describe distinctions and relations among the figures of the apocalyptic vision. In Thompson's view, the boundaries in Revelation are "not absolute, firm, or hard, but, rather, blurred and soft" (75), though as I will suggest below, this argument is as prescriptive as it is descriptive, marking a strong inclination to "soften" the text's violent edges. Because John's

---

[79] Aside from "the map" and "topography," another of Thompson's favorite tropes for Revelation is that of "the spatial arrangement of time in a musical score." "The conductor 'sees' all parts of the score, that which has been played, that which is being played, and that which will be played" (84). In this he reminds one of Farrer, who marveled at "the musical formality of the design" of Revelation (*Rebirth of Images*, 7–8).

vision is driven by an uncompromising monotheism, its oppositions inevitably collapse into unity, and the text is symbolically orchestrated by what Thompson calls "homologies," relations of similitude that underlie apparent differences. This pattern is especially evident on either side of the Christian and Anti-Christian divide, where, for instance, all the beasts are "variations on one another," but it is also true of the central antagonism itself: "Evil contrasts with the godly, but evil is not of a fundamentally different order from good" (80–81). Theologically, the homologies thus undermine any dualistic temptations. Structurally, they form an updated version of the synchronisms, making the text "homogeniall" by demonstrating that all its parts agree, no matter how antithetical or contradictory they appear.

Finally, even as Thompson imagines a much more fluid text than Mede did, with all parts blending and reblending into a unified, dynamic whole, he posits at the center of such symbolic transformations a set of fixed, intrinsic principles he dubs "ratios." This mathematical trope describes a bottom-line self-referentiality, whereby symbols become meaningful primarily in relation to one another; it marks the rules that govern the abundant textual play, a metaphysical center of the sort Derrida described as necessary to the classical idea of structure.[80] Appropriately, the leading examples of apocalyptic ratios are measurements and numbers. The number of the beast or the dimensions of the New Jerusalem involve little external or literal reference; instead, they "disclose inner structures" (Thompson, 88). "To grasp essential ratios is to comprehend aspects of an inner structure that unfolds to create a comprehensive vision of the world" (89). We have seen this before. Ever since John modeled his text on the spatial and numerical order of architecture, commentators have sought to reproduce the "canon" that, already outside historical contingency, would definitively measure the textual space of apocalypse, providing the "square and plumb-rule" as Mede put it. Newton supplemented his commentaries on Daniel and Revelation with "A Dissertation upon the Sacred Cubit of the Jews." Hurd celebrated Mede's "strictest forms of geometric reasoning" (128). Farrer drew his quadrilateral Sacred Diagram. Declaring that "we must interpret the text exclusively by the text itself," Jacques Ellul called his book-length study *Apocalypse: Architecture in Motion*.[81] Thompson stuffs

---

[80] "Even today the notion of a structure lacking any center represents the unthinkable itself. . . . Nevertheless, the center also closes off the play it opens up and makes possible. As center, it is the point at which the substitution of contents, elements, or terms is no longer possible." Jacques Derrida, "Structure, Sign, and Play in the Discourse of the Human Sciences," in *Writing and Difference*, trans. Alan Bass (Chicago: University of Chicago Press, 1978), 279.

[81] Jacques Ellul, *Apocalypse: The Book of Revelation*, trans. George W. Schreiner (New York: Seabury, 1977), 35. I have translated literally the French title *L'Apocalypse: Architecture en Mouvement*.

his analytical toolbox with similar squares and plumb lines, which he terms "boundaries," "homologies," and "ratios." Should it be surprising, then, that he sees in Revelation a "temporal map" in which time has taken on the qualities of a magnificently ordered space, a space best represented by "a city let down from heaven" (84)?

If all *The Book of Revelation* did was to reproduce a familiar spatialist reading of Revelation in a modern key, it would require little more than a footnote here. In attempting much more, however, it provides an unusually vivid instance of how a sophisticated literary formalism can operate to suppress the legitimacy of historical conflict. Thompson's rigorous close reading of Revelation's internal unity sets out explicitly to refute two rival readings: that the text's vexed, dualistic structure reflects an origin in historical conflict; or conversely, that its artificially integrative structure only disguises the social contradictions out of which it is generated. For Thompson, the harmony of form and content evident in Revelation makes both conflict arguments untenable; read carefully, the text puts forth a genuinely synthetic, monotheistic vision that gathers all apparent differences into "the coherence, integrity, and wholeness of Christian existence" (91), a phrase most reminiscent of that which Stephen Dedalus borrowed from Aquinas to describe the epiphany of the aesthetic in *Portrait of the Artist*.[82] This concrete evidence, relying only on the words on the apocalyptic page, makes arguments about conflict and violence seem irrelevant if not irresponsible, an ungrounded fantasia of the modern scholar's overwrought mind.

> This examination of the seer's vision of the world suggests that it does not contain fundamental conflicts. One element or dimension of the vision is not pitted against another; and terms such as *conflict, tension,* and *crisis* do not characterize his vision. Revelation discloses in its depth or innerness a wholeness of vision consonant with the intertexture found at the surface level of his language. At all levels, signifiers, signifieds, deep structures, and surface structures form homologies, not contradictory oppositions. The logic of the vision does not progress from oppositions to their resolution. Rather, in all its aspects the language speaks from unbroken wholeness to unbroken wholeness. (91)

These are the final words of "The Script" section of *The Book of Revelation,* and indeed, they lead seamlessly into the historical investigation that follows, where the author will demonstrate that "the seer and his audience did not live in a world of conflict, tension, and crisis" (95). By

---

[82] In the famous passage, Stephen translates Aquinas as writing, "Three things are needed for beauty, wholeness, harmony and radiance." "Wholeness" translates the Latin *integritas.* James Joyce, *A Portrait of the Artist as a Young Man* (New York: Viking, 1956), 211.

reading Revelation as a literary text, Thompson can virtually make conflict disappear from its pages, but this is merely to prepare the way for a more challenging task: to write conflict out of history itself.

Revelation, however, will not go gently into that good night of aesthetic harmony. There remains the thorny problem with which this chapter began, the graphic and nearly continuous textual violence that even the most mesmerizing formalist criticism cannot make go away. In the final chapters of his book, having argued both that Revelation is internally unconflicted and that it originates in unconflicted circumstances, Thompson must face up to John's unerasable anger. Despite all his evidence, "there are," as he puts it, "plenty of indications that the seer views the Roman Empire antagonistically" (189). And indeed, almost in direct contradiction to the earlier sections of the book, John gradually, almost inevitably, begins to resemble the typecast prophet of inspired, fiery opposition, he whose "deviant knowledge . . . does not depend upon public institutions and existing political power" and therefore "serves to censure the public order" (181). Even if all other conflicts disappear, what can one do about this recalcitrant antagonism between John's Christian inspiration and Roman authority? This question prompts the author's most delicate maneuvers. To begin with, Thompson recognizes conflict in Revelation only to the extent that he can psychologize it; at stake is a matter of "cognitive conflict" over "definitions of reality" which in fact have little to do with actual social or political circumstances (193). The problem lies in the prophet's mind. John sees a reality incompatible with that publicly endorsed by Rome, and his apocalyptic text attempts to force that incompatibility on his fellow Christians. Thus Revelation does not respond to an existing crisis, but as "revelatory literature" (192), it represents a vision of alternative knowledge, which, if accepted by the audience, anticipates a break with the public order. One of Thompson's most disturbing applications of this logic involves the representation of martyrdom in Revelation, which according to his view is purely symbolic, a formative image of Christian myth and identity, and not a reflection of actual persecution. The book's many scenes of suffering and tribulation do not "report social, political realities" (188). Rather, these scenes are meant to remind Christians of the redemptive power of Christ-like self-sacrifice; they are "linguistic and religious themes," "verbal symbolics" (189–90), that urge Christians to demonstrate their commitment to faith by seeking out clashes with the empire, clashes that do not as yet exist.[83]

---

[83] It is not that Thompson entirely ignores the evidence for real persecution. Rather, he argues that persecution became widespread *after* the turn of the first century; before that, "overt conflict between Christians and their non-Christian neighbors requiring official, legal action was rare" (*The Book of Revelation*, 132). Thus, while there was some actual

Even were one to accept this counterintuitive argument, there still remains a nagging problem: whether it is cognitive or sociopolitical, a sharp, irreconcilable dualism drives the representations in Revelation, which therefore cannot simply be the book of "unbroken wholeness" Thompson describes by means of his formalist reading. Thompson's resolution of this contradiction is his most revealing gesture, for it occasions the shift whereby his argument becomes prescriptive. Suddenly the ideological axe he has to grind becomes visible. How can one reconcile John's text of unbroken cosmic wholeness, in which all boundaries blur, with his positing of an absolute rift between the rightness of Christian "reality" and the wrongness of Rome? The problem, it would appear, lies not with Thompson's construction of the literary unity of Revelation, but with John's all-too-human involvement in the perpetuation of conflict. To put the matter simply, John almost got the Apocalypse right, but erred, contradicting the "soft" essence of his divine vision by retaining a set of stubborn, intractable convictions. "Must inclusive visions necessarily be uncompromising?" Thompson asks. "Would we belie his vision if we asked him to relativize slightly his rock-bottom orientation so that his knowledge was not absolutely identical to God's?" The answer to this rhetorical question is "of course not," for it is John who has misunderstood the deepest implications of his own text by violating its inherent, mollifying relativism. "The seer would be more faithful to his vision of an unbroken wholeness if he did subvert his cognitive exclusiveness. John's radical monotheism should leave a place for Roman knowledge" (200). Seen through the lens of literary unity, the Book of Revelation critiques the intolerant millenarianism of its own misguided author.

Once cleared of the human error of conviction, once the primacy of its aesthetic relations has been established, Revelation emerges from its misreadings to teach a remarkable lesson about the dangers of ideological commitment. In his introduction, where Thompson benevolently suggested that millenarians are indistinguishable from scholars because both see the world from their own points of view, he also managed to preserve one small distinction: scholars, for all their self-consciousness and hesitancy, recognize this limitation, while millenarians, who hastily mistake their perspective for truth and act on this conviction, do not. Some two hundred pages later, in Thompson's conclusion, it turns out that the real Apocalypse belongs on the scholar's side. By consistently undermining the grounds of objective knowledge, of a fixed vision of the way things really are, Revelation acts as a guardian against any

---

persecution, "the theme is more prominent in the religious commitments and psychosocial understanding of the seer" than in social reality (191).

violence perpetrated in the name of such visions. Illuminating all that precedes it, this polemical conclusion takes up the most stubborn of apocalyptic problems, "the place of revenge and retribution in the Book of Revelation" (200), and Thompson completes his disarming of the Apocalypse by locating those violent tendencies in the prophet's mistake of "rock-bottom certainty."

> Such certainty leads to the closing of the millenarian mind. In the Book of Revelation, countering that process, there is a continual softening of boundaries that leads to the opening of the millenarian mind: the boundaries between contrarieties are not as hard as they first appear; ironic and eschatological reversals separate appearances—including hard, impenetrable boundaries—from reality. In this process vengeance, exclusiveness, and certainty about the adequacy of particular human insight (even revelation) fade. (201)

The term "millenarian" has now been generalized to describe any person who believes herself or himself right, any person whose motivation is inadequate to the complexities of reality.[84] For Thompson, millenarianism poses nearly the same threat Mede and Hurd perceived, the threat of people acting, perhaps violently, on their beliefs. To counteract this dangerous tendency, Thompson must counteract belief itself, make it more self-conscious, more paralytic, and he does so by converting Revelation into a Bible of liberal pluralism. Nothing could be more revealing here than the allusion to Allan Bloom's *Closing of the American Mind*. Not only has Revelation been made to look nonviolent, it has also, in its very ideological task, been made to look apolitical, the purveyor of an open-minded humanism; moreover, it has become the text best able to produce readers who will transcend mere politics, the properly self-doubting citizens of a democratic social order who have learned to think in sophisticated shades of gray, who realize the subjective limitations of their own beliefs and therefore tolerate the equally limited beliefs of others, that is, so long as all consent not to act on their convictions. When the democratic citizen eats the apocalyptic book, reading Revelation closely, the result is a vision of the world so subtle and complex in its fluid totality that the most foolish response to one's corner of circumstance would be decisive action.

---

[84] Thompson's millenarian thus resembles the Jehovah's Witness who, at a Red Cross evacuation center, approaches the narrator of Don DeLillo's *White Noise* (New York: Penguin, 1984) with a pamphlet entitled, "Twenty Common Mistakes about the End of the World." "He was a serious man, he was matter-of-fact and practical, down to his running shoes. I wondered about his eerie self-assurance, his freedom from doubt. Is this the point of Armageddon? No ambiguity, no more doubt. He was ready to run into the next world" (137).

Like Mede's and Hurd's before him, Thompson's apocalypse is a prescription for inaction and consequently an endorsement of the existing social order. The book's final paragraphs openly address an audience of unspecified millenarians, those who should particularly benefit from its literary analysis of open and closed textual boundaries.

> Any serious reader of the Book of Revelation will want to reckon with that protean aspect of the work. Judgments and claims will still be made; convictions will still be held. But if attention is given to the transformational character of the Book of Revelation . . . judgments and convictions—even those on which we make decisions and take actions—may be subverted by the seer's language. Ultimately the boundaries of the seer's world are soft; they are points of transaction whereby religious promises, social encounters, political commitments, biological givens, and cultural demands undergo mutual adjustments and form homologous relations. (201)

The apocalyptic text's homologies describe with precision the preestablished unity of the pluralist social order, the stability and security of which require that its citizens willingly soften their convictions and "undergo mutual adjustments." The "transformational character of the Book of Revelation" is in fact its ability to transform character, to perform the subtle ideological work of making its readers forsake their unsubtle ideological commitments, which now begin to look untenable, the product of narrow understanding. Having read all the signs of conflict out of Revelation's formal harmonies, having read any residue of conflict out of the historical circumstances of its production, Thompson enlists the literary apocalypse within a contemporary liberal agenda, making its task the discrediting of conflict in the present and the future.[85] Putting out the fires of modern millenarian politics, Thompson's apocalypse imagines a social order beyond the dynamics of historical change, a world in which decisions to enact change are systematically subverted by higher claims. From Mede's scientism to Thompson's subjective relativism, the apocalyptic aesthetic continues to perform the canonical work of Revelation.

[85] In his introduction, Thompson states his aims in a disarming way: "In brief, I am interested in conversation in a pluralistic context, and I think that a 'scholarly' approach to a work such as the Book of Revelation can contribute to fruitful, pluralistic dialogue" (*The Book of Revelation,* 2–3). While the book thus engages millenarians and others in a generous, open-minded fashion, it does so by assuming that pluralism is a form of interaction able to accommodate all positions. By the end of the book, one realizes that pluralism in fact disables the grounds of millenarian action; for a millenarian to accept the terms of this debate would be to concede in advance that all he or she will ever do is debate.

Unbuilding Jerusalem

CHAPTER THREE

APOCALYPSE AND REPRESENTATION: BLAKE, PAINE, AND THE LOGIC OF DEMOCRACY

> When man liberates himself politically, he liberates himself by means of a detour, through the medium of something else.
> —Karl Marx, "On the Jewish Question"

From its beginnings, modern Blake criticism has placed apocalypse at the center of its investigations. We have never moved off that foundation, and for good reason: apocalypse is pervasive in Blake's words and images, from the most explicit representations of the Last Judgment to the most subtle infiltration of revelation into plates seemingly unconcerned with eschatology. What began as a primary topos in Frye's *Fearful Symmetry* and Bloom's *Blake's Apocalypse* remains central today, despite the obvious and dramatic shifts in theoretical climate. Just as Frye could extend his consideration of Blake's career to a comprehensive (and apocalyptic) theory of literature itself, so Jerome McGann has modeled his own multivolume, revisionist anatomy of criticism on what he calls "the structural parody of *Jerusalem*," Blake's tendency in that poem and elsewhere to refuse closure by representing "the same topics from slightly altered perspectives." For a great many critics, Blake's apocalypse poses fundamental and urgent questions about the nature of art and literature, questions that demand to be argued over and over again. And yet we sometimes seem caught within one wheel-spinning problem: Is Blake's work the building or the unbuilding of Jerusalem?[1]

[1] Northrop Frye, *Fearful Symmetry: A Study of William Blake* (Princeton: Princeton University Press, 1947); Harold Bloom, *Blake's Apocalypse: A Study in Poetic Argument* (Garden City: Anchor, 1959). Part three of Jerome McGann's tetralogy, *Social Values and Poetic Acts* (Cambridge: Harvard University Press, 1988), acknowledges early on its plan to reconfigure the work of Northrop Frye: "Frye's holistic imperative can be reinstituted, however, if his ahistorical 'anatomy' is replaced by a dialectical model of critical and literary practice" (14). More implicitly, McGann signals his relationship to Frye by depending as thoroughly

When a transcendental Blake was more in fashion, it was often argued that the final leap to Jerusalem requires one to leave the Golgonooza of language and images behind, that in the end Blake's text points to something above and beyond signs.[2] The more recent tendency, in part the result of increased attention to his production methods, has been to emphasize the fierce materiality of the plates. Even so, the emerging consensus on the significance of Blake's printing process has not settled questions about the status of his apocalypse, and one can quickly observe a stalemate in diametrically opposed essays from a recent collection of criticism. In "A Wall of Words: The Sublime as Text," V. A. de Luca locates an "equation of divinity and textuality" in Blake's work that the poet derives from the Book of Revelation; informed by this equation, Blake's text ideally "provides its own golden string, its own walls, its own gates, its own heaven." For Paul Mann, on the other hand, the dominant equation in Blake is that between the book and the fall, an equation that indicates a Derridean tumble from presence into writing: "*The Book of Urizen* asks whether the very forms in which a visionary poet works are not ultimately futile, whether poetic apocalypse is not a contradiction in terms, whether poets are not doomed from the outset to reproduce Urizen's body and (as) the fallen world."[3]

Does Blake's material text accompany or even embody apocalypse, or is it that which, as text, prevents apocalypse from occurring? The first possibility assumes that apocalypse and representation are compatible terms, as when Robert Essick speaks of Blake's "incarnational sign," the "immanence of the transcendental signified within the material signifier."[4] The second assumes that apocalypse and representation are

---

as Frye did on Blake's apocalypse for his critical model. "The structural parody of *Jerusalem*," he states in the preface, "organizes Part I" and "is an index of the overall form and content" of the book (ix).

[2] A superb rendering of this argument can be found in Robert Gleckner's "Most Holy Forms of Thought: Some Observations on Blake and Language," in *Essential Articles for the Study of William Blake, 1970–1984,* ed. Nelson Hilton (Hamden, Conn.: Shoe String Books, 1986), 91–117. For Gleckner, Blake, like other romantic writers, "twisted and strained language in such fashion that it finally militated against its own existence, aspiring toward that totality of unverbalizable communication, that act of pure intellection which we call (with a certain helplessness) silence" (96).

[3] V. A. de Luca, "A Wall of Words: The Sublime as Text," and Paul Mann, "*The Book of Urizen* and the Horizon of the Book," both in *Unnam'd Forms: Blake and Textuality,* ed. Nelson Hilton and Thomas Vogler (Berkeley: University of California Press, 1986), 231, 61.

[4] Robert Essick, *William Blake and the Language of Adam* (Oxford: Clarendon, 1989), 24. At one point, Essick nearly repeats Mann's question: "How then can Blake, any more than Los, escape replicating the Urizenic in the language necessary for representing it?"—but he holds out for a more optimistic solution, "the promise of discovering even in the language of *Urizen* an escape from Urizen's language" (156–57).

hopelessly antithetical, mutually exclusive. In a general way, moreover, this central quandary reflects the competing critical methods scholars most often bring to Blake's work. Those who emphasize Blake's faith in apocalypse try to respect the artist's cultural horizon, situating his work within the history of ideas available to him—eighteenth-century biblical scholarship, Protestant millenarian beliefs, esoteric traditions of Western mysticism, or, in Essick's case, language origin theory.[5] Those who emphasize Blake's resistance to apocalypse read in his work an anticipation of the theoretical problems related to the poststructuralist understanding of language; as David Simpson puts it, "Of all the major writers I know Blake is . . . the most open to analysis in terms set forth by Derrida."[6]

Cutting across this debate is a general agreement that may help reconfigure the key terms *apocalypse* and *representation:* namely, the understanding that Blake is a political poet whose interests coincide with those of the late eighteenth-century democratic revolutions. While Blake's antiauthoritarian strategies have found an especially receptive home in deconstructive criticism, they have always been celebrated in Blake studies, where scholars almost universally agree that he undermines the authority of his own representations in order to "rouse" his readers to act. "In the long run, any completed system, including even Blake's own, must be destroyed in order to be freshly recreated."[7] Steven Shaviro, the author of this statement, might well be a "boa-deconstructor," to borrow a phrase from Geoffrey Hartman, but the sentence could have been written by any of Blake's humanist champions, by anyone, for that matter, who believes activity is finally more important than structure in Blake's work. Tilottama Rajan has argued that building and unbuilding are simultaneous and tense operations in Blake's apocalyptic texts, which encourage both "canonical reading" and "resistance to it." The

---

[5] From the vast body of work in this vein I mention here only a few that have especially influenced my own work: Joseph Wittreich, *Angel of Apocalypse: Blake's Idea of Milton* (Madison: University of Wisconsin Press, 1975) and *Visionary Poetics: Milton and the Line of Vision* (San Marino: Huntington Library, 1979); Leslie Tannenbaum, *Biblical Tradition in Blake's Early Prophecies* (Princeton: Princeton University Press, 1982); from Morton Paley's extensive work I single out the especially pertinent essay "William Blake, the Prince of the Hebrews, and the Woman Clothed with the Sun," in *William Blake: Essays in Honour of Sir Geoffrey Keynes*, ed. Morton Paley and Michael Phillips (Oxford: Clarendon, 1973). David Erdman deserves special attention in this category for his historical rigor, his political investment, and his ability to remain skeptical of Blake's success despite his deep commitment to the poet's vision: *Blake: Prophet against Empire* (Princeton: Princeton University Press, 1954).

[6] David Simpson, "Reading Blake and Derrida—Our Caesars Neither Praised nor Buried," in *Unnam'd Forms,* ed. Hilton and Vogler, 13.

[7] Steven Shaviro, "'Striving with Systems': Blake and the Politics of Difference," in *Essential Articles for the Study of William Blake,* ed. Hilton, 271.

liberating aspect of Blake's work, its political force, is a direct product of its self-consciousness, its ongoing interrogation of its own images, its foregrounding of contradictions—what Rajan has so aptly called "Blake's heresies against his own system."[8]

What deconstructive readings have helped us to see, then, is that Blake's representational forms, with all the seeming inadequacies that make them incompatible with the universalizing transcendentalism of apocalypse, are as central to the artist's political ends as apocalypse would seem to be. More important, representation does its political work precisely *by blocking apocalypse*. In this chapter I set out to substantiate that claim and to situate it historically. In the late eighteenth century, with the formation of modern democratic politics, matters of literary representation and political representation were often inseparable. When Blake foregrounds the fallen nature of his representational acts and thus disables any claims to apocalyptic authority, he does so within an urgent historical context that defines representation primarily as a political issue, as *the* political issue, one might say.

Blake's career unfolded amid popular slogans that celebrated representation as the necessary counterforce to the royal or aristocratic abuse of power: "No taxation without representation," the Americans proclaimed, or as Tom Paine would later put it, "Representative government is freedom." In a profound sense, Blake's aesthetic practice is structured by the discursive assumptions of the new democratic politics, just as that politics itself emerged from a set of aesthetic and epistemological principles. The primacy of representation over apocalypse in Blake, so vital to his deconstructive practice, is not an anachronistic projection but rather a crucial indicator of the historical moment, the democratic moment, that enables his particular kind of literary work.[9] Too often in Blake criticism one finds a rather mechanical tendency to assume that his apocalyptic desires blend seamlessly with his democratic commitments. Apocalypse, however, has been as convenient to the ex-

---

[8] Tilottama Rajan, *The Supplement of Reading: Figures of Understanding in Romantic Theory and Practice* (Ithaca: Cornell University Press, 1990), 197–98.

[9] Another attempt to locate Blake's strategies of textual indeterminacy within the horizon of his own historical circumstances, and one very much consonant with my own argument, can be found in "The Idea of an Indeterminate Text: Blake and Dr. Alexander Geddes," in Jerome McGann, *Social Values and Poetic Acts*. For McGann, Blake self-consciously developed an indeterminate text in response to the new scholarship that was demonstrating the historicized, heterogeneous, and ideological nature of the redacted Bible. McGann makes a persuasive case that Blake would have learned of such controversies through Geddes, a Catholic priest and "a highly visible advocate of the most liberal ideas of the period" (160). Both Blake and Geddes were Christian believers "deeply marked by certain Enlightenment modes of thought" (163), readers of the Bible as interested in the liberating processes of skeptical critique as they were in discovering the textual grounds for faith.

ercise of authoritarian power as it has been to the rallying of opposition, and the first half of this book suggests why literary apocalypse in particular might provoke uneasiness on the part of a poet interested in advancing liberty. In this initial foray into romantic literature, I want to suggest that Blake's *political* millenarianism paradoxically required a resistance to literary apocalypse, and it is this resistance that aligns him most fully with the historical and political imperatives of his age.

This chapter, however, is not primarily a reading of Blake. Although I begin with some close, insulated analysis of texts and images to indicate why Blake seems to me more the poet of representation than of apocalypse, the chapter rather quickly opens onto a wider consideration of representation and apocalypse in the 1790s, especially in the writings of Paine, and beyond that, it opens onto its largest concern: the relation between modern concepts of representation and democratic politics, a relation we might call "counterapocalyptic" in its commitment to unbuilding the various authoritarian Jerusalems I have previously described. After considering the way representative democracy and a certain skepticism about language emerged together, I end the chapter by discussing the politics that structure our current theoretical and critical engagements. By situating Blake's deconstructive strategies, in other words, this chapter opens an angle onto our own situation. Blake's continuing appeal to contemporary readers, especially those using the general terms of poststructuralist theory to read him, in part depends on the continuum that links him to us, our joint participation in the two-century-old project of modern representative democracy. In the late eighteenth century, Blake, at some risk, explicitly made himself a democratic advocate, and certain democratic practices seeped so profoundly into his work that they became virtually indistinguishable from his most characteristic literary devices, devices that largely remain unchanged throughout his career. In the late twentieth century, we barely acknowledge the compatibility or even the symbiosis that exists between our critical and theoretical acts and the political institutions and assumptions that structure them, institutions and assumptions that may have outlived their capacity to initiate substantive social change, even as they allow a heightened pitch of subversive rhetoric. The fit between democratic politics and a theoretical skepticism about language which has persisted for the past two centuries now sustains itself invisibly. In the final section of this chapter, I turn to some recent Leftist and poststructuralist attempts to reinvigorate the democratic project. These defenses, by their explicit yoking of theory and democratic politics, help make clear the implicit politics of our various theoretical criticisms. More specifically, they help us see how the very desire to politicize criticism, to focus it as we now so often do on the issue of power and subversion, can turn even the most "radical" of our activities into new (if sometimes tacit) apologies for our existing democratic culture.

Blake's Babylon

"Rather than rhapsodizing about Blake's apocalyptic breakthrough as if it were easily attained, we might dwell instead on the bitter honesty with which he has dramatized the pre-apocalyptic condition, which may be the only condition we can ever know."[10] When Leopold Damrosch concluded his early and extraordinary deconstructive account of Blake with this warning, he was especially on target in one respect: Blake's entire aesthetic project can be described as a dramatization of the pre-apocalyptic condition. Among other things, this means that the Whore of Babylon has a strong, nearly ubiquitous presence in his work, both in her more explicit forms (Rahab or the Female Will) and in her general symbolic function as that which must be eliminated before the Logos can ascend to his throne at the Last Judgment.[11] Babylon is the immediately preapocalyptic condition. When the Renaissance exegete David Pareus divided Revelation into literary units, he called section 6 "Babylon" and section 7 "New Jerusalem."[12] In the Book of Revelation itself, Babylon is the last obstacle of history to be overcome, and in the linguistic allegory I outlined in the first chapter of this book, she bears within herself the fallen and divided language of Babel that calls forth the messianic power of the Logos. No wonder Damrosch talks about the "bitter honesty" involved in representing the cheerless possibility that we may know only Babylon and never Jerusalem.

And yet there is a problem in this assessment that goes straight to the paradoxical center of apocalypse in the 1790s. As a radical millenarian, Blake could easily and conventionally identify Babylon with the monarchical or ecclesiastical tyranny that perpetuates fallen history and pre-

---

[10] Leopold Damrosch, *Symbol and Truth in Blake's Myth* (Princeton: Princeton University Press, 1980), 371.

[11] For the link between Rahab and the Whore of Babylon, see chapter 2 of Patricia Parker's *Literary Fat Ladies: Rhetoric, Gender, Property* (London: Methuen, 1987), where she describes how Rahab is understood in church tradition "as dilation, expansion, and deferral, and used as a figure for the space and time of language, discourse, and history before a Master's apocalyptic return" (9).

[12] See Michael Murrin's "Revelation and Two Seventeenth Century Commentators," in *Apocalypse in English Renaissance Thought and Literature,* ed. C. A. Patrides and Joseph Wittreich (Ithaca: Cornell University Press, 1984), 129.

vents the imminent democratic apocalypse: "The Beast & the Whore rule without control."[13] At the same time, however, the democratic discourse of the English Jacobins with whom Blake aligned himself was intrinsically counterapocalyptic, setting up representation as a way to resist the authority of apocalyptic claims. It will take nearly all this chapter to argue that last point, but here I would simply entertain the possibility that Blake found himself pressed into a contradiction: his apocalyptic imagery consistently collides with one of his most characteristic political and textual strategies—the subversion of apocalypse through representation. Oddly enough, the preapocalyptic condition that ought to be transcended, the multiplicity of voices that is never subsumed into a commanding unity, perseveres in Blake's work not merely out of his "bitter honesty"; it remains intransigent because it is essential to the freedom and empowerment envisioned by democratic politics. To indicate the centrality of the preapocalyptic condition in Blake's work, I will look in this section at a Last Judgment drawing, the biblical source of the Four Zoas myth, and a proverb of hell. These brief examples, however, must be seen in the context of the large, growing body of criticism that is currently establishing a more or less deconstructive Blake. De Man apparently never wrote on Blake because he thought the poet's privileging of writing over voice made his work so openly and obviously deconstructive that it was relatively uninteresting to read; Blake left too little for the critic to do.[14] The abundant and excellent criticism of the last decade has proved de Man both right and wrong.[15]

"A Vision of the Last Judgment" is the title Dante Gabriel Rossetti

---

[13] Blake, "Annotations to *An Apology for the Bible,*" in *The Complete Poetry and Prose of William Blake*, ed. David V. Erdman (Garden City: Anchor, 1982), 611. All further citations of Blake are to this text. For another such representation, see fig. 6, Blake's watercolor *The Whore of Babylon*.

[14] W. J. T. Mitchell recalls that, in conversation, de Man once responded to a question about Blake's importance to poststructuralist criticism in this way: "Blake's privileging of writing makes him less interesting to deconstruction, because it makes his work less resistant to its strategies. Everything is open to view in Blake. There are no secrets and repressions." This illuminating comment appears in the question-and-answer section that follows Mitchell's essay "Visible Language: Blake's Wond'rous Art of Writing," in *Romanticism and Contemporary Criticism*, ed. Morris Eaves and Michael Fischer (Ithaca: Cornell University Press, 1986), 91. Mitchell's answers generally offer an interesting and sustained discussion of the relation between Blake and Derrida.

[15] Again, to list a few of the works most important to this study: Damrosch, *Symbol and Truth in Blake's Myth;* Shaviro, " 'Striving with Systems' "; Nelson Hilton, *Literal Imagination: Blake's Vision of Words* (Berkeley: University of California Press, 1983); Mitchell, "Visible Language"; Rajan, *The Supplement of Reading.* Valuable collections of Derrida-inflected readings can be found in two anthologies of Blake criticism: *Unnam'd Forms: Blake and Textuality,* ed. Nelson Hilton and Thomas Vogler (Berkeley: University of California Press, 1986), and *Critical Paths: Blake and the Argument of Method,* ed. Dan Miller, Mark Bracher, and Donald Ault (Durham: Duke University Press, 1987).

gave a collection of notebook fragments written in 1810 for an exhibition of paintings that never took place. Despite its unfinished state, it is widely considered Blake's most programmatic aesthetic statement. Nowhere else does he display so fully his notions of art, imagination, and apocalypse, as well as the tensions inherent among them. And in no other place does Blake attend so explicitly to Babylon. The ostensible purpose of these fragments is to explain the obscure symbolism of a major painting, and while that painting has been lost, three surviving drawings executed between 1806 and 1809 match his figure-by-figure description more or less closely. This fortunate circumstance allows us to observe Babylon in two places, in both the visual representation of apocalypse and its verbal cataloguing. In the maelstrom of activity represented in each of these small pictures, making it difficult to fix one's attention, Babylon plays as significant a role as any other figure (see figs. 3, 4, and 5). Naked and displayed, she sits toward the bottom of the image's dominant vertical axis, forming the visual counterweight to the Messiah seated directly above her. Her posture is serpentine, his upright; her gaze is indirect, his straightforward. In the earliest of these drawings (fig. 3), Blake placed Babylon underneath the Beast at the lowest point of the vertical axis, but in later versions, he inverted their positions, setting her on top of a grotto, as if her throne were the fallen world itself, perhaps again to emphasize her opposition to the Messiah enthroned above her and to frame the entire composition by their polarity.[16] In all the pictures, trumpeting angels and a cataract of fire distance the two dramatically, but these dynamic forces also bind the group of figures into a single, continuous configuration. Presumably Babylon is about to be consumed in the fire that descends upon her; a

[16] The fact that Blake tinkered with the placement of Babylon suggests her significance to him and his need to position her in just the right symbolic manner. In many ways it is surprising that Blake included her at all. Morton Paley has shown that "for Blake's contemporaries, *the* Last Judgment was of course Michelangelo's Sistine Chapel fresco"; therefore, deviations from that model were not only conspicuous but also important indicators of artistic purpose. Morton Paley, *The Apocalyptic Sublime* (New Haven: Yale University Press, 1986), 94. Babylon's significance increases not simply because Blake includes her and Michelangelo does not; it is rather how Blake incorporates her that calls attention to his difference from the universally acknowledged master. As Albert S. Rowe pointed out in 1957, while Blake retains some of the basic features of Michelangelo's general composition, the only specific element that he comes close to adopting is "the cavern-like mound which appears at the bottom of the drawing," directly beneath Christ. Of course, as Rowe again points out, Blake borrows this feature only to alter it, setting Babylon atop the cavern. The overall effect is to transform Michelangelo's relatively naturalistic landscape into what is for Blake a characteristically and idiosyncratically symbolic landscape, in some ways more reminiscent of medieval than Renaissance art. Albert S. Rowe, "A Drawing of the Last Judgment," reprinted in *The Visionary Hand: Essays for the Study of William Blake's Art and Aesthetics,* ed. Robert Essick (Los Angeles: Hennessey & Ingalls, 1973), 207.

Figure 3. William Blake, *A Vision of the Last Judgment*, 1806. Stirling Maxwell Collection, Pollok House, Glasgow Museums.

Figure 4. William Blake, *The Vision of the Last Judgment,* 1808. Petworth House, The Egremont Collection (The National Trust).

Figure 5. B-11082. *The Last Judgment,* c. 1809, William Blake, 1757–1827. National Gallery of Art, Washington, Rosenwald Collection.

pair of three-headed figures assists in the scorching by setting torches to the flesh about her loins (fig. 5). Babylon does not fare well in these drawings—and only slightly better than she does in Revelation. Blake retains the stripping and the burning that are part of her punishment but omits the eating of her flesh in John's account.

When one turns to the description of these images in the notebook essay, one finds that Blake continues to follow Revelation closely, though he adds a few idiosyncratic twists. At the top of the axis, Jesus is seated "with the Word of ⟨Divine⟩ Revelation on his Knees . . . the Heavens opening around him by unfolding the clouds around his throne" (555–56). Blake characteristically stresses the Messiah's function as Logos, he who brings about the divine order by means of the power of the Word. Apocalypse is a linguistic event; it amounts to a rewriting of the world (the new heaven and new earth descend "as a Scroll" [556]), and the divine text emerges only as the corrupt text of history (Babylon) is subordinated and finally destroyed:

> Between the Figures of Adam & Eve [on either side of Jesus] appears a fiery Gulph descending from the sea of fire Before the throne in this Cataract Four angels descend headlong with four trumpets to awake the Dead. beneath these is the Seat of the Harlot ⟨namd⟩ Mystery in the Revelations. She is [bound] siezed by Two Beings each with three heads they Represent Vegetative Existence. ⟨as⟩ it is written in Revelations they strip her naked & burn her with fire ⟨it represents the Eternal Consummation of Vegetable Life & Death with its Lusts The wreathed Torches in their hands represents Eternal Fire which is the fire of Generation or Vegetation it is an Eternal Consummation (558)

Leaving aside for a moment the confusion surrounding the words "consummation" and "fire," we can see that Blake's Babylon embodies a number of conventional evils associated with the preapocalyptic condition. She is "Mystery," that which is indeterminate, dangerously open to misinterpretation, and therefore in need of the kind of sure reading that only the Logos promises. In Revelation, one remembers, the text achieves its closure only as Babylon's hidden meaning is made singular and explicit, the hermeneutic equivalent of stripping her naked. Blake also underscores Babylon's prodigious sexuality. She seduces wayward men even as she invites wayward meanings; she is promiscuous and generative in many ways, all fatal to the New Jerusalem. Most simply, she is what Blake calls "vegetative existence"—life in the subhuman (and feminine) state of nature. The apocalyptic consummation of Babylon marks the end of all evils attached to material existence, from the imperfections of fallen language to the equally dangerous temptations of the female body.

None of this should be surprising; misogyny and asceticism are old companions in apocalyptic writings, and in Blake's work sexual hostility often increases as the text moves toward its apocalyptic moment. One approaches the climax of *Jerusalem,* for instance, by way of an increasingly virulent diatribe against sexual activity, first in the announcement that "Humanity is far above / Sexual Organization" (79:73–74), then in the suggestion that none can "consummate bliss without being Generated" (86:42; without, in other words, becoming enmeshed in the natural cycles that perpetuate death), and finally in the declaration that "Sexes must vanish & cease / To be" (92:13–14). *Milton* had already made clear that Beulah, the realm of female sexuality, is threefold and that only the fraternity of the Zoas is fourfold or completely human.[17] Describing the Logos enthroned directly above Babylon, "A Vision of the Last Judgment" seems to reproduce these apocalyptic conventions uncritically, and yet it also veers from them in unexpected ways. Babylon is not as easily consumed as the image initially suggests, and her persistence first appears with Blake's own confusion of tongues. How are we to distinguish among the various fires of this apocalypse? In the passage quoted, fire at once signifies the sexual desire (the fire of Generation) to be transcended and the apocalyptic means of that transcendence. The notebook fragments posit an absolute dichotomy between the apocalyptic "World of Imagination" and the "world of Generation" (555), but these two realms overlap, sharing the "fiery gulph" that touches both the Logos and Babylon in the Last Judgment drawings. Imaginative acts and sexual acts both burn in Blake's representation, making it impossible to determine whether "Eternal Consummation" indicates the pleasures of infinite apocalyptic energy or the permanent incapacities of an inescapably sexual history.[18] And given this ambiguity, it becomes impossible to distinguish definitively between Babylon and the Logos, the female and the male, the fallen world and the apocalypse that is supposed to supplant it.

The persistence of Babylon in Blake's apocalypse, her refusal to go easily, is not merely the result of one verbal aberration, the attempt to make the word *fire* do double duty. It is a governing logic of the image. On the whole, the Last Judgment picture suggests not asceticism but freedom from sexual restraint. Its ecstatic, swirling figures oddly resem-

[17] Despite a tendency to rely on reductive Freudian resolutions, Brenda S. Webster provides a valuable introduction to the issue of antifeminism in Blake. See "Blake, Women, and Sexuality," in *Critical Paths,* ed. Miller, Bracher, and Ault, 204–24.

[18] In his general treatment of sexuality in Blake, Damrosch remains acutely aware of such unresolved contradictions: "In some mysterious way the sexual act must be the entrance to an apocalypse in which fallen sexuality will be burned up and replaced by something else" (*Symbol and Truth in Blake's Myth,* 238). One of Damrosch's great achievements is to demonstrate in many different ways how Blake's monistic vision continuously depends on dualistic categories to sustain it (here, fallen and redeemed sexuality).

ble those in Blake's watercolor *The Whore of Babylon* (1809), in which a series of sensuous, Dionysian nudes float up from the Harlot's cup of fornication only to be trampled and devoured by the warrior beast she rides (fig. 6). The swirling motion also anticipates his Paolo and Francesca watercolor, where the concatenation of Dantean lovers is gathered up in the whirlwind of desire. In each of these pictures, "energy" is clearly sexual. More to the point, the "fiery gulph" that defines the primary axis in the Last Judgment series is distinctly, almost pornographically, vaginal. In each of the representations, but most clearly pronounced in the Petworth figure (fig. 4), the arrangement of the trumpeting angels suggests the labia. The Logos and Babylon are positioned at two ends of a vulva.[19]

That Blake's representation of apocalypse is organized by and centered on the female sex is as startling as it is fundamentally paradoxical. One can find other images of the vulva in his graphics (it amounts, in fact, to a minor fixation), but almost always these images are related to Vala or the specter, figures in his mythology who consistently represent accommodation to the fallen world, figures such as Babylon who block apocalypse. Typically, the vaginal form is winged and demonic, as in the notebook marginalia of *Vala* (fig. 7) or in plate 6 of *Jerusalem*, which depicts the specter centered directly above Los's phallic hammer. In *Milton*, moreover, Blake explicitly links the specter with Babel (fallen language), making the association of specter, Babel, Babylon, and vaginal form the oddest possible combination to represent the apocalyptic triumph of the Logos.[20] As the "fiery gulph," the vortex at the center of

[19] As can be seen most clearly in the Petworth apocalypse, the image is governed by a pattern of swirling, concentric forms (if one can use that phrase to describe what might be ovals or diamonds) moving outward from the central fiery gulf defined by the trumpeting angels; the endpoints of the outer oval are the thrones of Jesus and Babylon. In all three pictures, as well as in Blake's similar compositions (*The Day of Judgment* executed for Blair's *Grave*, for instance), the pattern might best be described as the vortex, with all the ambiguities of apocalypse and (vaginal) sexuality that figure implied for Blake. My reading of the Last Judgment images, then, differs considerably from the "three schematic diagrams" W. J. T. Mitchell once drew to initiate discussion of the *"range* of ambiguity . . . suggested by these forms." It does, however, suggest one possible answer to a question Mitchell raised about Blake's relation to the art historical tradition: given that a symmetrical design, with the saved rising on the left and the damned falling on the right, has been typical of Last Judgment representations almost from the beginnings of Christian art, "did Blake simply accept and imitate this dualism . . . or did he find some way of modifying and transforming it in his pictures?" Because the dynamic, symmetrical pattern already invoked the image of the vortex (see Michelangelo's *Last Judgment*, where the explosive motion encircles an empty center), it could rather easily be adapted to Blake's idiosyncratic symbolic concerns. See Mitchell's supplement to *Blake*, "Blake's Visions of the Last Judgment: Some Problems in Interpretation," printed for the December 1975 meeting of the Modern Language Association.

[20] Blake, "Babel / The Spectre of Albion," *Milton*, 6:23–24.

Figure 6. William Blake, *The Whore of Babylon,* 1809. Reproduced by Courtesy of the Trustees of the British Museum.

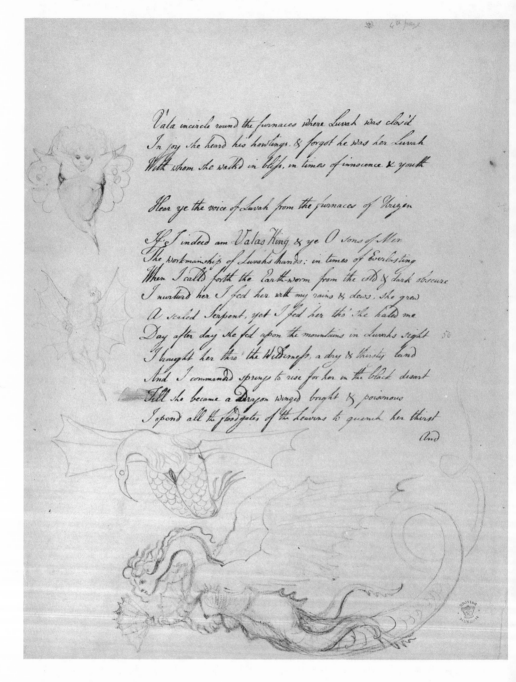

Figure 7.   William Blake, *Vala*, page 26. By permission of the British Library.

the Last Judgment picture, seems more and more to belong to Babylon, the promise of apocalypse becomes increasingly remote. The vortex itself is typical of Blake's ambiguity here; as Nelson Hilton argues, it can signal either passage into transcendence or, in its vaginal form, a return to generation.[21] In "A Vision of the Last Judgment," when Blake urges his (male) audience to engage his picture with prophetic imagination, he invokes a sexual act distinctly at odds with his apocalyptic hopes: "If the Spectator could Enter into these Images in his Imagination approaching them on the Fiery Chariot of his Contemplative Thought . . . then would he arise from his Grave" (560). To enter into this image of apocalypse, however, is to engage the Harlot, to become (in the words of Revelation) "drunk with the wine of her fornication" (King James Version, 17:2). And as we know already, none can "consummate bliss without being Generated." In the very attempt to imagine and to represent it, Blake's apocalypse returns us to the world of fallen acts and images.

Why should this be the case? Damrosch gives one answer; he reads in Blake an unresolved tension between apocalyptic truth and inadequate modes of representation: "Imaginative experience is valid because it is guaranteed by the divine Imagination, but its expressive symbols are contaminated by the fallen world from which they are drawn."[22] In this interpretation, all acts of representation are fallen acts, corruptions of a truth that is immaterial. To place Babylon at the center of a Last Judgment picture is to acknowledge with "bitter honesty" the inherent failings of art. At the same time, however, the incapacities of representation bear a certain benefit Damrosch does not acknowledge, a political benefit that has increasingly become a point of valorization among Blake's deconstructive critics. If one's own apocalyptic vision cannot be realized fully in any communicative medium, then neither can the apocalyptic visions of others. At the very moment one can no longer guarantee the expression of truth *to* others, one gains a freedom from truth imposed *by* others. The foregrounding of Babylon in Blake's apocalypse is in part a lesson in negation and critique; it ensures that any pretense to apocalypse can be refocused as a representation of apocalypse. The very composition of the Last Judgment images, shaped as they are by Babylon, serves notice that they are representational acts, that *because* they belong to the fallen world they cannot possess the absolute authority and privilege that presumably belong to the Logos. The very fact of representation—which is by definition partial, limited to the perspective from

[21] Hilton, *Literal Imagination*, 165–66, 209. For a detailed reading of the *Vala* marginalia, see John Grant's "Visions in *Vala*: A Consideration of Some Pictures in the Manuscript," in *Blake's Sublime Allegory*, ed. Stuart Curran and Joseph Wittreich (Madison: University of Wisconsin Press, 1973), 141–202.

[22] Damrosch, *Symbol and Truth in Blake's Myth*, 73.

which an object is re-presented—disallows any global claim of apocalypse, returning the Logos to the place of varied voices where it is one
preapocalyptic word or image among many. Thus in "A Vision of the
Last Judgment," Blake can speak of eternal forms, but only as they are
neutralized by a relativist and representational logic. The essay is paradoxically a testimony of faith and a prescription for releasing oneself
from the faith of others:

> Vision or Imagination is a Representation of what Eternally Exists. Really
> & Unchangeably (554)

> I have represented [Apocalypse] as I saw it [.] to different People it appears
> differently (555)

Along with its variants, *representation* is the most prominent word in "A
Vision of the Last Judgment," employed almost obsessively (nearly fifty
times).[23] As Blake makes his representational acts visible, as he thickens
them, the proliferating chain of mediation inherent within his apocalyptic project becomes self-evident. In the Book of Revelation, John masks
the necessity of representation (and so preserves his authority) by claiming immediate recourse to the revelatory power of the word of Christ.
Here, the illusion of apocalyptic transparency is explicitly and repeatedly denied. Blake's project consists of a series of conspicuous translations: the Last Judgment must first be envisioned, then represented in
an image, and finally described and glossed by a written commentary. As
one form attempts to explicate another, the layering of perspectives
insulates the audience from the aura of the event itself.

This process of undermining apocalyptic authority by calling attention to representation has been a central concern of Derridean readings
of Blake. By making deconstructive practices the means to distinctly
political ends, Blake's work seems to answer those who see deconstruction as just another nihilism or those who, as Rajan puts it, "see political
and deconstructive criticism as incompatible." Rajan's own definition of
Blake's "perspectivism" is characteristic: "It is simply an admission that
one's own point of view is not uniquely privileged and that there is no
synoptic point of view one can adopt to attain that privilege. This
renunciation of authority comes from the recognition that different
points of view cannot be 'smoothly combined' because they do not
necessarily bear on the same object. That we differ from each other
because we are talking about different aspects of the object, and that

---

[23] Dan Miller captures the paradox nicely: "At one moment, vision is the representation
of an eternal object; at the next moment, it indicates the direct disclosure of that object or,
more radically, becomes the object itself." "Blake and the Deconstructive Interlude," in
Critical Paths, ed. Miller, Bracher, and Ault, 156.

there is no 'object' apart from its appearance in discourse, is the surest obstacle to the creation of a common language that needs no further rereading."[24] Perspectival discourse is politically valuable; it is a good thing that objects cannot be severed from their representations—and that Blake, even when the "object" is the Last Judgment, makes certain that we see the inseparability of objects and their representations. Apocalypse, at least in the canonical Book of Revelation, marks the desire to exercise the authority attendant on a "common language that needs no further rereading," a language that, above and beyond historical differences, can speak universally and therefore can neither be added to nor subtracted from. The ubiquity of representation protects against just such apocalyptic intimidation.

For Rajan, the liberating quality of Blake's work is typical mainly of the early poems, with their investment in self-revision and intertextuality; the later epics turn increasingly to systematization and totalization, to building myth and canon. With this assessment, she joins Marilyn Butler in decisively reversing Frye's evaluation of Blake's career: the late epics mark not a cumulative and climactic literary achievement but a falling off from the more directly political engagements of the early 1790s.[25] Despite the real differences between early and late Blake, I cannot agree here, for throughout Blake's work there persists the same stubborn commitment to making representational acts visible. The effects of this political strategy are a matter of debate, something I take up later, but the dating of the Last Judgment pictures (1806–1809) suggests a certain continuity throughout Blake's career. Consider another instance, this brief (but typical) passage from the relatively late poem *Milton:*

Break not
Forth in your wrath lest you also are vegetated by Tirzah
Wait till the Judgment is past, till the Creation is consumed

[24] Rajan, *Supplement of Reading,* 213.

[25] Marilyn Butler articulated this argument in *Romantics, Rebels, and Reactionaries* (Oxford: Oxford University Press, 1981): "Most of [Blake's] best literary work" is done by 1795; afterward, it "has the flavour of private world-building, of internalized religious comfort," of "an increasingly private mythology, which is less topical," 40, 50, 51. If there is such a shift from political engagement to aesthetic withdrawal in Blake's career, we need to ask what allows it to occur—in other words, what allows the shift from his particular brand of politics (democratic) to his particular kind of aesthetic practice (deconstructive). The argument I develop throughout this chapter is that there is a relatively easy slide between the two, so that certain fundamental strategies of representation remain constant throughout Blake's career despite the real changes Butler describes. From this perspective, Blake's early political engagement will appear to have an aesthetic component already within it, and his later aesthetic withdrawal will appear to remain faithful to many of the political assumptions of the earlier work. Rajan raises the issue of early and late Blake most explicitly on 199–200 of *The Supplement of Reading,* though even there she acknowledges

> And then rush forward with me into the glorious spiritual
> Vegetation; the Supper of the Lamb & his Bride; & the
> Awakening of Albion our friend and ancient companion.
>
> (25:57–62)

Resisting the fallen world's snare of cyclical strife, and attempting to extricate apocalyptic redemption from the revolutionary violence that compromises it, Los recommends patience to his sons. Although the apocalypse that he imagines will follow their resistance to Tirzah involves a characteristic mixture of traditional and specifically Blakean elements, it also features a self-disabling gesture of the sort I have been describing: following "the Judgment," the sons of Los rush forth not into Jerusalem but "into the glorious spiritual / Vegetation." The enjambment is striking. After the idealized adjectives, one expects a noun more appropriate to the apocalypse the passage invokes. Instead, Los repeats the very term he used in such close proximity to represent the danger of Tirzah, a female figure who is Blake's version of preapocalyptic Babylon. One word represents both apocalypse and fall here, binding the two inextricably and reminding us that, despite the expression of apocalyptic desires, we have never left the limited realm of representation.

One could produce countless examples of this sort, but perhaps the best evidence of the inescapably preapocalyptic in Blake's work is the very myth of the Four Zoas, which organizes the late epics. Blake considered the Bible the great code of art, and his use of the first three chapters of Ezekiel says much about his understanding of art. Indeed, these chapters, which introduce the image of the merkabah, or chariot of God, might be read as a scene of instruction regarding acts of representation. An integral part of the merkabah image, the Zoas function in service of revelation, yet one could say that they consist entirely of revelation's antagonist—representation. In fact, the opening chapters of Ezekiel stage the conflict between the two. From the outset, Ezekiel insists on the simultaneity of presence and unmediated communication, and yet his discourse consists of layer upon layer of figuration. As the merkabah appears, the prophet first beholds "a fire infolding itself, and a brightness was about it, and out of the midst thereof as the color of amber, out of the midst of the fire" (1:4).[26] The fire is self-identical, acting on its own substance as both subject and object, dissolving any distinction between interior and exterior that might be symptomatic of division.

---

that the epics may involve some of the same processes of self-questioning she celebrates primarily in the *Songs*.

[26] Throughout this section, in citing Ezekiel, I have used the King James Version in order to follow the text Blake himself read.

Like the God of Exodus who, from a flame, declares, "I am that I am," Ezekiel's fire is the tautological presence that generates and grounds the metaphors that represent it ("as the color of amber"). Even further, the fire implicitly grounds the biblical text itself. When Ezekiel is later commanded to eat a scroll "written within and without" (2:10), that book parallels its source in the divine flame; it is writing acting on itself, writing that is internally consistent, self-referential, and undivided. John adopts this image in Revelation's book "written within and on the backside, sealed with seven seals" (5:1), and Blake does the same at the end of *Milton,* describing "a Garment dipped in blood / Written within & without in woven letters: & the Writing / Is the Divine Revelation in the Litteral expression" (42:12–14). In each case, the image speaks to an unmediated or "litteral" incarnation of the divine presence that not only inspires but also becomes the very text.

If the fire in Ezekiel's vision is meant to guarantee the authority of the text's metaphors, its task is enormous. In the first chapter alone, consisting of twenty-eight verses, Ezekiel employs the most obvious figures (in the form of "like," "likeness," and "as it were") twenty-seven times. The detours of visionary writing clearly reflect the Hebrew injunction against graven images of Yahweh, but they also teach a more general lesson about representation. Even the self-present fire from which metaphor originated eventually itself succumbs to metaphor. As Ezekiel approaches the center of vision, approaching the God that is its source, what once seemed to be present becomes trope: "And I saw as the color of amber, as the appearance of fire round about within it, from the appearance of his loins even upward, and from the appearance of the loins even downward, I saw as it were the appearance of fire, and it had brightness round about" (1:27). Fire, "as it were," has severed its theontological anchor. The chapter ends not with revelation but with a proliferation of figures, and the God that should have mastered the text is instead produced by it: "As the appearance of the bow that is in the cloud in the day of rain, so was the appearance of the brightness round about. This was the appearance of the likeness of the glory of the Lord" (1:28). It is difficult to know whether Ezekiel subsequently faints from his proximity to the divine or from the exhaustion of representing his distance.

The tension between apocalyptic presence and representation that informs this scene structures the element of it most important to Blake, the "four living creatures," or Zoas. Their definitive trait, repeated like a textual refrain, is that they never veer from a straight course.

Their wings were joined one to another; they turned not when they went; they went every one straight forward. (1:9)

And they went every one straight forward; whither the spirit was to go,
they went; and they turned not when they went. (1:12)

As Coleridge recognized, the Zoas primarily embody immediate communication: "The truths and the symbols that represent them move in
conjunction," he marveled.[27] The Zoas' unswerving motion responds
directly to the divine will that commands them; when the spirit says go,
they go. There is simply no margin of error, no resistance from an
imperfect medium that might result in even the slightest friction. For
Ezekiel, then, the Zoas are an idealized version of the prophet's own
relationship to God; he too is merely the divine vehicle whose words veer
from the truth of revelation no more than the Zoas veer from their strict
course. Just as the spirit set the Zoas upon "straight feet" (1:7), so,
Ezekiel explains, "the Spirit entered into me, . . . and set me upon my
feet" (2:2). A genuinely inspired prophet moves straight forward, especially in his speech. And yet the problem in Ezekiel's text is that everywhere language "turns" mercilessly, embarking on the necessary detour
of tropes, a word the root of which, as Harold Bloom often reminds us,
means "to turn." The Zoas, it seems, are constituted by a contradiction;
they consist of tropes, and yet they "turned not as they went." "Also out
of the midst [of fire] came the likeness of four living creatures. And this
was their appearance: they had the likeness of a man" (1:5). The paradox sets the medium of representation against the content of the vision,
and in doing so it opens the space of disbelief, allowing a response that
need not step in line.

Blake's own painting of Ezekiel's vision swerves precisely in this way
(fig. 8), making the problems inherent in the source the subject of his
image. In order to describe the Zoas' straightforward motion, Ezekiel
must rely on the antithetical disposition of trope. For Blake to represent
in paint the unswerving Zoas (here portrayed as a four-headed man
square to the canvas, proceeding directly toward the viewer), he must
necessarily relinquish the illusion of what Rajan calls a "synoptic point of
view." By virtue of the straightforward motion that defines them, one
head of the Zoas must be concealed. In Blake's dominant myth, the
withdrawal of one Zoa (Urizen) triggers the fall into generation. In "A
Vision of the Last Judgment," the three-headed creatures burning the
Whore of Babylon represent "vegetative existence." Representation, it
would seem, is inherently threefold, sexual, postlapsarian, and pre-
millennial, and thus never adequate to the fourfold vision. Any attempt

[27] Samuel Taylor Coleridge, *The Statesman's Manual* (1816), in *Lay Sermons*, ed. R. J.
White (Princeton: Princeton University Press, 1972), 29. For Coleridge, Ezekiel's Wheels
provide the best evidence that the books of Scripture can be considered "the living *educts* of
the Imagination," that "the Sacred Book is worthily intitled *the* WORD OF GOD."

Figure 8. William Blake, *The Whirlwind: Ezekiel's Vision of the Cherubim and the Eyed Wheels,* ca. 1803–1805. Purchased 1890. Courtesy, Museum of Fine Arts, Boston.

to represent that vision originates from a contingent position, from one place within the horizon of local perspectives. The failure of any single image aspiring to apocalyptic totality becomes plain when Blake includes the figures of four male profiles, two on either side of the painting. With this double exposure of the Zoas, Blake can fabricate the illusion of fourfold wholeness, but only as he makes manifest a set of internal contradictions. If one cannot have straightforward motion without sacrificing one of the Zoa's heads, then one also cannot have four heads without sacrificing the straightforward motion. Either way, one cannot escape the threefold or the swerving; either way, one cannot surmount a partial representation. To move from image to text, one finds the same self-subverting principle in Blake's use of the Zoas in the apocalypse that concludes *Jerusalem:*

> The Four Living Creatures Chariots of Humanity Divine Incomprehensible
> In beautiful Paradises expand These are the Four Rivers of Paradise
> And the Four Faces of Humanity fronting the Four Cardinal Points
> Of Heaven going forward forward irresistible from Eternity to Eternity
>
> (98:24–27)

As the Zoas rush forward to eternity, Blake's language turns and reveals itself; trope is as irresistible here as it is in Ezekiel's vision. The obstructed view of the Zoas is more subtle in print than in paint, but the fact remains that we can approach them only through the detours of so many Chariots and Rivers and Faces, through their likenesses, the figures that are all we have.

When Bloom once interpreted "London" in the shadow of Ezekiel, he argued that Blake's prophetic anxiety first appears as he wanders when he should progress straight forward. "To 'wander' is to have no destination and no purpose. . . . When [Blake] begins by saying that he *wanders* in London, his Jerusalem, his City of God, then he begins also by saying, 'I am not Ezekiel, I am not a prophet, I am too fearful to be the prophet I ought to be, *I am hid.*'"[28] Blake often worried more explicitly about swerving from the strict demands of inspiration. In a letter to his friend and patron Thomas Butts, he writes, "I am under the direction of Messengers from Heaven Daily & Nightly but the nature of such things is not as some suppose. without trouble or care. Temptations are on the right hand & left behind the sea of time & space roars & follows swiftly he who keeps not right onward is lost & if our footsteps slide in clay how can we do otherwise than fear & tremble" (724). Blake never shared Ezekiel's confidence that heaven had set him on "straight feet." And yet

[28] Harold Bloom, *Poetry and Repression* (New Haven: Yale University Press, 1976), 37.

the crisis of representation that makes both Blake and Ezekiel swerve away from apocalypse demonstrates not only the groundlessness of Ezekiel's confidence but the deceptive and authoritarian danger of his text as well. To say implicitly, "I am not Ezekiel," as Bloom has Blake say, may have little to do with anxiety. As John Brenkman argues, one can alternatively describe the wandering that is uncharacteristic of the biblical prophet as "a gesture of opposition."[29] When the foot slides in clay, and time and space (the preapocalyptic conditions of representation) overcome the visions of eternity, Blake fails to reproduce the power and authority of the prophet, but it is only by wandering, by erring, by turning, and finally by troping, that Blake allows, even invites, his reader to see his discursive practice. Blake goes out of his way, so to speak, to make himself conspicuous, to make sure that he is not "hidden" within an apocalypse that transcends his limited perspective. Only as Blake veers does he create a condition in which his reader can respond to apocalypse with something other than awe.

To put it another way, the wandering bound up with representation allows us to track the footprints of imperfection Blake leaves upon his work. Those critics concerned with the material constraints of Blake's printing methods have begun to take his "accidents" seriously, treating them as signifying elements that help "raise the question of mediation," thereby disrupting the reader's passive tendency to consider words and images transparent.[30] By making matters of representation unavoidable, Blake's self-critical apocalypse points to a necessary barrier between us and any truth claiming an unmediated communication, any truth that might be used to ground the exercise of power. As W. J. T. Mitchell has so persuasively argued, we can never forget "the specifically political character of Blake's commitment to making language visible."[31] Throughout his career, Blake is one of the great writers of suspicion; his discourse is consistently a lesson in surveillance, shaped as it is by so

[29] John Brenkman, *Culture and Domination* (Ithaca: Cornell University Press, 1987), 124. Brenkman is one of the most rigorously political readers of Blake: "Blake practiced the writing of poetry not in order to unveil objects of contemplation or to preserve the kernel of unvarying truth or to produce the harmonies of the beautiful illusion, but rather as the active imposition of 'imagination' or 'fantasy' as a form of discursive struggle against the dominant values organizing the social experiences and practices in which he participated" (111).

[30] Santa Cruz Blake Study Group, "What Type of Blake?" in *Essential Articles for the Study of William Blake*, ed. Hilton, 330. The Santa Cruz manifesto is vigorous in its antitranscendentalism, arguing that "the reader has the right to know that Blake made 'mistakes'" (306), and even more, that "Blake's production is itself a performance situation, a 'scene of writing' which continually draws attention to itself as graphological production" (323), thus producing many of its most disruptive, even subversive, effects by making the materiality of language intrude on the reader.

[31] Mitchell, "Visible Language," 51.

many devices for revealing the play of power within language, whether
his own or that of others. Although Blake may have been one of its most
ingenious practitioners, he did not invent the idea of a text that invites
resistance by calling attention to itself as text. The practice of a self-
questioning language adequate to both the multiplicity of conflicting
interests and the suspicion of all forms of centralized authority was so
common in the emergence of democratic politics that one is hard-
pressed to think of a writer associated with "the rights of man" who does
not at some time employ it.

The insistence on a wary vigilance, and the role that representation
plays in that vigilance, characterizes both Blake's texts and the democratic discourse that appeared simultaneously. Both saw politics everywhere, hidden in previously unsuspected places, and both consequently
demanded a new linguistic self-awareness, a sensitivity to the work of
representation in either the perpetuation or the critique of power. In
this context language takes on unprecedented significance as the field in
which power constitutes itself and gets resisted. The force and consequence of these assumptions are the subjects of the following two sections. For now, I want to suggest just how deeply embedded is Blake's
suspicion of apocalypse and the potentially dangerous authority of its
Logos, how his foregrounding of representation is nearly an automatic
function of even his most basic verbal operations.

In 1793, while he was still enthusiastic about the events in France,
Blake included the following proverb in The Marriage of Heaven and Hell:
"Truth can never be told so as to be understood, and not be believ'd"
(10:69). For Blake, matters of truth are always matters of apocalypse. In
"A Vision of the Last Judgment," he asserts that "whenever any Individual Rejects Error & Embraces Truth a Last Judgment passes upon that
Individual" (562), and later in the essay he associates the revelation of
truth with the conventional imagery of apocalypse: "Error is Created
Truth is Eternal Error or Creation will be Burned Up & then & not till
then Truth or Eternity will appear" (565). As Derrida has suggested, the
tendency to perceive knowledge in terms of an apocalyptic narrative is
pervasive in Western philosophy. "Truth itself is the end, the destination," he writes, "and that truth unveils itself is the advent of the end. . . .
The structure of truth here would be apocalyptic."[32] Truth displaces
error as new heaven and new earth displace the old; apocalypse is
internal, epistemological rather than phenomenal. This interior eschatology also binds apocalypse in a most explicit way to ideology. The Last
Judgment is an attempt to close the battle among conflicting judgments;

[32] Jacques Derrida, "Of an Apocalyptic Tone Recently Adopted in Philosophy," Oxford
Literary Review 6 (1984): 24.

it involves a restructuring of the way one thinks one's world, and to the extent that its truth is widely normalized as knowledge or belief, it stabilizes a particular order or Logos. The concise, epigrammatic form of Blake's proverb suggests how quickly truth can be understood and believed and thus amount to a minor apocalypse. Aphorisms offer the attraction of instant digestion; they subordinate the fact of their representation to a truth immediately and uncritically intuited, a truth which, as Wordsworth would say, is its own testimony, carried alive into the heart by passion.

Blake begins, then, with a form ideologically dangerous precisely because its truth seems to transcend representation. His proverb, however, does nothing of the sort. In the first place, its compact message would need no expression at all were it not for the implication that truth is often told, misunderstood, and disbelieved. The very existence of the assertion indicates that the transparency of communication cannot be taken for granted, leaving us no guarantee that this is a sentence we can understand, let alone believe. This initial opening of doubt is then enhanced by the strange surface of the sentence, which is anything but transparent. Blake might have written, "Truth told and understood must be believed," but instead he compels the reader to negotiate a double negative that complicates meaning as well as syntax. Blake goes out of his way, in other words, to ensure the possibility, even the probability, of being misunderstood. The sentence consists of a series of obstacles or negations that suddenly give way to a positive and perhaps unearned reversal at the end. The final clause arrives like the parousia; belief redeems truth, converting linguistic pessimism into plenitude. Just in time, the Logos displaces the preapocalyptic condition of Babylon. But do we believe it?

To write a narrative of the reading process involved in this proverb is to witness the obstacles to revelation. The proverb unfolds in four stages:

Truth
Truth can never be told
Truth can never be told so as to be understood
Truth can never be told so as to be understood, and not be believ'd

The reader begins with a confident presence, the thing itself, but by the end of the first complete thought truth has been severed altogether from verbal representation. The very assertion "Truth can never be told" performs its own content; it is a paradox of the type "This sentence is a lie" and so denies the possibility of determinate meaning. By the time the reader reaches the proverb's caesura—which Blake marked by a period and not the comma provided in modern, standard editions—the burden of indeterminacy expands to include interpretation as well as expression, audience as well as author.[33] If truth can be told, it cannot be received; there exists no means to secure the transmission of ideas without passing through the deflecting medium of language. Alternatively, Blake might be suggesting the need to camouflage his message; truth can never be told so as to be understood *right now,* at a time of counterrevolution in England. Indeterminacy deflects "Satan's watchfiends" as well as truth. According to David Erdman, Blake was deeply affected by the censorship campaigns of the 1790s; his combination of paranoia and self-aggrandizement created fears that were "related to the political realities of his time only in an exaggerated form that interpreted the possibility of jail as the probability of hanging."[34] Whether one sees the proverb's third phrase as evidence of historical pressures or as a comment on inherent linguistic limitation, Blake's subjection of truth to the contingencies of representation signals a direct contradiction of the proverb's overall and sanguine meaning, a meaning that can be completed, appropriately enough, only by introducing yet another negative. First slowing the reader by means of a tricky syntax and then internally commenting on his own representational act, Blake undermines the proverb's teleology and thus the closure of its apocalypse. Indeed, the very proverb that describes the simultaneity of truth and belief represents the distance between them, something Blake makes literal by placing the key terms (*truth* and *belief*) at the opposite ends of the sentence.

Given the crossing of linguistic and political subversion that occurs throughout his work, from its largest mythic formulations to its subtle, local assertions, is it any wonder that this romantic poet has proved irresistible to deconstructive readers and, moreover, that generally Derridean principles have found their way into so many discussions of his work, even among the critics resistant to anachronistic projections?[35] Has not a litany of critical assumptions achieved something like a working consensus among Blake scholars, at least in its broadest terms? One could begin with the notion that Blake's text demands interpretation rather than mere belief, an active rather than a passive reader. Its cultivated obscurity, its obvious undecidabilities (if not outright indeter-

---

[33] See the Santa Cruz Blake Study Group essay "What Type of Blake?" which addresses this example of David Erdman's editorial intrusions (in *Essential Articles for the Study of William Blake,* ed. Hilton, 313).

[34] Erdman, *Prophet against Empire,* 139.

[35] A perfect example of this currency is Essick's *William Blake and the Language of Adam,* which provides a rich historical survey of language origin theory available to Blake but is continually pressured (and for the better, I think) by Derrida's ideas on language.

minacies) initiate the reader into a process of critical awareness that undermines the possibility of arriving at a fixed, static meaning. Because it militates against closure, the work generates an exponential proliferation of imaginative—that is to say, textual—activity. Blake, we are frequently reminded, was "an indefatigable reviser of his pictorial works," assuring that no illuminated book might achieve a final or definitive form.[36] Just so, we are told, we must endlessly rework our readings, striving not for some encyclopedic understanding of "the system" but for a reproduction of the restless, creative process itself: "The insistence that criticism can never stand still but must constantly search to reformulate its utterances is only the assertion that it must know itself and the irony of its situation."[37] According to Hazard Adams, criticism joins Blake in the assault on teleology and thus necessarily in the assault on apocalypse; embracing the difficult path of irony means learning to live without the facile comfort of an ending. In an outstanding essay linking Blake and Derrida, Dan Miller suggests that more than anything else "Blake's revelation reveals . . . the intransigence of allegorical representation and the interminable analysis that allegory provokes." Prefacing his excellent reading of the apocalypse in *Jerusalem*, Miller writes, "There can be no moment at which the work of deconstruction is finished, no time when the analysis is complete. Derrida has spoken of interminable analysis."[38]

With its commitment to endless activity and the subversion of closure, with its deep suspicion of authoritative structures and meanings, deconstructive criticism has indeed been faithful to Blake's ideal of radical energy, perhaps too faithful. When Blake developed a practice that gave representation priority over apocalypse, he did so under the aegis of representative democracy, the political project that he believed capable of producing revolutionary social change. How fully that change was revolutionary is still a matter of debate among historians, but no one would deny that open republicanism carried certain risks in 1794, the real danger of arrest at least, even if the threat of execution was virtually nonexistent. As E. P. Thompson has made so unforgettable, English power protected itself by actively, violently suppressing its democratic opposition; and as Raymond Williams points out, "Democracy was still a revolutionary or at least a radical term" to the mid-nineteenth century.[39] Today, in those English-speaking universities where Blake is a fixture of

---

[36] Essick, *William Blake and the Language of Adam*, 163.

[37] Hazard Adams, "Synecdoche and Method," in *Critical Paths*, ed. Miller, Bracher, and Ault, 51.

[38] Miller, "Blake and the Deconstructive Interlude," in *Critical Paths*, ed. Miller, Bracher, and Ault, 167, 149.

[39] Raymond Williams, *Keywords* (London: Fontana, 1976), 96.

the curriculum, advocating democratic principles runs no such risks, and while everyone must be glad that this is true, one must also wonder to what extent, after two hundred years, democratic politics can still be considered a radical politics—especially as it has come almost exclusively to mean representative government and free speech.[40] Take, for instance, Paul Mann's charge that what he and others have called the Blake Industry sustains itself by endless self-criticism and the suspicion of fixed truth, the very cornerstones of intellectual freedom: "The consensually validated revelation of Blake's truth would put the industry out of business. Blake's 'truth' becomes a currency, a fluctuating exchange value in an economy whose survival depends not only on agreement but on disagreement, discord, dismissals, departures, the continual destruction and reconstruction of each appearance of that truth."[41] The perpetual activity of a counterapocalyptic aesthetic amounts to a furious running in place that simulates radical volatility even as it serves the academy's institutional and professional status quo. This very contradiction between intention and effect, moreover, results from intellectual and ethical rigor, the dogged insistence that no interpretation, no matter how ingenious, can function with absolute authority for others. Mann draws his metaphor from economics, but such resistance to imposition and authority has its source in the free market's historical companion—the politics of democratic representation. Within the horizon of modern democracy, what Blake and his deconstructive critics mainly share is the burden they place on the critical and supposedly liberating potential of discursive practices. From its beginnings, modern democratic culture has tended to confuse the subversion of truth and authority as they are represented in discourse with the subversion of power formations themselves. The collapsing of truth into representation is indeed a political act; it is an act that marks Blake's historical participation in the redefinition of politics. Like many of the critics who today follow his lead, however, Blake tends to exaggerate the consequences of his political act, erring only as he overestimates the significance of representation.

---

[40] Williams describes how the term *democracy,* after the late eighteenth-century revolutions and modeled especially on the American Constitution, came to mean "representative democracy" rather than "popular power" and how the former in fact was developed as a means of containing the latter, older, and more radical conception. "It would sometimes be easier to believe in democracy, or to stand for it, if the C19 change had not happened and it were still an unfavourable or factional term." *Keywords,* 97–98. In this chapter, I am talking almost exclusively of representative democracy, even and especially as it emerged from a more radical matrix. The importance of this transitional and politically constitutive moment for Blake is concisely indicated by Shaviro: "On the broadest historical level, Blake's discourse may be lodged in the contradiction between what the Enlightenment promised in the way of liberation and what the capitalism of which it was the harbinger actually produced." Shaviro, "'Striving with Systems,'" 296.

[41] Paul Mann, "Apocalypse and Recuperation: Blake and the Maw of Commerce," *ELH* 23 (1985): 1.

Revelation, Representation, and the
Emergence of Democratic Discourse

"I know not how a representative assembly can more usefully employ itself than in talk."[42] In 1861, when John Stuart Mill undertook to define "The Proper Function of Representative Bodies" as "talk," he acknowledged outright that what he valued in an elected assembly is exactly what the critics of representative democracy derided—that it is *only* capable of talk. Mill's statement is jarring, but by the time "On Representative Government" appeared, it was already part of a minor political tradition. If the statement seems to value language rather highly, it also serves to underscore a certain tautology central to the democratic culture Mill inherited: the proper function of representation (a form of government) is representation (the production of meaningful signs, here speech). For Mill, political and linguistic activity are indistinguishable, or even identical; while he might be able to imagine a linguistic activity that is not political, he cannot in turn imagine an authentic political activity that is not linguistic in nature. Consisting entirely of the sum of its verbal acts, democratic government is like a text open to perpetual revision; Mill's ongoing concern is thus the aesthetic "form" of good government (the titles of the first three chapters of his treatise are "To what extent Forms of Government are a Matter of Choice," "The Criterion of a Good Form of Government," and "That the ideally best Form of Government is Representative Government"). This particular identification between politics and language as they converge in the activity of representation has its roots in the democratic revolutions of the late eighteenth century; it is bound up with the strategies of aesthetic representation we saw in Blake, and as I will argue in detail, it is especially well articulated in the writings of Tom Paine. But before I turn to the emergence of modern democratic discourse, its sources and implications, perhaps it is best to continue *in medias res*, for Mill's "On Representative Government," although already a departure from earlier and more radical democratic politics, relies heavily on the definitive assumptions of the earlier generation.

It is important to recognize that Mill is essentially antiegalitarian; he favors, for instance, a type of representation whereby "the best minds" in the nation exercise more electoral say than merely ordinary minds. But it is equally important to realize that some of Mill's innovations evolve logically out of radical democratic principles and practices. Consider the firm distinction Mill advocates between the executive and

[42] John Stuart Mill, *Utilitarianism, Liberty, and Representative Government* (New York: Dutton, 1951), 322. Further references are to this edition.

legislative functions of government, that is, between acting and deliberating. The proper role of an assembly, as we have already seen, is talking; a representative body, hardly embodied at all, ought to be a mind, a mouth, and nothing more. This radical severing of representation and action would have seemed foreign to an earlier generation, which tended to see representation *as* action; Blake once claimed that Paine conquered European armies with a mere pamphlet, with writing. And yet, Mill's self-disabled assembly, his disempowered representative body that can only speak and that, moreover, encourages its citizens to accept speech as an act sufficient in itself, remains faithful to certain deeply embedded democratic assumptions that emerged in the revolutionary period. With confidence Mill can say that his talking assembly "is surely ample power, and security enough for the liberty of the nation" (321). Underlying his rhetoric is a belief central to the democratic culture he inherited from the likes of Blake and Paine: the nearly absolute faith in the power of language, in the power of representation, to secure freedom.

How, one might wonder, can language, speech, and representation possess such power when Mill differentiates "talking" so sharply from "doing"? Mill's answer is simple enough: even though representation cannot "do," it can "undo." Representation stands in a negative relation to power, the kind of absolute power embodied in previous centuries by the executive (the monarch). The utmost authority of a representative body, for Mill, is appropriately a negative one; it can impeach a member of the executive for wrongdoing, for an abuse of power. But this last resort is almost never necessary, since the negation of power is already achieved by the assembly's talking function, its ability "to check by criticism" (323), "to throw the light of publicity on [the executive's] acts: to compel a full exposition and justification of all of them which any one considers questionable" (321). The primary function of representation, then, is simply to give power a visible form, to make it pass through language and thus assume a shape that disarms it of its dangerous coercive tendencies. In *Milton,* Blake has the poet-prophet battle the tyrant Urizen by sculpting him, molding him with clay, giving him identifiable form.[43] For both Blake and Mill, power and representation are archetypal antagonists; they are antonyms, just as within the dominant liberal tradition power and liberty, according to Norberto Bobbio, "can be counterposed as antithetical terms."[44] Representation arises as

[43] "Silent Milton stood before / The darkend Urizen; as the sculptor silent stands before / His forming image; he walks round it patient labouring. / Thus Milton stood forming bright Urizen" (20:7–10). See also 19:10–14.

[44] Norberto Bobbio, *Liberalism and Democracy,* trans. Martin Ryle and Kate Soper (London: Verso, 1990), 15.

an answer to power, for to represent power is to collapse it into language. This process implies a remarkable rise in the prestige of language, a newfound faith in the capacities of signs; without such faith it is unlikely that the democratic revolutions would have taken the course they did. By midcentury, one symptom of the lingering prestige of language is the idea that parliament and the free press are redundant. Since parliament does not act but only undoes actions by representing them publicly and critically, the same function could be performed as effectively by a good newspaper. What matters in the end is that power gets verbalized.[45]

In Mill's model, then, representation stands as a buffer between a nation's people and their rulers. But if it guards against the abuse of power from above, preventing any return to the arbitrary and total discretion of a monarch, representation serves a different function in relation to the populace it represents. It signifies, in a familiar phrase, the power of the people, the institutional conditions of their self-governance. But representation offers the public a particular kind of empowerment, one that simultaneously neutralizes potential dangers. It offers people speech instead of power. This secondary, but still "talking," function of parliament turns the assembly into "the nation's Committee of Grievances, and its Congress of Opinions, an arena . . . where those whose opinion is overruled, feel satisfied that it is heard, and set aside not by a mere act of will, but for what are thought superior reasons" (321). According to this plan, grievances need not be redressed so long as they are addressed. Mill very much wants to channel national conflicts into the assembly's talking function, to give voice to as many people as possible without putting at risk the stability of the social order. As representation makes visible the activities of power above, it also diffuses power from below, but it does so in such a way that those below paradoxically "feel" themselves empowered. As his statement indicates, Mill is not particularly concerned with parliament's role in initiating social change. He is concerned, however, to create a mechanism whereby the potential agents of change "feel satisfied" with exercising speech, with the sense of empowerment one experiences in talking rather than doing. Representation is that mechanism; it works by transforming conflicting and even radical desires into a particular discursive practice, one that is regulated according to state-sponsored rules. Parliament literally becomes, as Mill states, "an arena"—a place where conflict gets repre-

[45] Mill himself cites an M. Salvador who likens the free press to the role the prophets played as unofficial critics of the absolute monarchy in ancient Judaea (269). Catherine Gallagher cites Disraeli's Coningsby as one who "wishes to replace the Parliament with the press." *The Industrial Reformation of English Fiction, 1832–1867* (Chicago: University of Chicago Press, 1985), 218.

sented in an artificially constructed space for the benefit of spectator-citizens, staged for an audience that experiences its freedom as the right to enter the performance and speak. In its fundamental drive to negate power, democratic culture depends on this enhancement of the status of language: to be able to speak is to be free—or in Paine's simple formula from *Rights of Man*, "representative government is freedom."[46] As always, freedom means freedom from power (hence the convergence of liberalism and democracy which Bobbio ascribes to the late eighteenth century), and the medium in which that freedom is constituted and experienced is language.

"On Representative Government" is not, so far as I can tell, an ingenious attempt to rid an elite executive of obstacles to its actions while seeming to erect precisely such democratic obstacles. Mill makes his case within an already established democratic culture that believes the function of representation is to collapse power into language. This rather utopian belief first appears with the emergence of a specifically democratic discourse in the late eighteenth century, and I want to turn now to the French and English debates about representation of that period. Political discussion in the 1790s is almost entirely centered on the appropriate form of government ("The Criterion of a Good Form," as Mill would later have it), but such matters are especially important to republicans because their rhetoric so often suggests that form itself is inherently antithetical to power, or as I put it earlier, that to represent power (to give it a visible form) is to render it essentially harmless.[47] The democratic discourse of the 1790s is characterized by a certain faith in its own formal elements, primarily a belief that principles, activities, and structures which stage the subversion of power actually subvert the exercise of power within a society. One of the great successes of the democratic revolution is to make power seem a matter of language, to make its appearance in discourse seem coterminous with its very existence. The 1790s is therefore marked by a heightened interest in all the demystifying activities of representation, from those traditionally considered aesthetic to those already accepted as political. Because representation means the nullification of power, such republicans as Paine set out to demonstrate that representation is ubiquitous, that nothing lies

---

[46] Tom Paine, *Rights of Man* (New York: Penguin, 1969), 201. Further references are to this edition.

[47] Patrice L.-R. Higonnet suggests that a fixation on form was already a trademark of Anglo-American radicalism by the time of the revolutions: "More than [any] other concern, institutional forms attracted the attention of eighteenth-century Anglo-American radicals: for them what mattered was the political setting of social change, rather than social change per se." *Sister Republics: The Origins of French and American Republicanism* (Cambridge: Harvard University Press, 1988), 181.

beyond its reach that might serve as power's foothold. In short, the unspoken democratic dictum is that everything, not simply "the people," must be represented.

From Power to Language

The attention to representation within democratic discourse necessarily blurs any distinctions we might create between aesthetics and politics. Indeed, the epistemological and aesthetic questions we associate with the new poetic forms of romanticism did not emerge arbitrarily in relation to the new republican forms of government that involved a restructuring of and a wider scope for representation. Political and aesthetic representation evolved together, and a poet such as Blake can only be understood in the context of this dual focus.

To begin with, the *beautiful* and the *sublime*, the leading aesthetic categories of the late eighteenth century, became increasingly politicized as they became the occasion of an implicit debate about representation. When Burke wrote his defense of aristocratic government, he relied, as Mary Wollstonecraft was the first to notice, on the terms of his forty-year-old treatise on the beautiful and the sublime. Ronald Paulson has shown that Burke was not alone; almost all interpreters of the Revolution constructed their narratives from the familiar forms of representation they knew through art or literature. The political implications of these forms, Paulson argues, thus quickly became apparent.[48] In Burke's case, the *Reflections on the Revolution in France* self-consciously enlists both the sublime and the beautiful, but it is the former that serves to reinvest the monarchy and the peerage with the aura of unfathomable authority he imagines they once possessed in a less aggressive, feudal era. As J. C. D. Clarke has amply demonstrated, the conservative case spearheaded by Burke in 1790 relied on the established traditions of Anglican ideology; it did not suddenly "return to the doctrine of divine right: it had never left it."[49] The sublime intimidates by its mystery, by the spectacle of a power that exceeds comprehension but is still mystically embodied in the presence of the king. In Kant's very differently motivated formulations of the same year, the sublime is that which cannot be represented because it is incommensurable, because it transcends any attempt to give form to its "greatness": "But if we call anything, not only great, but absolutely great in every point of view (great beyond all comparison), i.e.

[48] Ronald Paulson, *Representations of Revolution (1789–1820)* (New Haven: Yale University Press, 1983). See especially chapters 1–4.
[49] J. C. D. Clarke, *English Society, 1688–1832: Ideology, Social Structure and Political Practice during the Ancien Régime* (Cambridge: Cambridge University Press, 1985), 200.

sublime, we soon see that it is not permissible to seek for an adequate standard outside itself, but merely in itself. It is a magnitude which is like itself alone."[50] This spectacle of an unimaginable power beyond analogy provides a rhetoric easily appropriated by or for divine right (consider Kant's example of a sublime image: "Jupiter's eagle with the lightning in its claws"). The sublime rules by its mystery, and inseparable from its mystery is the idea that it transcends representation.

Juxtaposed with the sublime, the beautiful consists of securely bounded, identifiable form. Burke thus saw it as the necessary and pragmatic complement of the sublime, a softening of power that would produce love and consensus as well as respect and fear; without the beautiful, hegemony would be impossible.[51] At the same time, however, clear and distinct form could be employed not to supplement the sublime but to counteract its intimidation tactics, as in Blake's unwavering commitment to lucidity in drawing. Blake never rejected the sublime, only the leading version of it: "Obscurity is Neither the Source of the Sublime nor of any Thing Else" (658), he wrote in his annotations to Reynolds. The principle of clarity, which introduces self-conscious artifice into works given over to energy, seems to contradict many of Blake's own verbal and visual practices, especially his celebrated retort to Reverend Trusler: "That which can be made Explicit to the Idiot is not worth my care" (702). But the "firm and determinate lineaments" (530) Blake invariably described as the essence of good art serve a crucial function: they guarantee an awareness of representation in all his works. No element of Blake's practice reveals more clearly his adherence to Enlightenment politics, despite the problems it may pose for his typically "romantic" vision. The sublime and the unknowable must be given determinate forms; they must be brought out of darkness into light; they must, in other words, be represented. In the first flush of the Revolution, Richard Price laid out with characteristic clarity the formula for all who suffered under the mystique of power: "Remove the darkness in which they envelope the world, and their assumptions will be exposed, their power will be subverted, and the world emancipated."[52] Expose/Subvert/Emancipate: the inextricable link among these three

[50] Immanuel Kant, *Critique of Judgment*, trans. J. H. Bernard (New York: Hafner Press, 1951), 88.

[51] This argument has been put forth brilliantly by Terry Eagleton: "As a kind of terror, the sublime crushes us into admiring submission; it thus resembles a coercive rather than a consensual power, engaging our respect but not, as with beauty, our love. . . . The distinction between the beautiful and the sublime, then, is that between woman and man; but it is also the difference between what Louis Althusser had called the ideological and repressive state apparatuses." *The Ideology of the Aesthetic* (Oxford: Basil Blackwell, 1990), 54–55.

[52] Richard Price, *A Discourse on the Love of Our Country*, 2d ed. (Dublin, 1790), 18–19.

activities, the automatic passage from representation to subversion to liberation, was assumed not only by Price but by nearly everyone invested in the democratic project. "In the representative system," Paine himself would argue, "the reason for everything must publicly appear. . . . There is no place for mystery; nowhere for it to begin" (184). The final plate of *Jerusalem* begins by declaring "All Human Forms Identified" (99:1). The phrase may seem oddly repressive and totalizing to us, but set in its political context, it clearly indicates Blake's belief that everything must be represented before power can be subverted and emancipation can occur.

In the first few years of the 1790s, the immediate political analogue of this rivalry between the beautiful and the sublime was the debate over the English Constitution. Following Burke, the conservatives assumed that the Constitution transcended representation, that it belonged to the realm of "autonomous ideas," as Olivia Smith has put it, or to a metaphysical order, God's "Logos," in Steven Blakemore's phrase.[53] The Constitution had nothing to do with a particular written document and everything to do with "the order of things." When Coleridge addressed the issue years later in "Church and State," he opposed the English Constitution to both a democratic republic and an absolute monarchy, since each of these forms of government makes the mistake of delegating all its power at all times. "Nothing is left obscure, nothing suffered to remain in the Idea, unevolved and only acknowledged as an existing, yet indeterminable Right. A Constitution such states can scarcely be said to possess."[54] The English Constitution holds some of its power in reserve, in a realm of pure and mystical spirit that exceeds any reduction to representation.

According to Paine, however, without a written constitution, England

[53] Olivia Smith develops this idea in relation to Paine's sedition trial: "During Paine's trial for writing Part Two, the Attorney-General objected to Paine's discussion of the constitution, not only because Paine scorned the thing itself, but also because he thought of the word with too much historical specificity. While Paine discussed the constitution as an identifiable object which had been shaped by the historical process and the needs of various social groups, the Attorney-General presented it as an autonomous idea. The sense he conveyed of it, as changing according to its own life rather than human interference, was common to conservative pamphlets of the time. It 'has been growing—not as Mr. Paine would have you believe, from the Norman Conquest—but from time almost eternal,—impossible to trace.'" *The Politics of Language, 1791–1819* (Oxford: Clarendon, 1984), 44–45. Steven Blakemore writes that Burke thought of the constitutions as "reaffirming a world order, as if they were also separate clauses, separate paragraphs, in one essential corpus reaffirming forever God's order and Logos." *Burke and the Fall of Language: The French Revolution as Linguistic Event* (Hanover, N.H.: University Press of New England, 1988), 17.

[54] Coleridge, *On the Constitution of Church and State*, in *The Collected Works of Samuel Taylor Coleridge*, 16 vols., ed. Kathleen Coburn (Princeton: Princeton University Press, 1976), 10:96. I thank David Kaiser for pointing out this passage.

could claim no constitution at all: "The continual use of the word *Constitution* in the English Parliament, shows there is none; and that the whole is merely a form of Government without a Constitution, and constituting itself with what powers it pleases. If there were a Constitution, it certainly could be referred to; and the debate on any constitutional point, would terminate by producing the Constitution" (131). Paine's statement appeals to a positivist and pragmatic logic, but scholars have demonstrated that he was in fact substantially altering established definitions, which conformed much more closely to Burke's usage. Johnson's Dictionary defined *constitution* not as a written document but as a "state of being; particular texture of parts; natural qualities."[55] This argument, however, misses the point. As the first phrase quoted indicates, Paine insists that *Constitution* is a usage; no matter how one defines it, it is first and foremost a word. The Constitution is not sublime; it exists neither as an idea nor as a cosmic order beyond representation that can authorize the implementation of power. Underlying Paine's argument is the strategic assumption that language, or more precisely writing, precedes ideas, that any claim to a metaphysics of power rests upon a prior ground of representation, despite the conservatives' attempt to mask this fact and to portray representation as a dangerous innovation. Earlier in *Rights of Man*, before he addresses the issue of the Constitution directly, Paine anticipates himself with a telling analogy: "The American constitutions were to liberty, what a grammar is to language: they define its parts of speech, and practically construct them into syntax" (95). Not only does the analogy create the impression that writing (representation) is the necessary antecedent to liberty, but it also leaves no room in its equation (constitution is to freedom as grammar is to language) for anything that might be considered extralinguistic. Freedom is generated by and consists in representation.[56]

The specific debates about the Constitution or about the beautiful and the sublime are part of a wider phenomenon that touches nearly everything in the revolutionary period. What I have called the rise in the prestige of language, the will to representation as a means of undermining power, signals the emergence of democratic politics, or in terms

[55] See Blakemore, *Burke and the Fall of Language*, especially pages 5–6 and 10, and Smith, 44.

[56] Mitchell provides an excellent discussion of the constitution debate, which he argues established "the battle lines between the conservative oral tradition and the radical faith in the demotic power of printing and 'visible language'" ("Visible Language," 54). Mitchell also suggests the ways in which Blake subtly positioned himself between "radical and conservative views of writing" (61), refusing the romantic fetishization of the ineffable and the hidden, but also critiquing the exaggerated and coercive rationalism of the philosophes which eventually took political form in the Terror. In this way, as I will argue below, his strategies lie closest to those of Paine.

more consistent with those of François Furet, it *constitutes* the emergence of democratic politics. Furet has argued that the French Revolution created neither capitalism nor bourgeois culture, which were well under way without the Revolution. It did, however, create what he calls "democratic culture": "It was the beginning of what has ever since been called 'politics,' that is, a common yet contradictory language of debate and action around the central issue of power."[57] Politics came into being as a sharp proliferation of verbal production. Lynn Hunt has shown that the Revolution was accompanied in France by "a deluge of words, in print, in conversations, and in political meetings"; to cite just one of her examples, the number of periodicals grew from but a few dozen in Paris in the 1780s to more than five hundred by summer 1792.[58] Those familiar with the pamphlet war of the early 1790s know that something comparable occurred in England. The significance of the British "deluge of words" was felt by all parties involved, a fact indicated by the urgency with which the writers discussed the very propriety of political discussion. In England, debate itself often became the subject of debate. Samuel Horsley engaged in an already lost cause by the time he felt compelled to condemn "the freedom of dispute, in which, for several years past, it hath been the folly in this country to indulge, upon matters of such high importance as the origin of Government, and the authority of Sovereigns."[59] Authority had already been made a matter of representation, a rivalry of words. Republicans did not have to speak directly of emptying power into language (though Paine would do so explicitly in his critique of apocalypse a few years later). They enacted it by writing.

Although he was not the only one to recognize it, Paine seemed to understand most comprehensively that representation had an importance beyond the shape that a particular government should take. It was not until *Age of Reason* that he developed a formal principle to explain how representation undermines the imposition of authority and guarantees

---

[57] François Furet, *Interpreting the French Revolution,* trans. Elborg Forster (Cambridge: Cambridge University Press, 1981), 26.

[58] Lynn Hunt, *Politics, Culture, and Class in the French Revolution* (Berkeley: University of California Press, 1984), 19.

[59] Samuel Horsley: "A Sermon" (1793), in *Burke, Paine, Godwin, and the Revolution Controversy,* ed. Marilyn Butler (Cambridge: Cambridge University Press, 1984), 143. Blakemore makes the basis of his book the realization that "the debate over revolution and counterrevolution was often about the very meaning of [the traditional European world] and the language that sustained it. . . . It is this special linguistic self-consciousness that shapes their vision of the Revolution as, among other things, an astonishing linguistic event" (1–2). While Blakemore is absolutely right that the ideological battle was fought on the terrain of language, he underestimates the extent to which this very fact tipped the long-term balance in favor of the radicals.

a diffusion of power, but the role played by representation in his writing was evident the moment he decided to respond to Burke. Simply by responding, Paine and others achieved something of a victory. Burke's magisterial sublime had meant to awe the opposition into silence, but it quickly became obvious that his was not the only word. As soon as the Revolution became a matter of dialogue, it ceased to be a monolithic event; it consisted instead of competing interpretations. By offering what amounted to a representation of the Revolution, Burke did not close the linguist field; he opened it. In a fashion characteristic of the republicans, Joseph Priestley realized that Burke's own strategy of a written defense of the monarchy created an advantage for his opponents. In one of his public letters to Burke he first quotes the *Reflections*, "it has been our misfortune, and not, as these gentlemen think it, the glory, of this age, that everything must be discussed," and then wryly adds, "certainly such a publication as this of yours . . . must lead to much discussion."[60] In much the same way, Paine suggests that he would never have written *Rights of Man* without Burke's written provocation; Burke's "misrepresentations" of events made it necessary (35). The brilliance of Paine's strategy is that he need not convince his audience he is right in order to advance his cause; all he need do is make his readers uncertain, make them suspect that political and historical events are capable of alternative representations motivated by conflicting interests. By dissolving history and political philosophy into a multiplicity of voices, the debate already performs the fundamental activity of democratic culture; to the extent that Burke merely gets his "fair say," he forfeits his power.

As a practitioner of the "new" history, Furet has contended that, since events themselves are inaccessible, any reading of the French Revolution must be an interpretation of other interpretations. What matters is the way participants or later historians perceived and structured events. Claude Lefort adds the interesting twist that this adherence to a metacritical method was promoted by the Revolution itself; Furet works within the very conditions established by the historical moment he studies. Metacriticism itself is an instance of democratic politics at work; it subjects entities that might be considered closed or static—history, power, social status, language—to the open-endedness and indeterminacy of discourse.[61] When Paine refers to Burke's account of the October arrests at Versailles as "tragic paintings," merely rhetorical flourishes "calculated for theatrical representation," when he reminds

[60] Joseph Priestley, *Letters to the Right Hon. Edmund Burke*, 3d ed. (Birmingham: Thomas Pearson, 1791), Letter VI, 50.

[61] See especially part 1 of Furet's *Interpreting the French Revolution*, and Claude Lefort's "Interpreting Revolution within the French Revolution," in *Democracy and Political Theory*, trans. David Macey (Minneapolis: University of Minnesota Press, 1988), 89–114.

Burke that "he is writing history, and not *Plays*" (49), Paine not only anticipates modern theoretical assumptions regarding the positivist fallacy, he recognizes their immediate importance as democratic practices. Again, what matters most is not so much Paine's ability to persuade a reader that his history is unmotivated and therefore "real" but his ability to make clear that all history is narrative. Most of *Rights of Man* is given over to retelling the stories Burke told in the *Reflections*—the events leading up to 14 July, the taking of the Bastille itself, the October arrests. Accompanying this production of competing narratives is an ongoing emphasis on the constructed nature of all social experience, the way power secures itself by simultaneously manipulating representations and denying their status as representations: "It would seem, by the exterior appearance of such countries, that all was happiness; but there lies hidden from the eye of common observation, a mass of wretchedness that has scarcely any other chance, than to expire in poverty or infamy" (218); and "A vast mass of mankind are degradedly thrown into the background of the human picture, to bring forward with greater glare, the puppet show of state and aristocracy" (59). Those in power dictate what appears in the social picture, though the passive construction of the second sentence quoted indicates that power can deftly efface its agency in producing such representations. Controlling the means of representation, power erases the dispossessed while making itself seem preternaturally visible. Passages such as these prepare the way for Paine's frontal assault on the monarchy, that it is a mere show which might be represented otherwise: "Certain it is, that what is called monarchy, always appears to me a silly, contemptible thing. I compare it to something kept behind a curtain, about which there is a great deal of bustle and fuss, and a wonderful air of seeming solemnity; but when, by any accident, the curtain happens to be open, and the company see what it is, they burst into laughter" (182).

Paine's argument that the monarchy amounts merely to representation plays on Burke's own rhetorical appeals, which made quite clear the relation between the court's authority and its ability to produce moving spectacles. By calling attention to the monarch's theatrical aura, Burke suggested that its charismatic power, though temporarily threatened, was essentially secure; given the choice, people would always prefer a glorious medieval fiction to reality. But Paine does not quite oppose reality to the master spectacle. He instead invites the reader to participate in the production of representations that has always been the exclusive domain of the court: "The representative system of government," he explains in the paragraph following the one quoted above, "presents itself on *the open theater of the world*" (my emphasis). Paine accepts as a given that the world *is* representation; to see that this is the case, as Burke himself had already helped readers to see, was to move one step closer to the realization that the world is not a closed representation but instead is a matter of different performances reflecting different interests without any static or determinate meaning. Democratic government consists no less of representation than aristocratic government does; it simply opens its theater to more players and openly acknowledges its constructed status.

The Nature of Representation: From Apocalypse to Discourse

In her work on the Victorian novel, Catherine Gallagher has demonstrated that "a single tradition of thought about representation . . . persists throughout the nineteenth century" and that its earliest articulation appears in the writings of Coleridge. This tradition connects politics and verbal or literary meaning through a concept of "symbolic representation"; it is also both transcendentalist and distinctly antidemocratic. Because Coleridge feared the capitalist self-interest barely masked by an increasingly powerful utilitarian philosophy, he felt that the state should represent not the aggregate desires of the people below but the realm of metaphysical ideas and eternal values above. "Political meaning, like all meaning," writes Gallagher, "descends from higher and rarer, through representative symbols, to the lower and more numerous; it is not built up, as in the liberal model, from the facts, the political constituents representing themselves in the descriptive microcosm of Parliament."[62] In reference to this model, Paine decisively anticipates the liberal camp, building up representation from empirical facts, urging his readers to pull aside the curtain of rhetoric to see things "as they are," and always appealing to material nature as a readily visible and sure ground of value. Blake, on the other hand, shares with Coleridge the characteristic romantic desire to keep open a channel to "transcendental reality" through the symbol.

This distinction between descriptive and symbolic representation, which Hannah Pitkin discusses in great detail in *The Concept of Representation*, helps to place Blake and Paine in reference to what surely becomes a dominant nineteenth-century tradition in English politics and aesthetics, the one that leads straight to Arnold.[63] It does not, however, help us understand what Blake, a sometimes transcendentalist, and Paine, a sometimes empiricist, share as 1790s writers—how they are

---

[62] Gallagher, *Industrial Reformation of English Fiction*, 187–95.
[63] See especially chaps. 4–5 of Hannah Pitkin, *The Concept of Representation* (Berkeley: University of California Press, 1967).

united by a distinctly democratic practice of representation that lies just outside or beneath the polarity Gallagher identifies.[64] In order to explain their similarity, which goes beyond a mere republican sympathy and enters into some characteristic textual strategies, one must alter the very terms of the discussion; one must shift from a transcendentalist/empiricist orientation, which emphasizes the capacity of representation to provide access to truth (no matter how differently defined), to an orientation that emphasizes the capacity of representation to resist truth by opening it up to skeptical interrogation.[65] For Blake and Paine, this "deconstructive" practice of representation serves as a common counterweight to transcendentalism and empiricism respectively.[66] In the 1790s, this practice is hardly a well-defined tradition of the type Gallagher describes as dominant in the nineteenth century, but it is already a significant undercurrent, which itself eventually becomes dominant. It is this "undercurrent," after all, that anticipates our own conjunction of poststructuralist theory and pluralist, democratic politics. The antidemocratic model of representation Gallagher discusses may

[64] J. F. C. Harrison notes how consistently one finds Paine the deist linked to the seemingly opposite strain of radicalism to which Blake belonged—millenarianism: "If we dig into the history of popular radicalism almost anywhere before 1850, the chances are good that we shall unearth millenarian as well as Paineite references." "Thomas Paine and Millenarian Radicalism," in *Citizen of the World: Essays on Thomas Paine*, ed. Ian Dyck (New York: St. Martin's, 1988), 83.

[65] Gallagher acknowledges that many critics—Paul de Man, Frances Ferguson, Jerome Christensen among them—have already made this shift in orientation the characteristic theme of Coleridge studies. Such critics argue that Coleridge is unable to maintain his distinctions between symbol and allegory, and thus cannot "maintain his belief in the existence of eternal and transparent representations." Gallagher goes on to suggest that what is inadvertent and implicit in Coleridge becomes an explicit concern in Carlyle, who introduces "a gap between the symbol and its meanings as well as the possibility of the ironic degeneration of symbols" (195). I wish to suggest that this explicit concern, along with a set of *positive* political implications, was already a significant undercurrent of first-generation romantic writing.

[66] Florence Sandler, in " 'Defending the Bible': Blake, Paine, and the Bishop," offers a useful "reconstruction" of the argument between Paine's *Age of Reason* and Bishop Watson's *Apology for the Bible*, as well as Blake's response to that argument, which has been preserved in his annotations to Watson's text. Sandler is certainly right to see in Paine an advocate of the "Natural Theology" Blake despised, but she greatly underestimates the importance of Paine's refusal to impose his own beliefs: (1) his argument for an inviolable individualism—"My own mind is my own church" (*Age of Reason*, 8)—that Blake himself endorses, and (2) his proposal that representation protect against authority, something Blake himself practiced. For Sandler, Blake must finally have recognized in Paine "another Analytical Angel who would impose his phantasy." In *Blake and His Bibles*, ed. David Erdman (West Cornwall, Conn.: Locust Hill Press, 1990), 43. It is possible, however, that Blake saw something quite the opposite. See, for instance, Jerome McGann's very different account, in which Paine stands not only for an Enlightenment suspicion of received authority, including that of the Bible, but also for the primacy of individual conscience in matters of judgment. *Social Values and Poetic Acts*, 163.

find contemporary proponents in the cultural literacy camp, but it is the model of representation evolved out of the practices of Blake and Paine that wields "power" in current academic discourse.

To argue that Paine, despite his own empiricist longings, develops a deconstructive practice of representation is to argue against the widely accepted idea that Paine employed "an instrumental theory of language," that he believed "language is merely the vehicle for conveying knowledge and information."[67] Despite some growing recognition that Paine was as rhetorically astute as his adversary Burke, no one has acknowledged the extent to which his concern with representation undermines his image as a simple empiricist, let alone the political function it served in his campaign for representative government.[68] *Rights of Man,* I have argued, is on many levels a practical demonstration of the ubiquity of representation and of the principle that no single representation can assume authority over others on an a priori basis. And yet, what Paine seemed to understand as a fundamental premise of democratic culture was never directly expounded until he turned from a deliberation on government to one on religion.

In 1794, at the height of the Revolution controversy, Paine wrote his blunt but masterly critique of revealed religion, *Age of Reason.* According to the common explanation for this shift in targets, Paine grew increasingly disillusioned with the Revolution as it evolved into the Terror. He lost his hard-fought battle in the Assembly to save the life of Louis XVI, and as the Girondins lost their influence, he saw most of his friends imprisoned and ultimately guillotined. Thus Paine's turn from politics to religion, from a defense of democracy to a defense of deism, marked a desire to help restore the Revolution's original humanist principles. "The people of France were running headlong into atheism," he wrote to Samuel Adams, "and I had the work translated and published in their own language to stop them in that career, and fix them to the first article (as I have before said) of any man's creed who has any creed at all, *I believe in God.*" Paine himself was arrested the day he finished his book.[69] Despite these circumstances, *Age of Reason* is not an abandonment of politics for either the cheap rewards of priest-baiting or the platitudes of deistic faith; it is at once an extension of his attack on aristocratic

---

67 Blakemore, *Burke and the Fall of Language,* 79.

68 Butler notes that Paine "has only recently been taken seriously as a master of prose." *Burke, Paine, Godwin, and the Revolution Controversy,* p. 108. See also Smith, *Politics of Language,* chap. 2.

69 See Jerome D. Wilson and William F. Ricketson, *Thomas Paine* (New York: Twayne, 1978), 103, and George Spater, "European Revolutionary," in *Citizen of the World: Essays on Thomas Paine,* ed. Ian Dyck (New York: St. Martin's, 1988), 61.

government and a masked repudiation of his more immediate nemesis, Robespierre.[70] Moreover, it is Paine's most urgent plea for the necessity of representation. The driving concern of *Age of Reason* is to undermine the authority of any voice that claims to be identical to power, any voice, that is, which asserts its hold on an empowering truth by bypassing the intervention of representation. To demonstrate the necessary role of representation in acts of resistance, Paine applies its principles to a linguistic form that generates its power by claiming to transcend representation—the text of biblical apocalypse—but, as we will see, his eyes are always on Burke and Robespierre.

In many respects, *Age of Reason* is nothing more than a derivative popularization of eighteenth-century assaults on the Bible as literal history. Paine's chapter-by-chapter dismantling of sacred texts begins, however, with something genuinely new: a principle of subversive reading unavailable before the emergence of democratic discourse but central ever since. After explaining that all official religions ground their authority in one sort of revelation or another, Paine begins, with his inimitable clarity, to define revelation and to outline its consequences:

Revelation, when applied to religion, means something communicated *immediately* from God to man.

No one will deny or dispute the power of the Almighty to make such a communication, if he pleases. But admitting, for the sake of a case, that something has been revealed to a certain person, and not revealed to any other person, it is revelation to that person only. When he tells it to a second person, a second to a third, a third to a fourth, and so on, it ceases to be a revelation to all those persons. It is revelation to the first person only, and *hearsay* to every other person, and consequently they are not obliged to believe it.

It is a contradiction in terms and ideas, to call anything a revelation that comes to us at second-hand, either verbally or in writing. Revelation is necessarily limited to the first communication—after this, it is only an account of something which that person says was a revelation made to him; and though he may find himself obliged to believe it, it cannot be

---

[70] By emphasizing the strength of the Anglican Church in producing England's dominant eighteenth-century ideology, J. C. D. Clarke has helped explain the logic of Paine's turn from explicitly political matters to a critique of religion. "The theological basis of monarchical claims meant that republicanism and anticlericalism were logically linked"; "as Paine committed himself more and more bitterly against European regimes which defined themselves ever more clearly in religious terms, the element of theological heterodoxy assumed an even greater prominence in his work." *English Society, 1688–1832*, 292, 328.

incumbent on me to believe it in the same manner; for it was not a revelation made to *me*, and I have only his word for it that it was made to him.[71]

In what has become a central, if not the central, assumption of representative democracy, words protect us from the imposition of authority; when revelation passes through representation, it loses its hold on its potential subjects. If words thus intervene between us and power, they can do so precisely because in Paine's linguistic practice words are not simply transparent, the verbal equivalent of empiricism. For Paine language means discourse; it is necessarily mediated by contingencies that make it partial, limited, interested, and therefore variable according to speakers and circumstances. If language were unmediated by cultural factors, then revelation could retain a universal authority, then John's claim in the Book of Revelation that he merely records without loss the voice and visions of Christ would at least be plausible. By foregrounding the failings inherent in any verbal transmission, Paine circumscribes revelation so tightly that without ever denying the possibility of its existence he renders it harmless. In a way thoroughly compatible with Blake's art, he introduces the right to suspicion, insisting that the "fallen" nature of human language, what Burke derided as "the confused jargon of . . . Babylonian pulpits," releases us from an obligation to believe and thus ensures our right to dispute the claims of power.[72] No one ever so relished the obstacles to a determinate text: "The continually progressive change to which the meaning of words is subject, the want of a universal language which renders translation necessary, the errors to which translations are again subject, the mistakes of copyists and printers, together with the possibility of willful alteration, are of themselves evidences that the human language, whether in speech or in print, cannot be the vehicle of the word of God" (24). To put the matter simply, our contingencies, our linguistic imperfections, set us free. The very fact that we have interests, that our thoughts and our words are irresistibly informed by the accidents of local circumstance, makes an airtight communication of revelation impossible.[73] If, as Blakemore has argued,

[71] Thomas Paine, *Age of Reason* (New York: Pantheon, 1984), 9–10. Further references are to this edition.

[72] Burke's phrase appears in the following sentence from the *Reflections:* "We, on our parts, have learned to speak only the primitive language of the law, and not the confused jargon of their Babylonian pulpits." *Reflections on the Revolution in France,* vol. 3 of *The Works of Edmund Burke,* 9th ed., 12 vols. (St. Claire Shores, Mich.: Scholarly Press, 1965), 269.

[73] Paine does argue that nature is available in an unmediated fashion, that it is "an everexisting original, which every man can read." Nature thus represents a kind of transpersonal source of meaning, since through it God "speaks universally," without "human intervention." And yet, according to Paine's logic, natural perception must eventually go

Burke conceptually and metaphorically organized his discourse around the messianic triumph of the Logos over Babel, Paine organizes his around the counterapocalyptic resistance to the Logos by Babel.[74]

Age of Reason begins, then, by outlining a method of verbally disabling power that lies at the heart of the representative democratic project. This in no way, however, explains the urgency or the specificity of the text. Paine finished his book 27 January 1794, the day he was arrested by Robespierre's Committee for Public Safety. That very day, Bertrand Barère, speaking for the same committee, delivered a report to the National Assembly on the need to make French the universal language of the nation. This report, which proposed to install a teacher of French in every "département" where the common people spoke "un idiome étranger" (348), marked the culmination at that point of what Patrice Higonnet has called the unfolding of the Revolution's "linguistic terrorism."[75] In the early days of the Republic, the Assembly was marked by an unusual tolerance of France's widespread linguistic diversity—Breton, German, Italian, and Basque were spoken in various border regions, and nearly thirty distinct dialects, or "patois," made the French language itself an internal hybrid. Between 1790 and 1793 the Convention often weighed the necessity of translating its laws and decrees against the practical inconvenience and ideological irritation of doing so, but by the fall of 1793 nationalist momentum was building for declaring French the Republic's sole and official language.[76] In December, Paine was removed from the Assembly by a motion that denied foreigners participation in the government, and the January report of Barère not only decided that all government communication would henceforth appear only in French but also pronounced foreign languages and internal dialects the practice of "contre-révolutionnaires" (349). Barère's suspicion of the German speakers in eastern France carried significance for

the same path of mediation that revelation does; while nature "does not depend upon the will of man whether it shall be published or not," the communication of any sensory perception certainly does depend on such intervention. *Age of Reason*, 32.

[74] According to Blakemore, Burke's "controlling metaphor for this sinister new language is that of Babel, and Babel becomes the symbol and metaphor for all the insane chaos and confusion that threatens to darken and destroy the established 'written' monuments of civilization" (*Burke and the Fall of Language*, 91). These written monuments, in turn, "reflect and mime the cosmic ordering of the Logos" (102).

[75] The entire text of Barère's report can be found in *Procès-Verbaux du Comité D'Instruction Publique de la Convention Nationale*, ed. M. J. Guillaume, Tome IV of *Collection de Documents Inédits Sur L'Histoire de France* (Paris: Imprimerie Nationale, 1897), 4:3, 348–55. Further references are to this text; I have provided literal translations for extended passages.

[76] For an outline of these events, see Patrice L.-R. Higonnet, "The Politics of Linguistic Terrorism and Grammatical Hegemony during the French Revolution," *Social History* 5 (January 1980): 42.

anyone who, like Paine, spoke "un idiome étranger": "N'est-ce pas l'ha-
bitant des campagnes qui parle la même langue que nos ennemis, et qui
se croit ainsi bien plus leur frère et leur concitoyen, que le frère et le
citoyen des Français qui lui parlent une autre langue et qui ont d'autres
habitudes? [Isn't it the inhabitant of these regions who speaks the same
language as our enemies, and who thus believes himself more their
brother and compatriot than the brother and compatriot of the French
people who speak to him in another tongue and who possess different
habits?]" (351). English too, of course, was an enemy language; Barère
singles it out at the end of his report as "l'idiome d'un gouvernement
tyrannique et exécrable" (355), despite the fact that English was spoken
in no region of France. This movement toward the erasure of linguistic
diversity, which built up to the day of both Paine's arrest and Barère's
report, must have been particularly hard on Paine, one of whose conspicuous difficulties in the Assembly had always been his minimal knowledge of French.[77] On the very day the Assembly legislated the end of
written translation, Paine finished a dissenting book that he then arranged to have translated into French, a book moreover that describes
translation as an imperfection mandated by the inherent and untranscendable diversity of language: "The want of a universal language . . .
makes translation necessary."

The relation of Barère's report to the defense of imperfect representation in *Age of Reason* is even more striking than I have thus far indicated, especially concerning Paine's critique of apocalyptic revelation.
One takes for granted the millenarian inclinations of the National Assembly, which after all felt perfectly comfortable ending history and
declaring the day one, year one of an unprecedented era. And as we
have seen before, the desire for a universal language is commonly an
apocalyptic desire. Early in his report, Barère describes the history of the
French language as a providential narrative, which moves from a corrupt and fallen multiplicity that divides the nation to "une plus belle
destinée" (350)—a redemption characterized by social and linguistic
unity: "les hommes libres se ressemblent tous, et l'accent vigoureux de la
liberté et de l'égalité est le même [free men are all alike, and the vigorous
accent of liberty and equality is the same]" (350). Barère's logic here is
clearly that which Irigaray calls the logic of "le même," the teleological
desire to eradicate difference, to produce a homogenous social space
free of contradiction.[78] The confirmation of this undifferentiated social

---

[77] Like Paine, Joseph Priestley had been elected to the National Assembly in 1792, but
unlike Paine, he declined the invitation, offering as one excuse the fact that his French was
inadequate. See Clarke Garrett, *Respectable Folly* (Baltimore: Johns Hopkins University
Press, 1975).

[78] "Now, this domination of the philosophic logos stems in large part from its power to
reduce all others to the economy of the Same. The teleologically constructive project it takes on is

space, its very embodiment, becomes the extension of one language "sur toute la surface de la République [over the entire surface of the Republic]" (354), an extension that mirrors the victory of the self-identical Logos over Babel/Babylon in the paradigm established by Revelation. According to Barère, the time of linguistic difference is over, ended apocalyptically by the Revolution; all that remains is the spatial dissemination of the universal language. In this model, Paris becomes the expanding geographical center of the Logos. The linguistic dissenters, already literally marginalized, remain only at the borders of the Republic, "quelques frontières," where their differences might easily be erased: Barère speaks of "les idiomes étrangers ou barbares que nous aurions dû faire disparaître [the foreign or primitive idioms that we ought to make vanish]" (351). Not surprisingly, Barère hints at even a global destiny for French, since it is the language "chargée de transmettre au monde les plus sublimes pensées de la liberté [charged with transmitting to the world the most sublime thoughts of liberty]" (349).

Oddly enough, Barère's fantasy of one word for all reverses the roles of a conventional apocalyptic narrative convenient to power without altering the narrative's structure at all. While Burke defends the Logos of the monarchy against "the Babylonian pulpits" of the Revolution, Barère defends the Logos of the Revolution against the Babel of the ancien régime:

Dans la monarchie même, chaque maison, chaque commune, chaque province, etait en quelque sort un empire séparé de moeurs, d'usages, de lois, de coutumes et de langages. Le despote avait besoin d'isoler les peuples, de séparer les pays, de diviser les interêts, d'empecher les communications, d'arrêter la simultanéité des pensées et l'identité des mouvements. Le despotisme maintenant la variété des idiomes; une monarchie doit resembler à la tour de Babel; il n'y a qu'une langue universelle pour le tyran, celle de force. . . .

Les lois d'une République supposent une attention singulière de tous les citoyens les uns les autres, et une surveillance constante sur l'observation des lois et sur la conduite des fonctionnaires publics. Peut-on se la promettre dans la confusion des langues, dans la négligence de la premiere éducation du peuple, dans l'ignorance des citoyens? (354)

[During that same monarchy, each house, each community, each province, was in some sense a world separate in morals, usages, laws, customs, and languages. The despot needed to isolate the peoples, to separate the

---

always also a project of diversion, deflection, reduction of the other in the Same." Luce Irigaray, *This Sex Which Is Not One*, trans. Catherine Porter (Ithaca: Cornell University Press, 1985), 74.

regions, to divide interests, prevent communications, arrest the simultaneity of thoughts and the identity of movements. Despotism maintains a
variety of idioms; a monarchy has to resemble a tower of Babel; the only
universal language for the tyrant is force. . . .

The laws of a Republic suppose a single attention of all the citizens to
each other, and a constant surveillance regarding both the observation of
the laws and the conduct of public officers. Can one carry this out among
the confusion of tongues, in the neglect of the primary education of the
people, in the ignorance of the citizens?]

In this context, the specific strategy of *Age of Reason*, which is a linguistic
or hermeneutic strategy, becomes more apparent. Caught between the
Logos of Burke and the Logos of the Revolutionary Terror, Paine found
himself in the position of defending the confusion of tongues, offering
up Babel as the political means necessary to deflect the imposition of
power and to defer the apocalyptic moment when difference succumbs
to an imperial identity. It is remarkable how directly (if inversely) Paine's
investment in the protection of a "fallen" representation corresponds to
Barère's vision of a flawed linguistic state that must be transcended.
Indeed, Paine's language of democratic representation is exactly that
which Barère attributes to the deposed monarchy: it is divided among
conflicting interests and idioms, it prevents transparent communication,
and it resists any appeal to a "simultanéité des pensées" that bypasses
linguistic interference. In "la tour de Babel" lies freedom.[79]

Age of Reason, of course, is not a direct response to the Barère report;
the two are simultaneous. It is, however, a veiled but head-on confrontation with the Terror which made Barère's report inevitable and even
predictable. In its introduction, *Age of Reason* purports to defend the
"theology that is true" against the widening sweep of atheism, but it also
suggests an ulterior and specifically political motive: "All national institutions of churches," Paine states as he begins his description of
church authority, "appear to me no other than human inventions, set up

---

[79] The culmination of linguistic terrorism came shortly before the fall of Robespierre
with the Abbé Grégoire's report to the Assembly on 4 June 1794. Grégoire extended
Barère's assault on foreign languages into one against the patois, reporting on "la nécessité
et les moyens d'annéantir les patois et d'universaliser la langue Francaise [the necessity and
the means of destroying the patois and of universalizing the French tongue]." Again, the
contrast to Paine's approach to language could not be greater. Grégoire, feeling that the
present state of French led to many errors in communication, suggested several proposals
for perfecting the language: correcting and standardizing spelling, fixing "d'equivoques et
d'incertitudes [equivocations and uncertainties]," creating both a new grammar and a new
dictionary, eliminating irregular verbs and grammatical exceptions generally, and so on.
Procès-Verbaux du Comité D'Instruction Publique de la Convention Nationale, ed. Guillaume,
4:3, 494–95.

to terrify and enslave mankind, and monopolize power and profit" (7–8). "Terrify," especially in conjunction with the phrase "monopolize power," is an unmistakable buzzword. The Terror, one must remember, was public policy, openly advocated by that name in the National Assembly. At great risk to a man momentarily expecting incarceration and probably even execution, Paine implies by his statement that democratic government in France in 1794 is simply another form of church tyranny, concentrating a coercive power into a centralized authority and thus reversing the true basis of democracy, which diffuses power across conflicting sites. As Paine could acknowledge openly in the introduction to part 2, published in 1795 after his release from prison, *Age of Reason* was occasioned by his realization that "the intolerant spirit of Church persecutions had transferred itself into politics" (73). The critique of revelation as the ground of religious authority, then, is also a critique of revelation as the ground of political authority. Even more important, both critiques are enabled by the same form of resistance—representation.

Paine's dispute with Robespierre and the Terror went well beyond the issue of linguistic diversity; it went straight to the nature of democracy itself. Barère's proposal that French become a universal language was but one symptom of a much larger question regarding democracy and representation: are these two terms identical, or does democracy mean the transcendence of representation altogether? Paine's understanding came straight from his Anglo-American roots: as Higonnet asserts, he "wrote of republicanism and not of democracy, or—heaven forbid— social democracy."[80] Even more than his status as a foreigner, it was the belief in representation rather than direct popular rule that jeopardized his standing and that of other moderate republicans in France when the Revolution turned into the Terror. The Jacobins were able to seize power in Paris mainly because of *their opposition to representation,* because of their claim to embody *immediately* "the will of the people." The most radical assumption of the Terror, an assumption which far exceeded any such claims for popular power in America, was that the people could govern themselves directly without any mediation between them and power. Political representation, according to this view, lay closer to the old system of government than to the new; it simply reorganized an arbitrary and elite power without genuinely redistributing it. Legislators differed from kings in degree, not kind; they still ruled the people, who still obeyed. The only legitimate means of empowering the people lay in doing away with political representation altogether, in making the peo-

---

[80] Higonnet, *Sister Republics,* 190. Higonnet's lively comparative study of the two revolutions illustrates many of the differences between Jacobin democracy and the American model of representative government.

ple themselves identical to power. The fierce political struggles of 1793 and 1794 that led to the ascent of Robespierre involved each rival party's desperate assertion that it alone embodied rather than represented "the people."

Jacobin democracy is thus a politics inseparable from a set of linguistic premises, premises that differ sharply from those involved in either the American Revolution or British radicalism. In its widest significance, Barère's advocacy of a universal language reflects a desire to be free of language entirely, at least free of language as we know it, as we experience its inherent limitations in history. The universalization of French is merely one synecdoche for the Terror's governing ideal of social transparency. As Hunt has argued, the Assembly's fixation on national unity expresses "the revolutionary belief in the possibility and desirability of 'transparency' between citizen and citizen, between the citizens and their government, between the individual and the general will" (44). Barère manifests this belief when he sets "la confusion des langues [the confusion of tongues]" against an ideal of "la simultanéité des pensées [the simultaneity of thoughts]" or "une attention singulière de tous les citoyens les uns les autres [a single attention of all the citizens to each other]." Building on an obviously logocentric model, the Terror marked an attempt to govern without the mediating functions typically served by representation and made necessary by social differences: "It [the Terror] was not conceived as the arbiter of conflicting interests (agriculture vs. commerce, for example), but rather as the mechanism for ensuring that individual wills were forged into one, single, general, or national will" (Hunt, 47).

Paine's suspicion of revelation in the opening pages of *Age of Reason* is precisely a suspicion of social and linguistic transparency: "Revelation is necessarily limited to the first communication—after this, it is only an account of something which that person says was a revelation made to him." Addressed covertly to the Jacobin Tribunal, this says, "you claim to speak directly the will of the people, but neither I nor anyone else am obliged to believe your words." Robespierre had merely inverted the Book of Revelation; his unmediated inspiration came not from God above but from the people below. In either case, authority was generated by asserting one's access to (or even identity with) an absolute and total source of power. By disallowing the possibility of transparency, representation served two functions for Paine: it collapsed Robespierre's voice back into the multiplicity of social voices, into the welter of party or individual interests the Jacobins had claimed to transcend; and it denied the very existence of a single, self-identical national voice that could will the exercise of power. For Paine and like-minded republicans, power in any hands was dangerous; it could be justified under no circumstances.

Power had to be negated perpetually, and such negation could only be accomplished by exploiting inherent social and linguistic differences, by making the lack of a universal community the basis of liberation. Representation thus becomes the means by which diverse people simultaneously form a government and free themselves from coercive attempts to render them a single, uniform entity—"the people."

Paine's critique of revelation in *Age of Reason* exposes the irony that made the Terror so precarious: while the Terror attempted to ground authority in an autonomous and extralinguistic source, it could do so only through increasingly theatrical rhetoric. It persisted only so long as its orators could defend it. "The people," after all, was nothing but a verbal representation that could be sustained only on the crest of rhetoric. It "had no objective existence at the social level," as Furet points out; "it was but a *mental representation of the social sphere* that permeated and dominated the field of politics" (63). "The people" had to be created in words, and the process of creating "the people" became the burden of the Revolution's cultural dimension—the symbols, rituals, and staged spectacles that, as recent scholars have demonstrated, played a significant role in the unfolding of events. Higonnet suggests that even the campaign for a national language was an attempt to produce an image of social unity that would compensate for the real social contradictions (differences in private property) the Revolution could not (and never fully tried to) erase.[81] Of course the greatest irony of the Terror was that legislators who can only be called political representatives were the ones declaring the end of representation, producing resonant slogans like "Le peuple seul est souverain." "Exaltation of the people," Edmund Morgan writes, "can be a means of controlling *them*."[82] This inescapable paradox brought on what Hunt calls the Assembly's "crisis of representation" (88), an ongoing quandary that she finds epitomized in the problems the Assembly incurred when it attempted to use Hercules as a

[81] "The real rationale of linguistic terrorism lay in the desperate efforts of the bourgeois revolutionaries to reconcile their genuine craving for community or 'moral' equality with their equally serious determination not to give way on the social and economic hierarchy. The persecution of dialects served two ends: first, it could be seen as a genuine step towards a more equal society; second, it diverted attention from more material social problems, like the redistribution of land." Higonnet, "The Politics of Linguistic Terrorism," 49. An alternative point of view is held by R. R. Palmer, who sees the campaign for a national language as a genuine expression of democracy. *The Improvement of Humanity: Education and the French Revolution* (Princeton: Princeton University Press, 1985), 186.

[82] Edmund Morgan, "Government by Fiction: The Idea of Representation," *Yale Review* 72 (April 1983): 323. In his survey of the Anglo-American tradition of political representation, Morgan suggests that "it would perhaps not be too much to say that representatives invented the sovereignty of the people in order to claim it for themselves" (332). The paradox of the Terror was that it resisted this anti-democratic element of representation rhetorically while reproducing it in effect.

symbol for the people: "[Hercules] was an image-representation of the
people provided by the people's representatives, and as such it inherently included the representatives' interpretation of the people. This
implicit interpretive element threatened to reestablish in cultural form
the very relationship of political authority (authority outside the people)
that the radicals were promising to abolish. Thus, even as the image
proclaimed the supremacy of the people, it reintroduced the superiority
of the people's representatives" (100). For Paine, the resistance to power
lay not in transcending this "crisis of representation," and certainly not
in disguising it, but rather in deepening its self-critical tendency, in continuously assuring its visibility. In Paine's version of democratic government, the answer to the crisis of representation is to institutionalize it.

Democratic Government as Text

In *Rights of Man*, when Paine described the actual features of a democratic government, he generally relied on the innovations made by
James Madison four years earlier (1787) in *The Federalist,* during the
campaign to ratify the American Constitution. "By ingrafting representation upon democracy," he wrote, nearly echoing Madison, "we arrive
at a system of government capable of embracing and confederating all
the various interests and every extent of the territory and population"
(180). *Interests,* derived from a French root meaning "to differ," increasingly became a taboo word in France as the Republic advanced
toward the transparency/unity ideal of the Terror, but for Paine it
signified the basis of freedom in social differences, not the least component of which were differences in property.[83] There is no such thing as
disinterested representation for Paine, no ontologically or metaphys-
ically privileged word. In a way that derives from Madison and anticipates Mill, Paine's representative government gives political form to the
"crisis of representation"; it stages the contradictions inherent in the
realm of the social, makes a virtue of a decentralizing plurality, and at
the same time deflects conflict onto the plane of language.

Arnold later saw in representative democracy, with its idea of state
authority as an empty center, a prescription for "anarchy"; concerned
only with negating power and not with articulating universal values, it
fostered the illusion that "we are only safe from one another's tyranny
when no one has any power."[84] Arnold thus lamented precisely what

---

[83] For a history of the word *interest,* see Pitkin, *Concept of Representation,* 157.

[84] Matthew Arnold, *Culture and Anarchy,* ed. J. Dover Wilson (Cambridge: Cambridge
University Press, 1960), 95.

Madison saw as the value of representation in his proposals for the American Constitution. Much as it was for Mill in his "talking function" of government, representation for Madison was a way of giving people a political say without giving them unqualified power. In his famous argument, the sheer size and geographic diversity of the United States guarantee that power will be dissipated with the variety and inevitability of conflict: "Whilst all authority . . . will be derived from and dependent upon the society, the society itself will be broken into so many parts, interests and classes of citizens, that the rights of individuals, or of the minority, will be in little danger from interested combinations of the majority."[85] Madison, like the other federalists, hoped that the Constitution would create a national identity, that the diverse populace would unite around the political principle of popular sovereignty through representation—e pluribus unum—but such unity bore little resemblance to that which the Jacobins would later propose in France. After all, Madison's nation is defined not by a shared essence that makes it a homogenous whole but by its internal fractures, its hybridization, and its intractable particularity (the necessary philosophical counterparts to liberal individualism).[86] Representation then transforms this base of difference into a paradoxically healthy paralysis—or as Pitkin puts it, "the welfare of the nation is achieved by inaction and stability."[87] Madison's most decisive innovation marks an attempt to institutionalize the crisis of representation even further, to embed it deeply and unalterably within the form of democratic government. What is the system of checks and balances, if not a perpetually self-subverting formal mechanism, a way of "contriving the interior structure of the government as that its several constituent parts may, by their mutual relations, be the means of keeping each other in their proper places" (*The Federalist*, 85)?

Seven years later, when Paine built upon Madison's precedent to repudiate the Terror as an apocalyptic text, he demonstrated most clearly the way in which democratic politics had become implicated in

[85] Alexander Hamilton, James Madison, John Jay, *Selections from "The Federalist,"* ed. Henry Steele Commager (New York: Appleton-Century-Crofts, 1949), 88. Further references are to this edition.

[86] Bobbio suggests that liberalism, with its ideal of minimal state power and maximum individual liberty, involves a philosophical commitment to both heterogeneity and particularity on the one hand and the value of conflict on the other: "Associated with its counterposing of individual variety to state-sponsored uniformity, we discover a further original and characteristic theme of liberal thought: the insistence that conflict is fruitful. . . . [W]e find a growing emphasis on the idea that opposition between individuals and groups . . . is beneficent, being a necessary condition of humanity's technical and moral progress." *Liberalism and Democracy,* 22. In this regard, Blake, with his "minute particulars" and his claim that "opposition is true friendship," is certainly a child of liberalism.

[87] Pitkin, *Concept of Representation,* 195.

the problems of aesthetic form, both in terms of production and interpretation. Republican government, one could say, is structured like a
language or, taking a deeper risk of anachronism, one could say it
functions like a poststructuralist text. In this sense, representation is an
attempt to institutionalize, to give positive political form to, the decentering of meaning on the one hand and the decentering of power on the
other. In society, in language, and in government, representative democracy is defined primarily by what it sets out to deny: the idea of a
determinate and homogenous social order purged of conflicting interests. Paradoxically, its institutions are the positive form of an essentially
negative process, what earlier, in reference to Mill, I called "undoing":
the emptying out of power into the play (or self-canceling conflict) of
social differences that in turn has for its symbol the emptying out of the
Logos into the play of multiple and irreconcilable interpretations. In this
way, the deconstructive practice of foregrounding representation which
we saw in both Blake and Paine becomes a foundational principle of
political structure. Whether in text or government, what matters is the
way one undermines one's ability to produce determinate meaning and
thus one's own authority over others; what matters is the ability to affirm
a negative relation to power. The common denominator of democratic
practices, then, is the production of forms that enact their own incapacities, their own disabling contradictions, in deference to a freedom
constituted by untranscendable social and linguistic diversity. What has
become perhaps the leading methodological assumption of contemporary theory in so many of its guises lies at the foundation of the Western
governments under which such theory has been generated. Representative democracy—"a place of adverse discussion for all opinions relating
to public matters" (323), according to Mill—is that self-proclaimed radically plural text where all possible meanings can be articulated but none
can act with authority. And underlying this politics is the fundamental
assumption that power can be collapsed into indeterminate signs, that
freedom corresponds to the capacity for perpetual subversion in and by
language.

In the next section I will briefly discuss one form of the symbiosis
between decentered politics and contemporary theory—how, in a conspicuously circular manner, the poststructuralist critique of power generated under democracy has in turn undertaken a theoretical defense of
democracy. I want to conclude here, however, by simply pointing out the
fit between poststructuralist vocabulary and democratic politics.[88] When

[88] Another example of this "fit" can be found in both the method and content of Hunt's
Politics, Culture, and Class in the French Revolution, where she proposes to read the Revolution "as a text": "By its very nature, revolutionary rhetoric posed many of the same issues as
those common in literary criticism today. Standards of political interpretation were as
disputed in the 1790s as standards of literary interpretation are today" (25).

Claude Lefort, in *Democracy and Political Theory,* speaks of an indeterminacy fundamental to democracy, he reproduces the primary democratic assumption that power can be linguistically emptied: "The important point is that democracy is instituted and sustained by the *dissolution*
of the markers of certainty. It inaugurates a history in which people experience a fundamental indeterminacy as to the basis of power, law and
knowledge, and as to the basis of relations between *self* and *other,* at every
level of social life."[89] Before the democratic revolutions, power depended for its legitimacy on the belief in fixed certainties outside of
language, certainties that were symbolically centered on the material
presence of the king's body. The violent removal of the king initiated a
decentered and indeterminate social space; as Lefort's favorite phrase
has it, "The locus of power becomes *an empty place*" (17). This intersection of indeterminacy (a linguistic phenomenon, the dissolution of the
"markers" of certainty) and the absence of power is characteristically and
uncritically democratic. In *Rights of Man* Paine already knew that what
Lefort calls "disincorporation" (17) was necessary to uncharm the monarchical sublime: "A nation is not a body, the figure of which is to be
represented by the human body" (181). Remove the king's body, the
unified presence in which power *symbolically* appears, and, so the argument goes, power can *actually* be made to disappear. Blake's *Last Judg-*
ment drawing, which involves a coronation of absolute power, is dominated not by the Messiah on his throne but by the "fiery gulph" at the
picture's center, an empty place from which energy is diffused cen-
trifugally. And Madison's checks and balances, which deliberately emphasize the contradictions in the text of representation, do nothing if
not stage the emptying of power. Each of these instances demands a
symbolic reorientation. In democracy's self-representations, the locus of
power is indeed an empty place, or in another of Lefort's characteristic
formulations, power "is tacitly recognized as being purely symbolic"
(17), in other words, merely a matter of language or representation. In
the next section, I will briefly consider the unspoken corollary to this
definitive assumption: in representative democracies, it is also tacitly
recognized that the *subversion* of power is purely symbolic.

The New Apologists for Democracy

When one thinks of the crisis of representation today, at least in the
narrow setting in which this book will be read, one thinks of an epistemo-

[89] Lefort, *Democracy and Political Theory,* 19.

logical or aesthetic crisis, a crisis suggested by familiar phrases like the impossibility of the universal or Nietzsche's mobile army of metaphors and metonymies or Derrida's white mythology, a crisis initiated by the radically skeptical disregard of any absolute ground upon which a privileged representation may claim to be founded. Just as it did in the 1790s for Blake and Paine, this rupture in turn suggests a political possibility, an institutional possibility, namely the opening up of representation in all its forms to many voices, to collateral and competing interpretations that are not always (or desirably) reconcilable. Many of the most recent developments in literary theory and criticism (from canon and curriculum revision to writings concerned with dominant and marginalized discourses) reflect a desire to realize the political possibility implied by the poststructuralist decentering of representation, something one sees in a nearly innocent form when earnest students say they're no longer interested in theory unless it is related to actual practice. What I want to suggest, within the considerably limited scope of this section, is that theory for some time has been and continues to be bound up with an actual political practice, a democratic practice, and that no matter what claims are made for the subversive nature of a particular discourse, no matter what claims are made for the radical practice of a local textual or critical strategy, such claims are already structured by modern democratic politics, by the relatively stable and resistance-resistant context within which they participate. This context is indeed relatively stable; with its particular configuration of political and aesthetic representation, it retains many of the salient features we saw already operative in the writings of Blake and Paine.

The critique of liberal democracy has recently been called a "growth industry," and to some extent, this section merely adds to that growth, as I reproduce a few questions Marx asked of democratic politics that seem to me still unanswered.[90] My immediate concern, however, is the recent defense of democracy launched by various leftist thinkers more or less employing a poststructuralist vocabulary and what this tendency suggests about our current literary theory, especially as it grapples with issues of power and subversion. By making the symbiosis between poststructuralist assumptions and democratic politics their very topic, these defenses inadvertently reveal to literary or cultural theorists the politics that accompanies and structures those critical acts that rely on poststructuralist assumptions. By briefly turning to these explicit apologies for democracy, we might just see how we, as literary and cultural critics of many different persuasions, despite those differences and perhaps be-

[90] See Martin Stone, "The Placement of Politics in Roberto Unger's *Politics*," *Representations* 30 (Spring 1990): 78.

cause of them, are always already ourselves the tacit defenders of the democratic faith.

So many democratic apologias now flood the political scene that the first thing to do is to distinguish the poststructuralist version, with its own internal diversity, from the near euphoria on the right following the collapse of the Berlin Wall. In the context of both this chapter and recent historical events, perhaps the most decisive factor is that the leftist defenses are severely counterapocalyptic. Together they can be considered the group antithesis of the essay by Francis Fukuyama, "The End of History?", that achieved instant celebrity with its apocalyptic vision of an already triumphant liberal democracy:

> What we may be witnessing is not just the end of the Cold War, or the passing of a particular period of postwar history, but the end of history as such: that is, the end point of mankind's ideological evolution and the universalization of Western liberal democracy as the final form of human government. This is not to say that there will no longer be events . . . , for the victory of liberalism has occurred primarily in the realm of ideas or consciousness and is as yet incomplete in the real or material world. But there are powerful reasons for believing that it is the ideal that will govern the material world *in the long run*.[91]

All the leftist democratic revivals I am interested in—those of Roberto Unger, Claude Lefort, Ernesto Laclau, and Chantal Mouffe—preceded Fukuyama's essay, but they share a nearly phrase-by-phrase rebuttal of its apocalyptic tendencies, its millennial vision of an already achieved democratic ideal. Most important in this regard is that they are all rigorously nonteleological, denying not only the fantasy of an end to history but also the possibility of any form (cognitive or aesthetic or political) that might be considered final. In fact, the latent genius of democracy according to these accounts is its capacity to produce self-deconstructing institutional forms that ensure through their very instability a deep historical embeddedness, an ongoing invitation to change.

---

[91] Francis Fukuyama, "The End of History?" *The National Interest* 16 (Summer 1989): 4. The celebrity of Fukuyama, oddly enough a former student of Derrida turned State Department policy planner, was indeed instantaneous and astonishing. James Atlas summarized the phenomenon in a *New York Times Magazine* article: "George F. Will was among the first to weigh in, with a *Newsweek* column in August; two weeks later, Fukuyama's photograph appeared in *Time*. The French quarterly *Commentaire* announced that it was devoting a special issue to 'The End of History?' The BBC sent a television crew. Translations of the piece were scheduled to appear in Dutch, Japanese, Italian, and Icelandic." And so on. "What Is Fukuyama Saying and To Whom Is He Saying It?" *New York Times Magazine,* October 22, 1989, 38.

Thus "endlessness," whether in Unger's "revisability" or Lefort's "open-ended debate," is constitutive of democracy, and along with endlessness come a host of other counterapocalyptic premises that reflect a commitment to the genuinely historical and contingent: the denial of autonomous or immaterial ideas, the denial of universals, the denial of a universal language. Laclau and Mouffe echo all of these premises when they state, "The discourse of radical democracy is no longer the discourse of the universal; the epistemological niche from which 'universal' classes and subjects spoke has been eradicated, and it has been replaced by a polyphony of voices, each with its own irreducible discursive identity."[92] The emergence of radical democratic politics in the 1790s was accompanied by a thoroughgoing suspicion of apocalyptic authority, of any authority grounded in a space outside history. That suspicion remains a conceptual given among the leftist democratic writers that I discuss here.

Despite the shared aversion to apocalypse, and the correlative valuing of history, the project of revitalizing democratic politics differs greatly from Unger to Lefort and from Lefort to Laclau and Mouffe; it would demand an entire essay (or even a book) to negotiate the complications of any one articulation, let alone the differences among them. There is, however, a common tendency that can serve as a starting point here: the desire to extend the radical possibilities of democratic politics by institutionalizing, in a way deeper than has yet been accomplished, the crisis of representation, in other words, to lessen the distance between social relations as they exist and the model of nonhierarchical discourse promulgated by the disciplinary varieties of poststructuralism. Typically this desire first involves conceptualizing society negatively, that is, as a phenomenon without a fixed essence ("Society is . . . impossible," announces Laclau), and then proposing ways in which democratic social

[92] Ernesto Laclau and Chantal Mouffe, *Hegemony and Socialist Strategy: Towards a Radical Democracy* (London: Verso, 1985), 191. Rejecting transparency, "History in the singular," and the "Jacobin imaginary," Laclau and Mouffe describe their opposition to orthodox Marxism and their defense of democracy in terms remarkably parallel to those of Paine's counterapocalyptic resistance to the Terror: "What is now in crisis is a whole conception of socialism which rests upon the ontological centrality of the working class, upon the role of Revolution, with a capital 'r', as the founding moment in the transition from one type of society to another, and upon the illusory prospect of a perfectly unitary and homogeneous collective will that will render pointless the moment of politics. The plural and multifarious character of contemporary social struggles has finally dissolved the last foundation for that political imaginary. Peopled with 'universal' subjects and conceptually built around History in the singular, it has postulated 'society' as an intelligible structure that could be intellectually mastered on the basis of certain class positions and reconstituted, as a rational, transparent order, through a founding act of political character. Today, the Left is witnessing the final act in the dissolution of that Jacobin imaginary" (2). Further references to this text are cited as *HSS*.

arrangements might express the freedom inherent in such negativity.[93] What enables this project generally is the assumption, which we first saw in Blake and Paine, that language is disempowering because it makes inaccessible or nonexistent the "real" or the "true" (now bracketed) upon which power formerly depended for its authority. In his critique of apocalypse, one recalls, Paine strategically employed what we might designate as the two necessary components of the crisis of representation: (1) that because representation is ubiquitous we have no access to unmediated revelation, only to representations; and (2) that representations lack ontological or metaphysical authority and are therefore partial, interested, historically contingent, and indeterminate. When Laclau and Mouffe make their radical democracy dependent on a "rule of discursivity"—"every object is constituted as an object of discourse"— they apply relatively unchanged assumptions to approximately similar ends: "What is denied is not that . . . objects exist externally to thought, but the rather different assertion that they could constitute themselves as objects outside any discursive condition of emergence" (*HSS*, 107–8). Like Paine, Laclau and Mouffe want to capitalize politically on the unavoidable mediation of representation, realizing that anything laying claim to a reality outside discourse forfeits its authority as soon as it passes (or is made to pass) through discourse.[94]

No wonder Claude Lefort, whom Laclau and Mouffe cite as a kindred spirit, can champion democracy by saying that "the negation of what is assumed to be real is constitutive of the history of modern society," in other words, of democratic culture.[95] This fundamental premise—that the disempowering capacity of language, its essential negativity, can take a positive social and institutional form—appears as a varied chorus among the leftist champions of democracy. In Roberto Unger's version, for instance, the task of an "empowered democracy" is twofold. The first task is to disempower the "false necessities" that exist only in discourse but which have severely constrained our ability to imagine alternative social formations (false necessities seem roughly comparable to Blake's "mind-forg'd manacles"). Unger also calls this prerequisite activity "trashing the script." The second task is to institutionalize our Keatsean "negative capability," Unger's term for our ability to create social ar-

[93] Ernesto Laclau, "Metaphor and Social Antagonisms," in *Marxism and the Interpretation of Culture*, ed. Cary Nelson and Lawrence Grossberg (Urbana: University of Illinois Press, 1988), 249.

[94] A point of terminology: Laclau and Mouffe reject the term *representation*, which they feel has implied within the orthodox Marxist tradition a pseudoscientific rigor that relies on reductive and dualist allegories of surface-depth. They prefer the term *articulation* as one more open to indeterminacy and multiplicity. See *HSS*, 65.

[95] Lefort, *Democracy and Political Theory*, 114.

rangements open to skeptical challenge and perpetual revision precisely because they are recognized to be without any ontological or metaphysical foundation.[96] The romantic tint to Unger's rhetoric should not, at this point, come as a surprise. Similarly for Laclau and Mouffe, the first step toward a radical democracy is the realization that all existing social orders are "precarious and ultimately failed attempts to domesticate the field of differences," erected as they are on the prior "negative essence" of the social (*HSS*, 45); the second step is to "institutionalize a true pluralism," "true" in that it expresses more adequately the unanchored negative essence current social orders repress.[97]

More explicitly than any of the others, and for this reason I look at them in greater detail, Laclau and Mouffe make radical democracy inseparable from a set of linguistic assumptions and thus most clearly suggest the way democratic politics remains remarkably invested in the prestige of language. *Hegemony and Socialist Strategy* is a densely argued book, one that to an impressive degree makes good on its promise to advance critical theory toward a post-Marxian terrain. I will focus, however, on Mouffe's independent essay "Hegemony and New Political Subjects: Toward a New Concept of Democracy," where one can see in small the assumptions that inform the far more ambitious collaborative project. In all their work, Laclau and Mouffe tend to follow a consistent argumentative procedure: they begin with an idea of language (post-structuralist discourse), then use it as an explanatory model for the social (negative essence), and finally suggest ways to extend it politically, to realize it institutionally (in a radically plural democracy). It is not surprising, then, that Mouffe begins her essay by appealing to the fundamental indeterminacy of social agents and relations and the impossibility of reducing them to fixed, single categories (especially the category of class): "Within every society, each social agent is inscribed in a multiplicity of social relations—not only social relations of production, but also the social relations, among others, of sex, race, nationality, and vicinity. All these social relations determine positionalities or subject positions, and every social agent is therefore the locus of many subject positions and cannot be reduced to only one. Thus, someone inscribed in the relations of production as a worker is also a man or a woman, white or black, Catholic or Protestant, French or German, and so on. A

---

[96] *False necessity* and *negative capability* are terms that play a central role in Roberto Unger's epic rethinking of social theory and democratic political practice. *False Necessity: Anti-Necessitarian Social Theory in the Service of Radical Democracy* (Cambridge: Cambridge University Press, 1987).

[97] Chantal Mouffe, "Hegemony and New Political Subjects: Toward a New Concept of Democracy," trans. Stanley Gray, in *Marxism and the Interpretation of Culture*, ed. Nelson and Grossberg, 100. Further references to this text will be cited as "Mouffe."

person's subjectivity is not constructed only on the basis of his or her position in the relations of production" (Mouffe, 89–90). This analysis of overdetermined social relations is itself valuable, especially for de-mystifying the reduction of subjectivity to economic class, but at this point, Mouffe indulges in a telling rhetorical elision: "Furthermore, each social position, each subject position, is itself the locus of multiple possible constructions, according to the different discourses that can construct that position. Thus, the subjectivity of a given social agent is always precariously and provisionally fixed or, to use the Lacanian term, sutured at the intersection of various discourses" (Mouffe, 90). The paragraph begins with the subject inscribed within social relations; it ends with the subject inscribed within various discourses. Both of these constructions, of course, are necessary for any account of subjectivity. What gets blurred in the shift, however, is the precise relation between the social and the linguistic; it is not clear whether Mouffe describes two things that are related or two things she takes to be identical. This ambiguity continues a moment later when she states, "I affirm . . . the existence in each individual of multiple subject positions corresponding both to the different social relations in which the individual is inserted and to the discourses that constitute these relations" (Mouffe, 90). The "both . . . and" construction preserves at least some minimal distinction between social relations and discourses, but when Mouffe adds that discourses constitute social relations, she makes it seem as if social rela-tions are *entirely* linguistic in nature. As the essay progresses, Mouffe often refers to "discourses or practices" and "practices or discourses," as if these two things were coextensive, interchangeable without any remainder.[98]

Why is this elision not only important but definitive? Certainly all discourses are social practices, but is it equally true that all social prac-tices consist solely of discourse, as if signification were their only molecu-lar stuff? In the blunt rejoinder of a social historian still committed to historical materialism, "Language is not life."[99] I don't propose to ex-plain in any naively positivist sense what aspect of social relations or practices or "life" lies beyond discourse. Rather, I want to point out the surreptitious convenience, and self-importance, involved when the cul-

[98] Such interchange occurs often in the essay; I provide only one especially pertinent instance here: "Democracy is our most subversive idea because it interrupts all existing discourses and practices of subordination" (96).

[99] Bryan Palmer, *Descent into Discourse: The Reification of Language and the Writing of Social History* (Philadelphia: Temple University Press, 1990), xiv. In this spirited critique, Palmer is at his best in demonstrating that the turn to language as a means of superseding reductive materialist categories such as base and superstructure has often resulted in an unfortunate slide into idealism.

tural theorist assumes there can be no distinction whatsoever between language and life. Laclau also makes the identity between society and discourse absolute: the concept of discourse, which he claims to derive from Derrida's "Structure, Sign, and Play," "describes the ultimate non-fixity of anything existing in society."[100] Underlying this argument, I would suggest, is an old rhetorical trick—the collapsing of power into language. Once one accepts that social relations are exclusively linguistic in nature and that power is constituted within discursive formations, one can logically advance the argument that power can be subverted linguistically, that social relations can be radically altered by altering discourses. Richard Price's Enlightenment formula remains intact: expose, subvert, emancipate. Indeed, Laclau and Mouffe read the French Revolution not as a political illusion masking bourgeois economic interests but as the origin of a subversive, democratic discourse: "Our thesis is that it is only from the moment when the democratic discourse becomes available to articulate the different forms of resistance to subordination that the conditions will exist to make possible the struggle against different types of inequality" (*HSS*, 154). The historical drama of power and resistance is played out entirely upon a linguistic stage.

By no means do I wish to deny the deep interanimation of social relations and discourse. I merely want to question the idea that power is exhausted by language, that no aspect of social relations exceeds the multiple and conflicting discourses that represent and to some extent construct those relations. The great success of the democratic revolution, as I have suggested, was to make it seem that power and language were, so to speak, made of the same stuff, so that activities that staged the subversion of power in language seemed actually to subvert power in society. In this sense, Laclau and Mouffe belong squarely to the democratic revolution they hope to extend. Consider, for instance, this claim by Mouffe: "As long as equality has not yet acquired (with the democratic revolution) its place of central significance in the social imagination of Western societies, struggles for this equality cannot exist. As soon as the principle of equality is admitted in one domain, however, the eventual questioning of all possible forms of inequality is an ineluctable consequence. Once begun, the democratic revolution has had, necessarily, to undermine all forms of power and domination, whatever they may be" (Mouffe, 94). Even more than the necessitarian rhetoric or the dubious argument that equality in one domain irresistibly spreads to other domains, what concerns me here is the inflated status of language in this account of revolutionary politics.[101] To begin with, the act of subversion

[100] Laclau, "Metaphor and Social Antagonisms," 254.

[101] The inevitable spread of equality through the effects of democratic discourse is a favorite theme of Laclau and Mouffe's. They often cite the following quotation from

is a verbal act (questioning the forms of inequality); this verbal act is then automatically endowed with an efficacy (undermining the forms of power and domination); and finally, this efficacy involves the capacity to undermine, not power and domination per se, but *the forms* of power and domination. For Mouffe no distinction exists between form (discourse) and power; in fact, the disabling of power has already occurred by the time one assumes that power is indistinguishable from its verbal forms. But if one were to challenge this especially democratic assumption, isn't it possible that Mouffe's version of radical politics might become yet another activity played out on a field to some degree merely formalistic, the field of language that certainly penetrates or overlaps with or informs the social field (choose your metaphor) but does not absolutely equal it?

Which brings me to Marx and a momentary detour. In "On the Jewish Question," Marx developed a critique of democratic politics that to my mind has not yet been answered and thus bears remembering in a time of democratic revivalism. In one form or another, his critique underlies the common debate about formal and substantive democracy, the terms of which Norberto Bobbio summarizes well: "There is no question that historically the term 'democracy' has been interpreted, at least in its origins, in either one of two main senses, depending on whether the stress is laid more on the body of rules . . . which must be observed if political power is to be effectively distributed among the majority of the citizens, or on the ideal of equality in which democratic government should find its inspiration."[102] In this division, *formal democracy* concerns itself with the problem of political power and liberty, *substantive democracy* with the problem of equality, including economic equality. When in the late eighteenth century the liberal republicans instituted political representation as a formal mechanism for negating power, their distinctly formalist version of democracy evolved out of a rather limited notion of what needed to be negated. Within their conceptual universe, power meant one thing only: authoritarian state power. In the century-old liberal philosophy that is fully evolved in Paine's *Rights of Man*, coercion existed exclusively as a feature of despotic government and therefore

---

Tocqueville: "That men should be eternally unequal among themselves in one single respect and equal in others is inconceivable; they will therefore one day attain equality in all respects" (quoted in Mouffe, 89; *HSS*, 156).

[102] Bobbio, *Liberalism and Democracy*, 31. Raymond Williams provides an alternative way to describe the "two modern meanings of democracy": "In the socialist tradition, democracy continued to mean *popular power:* a state in which the interests of the majority of the people were paramount and in which these interests were practically exercised and controlled by the majority. In the liberal tradition, democracy meant open election of representatives and certain conditions (democratic rights, such as free speech) which maintained the openness of election and political argument." Williams, *Keywords,* 96.

had only to be eradicated from government to be eliminated altogether; alternatively, civil society was defined against the state as a spontaneous, natural realm of economic activity that fostered social relations devoid of anything that might be called power.[103] As Paine's slogan states, "Representative government is freedom." Representation annuls power in the only place it exists—the state—and consequently liberates the uncoercive activities of social exchange previously hindered by governmental imposition. Whether or not such a stark antithesis between the political state and economic civil society actually existed hardly matters. Recent work by John Brewer demonstrates conclusively that the central government in eighteenth-century England controlled and manipulated the nation's economic activities, making any distinction between public and private spheres factually ludicrous.[104] And yet that distinction bore the stamp of reality for English liberals like Paine, who felt that by ending arbitrary political power they could liberate society: "The instant formal government is abolished, society beings to act" (*Rights of Man,* 164).

For Marx, representative government could never fulfill its inflated promise to negate power per se, since it left untouched, and indeed encouraged, the already existing play of social power bound up with the interests of capital and its relations of domination. To believe in the liberal promise was to believe in the illusion that political freedom is sufficient freedom. The democratic revolutions yielded a civic schizophrenia that Marx likened to the persistent theological dualism of heaven and earth: citizens could experience freedom, equality, and the absence of power in the essentially formal or wish-fulfilling space of electoral politics only to live social lives in material spaces consisting of hierarchy, division, and coercion.

[103] Sheldon Wolin has described in great detail the enabling illusion of liberalism—that, in contrast to the realm of politics, social and economic activity lacked the element of authority and thus the exercise of coercion: "What was truly radical in liberalism was its conception of society as a network of activities carried on by actors who knew no principle of authority. Society represented not only a spontaneous and self-adjusting order, but a condition untroubled by the presence of authority." Wollin demonstrates how this liberal bias was especially pervasive among the new eighteenth-century economists, who believed in "the relative absence of coercion in economic transactions." *Politics and Vision: Continuity and Innovation in Western Political Thought* (Boston: Little, Brown, and Co., 1960), 301, 291. Certainly Paine was the most widely read proponent of these fundamental assumptions in his time: "I have been an advocate for commerce. . . . It is a pacific system, operating to cordialize mankind." *Rights of Man,* 212.

[104] Brewer describes the eighteenth-century development in England of the "fiscal-military state." He writes that an "ever-more ponderous burden of military commitments," supported by "a radical increase in taxation, the development of public deficit finance on an unprecedented scale," and public administration of "the fiscal and military activities of the state" led to the creation of a powerful central government that knew no separation between political and economic activities. *The Sinews of Power: War, Money and the English State, 1688–1783* (New York: Knopf, 1989), xvii.

When the political state has achieved its true completion, man leads a double life, a heavenly one and an earthly one, not only in thought and consciousness but in reality, in life. He has a life both in the political community, where he is valued as a communal being, and in civil society, where he is active as a private individual, treats other men as means, degrades himself to a means, and becomes the plaything of alien powers. . . . In the state . . . where man counts as species-being, he is an imaginary participant in an imaginary sovereignty, he is robbed of his real life and filled with an unreal universality.[105]

Democratic representation, according to this view, offers its citizens a heaven of political freedom to mask the earthly reality of their social inequalities. Thus Marx speaks of the detour of political emancipation, a detour that avoids the proper human medium (society) by taking people into an alternative and imaginary medium (politics).

I wish to add two things before I return to Laclau and Mouffe. First, democratic representation for Marx, as both his religious analogy and his use of the term *imaginary* suggest, is essentially apocalyptic in that it displaces the nightmare of history with compensatory illusions that are largely formal or aesthetic in nature. History ends not in a book, but in the Constitution, in the formal freedoms of representation. Second, the detour of political emancipation is a detour into language, into the talking function most fully elaborated in Mill. Citizens experience the freedom from power as the staged collapse of power into language— representation. They experience the freedom to act as the freedom to speak in the cause of self-determination—again, representation. Democratic government maintains itself, as I have argued all along, through the belief that disempowerment and empowerment are essentially linguistic activities, that freedom is a linguistic state. Extending Marx's idea of the double life under representative government, we might say that democratic citizens live a life in language that is never entirely identical to their lived experience of society.[106]

[105] Karl Marx, "On the Jewish Question," in *Karl Marx: Selected Writings*, ed. David McLellan (Oxford: Oxford University Press, 1977), 46. Paine provides a good example of the political illusion in *Rights of Man* when he holds up the United States as a model: "There, the poor are not oppressed, the rich are not privileged" (167). This sentence makes sense only if oppression and privilege are considered to be exclusively political terms.

[106] In opposition to Marx, the common argument has been that the formal nature of democracy preserves an indeterminacy and thus an openness to critique and change that are utterly lacking in totalitarian regimes, where the attempt to fix the social order begins with a collapsing of state and civil society, with an extension of absolute state power into civil society. Agnes Heller is an eloquent speaker on this front: "Formal democracy leaves open and undecided the problem of the concrete structure of society. It is formal for

The poststructuralist defenses of democracy I have been examining are certainly not oblivious to Marx's critique, and their negotiations of it say a great deal about the nature of their project. Much of Lefort's "Human Rights and the Welfare State" addresses this very issue—the contention that "human rights merely served to disguise relations established in bourgeois society" (21). And yet at the moment Lefort recognizes the problem of formalism he tends to deflect it by concentrating on that of individualism, arguing that democracy did not reduce society to atomized monads, as Marx claimed, but rather brought into existence "a new network of human relations" (32). This does nothing, however, to answer the argument that "the new network" is merely, to borrow one of Lefort's favorite words, "symbolic."[107]

Laclau and Mouffe confront Marx's critique more directly and more interestingly. They acknowledge that at the time of the eighteenth-century revolutions, politics indeed constituted an artificially constructed public space separated from the multifold injustices of private society, at least in the imaginations of the liberals who brought about the political formations we still live with. They go on to argue, however, that it is in the nature of democratic discourse, once initiated, to extend beyond its original confines, to infuse itself into areas of social inequality that had previously been considered outside the domain of the properly political. Thus the ideals of liberty and equality that had existed only symbolically in the formal space of democratic politics eventually (and inevitably) get realized within a full range of social practices:

> The public/private distinction constituted the separation between a space in which differences were erased through the universal equivalence of citizens, and a plurality of private spaces in which the full force of those differences was maintained. It is at this point that the overdetermination of effects linked to the democratic revolution begins to displace the line of demarcation between the public and the private and to *politicize* social

precisely that reason. When Ho Chi Minh stated that socialism as a whole is comprised in the Declaration of Independence, he was right if we consider the democratic-ideal type of socialism. . . . All those who want to replace formal democracy with so-called substantive democracy, and thereby reunify state and society in a totalizing way, surrender democracy as such." "On Formal Democracy," in *Civil Society and the State,* ed. John Keane (London: Verso, 1988), 130–31.

[107] This is Lefort's consistent strategy: he acknowledges Marx's critique of formalism (as on page 34 of *Democracy and Political Theory,* when he talks of democracy as "a theater for the noisy expression of opinions which, because they are merely the opinions of individuals, neutralize one another") and then does one of two things: (a) he rebuts Marx's other critique, that of atomized and competitive individualism, or (b) he reminds us that the benefits of democracy must always be valued in relation to the evils of totalitarianism. Marx himself of course recognized the latter; he never stated that the liberal-democratic state was politically worse than the ancien régime. He simply argued that we could do better.

relations . . . : this is the long process which stretches from the workers' struggles of the nineteenth century to the struggle of women, diverse racial and sexual minorities, and diverse marginal groups, and the new anti-institutional struggles in the present century. (*HSS*, 181)

The whole of Laclau and Mouffe's practical project is contained in this passage—to extend the radical possibilities of democracy by making the whole of social relations conform to the power-negating ideals that had previously been limited to an insular politics—in other words, to extend the reach of politics. What concerns me here is not the desire expressed but the mechanism proposed to accomplish this expansion of political ideals. How is it that the democratic discourse can pass out of the largely formalist sphere of politics and into the wider and more substantial social sphere? How does the heaven of linguistic forms become incarnated in actual social relations? It would be inescapably utopian to believe this process could be accomplished largely because social formations are themselves already and thoroughly linguistic and therefore are predisposed to linguistic transformation.

Laclau and Mouffe's preliminary assumption that society and discourse are indistinguishable permits the deepening of democratic subversion within their system; subversion takes place as a linguistic reconfiguration and can therefore disrupt any linguistic domain—which for them includes economic relations as well as sexual, racial, ethnic, and national relations. This preliminary move, however, leaves entirely open to question their success in circumventing Marx's critique. By extending the reach of language into the entirety of social relations, they have perhaps merely expanded the formal space of the political/linguistic illusion. If one can say of democratic representation in the 1790s that it provided only in language what it could not fully deliver in social relations, what is to prevent one from saying the same of Laclau and Mouffe's radical democratic proposals? Put another way: Why should we believe that the "polyphony of voices" they see as the basis of a utopian democracy is not another version of Marx's political detour, accepting representation (here "voice") as the sufficient substitution for a leveling of power?[108]

[108] In a thorough and bracing critique of *Hegemony and Socialist Strategy*, Donna Landry and Gerald Maclean have questioned its neoliberalism: "'Equality' and 'liberty' without 'revolution' in a socialist, i.e. anti-capitalist *and* democratic, sense, have been the watchwords of liberalism for too long to be easily recuperated by the feminist left. . . . Given the history of 'liberty,' particularly in the Anglo-American contexts where it has served a 300-year term naturalizing social and economic inequality in the name of the 'free' market, and been most often defined as the 'liberty' of the propertied to remain the propertied, some more thoroughly deconstructed notion of what a truly democratic, socialist, anti-individualist liberty might represent here is necessary." Forthcoming in *Rethinking Marxism*.

In a series of questions following a conference lecture, Mouffe was asked whether her privileging of discourse "as a way of transforming consciousness and agency" amounted to "a new form of idealism." Her answer says much about the relation between poststructuralist theory and democracy: "I must say that I cannot accept the opposition between idealism and materialism—it doesn't pertain to my semantic world."[109] The ambiguous mix of idealism and materialism characteristic of the leftist approach to democracy appears most immediately in the use of the fashionable term *discourse*. Although this term suggests the materializing of language, in that language is now understood to consist entirely of historically contingent social practices, it may inadvertently and ironically mark an idealizing of social practices, in that they are now understood to consist entirely of language. In the subtle way that language gets substituted for matters of power one sees at work the relatively unchanged assumptions of a stable and stabilizing democratic context.

I began this discussion of poststructuralist defenses of democracy by noting their counterapocalyptic vehemence, their conviction that political radicalism is consistent only with a deep historicism, with a refusal to substitute aesthetic or ideal forms for history. In the old apocalypse, history ended when it passed into the order of the Logos. Poststructuralism, in its counterapocalyptic turn, has thoroughly rejected the Logos in favor of discourse. But aren't we on the verge of an apocalyptic return when history, the medium of social conflict, becomes entirely a matter of discourse, when it threatens to become *merely* political? We must not underestimate the capacity of democratic culture to deflect matters of power onto the plane of language and so ensure the relative stability of its social relations by exaggerating the relative instability of its linguistic dynamic. Until Marx's critique is more adequately answered, we face the possibility that representative democracy, which, according to Paine, was supposed to negate the authority of apocalypse, is a new, more subtle version of apocalypse, an invitation to a life of formal possibility that, while not exactly outside of history, is not commensurate with the full force of history either.[110]

---

[109] This exchange is printed after Mouffe, "Hegemony and New Political Subjects," 104. As Mouffe develops her answer, she reverts in an interesting way to the ambiguity I earlier targeted: "By discourse," she states, "I understand not only speech and writing but also a series of social practices, so discourse is not just a question of ideas" (104). This statement reflects the widening of discourse that, in its absolutist form, I have called into question. Here she merely suggests (unobjectionably) that a number of nonlinguistic social practices might be considered as participating in the field of signification and thus discourse. Moreover, when Mouffe says "a series of social practices" she specifically avoids saying "all" social practices, thus again leaving open the possibility that some elements of practice lie outside of language.

[110] Landry and Maclean instructively demonstrate how Laclau and Mouffe substitute

At this point, the implications of this discussion for current critical practices should be apparent. At the very least, we ought to recognize that critical and theoretical acts like the writing of this book are, for better and for worse, contained by the democratic culture within which they are generated. The desire to politicize criticism is already framed by existing political constructions. Let me be more specific. The current concern with issues of cultural power and subversion might be conveniently, if somewhat absurdly, divided into two types of criticism: the vaguely political and the directly political. By the vaguely political I refer to theoretically inclined criticism that concentrates on the undermining of authority within language systems and that describes this linguistic activity in a loosely political vocabulary of insurrection and freedom. Much early deconstructive criticism is of this type and certainly much contemporary romantic criticism as well. A variety of examples might be found in the Blake studies I have already mentioned. Passages from works of Hazard Adams and Nelson Hilton provide typical instances:

> The Blakean conception of synecdoche that opposes the negations open/ closed and miraculous/figurative I shall call *radical* and *progressive,* adopting the second term from Blake's well-known aphorism "Without Contraries is no progression."

> Blake's intellectual allegory shaped by synecdoche is an endlessly exfoliating potentiality of identities, carrying ethical implications of the greatest urgency.[111]

> Though perception necessarily begins enchained, linked to a past and context, in realizing the nature and operations of its restraint—the psychic and cultural fetters, locks, and manacles—perception may to some extent unchain itself.[112]

Within the context of my discussion, one political effect of such criticism is to create a tacit analogy between the function of representation in texts and the function of representation in government: to stage the subversion of authority and power in the formal space of the text is to affirm the analogous tendency in politics. Moreover, because this criticism invites, indeed demands, the conflict of multiple interpretations,

---

formal, theoretical abstractions for the specificities of actual historical movements and in the process reproduce some patently ethnocentric myths. In one of their most persuasive objections, Landry and Maclean argue that *Hegemony and Socialist Strategy* privileges the struggles of postmodern, industrial politics over those of neo- and postcolonialism.

[111] Adams, "Synecdoche and Method," in *Critical Paths*, ed. Miller, Bracher, and Ault, 47–48, 71.

[112] Hilton, *Literal Imagination*, 56.

each lacking in authority ("Interpretations are to be made and endlessly remade" [Adams, 50]), it reproduces within academic and professional organizations the pluralist deadlock guaranteed within democratic government by the crisis of representation, the deeply embedded system of checks and balances. The capacity of democratic pluralism to absorb all acts of critique often pits the radical pretensions of a particular critical act against the unacknowledged conditions of institutional stability within which it emerges.

Of wider interest at this intellectual moment are the varieties of directly political criticism which not only describe specific instances of cultural domination but set out to contribute to the struggle for change. With all its diverse forms—feminism, ethnic and racial empowerment movements, Marxism, postcolonialism, sexual-orientation movements (the list corresponds roughly to what Laclau and Mouffe call "the new social movements")—this criticism to varying degrees involves a focus both on dominant discourses that produce ideological norms and on the marginalized but potentially subversive discourses that elude and challenge those norms. In both types of study, the often urgent and necessary work emerges from and reproduces crucial democratic assumptions. On the one hand, analysis of dominant discourses—exposing the subtle ways in which they naturalize power of all sorts—suggests that power can be disentrenched by representing its verbal operations. Even the most pessimistic Foucauldian discussions of totalizing power take some refuge, at least implicitly, in the idea that a measure of freedom exists in giving power a knowable, linguistic form. I begin with the assumption that these studies of dominant discourses are of vital importance; they become problematic only when they imply the coextensiveness of social and discursive practices and thus overestimate the extent to which representing power discursively might form an adequate resistance to it.

On the other hand, the passionate advocacy of discourses that lie outside and challenge dominant cultural norms suggests the familiar belief that the socially marginalized are genuinely empowered as they develop the subversive potential of self-representation. Again, this practice is only problematic when one substitutes linguistic for complete empowerment. The countless radical discursive strategies ingeniously and compellingly championed since the late 1960s—from différance to "l'écriture feminine" to signifyin', just to name a few—all represent significant political challenges to some aspect of cultural domination, but at their outer limits they may simultaneously affirm and deepen the democratic context that was compatible with those forms of domination in the first place. Both instances of directly political criticism—the critique of dominant discourses and the celebration of marginalized discourses—

extend into the realm of cultural interpretation the basic activities described by Mill's "talking function" of representative government: one throws the light of publicity on abusive acts of power, the other makes culture a committee of grievances, a congress of opinions, where different voices can advance different interests, but where all in the end are tempted to "feel satisfied" that their voices are heard, tempted to feel satisfied with, for instance, their new places within the democratic curriculum. Criticism has indeed become more political and has achieved tangible political objectives (such as canon reformation); whether it has become more radical can only be measured by the extent to which the freedom in language promoted by politics gets translated into the somewhat different medium of social relations.[113]

In his critique of Western representative democracy, Marx took for granted that "political emancipation is of course a great progress."[114] One can certainly say the same of political criticism, and the last thing I would want to suggest is that the variety of political criticisms are lacking in real and immediate value. Nor would I want to hold them or myself to some impossible standard of producing all-or-nothing transformative results. I merely wish to ask the questions Marx asked of democratic representation: First, is it enough? and second, how does it come to seem enough? Laclau and Mouffe reveal a certain symbiosis between poststructuralist ideas of representation and democratic culture, and thus they invite a necessary question: Are they deepening the radical potential of democracy and the crisis of representation, or are they reproducing its formalism, enacting its capacity for perpetual subversion in the designated space of language that leaves power to some significant degree untouched?[115] The same question might then be put to our

[113] One of the most vocal critics of the way in which power struggles get reworked into the formalist "talking function" of the university has been Edward Said. In "Representing the Colonized: Anthropology's Interlocutors," Said describes "the domesticated result" that occurs when social struggle enters academia and becomes "Bakhtinian dialogism and heteroglossia": "The point I am trying to make is that this kind of scrubbed, disinfected interlocutor is a laboratory creation with suppressed, and therefore falsified, connections to the urgent situation of crisis and conflict that brought him or her to attention in the first place. . . . To convert [subaltern figures] into topics of discussion or fields of research is necessarily to change them into something fundamentally and constitutively different." *Critical Inquiry* 15 (Winter 1989): 210.

[114] Marx, "On the Jewish Question," in *Karl Marx: Selected Writings*, ed. McLellan, 47.

[115] To their credit, Laclau and Mouffe make perfectly clear that they consider their radical project to take place *within* democratic politics. *"The task of the Left therefore cannot be to renounce liberal-democratic ideology, but on the contrary, to deepen and expand it in the direction of a radical and plural democracy"* (*HSS*, 176). With this kind of claim Laclau and Mouffe are vulnerable to the charge that their new philosophy "can only insist on what is already the case in modern societies—that they remain democratic and pluralist." See Dick Howard's "Another Resurrection of Marxism," in his *Defining the Political* (Minneapolis: University of Minnesota Press, 1989), 90.

newly politicized academic culture: Is criticism, to borrow Unger's terms, a context-disturbing activity or a context-affirming routine?

Some time ago it was common to describe the development of criticism in terms of a change from ambiguity to indeterminacy. The latter seemed to be a more radical version of the former, pushing the logic of ambiguity to an extreme by denying the saving comforts of a mythical controlling context. Recent criticism has in turn taken radicalism literally and more seriously, insisting that it move out of the text and into the political struggles concerning the exercise of power. From ambiguity to indeterminacy to politics—or from the new criticism to deconstruction to cultural critique—one common denominator remains an essentially unchanged set of democratic principles regarding the issue of representation. When Cleanth Brooks once suggested that by participating in the ambiguity of poetry "we doubtless become better citizens," he articulated more explicitly than anyone after him the good citizenship that is perhaps a regular feature of criticism in the democratic West.[116]

[116] Cleanth Brooks, "Irony as a Principle of Structure," in *Critical Theory since Plato*, ed. Hazard Adams (New York: Harcourt Brace Jovanovich, 1971), 1048.

CHAPTER FOUR

APOCALYPSE AND POLITICS:
PERCY BYSSHE SHELLEY'S 1819

Shelley loved the people.

—Mary Shelley, note to "The Mask of Anarchy"
in *The Complete Works of Percy Bysshe Shelley*

[The redeemed in Michelangelo's *Last Judgment*] ought to have been what the
Christians call *glorified bodies;* floating onward and radiant with the everlasting
light (I speak in the spirit of their faith), which had consumed their mortal veil.
They are in fact very ordinary people.

—Percy Bysshe Shelley, letter, in
The Complete Works of Percy Bysshe Shelley

Is a philosophical movement properly so called when it is devoted to creating a
specialized culture among restricted intellectual groups, or rather when, and
only when, in the process of elaborating a form of thought superior to "common
sense" and coherent on a scientific plane, it never forgets to remain in contact
with the "simple" and indeed finds in this contact the source of the problems it
sets out to study and to resolve? Only by this contact does a philosophy become
"historical."

—Antonio Gramsci, "The Study of Philosophy
in the History of Culture"

Of the two apocalyptic projects that occupied Percy Bysshe Shelley in
1819 only one embarrassed Mary Shelley when she later wrote the
headnotes for a posthumous edition of her husband's poems. Anticipating the reception of Shelley's poetry to this day, Mary Shelley felt compelled to apologize for the millenarian lyrics her husband simply called
"Popular Songs," although the apocalyptic rhetoric of *Prometheus Unbound* posed no such discomfort. Despite the poet's efforts, his abrasively
political poems were not published until the securing of the 1832 Reform Bill, and, when they did appear, Mary understood they would not
rest comfortably alongside the works that were already establishing her
husband as a Victorian poet-hero. In making the "Popular Songs" ac-

ceptable to the public, she needed to account for the outright vulgarity of their language, something she explained as a kind of exercise in poetic slumming: "They are not among his best productions, a writer being always shackled when he endeavours to write down to the comprehension of those who could not understand or feel a highly imaginative style."[1] To some extent, Shelley apparently agreed; his hastily written poems of September and October 1819 responded to a specific crisis, the Peterloo Massacre, in which eleven political protesters were killed and hundreds of others wounded, and he never once indicated that he considered them on a par with the more universal political vision of *Prometheus Unbound.* And yet, the moment Shelley chose to address a working-class audience in the coarse language of millenarianism, the moment he lowered his apocalyptic register to speak in a common voice, the moment he turned away from a richly aestheticized presentation of political themes to an act of political participation, he opened an angle of critique on *Prometheus Unbound* and its celebrated social vision that is as often ignored today as it was by his nineteenth-century admirers.

Shelley wrote his "Popular Songs" as an act of political expediency, and since they fulfilled a function that *Prometheus Unbound* could not, they immediately pointed to the real limitations of his lyrical drama, a visionary work written for all time but in fact largely irrelevant for the needs of a specific time, that of late summer 1819. If the "Popular Songs" did not quite displace the "highly imaginative style" they had to supplement, they did initiate what we might consider a dialogue, expressed through competing types of apocalyptic representation, about the relation between literature and politics. At the very least, these poems indicate that *Prometheus Unbound* has no monopoly on the meanings and functions of apocalypse; more significantly, by establishing an alternative reference point, they allow us to see that the vision and the practice of *Prometheus Unbound* coexist uneasily, that what the play *says* about a politics of apocalyptic redemption and what it *does* politically are two different things. In 1963 Edward Bostetter pointed out that, despite his determination to play the prophet, to envision and advance human liberation, Shelley often exhibited "an indifference to, even a dislike of, human beings as the novelist or dramatist would be interested in them."[2]

---

[1] *The Complete Works of Percy Bysshe Shelley,* 10 vols., ed. Roger Ingpen and Walter E. Peck (New York: Gordian Press, 1965), 3:307. Because these poems were never published, there is no authorized title for the collection. I have adopted "Popular Songs" from a casual reference in one of Shelley's letters: on 1 May 1820 Shelley wrote to Leigh Hunt, "I wish to ask you if you know of any bookseller who would like to publish a little volume of *popular songs* wholly political, and destined to awaken and direct the imagination of the reformers." *Complete Works,* 10:164.

[2] Edward Bostetter, *The Romantic Ventriloquists* (Seattle: University of Washington Press, 1963), 218.

This observation bears particularly on the contradictions involved in Shelley's attempt to rewrite the Book of Revelation through his epic drama. Despite his ideal of an apocalypse of art and love, Shelley's imagination bears a certain violence toward those he would see transfigured, something evident not only in the literary representations of early 1819 but also in his social interactions of the same period. Shelley, for instance, could pursue his drama of universal human redemption with regard for only the slightest of audiences.[3] As the title of an essay by

[3] There has been so much outstanding work done on the political vision of *Prometheus Unbound*—its relation to the ideals and failures of the French Revolution and the liberating imaginative effects its creates for its readers—that acknowledgment would amount to listing much of Shelley criticism since the late 1950s. As Stuart Curran has definitively stated, "The romantic Prometheus is a political icon." "The Political Prometheus," *Studies in Romanticism* 25 (1986): 430. Since my aim is not to contest this judgment but to qualify it, I ought to explain why I have veered from it. It seems to me that the always illuminating discussion of the politics of *Prometheus Unbound* has too often confined itself to the play's self-representation, what it has to say about servitude and liberty (its thematic content) or how it performs an act of imaginative liberation (its communicative work as poetic form). In either account, the play's internal political dynamics are taken to be one and the same as its political effects, by which I mean the way it participates in actual social struggles regarding the relations of power. The limitations of this otherwise valuable approach appear as soon as the liberating impact of the play is made to depend on readers, for indeed Shelley's actual audience was and is very small and remarkably homogeneous. My argument is that Shelley came to recognize this problem in a way that those of his critics who read the play as a source of tremendous transformative power often do not.

In lieu of a list of political criticism of *Prometheus Unbound*, let me provide a few instances of the inadvertent idealization that occurs when readers minimize the reality of Shelley's limited audience. One such course has been to emphasize the role of drama and performance in the work, which has prompted Jean Hall to speak of the "socialized imagination" that "remains an idealizing force only insofar as it is open to all." "The Socialized Imagination: Shelley's *The Cenci* and *Prometheus Unbound*," *Studies in Romanticism* 23 (1984):347. Arguments about the play's democratic and monumental inclusiveness, its performative, communal desires, rarely take into account its actual dissemination. The same might be said of the deconstructive readings of Shelley that see in his destabilizing linguistic strategies a liberating force that works through individual readers to transformative social effects. Thus Tilottama Rajan can acknowledge early in an essay that *Prometheus Unbound* claims nearly omnipotent powers for words only as it remains "at a certain distance from actuality," but can conclude that it belongs "with works that assume the interaction of fiction and sociopolitical reality, fiction and personal life. . . . In choosing the mode of drama, Shelley departs from *Alastor* to set his work in the space of historical difference." *The Supplement of Reading: Figures of Understanding in Romantic Theory and Practice* (Ithaca: Cornell University Press, 1990), 303, 322. By no means is this wrong, but it implicitly defines historical difference and sociopolitical reality rather narrowly. Any reader-oriented criticism ought to consider the play's real readers, not merely hypothetical effects intrinsically required or invited by the text. Even in interpretations that recognize the small circle of Shelley's audience there remains a nearly irresistible tendency to speak of large results commensurate with the poem's grand vision. Thus in an excellent essay Marlon Ross begins by asking, "If [Shelley's] aim is reform, even if indirectly, why does he address the poem to those whose imaginations are already refined?" He then analyzes the effects *Prometheus Unbound* ought to have on its readers, making them conscious of the linguistic processes constitutive of the world, helping them maintain a utopian vision of

Carol Jacobs suggests, apocalypse in *Prometheus Unbound* refers to the imaginative process of "Unbinding Words," freeing language and its human values from the weight of historical determination; at the same time, however, the imaginative work of transcendence, of building Jerusalem—even when it is conceived not as Platonic retreat but as the work of social rehabilitation—requires a process of disengaging oneself from the reality of others.[4] It is precisely this leaning toward an apocalyptic but peopleless space, an autonomous space of words, that the experiment of the "Popular Songs" puts into question, for when Shelley turned again to apocalypse late in the summer of 1819, he did so in order to adopt the historically embedded idiom of a particular people engaged in struggle. Only in the light of this functional apocalyptic rhetoric, in which literary form is subordinated to political consequence, does the "highly imaginative style" of *Prometheus Unbound* begin to seem dysfunctional.[5]

---

the future while remaining mentally equipped to endure and to reform reality now. In his conclusion, Ross argues that the poem might even "have a modicum of success with any reader," and while this is already to scale back the claims made earlier, it then honestly retreats another step: "The poem's primary audience, however, is not such unimaginative readers, but those readers who can image the poem and envision the dream." For Ross, the poem's contribution to social transformation depends on its ability to provide "much needed exercise for the mental muscles," but in the end it seems to exercise an audience already "fit . . . though few." "Shelley's Wayward Dream-Poem: The Apprehending Reader in *Prometheus Unbound*," *Keats-Shelley Journal* 36 (1987): 111, 132–33, 123. The general problem, then, is twofold: first, terms like *egalitarianism, heterogeneity,* and *inclusiveness* can become merely abstract or formal in discussions of *Prometheus Unbound;* second, the large claims made for the play's impact on individual imaginations and social relations as a whole are often inversely proportionate to the small number of people who can or do read the play. Shelley had no obligation to write for a mass audience, but we have an obligation to temper our enthusiasm with a measure of realism. Most of all, we need to guard against the temptation to see a relatively small body of educated elite as the representatives of a universal humanity, to mistake the community of intellectuals for an audience sufficiently capable of realizing Shelley's utopian vision.

[4] "Unbinding Words" is in fact the title of Carol Jacobs's chapter on *Prometheus Unbound* in her *Uncontainable Romanticism* (Baltimore: Johns Hopkins University Press, 1989), 19–57.

[5] In a classic essay of 1957, G. M. Matthews argued against those symbol-hunting scholars who saw in *Prometheus Unbound* a treasure of Platonic thought disconnected from sociopolitical concerns. "One of two things must be true," he wrote, "either the writer's political dedication, so often repeated, was essentially superficial and the 'symbolism' proves it, or else the 'symbolism' involves more than its interpreters suspect." Matthews went on to reconstruct brilliantly and meticulously the reference of Shelley's volcanoes to revolution. In this chapter I attempt to push Matthews's polemical argument one step further; as Matthews questioned the Platonists, so I question those who now uncritically accept the revolutionary nature of *Prometheus Unbound.* Although the symbols of *Prometheus Unbound* are politically laden, what a poem represents internally, theoretically, fantastically and what it does as an action in the world can be two very different things. At the end of his essay, Matthews chided the Platonists: "The pursuit of 'symbols' can become an evasion of reality." Isn't it also true, however, that a satisfaction with symbolic politics can also become an evasion of reality? "A Volcano's Voice in Shelley," *ELH* 24 (1957): 191, 227.

In this chapter I unfold the dialogue on literature and politics that led Shelley from *Prometheus Unbound* to the "Popular Songs." Shelley's intellectual peregrinations are especially instructive, for they indicate how uncertain the political valence of apocalyptic representation is; one can never assume, as romantic criticism has too often assumed, that there exists some automatic link between apocalyptic literature and progressive effects. Even when the apocalyptic images of the radical millenarian tradition are restored to their place in political engagement, as Shelley restored them in the "Popular Songs," their transformative power may still be limited and contained. Therefore, after charting Shelley's changes through what Stuart Curran once called his annus mirabilis, in the final section of this chapter I pick up where the last chapter on Blake and Paine left off—with the fortunes of apocalyptic discourse when it is inscribed within the imperatives of democratic revolution.[6]

Prometheus Unbound and the Scene of Annihilation

Although apocalypse has been a central term in Shelley criticism and has served to describe everything from the poet's visionary idealism to his honest and unrelenting skepticism, I want to begin with an underappreciated aspect of his apocalyptic concerns: Shelley relished a scene of annihilation.[7] To be sure, Shelley was not and is not alone in this fetish. After the turn of the nineteenth century, European culture widely ad-

[6] I refer to the title of Stuart Curran's *Shelley's Annus Mirabilis: The Maturing of an Epic Vision* (San Marino: Huntington Library, 1975).

[7] The classic statement on Shelley's apocalyptic idealism is Ross Woodman's *The Apocalyptic Vision in the Poetry of Shelley* (Toronto: University of Toronto Press, 1964), though this aspect of Shelley has exerted a wider influence on literary studies through M. H. Abrams's comments in *Natural Supernaturalism* (New York: Norton, 1971) and Northrop Frye's use of an image from "A Defence of Poetry" (poetry "is at once the centre and circumference of knowledge") to describe the anagogic phase of literature in *Anatomy of Criticism* (Princeton: Princeton University, 1957), 119. The inversion of this transcendental Shelley takes characteristic shape in J. Hillis Miller's essay "The Critic as Host," where Shelley's desire for apocalypse is consistently undermined by his inability to extricate himself from the limitations of language: "Shelley's poetry is the record of a perpetually renewed failure. It is the failure ever to get the right formula and so end the separate incomplete self, end lovemaking, end politics, and end poetry, all at once, in a performative apocalypse in which words will become the fire they have ignited and so vanish as words, in a universal light. The words, however, always remain, there on the page, as the unconsumed traces of each unsuccessful attempt to use words to end words." Harold Bloom, Paul de Man, Jacques Derrida, Geoffrey H. Hartman, J. Hillis Miller, *Deconstruction and Criticism* (New York: Continuum, 1979), 237.

mired a jolting apocalyptic image, especially in those pictures of modern cities reduced to ruins, and such images have continued to exercise a fascination well into our nuclear era. But in Shelley this tendency to imagine destruction on a vast scale, though explicit only on occasion, becomes embedded in his most characteristic forms of expression; hardly an aberration, it is a symptomatic and habitual thought. As a popular topos (the sublime would be the generic category), the scene of annihilation serves various functions not incompatible with a philosophical or political idealism. By representing things radically other than they are, it manifests a utopian impulse; the urban environment that seemed nearly permanent can be thought away in an image that leaves only a trace of the city's oppressive weight and solidity—the shell of a building here, the broken arch of a bridge there. This utopian desire delights in its naïveté; it worries little about what comes next and simply exercises a blind, directionless blow to the contemporary, creating a relatively blank future that is better than a complicated and burdensome present. At the same time, however, this playful leap to apocalyptic freedom quietly bears an unthinkable violence, for the image's pleasure and horror, what makes it sublime, is that it imagines *freedom from people*.

This always conspicuous motif can enter Shelley's writing so casually, so unburdened with discomfort, that we sometimes pay it little attention. The most conventional representation of the tendency that I know of appears in the least likely place: "Peter Bell the Third," a scathing doggerel satire on Wordsworth's political and artistic decline and perhaps Shelley's least sublime poem. Byronic wit colors the entire piece, even the scene of annihilation that caps the nearly slapstick dedication to fellow satirist Thomas Moore. Wishing himself and Moore the good fortune of a posterity that survives London itself, Shelley accentuates his point by delightedly representing the city, from the far reach of time, as a desolate ruin: "when London shall be an habitation of bitterns, when St. Paul's and Westminster Abbey shall stand, shapeless and nameless ruins in the midst of an unpeopled marsh; when the piers of Waterloo bridge shall become the nuclei of islets of reeds and osiers and cast the jagged shadows of their broken arches on the solitary stream,—some transatlantic commentator will be weighing . . . the respective merits of the Bells and the Fudges."[8] One could account for this apocalyptic vision in any number of ways—the prevalence in painting of the *Paris-morte* motif, the fascination of British travelers with such museum cities as Rome, the visualization of transiency that reinforces the satire's em-

---

[8] "Peter Bell The Third" in *Shelley's Poetry and Prose*, ed. Donald Reiman and Sharon Powers (New York: Norton, 1977), 325. All further citations, unless otherwise indicated, are to this text.

phasis on humility—but I would add to this list of accounts the grati-
fication Shelley likely found in the instant depopulation of the early
nineteenth-century urban landscape, the "unpeopling" of a crushingly
dense and familiar scene that returns the city to nature in the form of an
uninhabitable marsh. Within the fiction, such alteration is hardly sudden; the scene reveals the gradual processes of decay and growth that
have made the Thames a solitary stream. But it is the lightning speed
with which one can imagine such a thorough emptying of what is now
saturated that invests the scene with pleasure. This vision of London
ruined would have considerably less effect, for instance, without the
complementary image of London that appears in the poem itself, an
image that lies closer to the lived claustrophobia of Oxford and other
streets: "And this is Hell—and in this smother / All are damnable and
dammed; / Each one damning, damns the other; / They are damned by
one another, / By none other are they damned" (217–21). The over-
crowded, industrial site ("Hell is a city much like London— / A popu-
lous and a smoky city" [147–48]) demands the utopian blank slate, the
breathing room, of the other, especially in the mind of a poet who could
never completely resist the gentility of his landed upbringing, who
continued to associate freedom with the privilege of an open field. When
the poem goes on to catalogue the London damned, Shelley includes
himself among those few who "believe their minds are given / To make
this ugly Hell a Heaven" (244–45). If imagining annihilation is not
exactly to transform hell into heaven, it is, at least in the pleasure of
fantasy, one way to dispose of hell. The utopian scene remains comic, of
course, only because it bypasses the violence of destruction to focus on
the picturesque result. We do not have to imagine people dying simply
to imagine them blissfully, harmlessly gone. And Shelley does not indulge in a misanthropic fantasy of global annihilation (some "new and
now unimagined" [p. 325] culture will supersede that of Europe); he
simply prefers future and transatlantic populations to those present.

More at home with the sublime than with the comic, Shelley rarely
passed up an opportunity to contemplate the agents and acts of annihilation. The province of Kant's dynamic sublime recurs in his writings
as so many Mont Blancs and Vesuviuses, sources of power defined by
their capacity to destroy the monuments of culture, to obliterate human
works. Three years before "Peter Bell," and in a setting more compatible
with such meditations, Shelley imagined the adversarial relation between civilization and sheer destructive power, but oddly, and perhaps
inadvertently, he did so in a way that suggests a hidden interdependence
between them. Part IV of "Mont Blanc" begins by establishing an un-
bridgeable gap between human endeavor (indeed, any organic activity)
and a Power "remote, serene, and inaccessible" (97). As the section

progresses, it steadily visualizes this opposition as a hierarchy in which Power descends from its glacial prominence and enters the subordinate world of the living as annihilation. High atop Mont Blanc

> . . . many a precipice,
> Frost and the Sun in scorn of mortal power
> Have piled: dome, pyramid, and pinnacle,
> A city of death, distinct with many a tower
> And wall impregnable of beaming ice.
> Yet not a city, but a flood of ruin
> Is there, that from the boundaries of the sky
> Rolls its perpetual stream; vast pines are strewing
> Its destined path, or in the mangled soil
> Branchless and shattered stand: the rocks, drawn down
> From yon remotest waste, have overthrown
> The limits of the dead and living world,
> Never to be reclaimed. The dwelling-place
> Of insects, beasts, and birds, becomes its spoil;
> Their food and their retreat for ever gone,
> So much of life and joy is lost. The race
> Of man, flies far in dread; his work and dwelling
> Vanish, like smoke before the tempest's stream,
> And their place is not known.
>
> (102–20)

In the most characteristic feature of the scene of annihilation, the passage imagines the slow erosion of humanity as an instantaneous erasure of humanity. In this case, however, one is hard-pressed to determine just how the sublime image yields its satisfaction. The London-in-ruins of "Peter Bell" represented a crowded metropolis instantly emptied. Here, the image of lordly Mont Blanc as an icy, vacant city provokes pathos, not pleasure. The poem seems to mock the vulnerability of the built environment (the human "dwelling" that vanishes like smoke) by representing the glaciers as an alternative, nearly supernatural architecture. In the cruelest of ironies, the terms of a resplendent human culture—reminiscent of Wordsworth's "towers" and "domes," "All bright and glittering in the smokeless air"—describe the inhuman agent of annihilation. How can Mont Blanc at once be so beautiful and so devastating, an object that commands both the attraction and the repulsion characteristic of the sublime?

And yet the interwoven capacities for formal perfection and destructive power are what make Mont Blanc an object of aesthetic fascination. Put another way, the severity of Mont Blanc's beauty corresponds to its violent detachment from that which surrounds it, something Shelley figures as its capacity to make competing, unworthy objects of perception vanish. In this description, two events frame the "destined path" of apocalyptic power: Mont Blanc appears as an archetypal city and actual cities, inferior cities—populated cities, one might say—disappear, like smoke. With its pristine architecture that resembles the New Jerusalem just before it is inhabited, Mont Blanc is an image of heaven without people. In this way, the vertical arrangement of the scene indicates, in an allegory of idealist aesthetic production, the role imaginative violence plays in the desire for autonomous aesthetic objects that transcend circumstance. "For on that superior height / Who sits, is disencumbered from the press / Of near obstructions, and is privileged / To breathe in solitude."[9] So Wordsworth once described not an alpine peak but the "Eminence" of the superior subject, the perch of disinterested wisdom. In Shelley's poem disencumbrance does not occur passively; it must be willed. The sublime experience itself occurs only by means of the traveler's cultivated detachment, the ability to fabricate solitude by deliberately removing oneself from social context, by pretending for the moment that no one else exists. Thus the poem schematizes its own imaginative act; it is the power to erase the human context beneath the summit that *allows* one to imagine Mont Blanc as perfect architecture above. Hardly a power oblivious to human culture, Mont Blanc is paradoxically *the* high cultural effect, an image that derives its force from a poet's capacity to render context insignificant, invisible.

The last scene of annihilation I want to consider in this series of tableaus takes us into *Prometheus Unbound* and complicates the issue of aesthetic production by introducing the role of language. The fourth act of *Prometheus Unbound* is haunted by the force of history it claims to have overcome. When the renovated earth rolls in as the merkabah, the divine and apocalyptic chariot, it generates a light that reveals not the unhindered future but the scars of the past, the "ruin within ruin" (4.295) of history that mocks the chariot's transcendental (and conventional) "sphere within sphere" (4.243). As Shelley first reads the archaeological and then the paleontological strata of the earth, the historical record hangs its dead weight on utopia. In this remarkable passage there are two explicit images of annihilation, each suggesting that no matter how far one recedes into the past one discovers the inevitability of disaster. The most recent casualty, as in "Mont Blanc," is the human landscape; buried in the ground are "the wrecks beside of many a city vast, / Whose population which the Earth grew over / Was mortal but not

[9] William Wordsworth, *The Excursion*, 9. 69–72, in *The Poetical Works of William Wordsworth*, ed. Ernest de Selincourt and Helen Darbishire (Oxford: Clarendon, 1949), 5: 288.

human" (4.296–98). The prior casualty is that of prehistoric species, "prodigious shapes / Huddled in [the] grey annihilation" (4.300–301) of so many fossils. As Shelley dwells on the varieties of extinction, the burden of ruin increases in sheer mass until it suddenly calls forth an alternative act of annihilation, one that is oddly liberating, one that apocalyptically ends rather than perpetuates the sequence of history:

> . . . and over these
> The jagged alligator and the might
> Of earth-convulsing behemoth, which once
> Were monarch beasts, and on the slimy shores
> And weed-overgrown continents of Earth
> Increased and multiplied like summer worms
> On an abandoned corpse, till the blue globe
> Wrapt Deluge round it like a cloak, and they
> Yelled, gaspt and were abolished; or some God
> Whose throne was in a Comet, past, and cried—
> "Be not!"—and like my words they were no more.
>   (4.308–18)

In this series, natural agents of extinction—flood and comet—yield to a linguistic agent, and so the sequence enacts the displacement of nature by language that generally characterizes act 4's eschatological desires, its attempt to imagine a self-sustaining verbal universe. After this linguistic moment, in which a command is tantamount to an act of negation, "ruin" never again bothers the utopian celebration of act 4. History in general and behemoth in particular abruptly disappear under the spell of "Be not!" If in Genesis Yahweh could simply say "Let there be . . ." and there was, so that the Logos was instantaneously performative of creation, then he also commands by his words the instantaneous performative of "Be not!"—what we might call the decreative Logos. The two are often inseparable. The story of their inseparability is told not in Genesis, however, but in Revelation, where Christ must shatter the old before he can create a new heaven and new earth. If Christ is the Logos and the New Jerusalem his work, that city's ideal architecture is built on an act of linguistic violence. Of course, this idea was never far from Revelation's image of a Christ who does battle by means of the two-edged sword that issues from his mouth. Immediately following the liberating "Be not!" of the passage quoted, Earth sings a lyric of triumphant, weightless euphoria. But the utopian "animation of delight" that "wraps [the earth] like an atmosphere of light" (4.322–23) does so only in tandem with the "Deluge" that "Wrapt" the blue globe in annihilation, only as it recalls that moment when prehistoric creatures "Yelled, gaspt and were abolished."

When M. H. Abrams argued that the romantics responded to the terrors and disappointments of revolution by internalizing apocalypse, by making millenarianism a function of imagination, he accepted that imaginative acts differ from political acts in their freedom from violence, and to some extent they do. One of the most common responses to the violence of 1793 and beyond was to blame it on the revolution's prematurity: abstract social ideals had been forced on real people not ready to receive them. This explanation allowed various intellectuals from Schiller to Arnold to preserve what they valued of 1789 while transferring the mechanism of accomplishment from the precipitous work of politics to the gentler processes of culture. Schiller anticipated the social mission of much nineteenth-century aesthetic theory when he argued in 1795: "If man is ever to solve the problem of politics in practice he will have to approach it through the problem of the aesthetic, because it is only through Beauty that man makes his way to Freedom."[10] My brief sampling of Shelley's scenes of annihilation suggests, however, that in transferring apocalypse from politics to art and imagination, these writers did not so much suspend the problem of violence as alter its form. The internalization of apocalypse brought with it an internalization of apocalyptic violence, something particularly evident in English romanticism's great belated monument to political and aesthetic idealism, *Prometheus Unbound*. Shelley's play relies on a revealing sleight of hand; its millennial events cannot occur without the acts of violence it condemns, but it sidesteps this contradiction by projecting violence onto a nonhuman agent—Demogorgon. As Harry White points out, Demogorgon, by doing the dirty work of revolution, protects the integrity of Prometheus's ideal of love: he does "what the virtuous man could not do, both because of his particular ethic of suffering, and because, as luck would have it, he happened to be chained to a rock when the revolution got under way."[11] This wishful splitting of love from violence, and the attempt to contain the latter within a nonhuman agency, calls attention all the more forcefully to their interdependence. Without Demogorgon, Prometheus's internal action, his change of heart in the opening act, might simply be that—a change of heart that changes little else. Jupiter does not yield power until Demogorgon drags him down, suggesting that, despite his utopian inclination, Shelley still cannot imagine revolutionary change without revolutionary violence. But if Demogorgon doubles Prometheus—if he is the element of Promethean fire that does not

[10] Friedrich von Schiller, *On the Aesthetic Education of Man, in a Series of Letters*, ed. and trans. Elizabeth M. Wilkinson and L. Willoughby (Oxford: Clarendon, 1967), 9.
[11] Harry White, "Relative Means and Ends in Shelley's Socio-Political Thought," *SEL* 23 (1982): 628.

illuminate but burns—he similarly doubles Asia, which concerns me more. It is Asia, after all, who comes to signify the liberating innocence of the aesthetic in the drama; through Asia one witnesses the work of culture that is supposed to represent a nonviolent path to the millennium.

Asia and Demogorgon at first seem to belong to different domains, and Shelley persistently emphasizes their differences. Thus Asia must be summoned from her surface world to Demogorgon's den, buried deep in the earth's cavity. But from another perspective, we might imagine the characters to form overlapping or homologous images. According to Panthea, Demogorgon is an immaterial force that must be intuited; like Milton's darkness visible, he can be seen only paradoxically: "I see a mighty Darkness / Filling the seat of power; and rays of gloom / Dart round, as light from the meridian Sun, / Ungazed upon and shapeless— neither limb / Nor form—nor outline; yet we feel it is / A living Spirit" (2.4.2–7). By the end of act 2, Asia comes to resemble the spirit that instructs her, so much so that Panthea can say, "I feel, but see thee not" (2.5.17). One all light, one all dark, both characters are versions of "the deep truth [that] is imageless," the truth that is so deep it escapes fixed embodiment. Although they reflect one another, Asia also fulfills a conspicuous lack in Demogorgon, and she does so by becoming poetry. Demogorgon justifies his inability to answer Asia's questions fully by complaining, "a voice / Is wanting" (2.4.115–16); he thus suggests that his essence is mute as well as invisible. Asia, meanwhile, can sing, and her songs give this fundamental indeterminacy form. In the exquisite lyrics that conclude act 2, Asia, "by the instinct of sweet Music driven" (2.5.90), paradoxically becomes the very representation of disembodiment. This etherealization of Asia, her ascent into the pure form of music and light, invites us to forget her complicity in the power of Demogorgon's emboweled darkness. Asia's music is so dazzling that, once she begins to sing, Demogorgon disappears until the following act; in fact, we never see the two together again.

And yet the liberation of creative imagination occurs only in conjunction with the release of destructive power. Shelley tries to keep these functions apart, carrying his two characters out of the chasm and into the world in separate chariots, but they ascend as two manifestations of the same activity. First arrives the vehicle that conveys Demogorgon to Jupiter, where he "wrap[s] in lasting night Heaven's kingless throne" (2.4.149), initiating the scene of annihilation I have been calling an allegory of idealist aesthetic production. As Panthea's description makes clear, Demogorgon is an ascending version of the power that descends from Mont Blanc: "That terrible shadow floats / Up from its throne, as may the lurid smoke / Of earthquake-ruined cities" (2.4.150–52). And the effects of such power are almost predictable: following fast on the chariot of annihilation is the chariot of art meant to bear Asia. "See, near the verge another chariot stays; / An ivory shell inlaid with crimson fire / Which comes and goes within its sculptured rim / Of delicate strange tracery" (2.4.156–59). Asia's pure poetry, like Mont Blanc's architecture, is accompanied, if not enabled, by an act of violence.

As that which accompanies aesthetic production, Demogorgon might well be a name for another sort of violence, the disinterestedness we associate with Kant's third *Critique,* a term not unrelated to that which many critics employ in accounting for him: "potentiality."[12] Disinterestedness refers to a mental state in which special interests are negated, a mental state dislocated from a complex and particular set of worldly relationships—that is, unconditioned by the demands of this set of relationships rather than another. Demogorgon belongs to *Prometheus Unbound* as a source of pure negativity, an originary worldlessness unencumbered by the determinants of place or circumstance and free from the weight of a particular body: "Ungazed upon and shapeless—neither limb / Nor form—nor outline." Without any particular coordinates, he can only be defined by what he is not. Most important, Shelley imagines that this pure negativity is a restorative agent, that by drawing on its resources, both society as a whole and the individual human being experience liberation. Perhaps Schiller best illuminates the relationship between Asia and Demogorgon, for he could not be more explicit about the link between art and the healing power of the negative. *On the Aesthetic Education of Man* identifies the aesthetic as that which unites presence and absence—the state where "man" simultaneously is and is not:

> In the aesthetic state, then, man is naught, if we are thinking of any particular result rather than of the totality of his powers, and considering the absence in him of any specific determination. . . . [N]othing more is achieved by [aesthetic culture] than that he is henceforth enabled by the grace of nature to make of himself what he will—that the freedom to be what he ought to be is completely restored to him.

[12] Of many such interpretations perhaps Earl Wasserman's is the one most often cited. He considers the withdrawal to Demogorgon's cave "a withdrawal from the mutable actuality of space and time into the containment of potentiality." *Shelley: A Critical Reading* (Baltimore: Johns Hopkins University Press, 1971), 346–47. This vexed description already indicates that potentiality can only be imagined as something negative, the absence altogether of location in time and space. In his 1963 article, D. J. Hughes also identifies Demogorgon as potentiality, but unlike Wasserman, he suggests that potentiality in the poem coincides with an act of erasure: "The characteristic movement of mind in the poem [is] the cleansing of the actual that a new potential may emerge." "Potentiality in *Prometheus Unbound*," *Studies in Romanticism* 2 (1963): 122.

But precisely thereby something infinite is achieved. For as soon as we recall that it was precisely of this freedom that he was deprived by the one-sided constraint of nature in the field of sensation and by the exclusive authority of reason in the realm of thought, then we are bound to consider the power which is restored to him in the aesthetic mode as the highest of all bounties, as the gift of humanity itself. True, he possesses this humanity *in potentia* before every determinate condition into which he can conceivably enter. But he loses it in practice with every determinate condition into which he does enter. And if he is to pass into a condition of an opposite nature, this humanity must be restored to him each time anew through the life of the aesthetic.[13]

The aesthetic state makes particular "man" disappear, dissolving "him" into the infinite but negative freedom of pure, undetermined human potentiality. Similarly, *Prometheus Unbound* 4 will sing of its utopian ideal in terms of simultaneous presence and erasure: "Man, oh, not men" (4.394). Asia and Demogorgon mirror each other, then, because her full presence, the positive freedom of her universal beauty, is bound up with the power of an absolute absence to relieve one of contingencies, to free one from what Schiller in another essay called "the world, as a historic object."[14] One must converse with Demogorgon before one can rise with Asia in transcendental song. To descend to Demogorgon, then, is like suddenly leaping to the London-in-ruins of "Peter Bell" or the pristine architecture of Mont Blanc; it is to experience the emptying out of that which exists, to return to a state prior to all conditions. Moreover, to descend to Demogorgon is to experience worldlessness as a freedom not just from circumstantial definition but from social relation, a freedom from people that implies an imaginative violence of the sort I attribute to Shelley's scenes of annihilation. According to Schiller, the aesthetic restores to us an absence of determination *already there*, a negative freedom that, like Demogorgon, resides beneath our everyday existence and only awaits our discovery of it. But absence is not a lost original and worldlessness is not an already existing negative space waiting to be found—they must be imagined. The freedom Schiller describes, which is tantamount to free will (the power "to make of [oneself] what [one] will"), requires that one first think oneself free of others, people who, by imposing on us, constitute a large part of the determinate conditions in which we find ourselves entered.

In *Prometheus Unbound*, the principle of negative freedom, what we

---

[13] Schiller, *On the Aesthetic Education of Man*, 145–46.

[14] Friedrich von Schiller, "On the Sublime," in *Essays Aesthetical and Philosophical*, trans. unknown (London: George Bell and Sons, 1879), 140.

might call the Demogorgon principle, is ubiquitous, represented mainly by the absence of people in a text about humanity. As Dana Polan contends in an essay that has received too little attention, "If there is one lesson, one overarching concern of the text, it is to suggest that progress, the elevation . . . of men into Man, can only occur by a quasi-Platonic capturing of essences, by the denial of the actual."[15] Demogorgon's world-dissolving force gets released toward the end of act 2, but in a sense it structures the entire play. Demogorgon seems to have performed his work even before the drama begins, for the power of absence appears as early as the negatives inscribed within the opening act's landscape: "Black, wintry, dead, unmeasured; without herb, / Insect, or beast, or shape or sound of life" (1.21–22). To be sure, this desolate scene externalizes Prometheus's inner torment, but would it be perverse to consider it also something of an unearned opportunity? After all, no one begins from scratch; no one initiates action within an empty and uncluttered space open to private figuration. *Prometheus Unbound* begins by representing psychological and social servitude, Prometheus's subordination to Jupiter, but it already stacks its deck in favor of freedom. The hero's prison amounts to an absence of material conditions, a zero-ground as much as anything positively oppressive. This setting is undeniably severe, but even more it is empty—and such emptiness comes close to guaranteeing that Prometheus's will is already self-determinate, that his acts of consciousness dictate the nature of his conditions precisely because those conditions possess no independent reality. It seems fair to say of this deadly landscape that there is nothing to it. Even the anguish of solitude itself, so central to act 1, opens the path to free will, for no network of established social relations stands in the way of the hero's decisions. This precondition allows him "to make of himself what he will." If we tend to say that the entire action of the play occurs in the first seventy-five lines, in Prometheus's transformation of hate into love, it would be more accurate to recognize the dependence of this decisive, psychological moment on the action that enables it: the reduction of reality to the blank page upon which the hero can inscribe his own destiny. The entire redemptive apparatus of *Prometheus Unbound* cannot be set in motion without the poet's first having narrowed the world to a barren slope of rock, and in so doing, at a single stroke, having made the density of existing human relations insubstantial. One might even say that an unrecorded scene of annihilation precedes this play, for when the curtain rises, the people and things that might contradict or limit Prometheus's desires have utterly disappeared.

[15] Dana Polan, "The Ruin of a Poetics: The Political Practice of *Prometheus Unbound*," *Enclitic* 7 (Fall, 1983): 39.

As readers have long recognized, the people of *Prometheus Unbound* reside only off-stage, reported on by a variety of "spirits." Strangely, however, the play couples this dislocation with the recurrence of the word *people*, a word which functions in one of two ways: either as a noun signifying a cluster of mental images ("The ghastly people of the realm of dream" [1.37]) or as a verb signifying the production of such images ("every space . . . / Peopled with unimaginable shapes" [4.243–44]). This dematerializing effect generally transforms people into the thoughts and thought processes of Prometheus and Asia. The Furies, for instance, those "foul or savage fiends / [that] People the abyss" (1.369–70), express the darkest fears and insecurities of Prometheus. And yet they also possess more material coordinates; they are, among other things, the surrogate of "the people," the dense masses of the industrial, urban scene. As we know from "Peter Bell," hell is a crowd, and that is exactly the figure Shelley employs to describe his devils: an "endless crowd," "a vain loud multitude," a "monster-teeming Hell," "legions from the deep," and so on (1.330, 486, 447, 462). Prometheus triumphs as he controls and disperses these phantoms, as he shrinks them to insignificance by establishing his subjective detachment from them ("Yet am I king over myself" [1. 492]). Asia's visionary journey back to the human origin, before Jupiter reigned, leads to "A Paradise . . . Peopled by shapes too bright to see" (2.5.104–8). One recalls Shelley's lament that Michelangelo's *Last Judgment* was not apocalyptic enough, that its rather ordinary people ruin an effect better achieved by "radiant . . . glorified bodies." Here, the pure potentialities of Asia's song can be thought only in conjunction with a self-induced blindness: paradise consists of immaterial thought-people who displace the ordinary people we see around us.

Displacement, of course, is a function intrinsic to all acts of representation, but its operation seems especially significant here. According to the *OED*, the first English use of *people* as a verb—to fill a space with people—appears in the sixteenth and seventeenth centuries; it corresponds to the nascent colonial project, the discovery of new and "vacant" lands that could be peopled. The *OED* places the earliest figurative use of the verb at the beginning of the nineteenth century (in fact, it cites Shelley's *Rosalind and Helen* as its first instance), when it corresponds to romantic subjectivity: to fill psychological space with images, to imagine.[16] Although widely separated in history, the literal and the figurative

---

[16] Although the *OED* cites *Rosalind and Helen* as its first listing, the figurative use of *people* as a verb was relatively common in the eighteenth century. At midcentury, Richard Hurd wrote that poetry "peoples all creation with new and living forms." "A Dissertation on the Idea of Universal Poetry," in *The Works of Richard Hurd* (1811; reprint, Hildesheim: Georg Olms Verlag, 1969), 2:9.

verb share a common denominator. Both colonize spaces that are in fact already populated and both represent that act as if they were introducing elements into spaces that are empty.[17]

The ease with which one can imagine others gone, even as a prelude to their transfiguration, is what I have been calling the violence of Shelley's apocalyptic imagination. By using the term *violence* or by alluding to the ideologies of imperialism, I mean neither to exaggerate the force of Shelley's text nor to blur the distinction between violence inside and outside a text. If a common objection to Shelley's idealism has been that it consists of words only, then this darker side might seem similarly airy and inconsequential. Shelley is as ineffectual a terminator as he is an angel; he is neither Prometheus nor Demogorgon. At the same time, however, the social imagination within Shelley's texts bears a relation to his nonliterary activities worth examining, for that relation indicates something of the everyday practices that inform and are informed by esoteric imaginative acts. In Shelley's travels in Italy of late 1818 and early 1819, the period leading up to and including his writing of the first three acts of *Prometheus Unbound,* one finds that in his pursuit of the "wonders of nature" and the "wrecks of . . . magnificent . . . ancient art"[18] he eerily displays the same imaginative activity exaggerated in his scenes of annihilation.

Shelley was an unashamed tourist (he once broke off a fragment from Tasso's prison door as a souvenir for Peacock), and like most tourists of that period or any other he expected certain effects, an Italian image. The letters of his first year in Italy are mainly a sight-seeing record, an enthusiastic guidebook to locations of the beautiful and the sublime. Accompanying the deep pleasure he takes in Italy's cataracts and broken columns, however, is a disturbing refrain: the captivating scenery, he repeatedly complains, is marred by the intrusion of the local Italians. Shelley indicates this problem most bluntly in a letter to Leigh Hunt: "There are *two* Italies—one composed of the green earth and transparent sea, and the mighty ruins of ancient time, and aerial mountains, and the warm and radiant atmosphere which is interfused through all things. The other consists of the Italians of the present day, their works

[17] Just before starting *Prometheus Unbound,* Shelley completed his "Lines written among the Euganean Hills." Two of the poem's phrases are especially pertinent. Shelley describes the poetic mind as "Peopling the lone universe" (319), and moments later he adds the hope that poetry might heal "The polluting multitude" (356). As I have argued, to consider the universe a "lone" space to be imaginatively peopled already requires a wishing away of the existing and undesired multitude.

[18] *The Complete Works of Percy Bysshe Shelley,* 10:7. All further citations to Shelley's letters will appear in the text as *CW,* followed by the volume number and page number.

and ways. The one is the most sublime and lovely contemplation that can be conceived by the imagination of man; the other is the most degraded, disgusting, and odious" (*CW*, 10:10). The same lament informs countless details of Shelley's correspondence, from his disgust with Italian women who eat garlic to his disappointment in the "very ordinary people" of Michelangelo's *Last Judgment*. Shelley would have preferred one Italy, his Italy, a depopulated land compatible with the solipsistic pleasures of the sublime; in the most immediate way he desired what we have seen Wordsworth call the privilege "to breath in solitude," to be "disencumbered from the press / Of near obstructions." And this longing occasionally took the form of a rather brutal disregard for the day-to-day existence of others. "In Italy," he writes to Hogg, "it is impossible to live contented; for the filthy modern inhabitants of what aught to be a desart sacred to days whose glory is extinguished, thrust themselves before you forever" (*CW*, 10:8). The resemblance between the ruin-sprinkled desert Italy ought to be and the uninhabited London-in-ruins of "Peter Bell" is startling.

When these letters were published years later, Mary Shelley anticipated the reaction they might provoke and tried to soften their effect. She explained in a note that Shelley was deceived in his earliest impressions of the Italians, that he "quickly" realized their vices were imposed rather than inherent, the result of centuries of church and state domination.[19] And yet, perhaps the best evidence that the letters represent more than a temporary misjudgment, that they go some distance toward the center of Shelley's habitual thought, lies in the way Mary Shelley anticipated them in *Frankenstein*, where she seems to parody her husband by playing Victor's preference for the desolate Alps off of Clerval's love of the social landscape along the Rhone. A letter from Percy Shelley to Hogg may as well have been a letter from Victor to Clerval: "You are more interested in the human part of the experience of travelling; a thing of which I see little, and understand less."[20] Shelley did alter his stance over his years in Italy, but these vituperative statements persisted for more than a year. Most important, he wrote the worst of them while preparing to write *Prometheus Unbound*, acts 1–3.

[19] *The Complete Works of Percy Bysshe Shelley*, 9:300 n.

[20] *Complete Works*, 9:307. Reciprocally, Clerval's lecture to Victor in the novel might as well be a letter from Hogg to Shelley: "I have seen . . . mountains descend almost perpendicularly to the water, casting black and impenetrable shades. . . . I have seen the mountains of La Valais, and the Pays de Vaud: but this country, Victor, pleases me more than all those wonders. The mountains of Switzerland are more majestic and strange; but there is a charm in the banks of this divine river, that I never before saw equalled. . . . Oh, surely, the spirit that inhabits and guards this place has a soul more in harmony with man, than those who pile the glacier, or retire to the inaccessible peaks of the mountains of our own country." Mary Shelley, *Frankenstein*, ed. James Rieger (Chicago: University of Chicago Press, 1974), 153.

More fully than any others, two consecutive letters written to Peacock in December 1818 and January 1819 suggest the nexus of concerns that occupied Shelley just before he began his lyrical drama. Shelley took his correspondence with Peacock seriously, more so than that with other friends, even Hunt; at one point, Mary Shelley asked Peacock to preserve the letters so that she might later copy them, suggesting that Shelley believed they had "literary" merit. The December letter (*CW*, 10:12–19) begins inauspiciously, gossiping about Byron's moral decline in Venice, but it also introduces the characteristic disdain for the contemporary Italians that either directly or indirectly enters into each of the letter's themes. The "contempt and desperation" of the latest *Childe Harold* verses, Shelley explains to Peacock, derive primarily from Byron's escapades with lower-class Venetians, especially his homosexual involvements. Yet despite this influence, Shelley concludes, Byron is "not yet an Italian"; he remains "a great poet." It is worth pausing a moment on this double conclusion, not only because it implies that "poet" and "Italian" are mutually exclusive categories, but because it also implies that remaining a poet has something to do with remaining an Englishman. In fact, Shelley's barely restrained nationalism frames the whole discussion: "for an Englishman to encourage such sickening vice is a melancholy thing"; vaguely described practices in Italy—again, probably gay sex—"are not only not named, but I believe seldom even conceived in England"; "Countesses smell so of garlic that an ordinary Englishman cannot approach them."[21] One forgets for the moment that Shelley had utterly rejected England, choosing a vagrant self-exile rather than accommodating himself to his native land's stifling morality. The irony is painful: having left England for the Italy of ancient art and nature, Shelley still preferred the English to the Italians. It is precisely this stubborn bias that allows him to adopt the arrogant posture of the touring Englishman who believes the genuine Italy belongs to him by right of cultural superiority.

As the letter describes the sights of Rome—the Coliseum, the Arch of Trajan, the Forum, the treasures of Italy's cultural paradise lost—it steadily narrows its attention to the timeless ideas and values that survive the passing of whole populations: "Behold the wrecks of what a great nation once dedicated to the abstractions of the mind! Rome is a city, as it were, of the dead, or rather of those who cannot die, and who survive the puny generations which inhabit and pass over the spot which they have made sacred to eternity." Shelley's preference for the long-buried, for

---

[21] Louis Crompton states that Shelley's circumlocutions are usually taken to imply a "homosexual coterie," though his words remain too vague to draw absolute conclusions. *Byron and Greek Love: Homophobia in Nineteenth-Century England* (Berkeley: University of California Press, 1985), 244.

those who cannot interfere with his imagining of them, leads to his central inversion: the dead are living and the living are dead. It is this judgment on the living that allows Shelley to will their absence so casually, so guiltlessly, to reduce them to what he describes elsewhere as their already inherent condition. In an earlier letter, Shelley considers the Italians a people defined by their lacks, by their internal emptiness: "The modern Italians seem a miserable people, without sensibility or imagination, or understanding. Their outside is polished, and an intercourse with them seems to proceed with much facility—tho it ends in nothing and produces nothing. The women are particularly empty, and though possessed of the same kind of superficial grace, are devoid of every cultivation and refinement" (*CW*, 9:318). One recalls the scholastic definition of evil as a nonexistent, purely negative phenomenon, the definition to which Shelley alludes when Prometheus says of Jupiter, "let the hour / Come, when thou must appear to be / That which thou art internally" (1.297–99). Jupiter vanishes because, despite his all-powerful appearance, he is insubstantial, literally a "phantasm." Equally phantasmatic, the Italians can also be made to disappear, though this requires a self-conscious visual technique. In the letter to Peacock Shelley continues: "In Rome, at least in the first enthusiasm of your recognitions of ancient time, you see nothing of the Italians. The nature of the city assists the delusion, for its vast and antique walls describe a circumference of sixteen miles, and thus the population is thinly scattered over this space, nearly as great as London." The antique walls become the frame of a Roman "scene." By an act of imaginative will, by manipulating the mode of half creating and perceiving, the tourist pretends to be alone among the ruins, making Rome a hallucinatory field in which the living seem to vanish into the oblivion of open urban space.

As people thus recede into the thin air of invisibility, as the dead come to occupy the foreground Shelley believes they merit, an associative logic moves the letter from various Roman ruins to another of Shelley's favorite locations, the Protestant cemetery. Shelley's description of the windblown trees and "sun warm earth" that make this spot "the most beautiful and solemn cemetery [he] ever beheld" develops into a lyrical climax that gathers together the letter's various thematic strands. At first, the passage prolongs the inversion that steers Shelley's thought throughout: removed from the city's social thoroughfares, Shelley can represent the dead as the genuine living; he imagines them sleeping, at peace with their picturesque surroundings. At the same time, however, the meditation begins to call into question this central inversion of life and death, ending with a sober self-reflection on imaginative projection, on the inevitable illusion involved in personifying the dead: "Such is the human mind, and so it peoples with its wishes vacancy and oblivion."

Shelley, in other words, finally acknowledges that the dead are dead, but his recognition goes only half the distance: if the imagination can "people" vacancy and oblivion, filling an empty space, it also exercises its desires by willing an empty space, by reducing real people to imaginative vacancy and oblivion. The first allure of the Protestant cemetery is precisely the vacancy of the dead, their blank inability to resist personification. As the entire letter indicates, the sublime imagination seeks out such vacancy and oblivion, and where it cannot find them it creates them. The second allure, one not to be underestimated, is that this space free of the Italian living houses a large body of the *English* dead.

The last third of this letter belongs with a sequel, Shelley's next letter to Peacock (24 January 1819, *CW*, 10:20–28). Following the reverie on the English cemetery, Shelley describes an excursion to Vesuvius, a sight surpassed in its horrible sublimity only by the glaciers of Mont Blanc. This transition merely follows the sequence of Shelley's travels, but it also bears a thematic logic; it introduces the agent of a famous scene of annihilation, something that becomes especially significant with the following letter's account of a visit to Pompeii. If in Rome depopulation could occur only by a visual trick, Pompeii provided the ideal site to meditate on culture unburdened by people. Pompeii's impact on Shelley's thought was immediate. The city's lifeless ruins helped foster his understanding of the Greek ideal (Pompeii, he informs Peacock, was a Greek city), and, not surprisingly, the city found its way directly into *Prometheus Unbound* as a model for human life. With Vesuvius always visible or audible in the background, Shelley toured the empty streets, entering the remains of once inhabited homes to contemplate living arrangements, furniture, decorations, courtyards, mosaics, and fountains—the material signs of human life liberated from ordinary human use, transfigured into the property of a generalized "mental beauty." "There is an ideal life in the forms of these paintings," he states of the murals not yet removed to museums, ideal because aesthetic form had become independent of passing human life. A single, violent disaster had achieved two remarkable effects: the eruption of Vesuvius fixed Pompeii's forms permanently while it simultaneously erased the merely transient population that occupied them like tenants. Shelley briefly considers this violence early in the letter, but he discusses it only as it affected architecture, *as if people had never really mattered:* "[My idea of] the mode of its destruction was this:—First, an earthquake shattered it, and unroofed almost all its temples, and split its columns; then a rain of light small pumice-stones fell; then torrents of boiling water, mixed with ashes, filled up all its crevices." Architecture topples in this detached, scientifically fascinated account, but people do not die. Shelley effaces the horror of violent death by focusing almost exclusively on the fortuitous results—the preservation of Pompeii, the remains of which he was surprised and delighted to find so "perfect."

With the excursion to Pompeii, Shelley began to consolidate his image of an ideal human origin, anticipating the one "peopled by shapes too bright to see," that he would soon have Asia rediscover in *Prometheus Unbound*—or the one that is simply without actual people. Pompeii struck him like a revelation, he tells Peacock, but this revelation had been well prepared by his cumulative experience of "ancient time" in Italy.

> I now understand why the Greeks were such great poets; and above all, I can account, it seems to me, for the harmony, the unity, the perfection, the uniform excellence, of all their works of art. They lived in a perpetual commerce with external nature, and nourished themselves upon the spirit of its forms. Their theatres were all open to the mountains and the sky. Their columns, the ideal types of a sacred forest, with its roof of interwoven tracery, admitted the light and wind; the odour and the freshness of the country penetrated the cities. Their temples were mostly upaithric; and the flying clouds, the stars, or the deep sky, were seen above. O, . . . but for those changes which conducted Athens to its ruin—to what an eminence might not humanity have arrived!

This architectural ideal frames *Prometheus Unbound* as both the origin and telos of its grand utopian myth; it precedes and follows the lived experience of people. Before the tyranny of Jupiter and under the guidance of Prometheus, "Cities . . . / Were built, and through their snow-like columns flowed / The warm winds, and the azure aether shone, / And the blue sea and shadowy hills were seen" (2.4.94–97). After Jupiter falls, Prometheus and Asia advance to their eschatological home at the "far goal of time," a destination marked by a classical temple, "Distinct with column, arch and architrave," populated by "living imagery— / Praxitelean shapes," but "deserted now" (3.3.162–67). This ideal and vacant space stands at the end of time, waiting to be "peopled," but given the persistent concerns of Shelley's apocalyptic imagination, one must wonder whether it could survive occupation, whether it is ideal only so long as it is without inhabitants.

In the same letter in which he informs Peacock that he has finished *Prometheus Unbound* (6 April 1819), Shelley once more describes the two Italies. Again he focuses on an architectural monument, but this time the disruptive presence of contemporary Italians yields a valuable insight into the interdependence of the social and the aesthetic.

> In the Square of St. Peter's there are about 300 fettered criminals at work, hoeing out the weeds that grow between the stones of the pavement. Their

legs are heavily ironed, and some are chained two by two. They sit in long rows, hoeing out the weeds, dressed in party coloured clothes. Near them sit or saunter, groupes of soldiers, armed with loaded muskets. The iron discord of those innumerable chains clanks up into the sonorous air, and produces, contrasted with the musical dashing of the fountains, and the deep azure beauty of the sky, and the magnificence of the architecture around, a conflict of sensations allied to madness. It is the emblem of Italy: moral degradation contrasted with the glory of nature and the arts. (*CW*, 10:47–48)

The scene jars the observer not so much because the reality of coerced labor contradicts the piazza's architectural beauty but because such labor serves precisely to sustain that beauty, to preserve the piazza's weedless aesthetic effect. In other words, Shelley momentarily represents how unideal social relations and practices lie within, not outside, works of art, how the ordinary and degraded people who seem to intrude on cultural beauty like parasites can indeed be the very condition of its production and maintenance. The dissonant image of St. Peter's thus recalls Benjamin's famous argument in the most literal way: "For without exception the cultural treasures [the historical materialist] surveys have an origin which he cannot contemplate without horror. They owe their existence not only to the efforts of the great minds and talents who have created them, but also to the anonymous toil of their contemporaries. There is no document of civilization which is not at the same time a document of barbarism."[22] And yet, what Shelley sees at St. Peter's he cannot see elsewhere in Italy, and his vision remains especially selective in the production of his own great cultural treasure. Already by the end of the passage, as he generalizes from St. Peter's to Italy at large, he begins to separate social reality ("moral degradation") from the autonomous "glory of nature and the arts." This division may be difficult to sustain at the Vatican, where the aesthetic is so explicitly bound up with violence, but outside the papal walls, in the vast spaces of depopulated Rome, for instance, one can momentarily delude oneself into believing that beauty has no people in it.[23]

[22] Walter Benjamin, "Theses on the Philosophy of History," in his *Illuminations*, trans. Harry Zohn (New York: Schocken, 1969), 256.

[23] John Brenkman's statements on art and social relations speak particularly well to the paradoxes of *Prometheus Unbound:* "There is no basis for presupposing that social domination figures in the production of art merely as the contingent historical condition which has made art as 'free creation' possible. Or for presupposing that the divisions of society are merely external to the 'work itself,' leaving no imprint on its form and inner logic. Art . . . constitutes itself *within* and *against* the forms of domination that organize the society in which the work is produced and the one in which it is received." *Culture and Domination* (Ithaca: Cornell University Press, 1987), 24.

Common Apocalypse

Not unlike *people, popular* is a curious word in Shelley's lexicon of 1819; it helps us chart the changes from *Prometheus Unbound* to the "Popular Songs" Shelley wrote in response to the Peterloo Massacre. The word enters his correspondence often (and without pejorative connotations) only after he believed *Prometheus Unbound* was finished, and it marks a growing concern with the practical functions of literature, with the realities of audience. Toward the middle of the summer, Shelley began to recognize that his lyrical drama, "the most perfect of [his] productions" (*CW*, 10:95), was destined also to be an unpopular production, that for all of its interest in representing a universal humanity, it was in fact written for a select circle of twenty auditors.[24] In a sense, Shelley's writing practice of early 1819, with its disregard of a wide readership in favor of a coterie of like-minded intellectuals, paralleled his detachment as a tourist in Italy, his effort to remove aesthetic experience from the complex social context in which it functions. The paradox that results in manifest: although *Prometheus Unbound* remains theoretically committed to a vision of utopian social harmony, it reaffirms in practice a social hierarchy between intellectual elites and the reading public. In act 4, Shelley would have his chorus sing of "Man, one harmonious Soul of many a soul" (4.400), but this elevated social vision requires a cautious response of the sort recommended by Gramsci:

> And is it not frequently the case that there is a contradiction between one's intellectual choice and one's mode of conduct? Which therefore would be the real conception of the world: that logically affirmed as an intellectual choice? or that which emerges from the real activity of each man, which is implicit in his mode of action? And since all action is political, can one not say that the real philosophy of each man is contained in its entirety in his political action?[25]

To think of *Prometheus Unbound* in Gramsci's terms as a "political action" is to recognize that Shelley wrote it much in the way he wrote his private correspondence—for Peacock and a few others only. In the same letter describing his inspired walk through the empty streets of Pompeii, he explained to his friend, "In my accounts of pictures and things I am

---

[24] "*Cenci* is written for the multitude, and ought to sell well. I think, if I may judge by its merits, the "Prometheus" cannot sell beyond twenty copies." *CW*, 10:148.

[25] Antonio Gramsci, "Notes for an Introduction and an Approach to the Study of Philosophy in the History of Culture," in *An Antonio Gramsci Reader*, ed. David Forgacs (New York: Schocken, 1988), 328.

more pleased to interest you than the many; and this is fortunate, because, in the 1st place, I have no idea of attempting the latter, and if I did
attempt it, I should assuredly fail" (*CW*, 10:21). This judgment, with its
antipopulist pride, changes decisively during the summer of 1819. After
the death of his son, William, in early June, Shelley briefly stopped writing letters altogether, and on the other side of this silence, when he re-
sumed his correspondence with Peacock ten weeks later, he began to express an unexpected interest in audience, something especially evident
in his desire to see his new tragedy, *The Cenci*, performed in London.

The broad outlines of this shift are not difficult to indicate. Early in
the summer Peacock sent Shelley a copy of *Nightmare Abbey*, the novel
that affectionately satirizes Shelley's vanguard elitism in the character
Scythrop:

> "Action," thus [Scythrop] soliloquised, "is the result of opinion, and to
> new-model opinion would be to new-model society. Knowledge is power; it
> is in the hands of a few, who employ it to mislead the many, for their own
> selfish purposes of aggrandisement and appropriation. What if it were in
> the hands of a few who should employ it to lead the many? What if it were
> universal, and the multitude were enlightened? No. The many must be
> always in leading-strings; but let them have wise and honest conductors. A
> few to think, and many to act; that is the only basis of perfect society."[26]

Shelley seems to have taken the criticism seriously. He began to call his
own study "Scythrop's Tower," thus acknowledging that the novel's
parody was fundamentally on target, and he began to admire Peacock's
easily accessible prose, which he interpreted as a rhetorical lesson aimed
squarely at himself: "I suppose the moral is contained in what Falstaff
says—'For God's sake, talk like a man of this world'" (*CW*, 10:58). The
influence of this lesson appears everywhere in Shelley's writing at the
time, from his growing appreciation of lowbrow authors as diverse as
Boccaccio and Cobbett to his conviction that *The Cenci*, unlike his previous work, would "produce a very popular effect" (*CW*, 10:79). In direct
opposition to the lyrical idealism, the pure poetry which bore some
unspecified relation to social change in *Prometheus Unbound*, Shelley now
openly embraced the Wordsworthian creed, proclaiming in the tragedy's
preface that "in order to move men to true sympathy we must use the
familiar language of men" (241). Not "a detached simile or a single
isolated description" appear in the play, he declared with apparent
pride. And curiously enough, with this new attention to the social position of literary language comes an alternative to Shelley's characteristic

---

[26] Thomas Love Peacock, *Nightmare Abbey* (New York: Penguin, 1969), 47.

scene of annihilation. No longer something to be transcended by the apocalyptic imagination, society itself becomes the human telos. "Social enjoyment," he writes to Peacock in August, "is the alpha and the omega of existence. All that I see in Italy—and from my tower window I now see the magnificent peaks of the Appennine half enclosing the plain—is nothing—it dwindles to smoke in the mind, when I think of some familiar forms of scenery little perhaps in themselves over which old remembrances have thrown a delightful colour" (*CW*, 10:73). This small and fanciful scene, in which the mountaintop sublime vanishes (goes up in smoke, no less) in favor of a modest, social landscape, would have been unimaginable only a few months earlier. By November, even the ancient dead have lost their appeal, and Rome seems "more like a sepulcher than a city; beautiful, but the abode of death" (*CW*, 10:128).

From Prometheus Unbound *to the "Popular Songs"*

Well before Peterloo occasioned his first political poems in a popular idiom, Shelley was already beginning to see his work according to its social situation, and this change bore directly on his use of poetic language. *Prometheus Unbound* had staked its "beautiful idealisms" (135) upon the power of language to transcend local contingencies, to empty itself of all but general significance. One might say of the drama, as Pater said of all art, that it aspires to the condition of music. Before Jupiter's tyranny, under the guidance of Prometheus, "the harmonious mind / Poured itself forth in all-prophetic song, / And music lifted up the listening spirit / Until it walked, exempt from mortal care, / Godlike, o'er the clear billows of sweet sound" (2.4.75–79). The liberation narrative that constitutes most of the play involves a return to this ideal linguistic origin: the apocalyptic moment itself occurs when the Spirit of the Hour blows the Protean conch and loosens "its mighty music" (3.3.81), releasing the harmonies that would eventually become the monumental and millennial hymn of act 4. Music, in other words, is both origin and end in the play, making it analogous to the evacuated architecture I discussed in the preceding section, an ideal voice emptied of worldly attachments, standing at the far goal of time with all the fantastic beauty of an uninhabited temple. It is hardly surprising, then, that Shelley gives the play's last word to Demogorgon, that consummate figure of negativity. When Ione signals his return at the conclusion of act 4, saying, "there is a sense of words upon mine ears," Panthea corrects her: "A universal sound *like* words" (4.517–18; my emphasis). In the play's final utopian vision, language has catapulted itself into the universal by becoming pure sound, a richly playful and diversified aesthetic form disencum-

bered of specific content. Demogorgon's nonreferential language resembles what Kant called an "aesthetical idea"—"that representation of
the imagination which occasions much thought, without however any
definite thought."[27] Or put another way, one is reminded of De Quincey's friend, who objected that he could "attach no ideas" to "a succession
of musical sounds"—to which De Quincey responded, "Ideas! my good
sir? there is no occasion for them."[28] To transform language into music
requires a similar canceling of content, just as it requires a dislocation
of words from the specific social contexts in which they function. De
Quincey claimed to take his greatest "musical" pleasures from eaves-
dropping on Italian conversations he could not understand.

In its desire for a universal language in music, *Prometheus Unbound*
rehearses the apocalyptic narrative I have observed throughout this
book, the narrative of a final communal redemption accompanied by, or
even occasioned by, the transcendence of social, historical, and linguistic
differences.[29] As Shelley tells the tale of an apocalyptic return from

[27] Immanuel Kant, *Critique of Judgment*, trans. J. H. Bernard (New York: Hafner, 1951),
157.
[28] Thomas de Quincey, *Confessions of an English Opium-Eater* (Oxford: Oxford University Press, 1985), 45.
[29] Shelley's leading critic, Stuart Curran, has argued that the music of *Prometheus
Unbound* comes to represent difference without hierarchy, that its profusion of literary
forms is at one with the play's democratic ideals. Writing of act 4, Curran states, "The
explosion of lyric forms reflects not only the vital energy of the regenerated world but also
its inexhaustible variety. No element, no perspective, escapes the universal harmony. The
virtuoso flair by its very nature conveys inclusiveness . . . [and] each [lyrical form] is an
integral prism of perspective coexisting, much like musical cadences, in democratic equality." Curran goes on to conclude that there is no "major experiment equal to *Prometheus
Unbound* in the formal ramifications of its democratic ethos. No sense of generic hierarchy
is allowed to intrude upon Shelley's drama: whatever form they assume, hierarchies are
still the creations of Jupiter. Rather a mixture of genres implies an uncompromising
multiperspectivism, a constant process whereby the mind reorders the elements that
constitute its universe. In so wholly honoring received generic traditions, Shelley paradoxically creates a monument of revolutionary art whose concern is the nature of the ultimate
human revolution. . . . Genre so self-reflexively considered becomes virtually a metaphor
for the poem itself, the purpose of whose mixture of forms is to celebrate human inclusiveness." *Poetic Form and British Romanticism* (Oxford: Oxford University Press, 1986), 202–3. I
cannot imagine a more eloquent statement of the democratic ideals that the literary form
of *Prometheus Unbound* is intended to express. At the same time, however, does not this
inspired argument conflate the poem's magnificent poetic achievement with a genuine
political achievement? How can one speak of inclusiveness, universality, multiplicity, heterogeneity—all of which describe aesthetic features but are meant as allegories of a social
utopia—without considering the reality of the play's distinctly (and forthrightly) anti-
democratic practice, not what it is *about* but what it *does* as a social act of communication?
Shelley's representation of a vitally diverse totality of voices, inviting all perspectives to join
in equal participation, would seem anything but inclusive to most of the reading public,
and the point is that *Prometheus Unbound* was written without "them" in mind, or, rather, by
working to keep "them" out of mind. The "galaxy of *lyric* differentiation" Curran celebrates within the play speaks to a very small sector of the *social* differences outside the play.

division to all-encompassing harmony, he reproduces Revelation's central linguistic myth, the victory of the messianic Logos over the fallen condition of Babylon. Even more pertinent historically is the way that *Prometheus Unbound,* while trying to extricate the abiding revolutionary values from their entanglement in the Terror, reproduces the very linguistic ideals that inspired Barère and Grégoire in their campaign against the patois. In each of these apocalyptic variations, words come to represent a collective humanity by transcending social differences, by entering a formal space in which historical contingencies and local interests are deemed insignificant. This idealized self-representation, however, must be perpetually questioned, just as Shelley himself engaged in such questions during the summer of 1819. Apocalyptic language asserts its universality not by transcending but by *suppressing* social differences; it asserts its authority *over* social situations by claiming to be free *from* social situation. The remarkable feature of Shelley's poetry in 1819, as it veers away from *Prometheus Unbound,* is that it begins to challenge the very idea of a context-free language liberated from the content and purpose of particular social circumstance. By September, the universal music of *Prometheus Unbound* that was paradoxically written for so slight an audience would be replaced by the "Popular Songs" Shelley wrote for his widest audience yet, thus altering the function and representation of his apocalypse considerably.

The summer's first and most dramatic reconsideration of *Prometheus Unbound* occurred with *The Cenci,* though the full significance of this change has been overshadowed by the tendency to read the tragedy as Shelley's disillusioned response to his earlier and overinflated optimism. While this interpretation, invited by the author himself, is valuable and necessary, it obscures the extent to which writing *The Cenci* liberated Shelley from the severe social detachment he had imposed on himself with *Prometheus Unbound.* For all its morbid investigation of "sad reality" (237), *The Cenci* restored a healthy pragmatism regarding audience; after indulging so fully in closet drama, Shelley clearly found the prospect of public theater enabling. Moreover, the new concern with the actual (rather than purely theoretical) function of literary work—Shelley's attention to the participation of his own productions within a wider social setting—corresponds to a new representation of language *within* the play. One of the primary concerns of *The Cenci* is to demonstrate that all language is embedded in specific social circumstance, or more accurately, in the historical relations of power. Beginning with the opening line of the play—"That matter of the murder is hushed up"—Shelley foregrounds the actual politics of language that in *Prometheus Unbound* had taken a highly abstract, ahistorical form. As the tragedy's conflicts unfold, what matters more and more is the ability to control access to speech, the ability to assert one's power by diminishing the linguistic capacities of others. Anticipating the broad political issues that will emerge most forcefully in the "Popular Songs," *The Cenci* demonstrates Shelley's deepening appreciation of the way silence functions as a register of disempowerment. Thus act 1 consistently represents how those with relative power threaten to silence those without: the pope can hush a murder, Orsino can suppress a petition, and Cenci boasts that he can choke the throat of any challenger with dust. Appropriately, Beatrice's final offense, the one that brings the full force of Cenci's violence upon her, is her blatant disregard of her father's public speech. When Cenci celebrates the death of his sons at the infamous banquet that concludes act 1, he quiets his offended guests with his characteristic threat—"my good friends . . . Will think . . . perhaps / Of their own throats" (1.3.129–31)—but he cannot silence his own daughter, who continues to plead for help despite his attempts to interrupt her. Beatrice willfully ignores her father's voice, *"not noticing the words of Cenci"* (1.3), as Shelley's stage directions state. The realization that language is the field in which the competition for power plays itself out is hardly lost on Cenci, who subsequently recalls his daughter's disobedience in the following terms: "Then it was I whose inarticulate words / Fell from my lips, and who with tottering steps / Fled from your presence, as you now from mine. . . . Never again . . . Shalt thou strike dumb the meanest of mankind; / Me least of all" (2.1.112–20).

By raping Beatrice, Cenci literally strikes his daughter dumb; the sign of power's triumph is its capacity not merely to limit but to destroy speech. Perhaps the most startling gloss of Beatrice's oppression appears in Elaine Scarry's recent phenomenology of torture: "The tendency of pain not simply to resist expression but to destroy the capacity for speech is in torture reenacted in overt, exaggerated form. Even when the torturers do not permanently eliminate the voice through mutilation or murder, they mime the work of pain by temporarily breaking off the voice, making it their own, making it speak their words, making it cry out when they want it to cry, be silent when they want its silence, turning it on and off."[30] At the structural center of *The Cenci*—act 3, scene 1—is Beatrice's agonized silence, the staggering incoherence that immediately follows her rape. Beatrice is unable to articulate the crime: "What are the words which you would have me speak?"; "there is none to tell / My misery"; "[my] sufferings . . . have no tongue" (3.1.107, 113–14, 142). The entire tragedy pivots on this moment of linguistic deprivation, for without the power of self-representation Beatrice experiences a

[30] Elaine Scarry, *The Body in Pain: The Making and Unmaking of the World* (Oxford: Oxford University Press, 1985), 54.

collapse of agency itself, an utter evacuation of the self. After the rape, she cannot complete a simple sentence of self-identification: "I am . . . [*her voice dies away faintly*]" (3.1.68 and stage direction). In the remaining scenes, Beatrice goes on to speak at length, but she never recovers her own voice. She emerges from the empty center of incoherence to chart a course of violence, but she speaks in a new voice that distinctly resembles her father's. Cenci dies only after having displaced his daughter's voice with his own, "making it speak [his] words," as Scarry puts it; in one of the tragedy's most painful ironies, he secures the reproduction of power through the ventriloquism that brings about his own murder.

The anatomy of language and power in *The Cenci* marks the divide of 1819 for Shelley; it departs from the idealist aesthetics of *Prometheus Unbound* as it makes possible the gritty politics of the "Popular Songs," leaving an especially vivid imprint on the apocalyptic themes to which Shelley returned after Peterloo. When Shelley first received news of the massacre of working-class protesters at a Manchester political rally, his immediate response was to quote his own play, to draw on the very scene I have discussed. In a letter to his publisher Ollier, he adopted Beatrice's lines from the pivotal third act: "Something must be done. What, yet I know not" (*CW*, 10:80). Shelley knew, of course, that Beatrice, having lost her power of self-representation, would eventually take the self-destructive path of vengeance. "If I try to speak / I shall go mad," she says in lines just preceding those Shelley quoted for Ollier (3.1.85–86). Without access to language and the self-determination such access promises, Beatrice's only recourse is to reproduce the violence that has been imposed on her. Shelley's great insight was to observe how thoroughly the victimized English workers occupied a similar position and therefore risked the same disastrous outcome. After all, the Manchester reformers had gathered at St. Peter's Field in order to protest their deprivation of voice, to challenge the parliamentary injustices that systematically dispossessed them of political expression. As many as one hundred thousand people met to hear Orator Hunt address the problem Tom Paine had singled out a generation earlier, that they had been virtually silenced from the public sphere; although a sprawling industrial center like Manchester sent but one representative to Parliament in 1819, a rotten borough like Old Sarum could send two.[31] The English parliamentary reform movement of 1818 and 1819, which reached its climax with the Manchester meeting in August, urged empowerment through democratic representation, self-determination through wider and equitable access to the electoral system. Peterloo, it would appear, prompted Shelley to translate his analysis of power and language from the sphere of individual tragedy to that of political structure itself.

[31] See Thomas Paine, *Rights of Man* (New York: Penguin, 1969), 74.

In his hastily composed "Popular Songs" Shelley consistently organized the representation of social conflict according to a stark opposition between speech and silence—and the figure that he used to signify empowerment, the transformation of the silent into the speaking, was apocalypse. Throughout these informal, brazenly sloganeering poems, figures fit for a Last Judgment canvas shake their slumber, rise from the dead, and inevitably enter a new life of self-determination by discovering their ability to speak or to sing. The final stanza of "A New National Anthem," which celebrates Liberty as the true Queen of England, is typical: "Lips touched by Seraphim / Breathe out the choral hymn / God save the Queen! / Sweet as if Angels sang, / Loud as that trumpet's clang / Wakening the world's dead gang,— / God save the Queen!"[32] Death is Shelley's persistent image of the disenfranchisement that accompanies voicelessness, as the chilling off-rhyme of another poem indicates: "Corpses are cold in the tomb, / Stones on the pavement are dumb."[33] And as surely as silence is a type of death, speech is a type of resurrection, an association that allows Shelley to recast in political terms the apocalyptic literature familiar to his Bible-reading audience. In one of several biblical allusions, "An Ode: Written October 1819" invokes a famous passage from Isaiah:

> Awaken, awaken, awaken!
> The slave and the tyrant are twin-born foes;
> Be the cold chains shaken
> To the dust where your kindred repose, repose:
> Their bones in the grave will start and move,
> When they hear the voices of those they love,
> Most loud in the holy combat above.
>
> (8–14)[34]

Writing in exile, Second Isaiah called on Yahweh to liberate the Jews from Babylon as he once liberated them from Egypt: "Awake, awake, put on strength, O arm of the Lord; awake, as in the days of old, the generations long ago" (51:9). In Shelley's revision, the oppressed put on their own strength, engaging in a form of apocalyptic battle that for Shelley is clearly a matter of linguistic confrontation. Bones stir to the sound of newly awakened voices; as in "A New National Anthem," the

---

[32] Percy Bysshe Shelley, "A New National Anthem," in *Complete Works of Shelley*, ed. Ingpen and Peck, 3:292.

[33] Percy Bysshe Shelley, "Lines Written during the Castlereagh Administration," in *Complete Works of Shelley*, ed. Ingpen and Peck, 3:287.

[34] Percy Bysshe Shelley, "An Ode: Written October 1819, Before the Spaniards Had Recovered Their Liberty," in *Complete Works of Shelley*, ed. Ingpen and Peck, 2:297–98.

acquisition of speech and the resurrection from political death occur simultaneously.

By making the human voice the agent of apocalyptic liberation, Shelley sought to fit his "Popular Songs" into the agenda of the parliamentary reform movement, lending support to one of its primary objectives: the convening of a national assembly in which those deprived of representation would assert their right to speak outside the jurisdiction of Parliament. Shelley endorsed this platform explicitly—"Let a great Assembly be / Of the fearless and the free"—and each of his appeals to resurrected speech must be seen according to this reference point.[35] The apocalyptic rhetoric of the "Popular Songs" aimed not at some vague millennial kingdom but at an entirely specific historical objective. The campaign for an alternative assembly, which had been initiated by Paine and Thelwall in the 1790s, gained momentum early in 1819, and the Manchester rally, the largest of several that year, was viewed as preparation for a truly national meeting. This prospect threatened a return to the Jacobin politics of the previous generation, something that helps to explain why the administration ultimately refused to condemn the events that became known as Peterloo. After the massacre, the radical printer Richard Carlile typified the opposition outrage that made August 1819 the climax of the reform movement prior to 1832: he changed the name of his paper from *The Register* to *The Republican;* he began to reprint Paine's radical pamphlets; and he campaigned vigorously for the people's assembly. Because of such activities he was promptly jailed, and Shelley was inspired to write a letter in his defense intended for Hunt's *Examiner.* With these events one begins to understand the urgency of Shelley's association between speech and apocalypse. Even the impassioned slogan of "The Mask of Anarchy"—"Rise like lions after slumber / In unvanquishable number . . . / Ye are many—they are few" (lines 151–55 and elsewhere)—should probably be read in this light. Rather than a direct appeal to force that would contradict Shelley's ideal of nonviolent resistance, it seems to endorse the idea of a massive national convention; as the "Popular Songs" repeatedly assert, to rise from sleep is to awaken to the apocalyptic power of politics, the roar of collective speech.[36]

Given Shelley's deepening concern with the pragmatic politics of

---

[35] Percy Bysshe Shelley, "The Mask of Anarchy," in *Shelley's Poetry and Prose*, ed. Reiman and Powers, p. 308, lines 262–63. Further citations are to this text and indicated by line number only.

[36] John Belchem's "Republicanism, Popular Constitutionalism, and the Radical Platform in Early Nineteenth-Century England" is an informative source on the place of the campaign for the national assembly within the parliamentary reform movement. *Social History* 6 (1981): esp. 11–16.

language, given the fact that his intervention in a local crisis required addressing an audience made up largely of English workers with limited education, it is hardly surprising that the "Popular Songs" involve Shelley's fullest experimentation with poetry in a popular voice. What is surprising, and what measures the distance between the apocalyptic rhetoric of *Prometheus Unbound* and that of these small, passionate poems, is that Shelley seems to have found such political engagement liberating. At the very moment in which he urged others to awaken to the power of language, he described his own parallel awakening as a poet: "As I lay asleep in Italy / There came a voice from over the Sea, / And with great power it forth led me / To walk in the visions of Poesy" (lines 1–4). Before he had word of Peterloo, it seems, Shelley too had been asleep; and when he awoke, the bankrupt linguistic universals of *Prometheus Unbound* faded like a dream. The new poetic voice that led him by its "great power" into "The Mask of Anarchy" is a remarkably accessible voice, indeed rather common, "crude" in the disparaging language of some Shelley criticism; largely indifferent to aesthetic matters, it is above all concerned with communication. When this voice takes on an apocalyptic rhetoric, it does so not in pursuit of words that transcend history, but to speak to an audience of working people who traditionally expressed their discontent and their struggles in the language of radical Protestant millenarianism; it adopts *their* language, investing itself in the imagery through which "minority groups have articulated their experience and projected their aspirations for hundreds of years," as E. P. Thompson put it.[37] Apocalypse in these poems is a popular idiom, a local discourse, a means of voicing particular social desires that might otherwise be left inarticulate. It is Shelley's attempt to take the language of others seriously. If in *Prometheus Unbound* particular interests seem to disappear into the universal sound of apocalyptic music, then in these simple songs apocalyptic rhetoric sets out to represent just such forgotten interests.

In turning from one apocalyptic project to another in the summer of 1819, Shelley exercised the kind of critical awareness that Bakhtin would eventually come to represent; he began "to regard one language . . . through the eyes of another language."[38] On the either side of *The Cenci*, one finds Shelley employing the same apocalyptic images as if they belonged to different languages, with remarkably different results. In its attempt to imagine life as a form liberated from the constraints of

[37] E. P. Thompson, *The Making of the English Working Class* (New York: Penguin, 1963), 54.

[38] M. M. Bakhtin, *The Dialogic Imagination,* ed. Michael Holquist, trans. Caryl Emerson and Michael Holquist (Austin: University of Texas Press, 1981), 296.

history, *Prometheus Unbound* channels its political hopes into a desire to transcend the political altogether. As we have seen, the language of that desire is music, which seems to cancel sociolinguistic differences and hover above ideology. In *Prometheus Unbound*, the Antichrist is nothing other than history itself—or what the spirits who encourage Prometheus call "Ruin":

> Though Ruin now Love's shadow be,
> Following him destroyingly
> On Death's white and winged steed,
> Which the fleetest cannot flee—
>
> . . . .
>
> Thou shalt quell this Horseman grim,
> Woundless though in heart or limb.
> (1.780–83; 787–88)

When "The Mask of Anarchy," the centerpiece of the "Popular Songs," employs the same image, the object of apocalyptic desire has altered significantly. Anarchy rides a white horse "Like Death in the Apocalypse" (33), but he possesses an identity far less generic, far more local than "Ruin"; he is the English government of Castlereagh, Eldon, and Sidmouth (all named in the poem), an administration that has perpetuated tyranny by depriving its people of just representation. By invoking the Book of Revelation here, Shelley calls not for a leap out of history but for action against a particular instance of oppression that can be challenged only within history. History meant something different to the audience addressed by the "Popular Songs" than it did to the twenty mythographers Shelley imagined would read *Prometheus Unbound*: for the community of English workers, history was something still to be entered, not something to be left behind by the flight of transcendence.

The Moment of "The Mask of Anarchy"

As the allusion of its title to the Renaissance masque suggests, "The Mask of Anarchy" is more self-consciously "literary" than the other "Popular Songs," which perhaps explains why it has generated more critical interest than all the other songs combined. In her note to the poem, Mary Shelley promoted this disproportionate attention: "Many stanzas are all his own," she wrote, implying that one could sift Shelley's characteristic literary strengths out from the poem's merely propagandistic setting. Recently, Michael Scrivener has helped to counteract this tendency by demonstrating the extent of the poem's debt to popular iconography, but little has yet been said about the way its commitment to popular discourse enables the poem to critique the high rhetorical mode of *Prometheus Unbound*.[39] "The Mask of Anarchy" draws together nearly all the prominent concerns and procedures of the "Popular Songs," but, in a way the other poems do not, it explicitly addresses the relation between the literary and the political. Resisting any effort to separate aesthetic qualities from immediate social purposes, the poem presents an allegory of *the subordination* of the literary to the political. In doing so, moreover, it situates with greater historical specificity the objectives of the "Popular Songs."

"The Mask of Anarchy" consists of three distinct sections of uneven length, each of which represents a different linguistic practice. As they unfold sequentially, these sections narrate the passage from language under tyranny to language as democratic self-representation, a passage mediated by the intervention of poetry. Thus the first part of the poem, dominated by the pageant of Anarchy, describes the uneven distribution of public voice as it is manipulated by power. The adoring but trampled multitudes possess almost no means of expression here, for only those in league with authority have access to speech. Not only does Anarchy restrict language hierarchically in this fashion, but he also promotes the illusion that speech (as well as the power accompanying it) is fixed, determined, and unalterable. On his brow Anarchy bears the mark, "I AM GOD, AND KING, AND LAW" (37). Every spoken line in the poem's first section merely rearranges this official declaration, as if its terms were the necessary and immutable givens of discourse and social relation. Anarchy's cohorts, for instance, sing, "Thou art God, and Law, and King" (61), and lawyers and priests together whisper, "Thou art Law and God" (69). As if to confirm the tautological unity of the official lexicon, the echoing voices join forces: "Then all cried with one accord; / 'Thou art King, and God, and Lord'" (70–71). The stifling repetition encourages belief that words are limited in supply, belong to few, and can be combined only in prescribed, mechanical ways that endlessly reproduce the structure of power.

In order for the silenced to recover voice, the overdetermined order

---

[39] See Michael Scrivener's useful discussion of popular iconography in *Radical Shelley: The Philosophical Anarchism and Utopian Thought of Percy Bysshe Shelley* (Princeton: Princeton University Press, 1982), 199–246. Scrivener acknowledges that his work on "The Mask of Anarchy" grew out of a suggestion by Stuart Curran in *Shelley's Annus Mirabilis*. Curran has read the "Popular Songs" with great care and has paid particular attention to their apocalyptic rhetoric. These poems, Curran argues, "are written quickly, are written down, it would appear, to play upon superstitious millenarian expectations which Shelley himself did not share. In the presence of political crisis Shelley apparently thought it of some value to remind the religious of their last days" (183–85). One purpose of this section is to take that last sentence more seriously than Curran probably intended.

of language that excludes them must first be ruptured, its vulnerability demonstrated; this role Shelley reserves for poetry and its characteristic figure, metaphor. In the poem's second section, civil disobedience (represented by the character "Hope") releases a mysterious Shape that by eluding any identification challenges the very integrity of linguistic determinacy. In this Shape, the source of which Shelley never indicates, language is both decentered and liberated from fixed reference. If the first section of the poem depends on fixed allegorical relations—Murder like Castlereagh, Fraud like Eldon, Hypocrisy like Sidmouth—the second releases the signifier with the abundant troping we usually expect from Shelley. The indeterminate Shape that appears between Hope and her enemies as "A mist, a light, an image" (103) can be named in the poem only by linguistic excess, as an outpouring of shifting figuration that disturbs the pretense of linguistic closure.

> With step as soft as wind it past
> O'er the heads of men—so fast
> That they knew the presence there,
> And looked,—but all was empty air.
>
> As flowers beneath May's footstep waken
> As stars from Night's loose hair are shaken
> As waves arise when loud winds call
> Thoughts sprung where'er that step did fall.
>
> And the prostrate multitude
> Looked—. . .
> . . . .
> And Anarchy, the ghastly birth,
> Lay dead earth upon the earth. . . .
>   (lines 118–27; 130–31)

The Shape's simultaneous absence and presence recall Demogorgon's aesthetic function, just as the central image of the wind anticipates the traces of poetic inspiration Shelley will later describe in the "Defence."[40] Poetry and authority are as antithetical as Demogorgon and Jupiter, indeterminacy and dogma. Shelley avoids direct description of Anarchy's death, but the passage seems to imply that tyranny is a linguistic

---

[40] Jerrold E. Hogle describes the function of metaphor in "A Defence" in terms appropriate to the role of the Shape in "The Mask of Anarchy": "For Shelley the socialized psyche must always be forced back into the shifting depths of metaphor from which it came, else the mind will fabricate ways to enchain itself." "Shelley's Poetics: The Power as Metaphor," *Keats-Shelley Journal* 31 (1982): 185.

fabrication dissipated the moment language returns to its inherent troping process. There are as many meanings as metaphors within this
elusive Shape, a messianic figure whose power derives from the discursive freedom of its multiple voicing.

Were "The Mask of Anarchy" to end with its eponymous tyrant's
sudden demise, which it could, the poem would be little more than
Prometheus Unbound broadened for mass consumption. Like Anarchy,
Jupiter is also a mind-forg'd manacle, the product of a consciousness
trapped within a deadening verbal structure, the curse. By exorcising
the language of hatred, Prometheus releases Demogorgon, who, like the
Shape, dissolves the influence of power. In each poem, the release from
linguistic tyranny results in the liberation of metaphor and a profusion
of lyrical free play. But here the similarity begins to collapse, for "The
Mask of Anarchy" refuses to end with this type of linguistic victory. The
"perpetual Orphic song" (4.415) that *Prometheus Unbound* (in its finished
version) places in conclusion, "The Mask of Anarchy" sets in the unfinished business of the middle. As Barbara Johnson has written in an
essay on the politics of deconstruction, indeterminacy, as an end in itself,
can produce just the opposite practical effect of the radical freedom it
enables in texts, inducing paralytic indecision rather than the capacity
for committed, decisive action. But Johnson preserves a place for deconstructive linguistic processes (what she generally calls, after Barthes,
"writerliness") by subordinating them to the more pragmatic political
ends they might be made to serve.

> If writerliness is defined as attention to the trace of otherness in language,
> as attention to the way in which there is always more than one message,
> then it is hard to see how a true instatement of the power of other voices is
> possible without something like a writerly apprenticeship. . . . If writerli-
> ness cannot be set up as an *ultimate* value without neutralizing itself, it
> nevertheless seems to stand as the un-bypassable site of the *pen*ultimate.[41]

Deconstructive criticism, at least in America, has made much of its
spectacular living off the Shelley of *Prometheus Unbound* or "The Triumph of Life," but here Johnson comes close to describing the relation
between poetry and politics in "The Mask of Anarchy." The death of
Anarchy through poetic indeterminacy occurs before the poem's mid-
point; it marks the opening up of language, but only so that the rest of
the poem can advocate a specific political program, a realization of
linguistic difference in the shape (not the Shape) of an actual social

---

[41] Barbara Johnson, "Is Writerliness Conservative?" in her *World of Difference* (Baltimore: Johns Hopkins University Press, 1987), 31.

practice. In the poem's third section, a voice fills the gap left by poetry with a two-hundred-line speech on the realities of economic exploitation and the nature of genuine freedom. Immediately, one becomes aware that Anarchy's allegorical death by metaphor solves none of the problems *outside* the poem. This new voice, just the opposite of a lyrical end in itself, only *begins* to instruct its audience how to put language to work. The final linguistic form envisioned by the poem, political self-representation, remains a goal still to be achieved by collective action. Thus the third section calls on the politically inarticulate—those who "suffer moan" (273), who "groan for pain" (278), who "murmur [in] distress" (284), who, in sum, "suffer woes untold" (291)—to join in the campaign I earlier described as the reference point of the "Popular Songs," the campaign for an alternative national assembly. By poem's end, the power structure Anarchy represents has yet to be challenged.

Schematically, the three-part linguistic allegory of "The Mask of Anarchy" looks like this: (1) dominant discourse; (2) poetry; (3) democratic representation. Shelley continues to mystify poetry—it seems to come from an ideal place outside ideology—but nonetheless he now assigns it an intermediate role in the service of ideological conflict. In the following section, I discuss some of the consequences of Shelley's lingering utopianism, but for the moment I want to consider the political pragmatism of "The Mask of Anarchy," the fact that it considers poetry's absolute and inherent freedom significant only to the extent that it achieves some form of social realization. At the same time that Shelley adopted the apocalyptic rhetoric of his audience in order to motivate collective action at the moment of the Peterloo crisis, he also sought to direct that audience toward a more effective political discourse, which would supersede the limited traditions of millenarianism. In "The Mask of Anarchy," in other words, poetry mediates not simply between authoritarian and democratic discourses but between two languages of resistance. The poem's most explicit apocalyptic rhetoric, including the extended pattern of allusion to the Book of Revelation, appears primarily in the elaborate description of Anarchy, as part of the first section; despite the stifling official lexicon, with its claim to have exhausted all linguistic possibilities, there already exists a discourse of popular resistance that exceeds the administration's vigilance. By characterizing oppression in apocalyptic terms of ultimate evil, Shelley taps that discourse. He does so, however, only as his starting point. By the end of the poem, Shelley describes oppression almost entirely in terms of economic and political exploitation, giving the poem's linguistic narrative an added dimension: (1) apocalyptic rhetoric; (2) poetry; (3) economic/political analysis. It is this second dimension that allows us to situate the poem historically, for as it mediates between a type of resistance based on passionate superstition and a type based on the analysis of labor, "The Mask of Anarchy" marks a pivotal moment in the English reform movement.

The year 1819 was perhaps the last of the English romantic period in which traditional apocalyptic rhetoric carried wide political significance. Shelley was late in his choice of imagery but not anachronistic, and his cautious use of a radical discourse that had dominated the years following the French Revolution suggests his awareness that the nature of popular resistance was fundamentally changing. In the late eighteenth and early nineteenth centuries, political activism in England typically centered on communities attempting to redress the local disturbances industrialization wrought on their lives; it rarely if ever involved the more abstract affiliations of class. In his valuable reconsideration of Thompson's standard history of the period, Craig Calhoun has argued that "in the early part of the industrial revolution, community was the crucial social bond unifying workers for collective action. . . . [T]raditional values, not a new analysis of exploitation, guided the workers in their radicalism."[42] Acts of political violence were more likely to occur out of a desire to preserve established social arrangements than from an interest in advancing natural rights (Jacobinism) or securing a share of the material advantages brought to a few by industrialism. Calhoun expresses a central paradox by calling the independent craftsmen, shopkeepers, and others who resisted economic change "reactionary radicals." Not until the early 1820s, then, does one find evidence of the genuine working-class consciousness Thompson ascribed to an earlier period. The years between 1810 and 1820 saw the shift from Luddism to the parliamentary reform movement, from local, informal organization to protest campaigns organized regionally and nationally, from activism scattered across provincial sites to activism concentrated in the urban industrial centers. Most significantly for Shelley, the decade marked a transition from resistance based on traditional values to resistance based on a pre-Marxian analysis of economic exploitation.

Written at the end of this pivotal decade, "The Mask of Anarchy" draws on the language and convictions of traditional populism while trying to transform them into the political and economic critique that would enable workers both to represent more rigorously the frustrations they experienced and to identify the most effective means of empowerment. Reading the newspapers forwarded by Hunt and Peacock, Shelley knew well the rhetoric of the parliamentary reform movement, including the contradictions that often kept it a backward-looking movement; he understood the importance of traditional values to large-scale mobili-

---

[42] Craig Calhoun, *The Question of Class Struggle: Social Foundations of Popular Radicalism during the Industrial Revolution* (Chicago: University of Chicago Press, 1982), 7.

zation, recognizing that people acted when they saw themselves preserving or restoring those values. In 1816, Cobbett struck a lasting chord when he wrote, "There is no principle, no precedent, no regulations (except as to mere matter of detail), favorable to freedom, which is not to be found in the Laws of England or in the example of our Ancestors. Therefore, I say we may ask for, and we want *nothing new*. We have great constitutional laws and principles, to which we are immoveably attached. We want *great alteration,* but we want *nothing new.*"[43] Following Cobbett and others, Shelley couched his advocacy of the national assembly in terms of a nostalgic restoration of uncorrupted law, as if it involved no real innovation:

> "Let the Laws of your own land
> Good or ill, between ye [and your oppressors] stand
> Hand to hand, and foot to foot,
> Arbiters of the dispute,
>
> "The old laws of England—they
> Whose reverend heads with age are grey,
> Children of a wiser day;
> And whose solemn voice must be
> Thine own echo—Liberty!"
>
> (lines 327–35)

Similarly, the poem's apocalyptic rhetoric must be understood as an appeal to the movement's "reactionary radicals"; it allows anger and protest to surface in a way compatible with established community traditions. At the same time, however, Shelley seems to have realized the real cost of such popular appeal, what Calhoun calls the inability of millenarianism "to develop a deeper understanding of the dynamics of a social or economic system."[44] Although he is a figure more specific than history or "ruin," Anarchy is still too vague an Antichrist, the nebulous symbol of any and all official evils. Even as he bears Castlereagh, Eldon, and Sidmouth in his entourage, Anarchy is more the proverbial "them" of big government than a focused target for resistance. Precisely for this reason the poem must grind him to dust before it can get on to its real work. As an image of the inevitable demise of power, the death of Anarchy serves to encourage and sustain the dispossessed in their struggle, but that death is also the poem's necessary means of superseding its own apocalyptic rhetoric. With the Antichrist invoked and overcome in

---

[43] Cobbett, quoted by Calhoun, ibid., 103.
[44] Calhoun, *The Question of Class Struggle,* 72.

utopian fantasy, the poem proceeds to specify a series of crippling economic abuses, from the systematic deflation of wages and the alienation of labor to a vivid critique of wage slavery—"'Tis to work and have such pay / As just keeps life from day to day / In your limbs, as in a cell / For the tyrant's use to dwell" (lines 160–63). After the death of Anarchy, the Book of Revelation and its imagery simply disappear from the poem.

Throughout his career, Shelley viewed millenarianism with ambivalence. He feared that with its focus on divine intervention, the inevitability of providential victory and the heavenly kingdom, millenarianism might cultivate passivity on behalf of those who most needed to act for themselves. But as the "Popular Songs" demonstrate, he also understood that the oppressed, without an independent language of resistance, adapted to their own purposes the language that was available. At times, providentialism might be the best means for a severely deprived community to articulate its vision of an alternative life. At other times, apocalyptic faith can interfere with the work of economic analysis and the implementation of political programs. The unusual power of "The Mask of Anarchy" results from its placement between such moments, from the way it seizes the historical opportunity to transform desperate hope into self-directed action.

In the years following the Russian Revolution, Gramsci, like Shelley before him, acknowledged the cultural if not the metaphysical validity of apocalyptic providentialism: "When you don't have the initiative in the struggle and the struggle itself comes eventually to be identified with a series of defeats, mechanical determinism becomes a tremendous force of moral resistance, of cohesion and of patient and obstinate perseverance. 'I have been defeated for the moment, but the tide of history is working for me in the long term.' . . . Indeed one should emphasize how fatalism is nothing other than the clothing worn by real and active will when in a weak position."[45] Gramsci knew that the transition from wishful but passive optimism to active and effective struggle can occur only when the means of empowerment are at hand; it cannot simply be willed. The dispossessed become agents when circumstances permit, or in terms of the intellectual tradition Gramsci advanced, when those without privilege become indispensable to a given economy's mode of production. At such times, they are already empowered without knowing it. "But when the 'subaltern' becomes directive and responsible for the economic activity of the masses, mechanicism at a certain point becomes an imminent danger and a revision must take place in modes of thinking because a change has taken place in the social mode of existence. . . . [I]f yesterday the subaltern element was a thing, today it is no

45 Gramsci, "The Study of Philosophy in the History of Culture," 336–37.

longer a thing but a historical person, a protagonist" (336). In the years before Marx, "The Mask of Anarchy" moved resistance away from the discourse of apocalypse (historical "mechanicism") because Shelley observed just such a change in "the social mode of existence." In the aftermath of Peterloo, he urged English workers to see themselves as active agents, as "Heroes of unwritten story" (148), because the time was right for them to assume the role of self-determination. All the nation's wealth and power, the poem contends, already depends on the productivity of their labor:

> The seed ye sow, another reaps;
> The wealth ye find, another keeps;
> The robes ye weave, another wears;
> The arms ye forge, another bears.
>
> Sow seed,—but let no tyrant reap;
> Find wealth,—let no imposter heap;
> Weave robes,—let not the idle wear;
> Forge arms,—in your defence to bear.[46]

The year 1819 was exactly the moment to supplement apocalyptic discourse with an analysis of labor and capital.

Protest Poetics in the Age of Democracy

In the postapocalyptic universe of *Prometheus Unbound*, act 4, words are the agents that perform human desire, language the transformational medium in which history dissolves and a liberated world of human making emerges. The first figures to appear in the play's fantastic millennial scene are the last vestiges of temporality itself, the ghosts of transcended time who announce themselves with a lyric introducing Shelley's governing principle: apocalypse through the play of language.

> Here, oh here!
> We bear the bier
> Of the Father of many a cancelled year!

---

[46] Percy Bysshe Shelley, "Song to the Men of England," in *Complete Works of Shelley*, ed. Ingpen and Peck, 3:288–89.

>   Spectres we
>   Of the dead Hours be,
>   We bear Time to his tomb in eternity.
>   (4.9–14)

The boisterous melody of these lines hints at the dazzling verbal technics to come, but I want to focus for the moment on two obvious, exemplary puns. In the second line, "bear" carries or conceives "bier," so that an arbitrary play of the signifier becomes thematically linked to the death of time. Similarly, in the last line, "Time" modulates into "tomb," just as if phonic metamorphosis were itself capable of bringing ("bearing") time to its teleological end, opening the portals of posthistory. Within another fifteen lines, these last temporal reminders themselves "melt away / Like dissolving spray" (4.24–25), and the millennial hymn of act 4, the "mystic measure / Of music and dance," is underway. After the pragmatic social commitments Shelley demonstrated in the summer of 1819, the unembarrassed wishfulness of this linguistic apocalypse might seem rather self-indulgent or, even worse, trivial. Moreover, having already shown that Shelley veered away from his lyrical drama, why do I once more raise the specter of utopian music? The answer is simple: Shelley wrote act 4, with its exponential leap into the visionary imagination, *after* he wrote his "Popular Songs." If in the September of political engagement Shelley relegated the literary to a penultimate role, in December, poetry once again occupied the site that cannot be superseded, the New Jerusalem in which linguistic freedom becomes an end in itself. Why?

The easiest path to an answer lies through the events that followed Peterloo, a tragedy that might have ignited the reform movement but instead signaled its dissolution. The refusal of the administration to investigate the massacre, the long, toothless debate in Parliament about whether the administration should investigate, the gradual loss of reformist momentum—all have been well-documented.[47] By the time Shelley returned to his lyrical drama, Parliament had turned decisively against the opposition cause, passing legislation that severely curbed the rights of reformers to assemble and to disseminate information. Thompson has asserted that the Six Acts of December 1819 marked only the beginning of "the most sustained campaign of prosecutions in the courts in British history."[48] Even in Italy Shelley felt the chilling effect of repression when Hunt, the closest of his political allies, refused to publish the "Popular Songs," abruptly ending Shelley's hopes of reaching a

---

[47] See Thompson, *The Making of the English Working Class*, 746–68, and Belchem, "Republicanism, Popular Constitutionalism, and the Radical Platform," 16.

[48] Thompson, *The Making of the English Working Class*, 768.

mass audience.[49] The short answer, then, is that Shelley reverted to *Prometheus Unbound* when the moment of political opportunity collapsed. Depending on one's idea of literature and politics, his decision to do so might seem either an escape into imaginary compensations (Polan, in an especially harsh judgment, calls act 4 "an effusive gush of signifiers, all of which substitute for the processes of human life") or a healthy realization that, after political disappointment, literature and its vision of a better society abide.[50] But as short answers typically do, this one goes only so far; it might describe Shelley's final swing of 1819, but it doesn't explain why, in the first place, the pendulum of that eventful year should consist of the political at one end and the literary at the other. If my pendulum metaphor suggests the opposition of Shelley's divided loyalties, it is also meant to invoke regular, continuous motion; in this last section I ask what assumptions aligned the political and the literary that allowed Shelley to pass so readily from one to the other and back again. With that question, we can begin to see that *Prometheus Unbound* and the "Popular Songs," despite the real differences of their apocalyptic rhetoric, belong to a smooth space, a cultural space in which the literary and the political converge in a faith in the work of representation. Shelley's changes of 1819 occur within the limits of the developing democratic culture that gave shape to his social vision, a culture that locates freedom and empowerment in linguistic agency, in the power of words.

Shelley turned from *Prometheus Unbound* in large part because he recognized that without readers even the most elevated imaginative vision remains ineffectual, amounting to nothing more than the autonomous sum of its verbal parts. Girded by this understanding that words in and of themselves accomplish little, the "Popular Songs" entered into politics with a particular kind of caution, urging their audience of English workers to lift themselves out of silence, but also warning them not to become too enamored of words in the process. "Let deeds, not words, express / Thine exceeding loveliness" (lines 260–61), "The Mask of Anarchy" exhorts, just before it recommends its particular plan of action: "[L]et a great Assembly be / Of the fearless and the free" (lines 262–63). There is, however, an obvious paradox here: although Shelley calls for direct political action rather than mere talk, the action he endorses consists mainly of words, for what is an assembly if not a place of speech

---

[49] Paul Foot has been particularly sharp in condemning Hunt, who refused to publish the Carlile letter as well as the "Popular Songs" and seems to have generally ignored Shelley's inquiries about these writings: "And so Leigh Hunt, the warm-hearted liberal and supporter of free speech, became, uncomfortably but firmly, the censor of some of the most powerful political writing in the English language." *Red Shelley* (London: Sidgwick and Jackson, 1980), 219.

[50] Polan, "The Ruin of a Poetics," 42.

and debate, a place where those who are represented have their say? As Jerrold Hogle, the most recent champion of a deconstructive approach to Shelley, aptly puts it, the poet-reformer sought "a wide-open public forum of continual negotiation," with "an awareness of history and experience as its guide and the malleability of language as its principal tool."[51] The strength of the reform movement in 1819 lay in the sheer numbers it mobilized, the huge protest crowds at Norwich, Birmingham, and Manchester that for the most part listened peacefully to speeches, but provoked widespread fear mainly because of their potential for violence. The challenge for reform leaders was to exploit that threat while at the same time directing the passionate anger of their constituents into forms of nonviolent resistance, such as the convening of the national assembly. Underlying "The Mask of Anarchy," then, is Shelley's conviction that the very distinction between words and action is a false one, that by encouraging the workers to use speech as the vehicle of change, he was in fact directing them toward their most effective weapon in the struggle for power: "Be your strong and simple words / Keen to wound as sharpened swords" (lines 299–300). The assembly would be the word made deed, language transformed from image to action; the sole purpose of seizing the right to collective speech would be to produce tangible results, to redress the power imbalance that enables a few with shared interests to speak while the many remain silent.

Set against the wordplay apocalypse that opens act 4 of *Prometheus Unbound*, the functional linguistic politics of "The Mask of Anarchy" seem to belong to a different verbal universe. And yet, despite the swing from literary detachment to political engagement, it seems important to point out that the political objectives Shelley envisioned remain firmly inscribed within a *verbal* universe. One of the most visible marks left on Shelley as the second-generation heir to the democratic legacy is his confidence, cutting across his literary and political endeavors, that linguistic agency is sufficiently capable of disabling power and securing self-determination. Here, so to speak, is where his literary and his political wires cross. By making more expansive representation its primary form of contesting tyranny, Shelley's assembly reproduces the faith in symbolic forms which, in swinging away from *Prometheus Unbound*, it was meant to correct. In 1819, Shelley had no way of knowing the course representative democracy would take in later years; for him, as for others participating in the parliamentary reform movement, it remained an unrealized radical proposal genuinely committed to a redistribution of power. And yet, even in a poem like "The Mask of Anarchy," one can

---

[51] Jerrold E. Hogle, *Shelley's Process: Radical Transference and the Development of His Major Works* (Oxford: Oxford University Press, 1988), 250.

already perceive the exaggerated investment in language that would eventually lead to Mill's celebration of the "talking function" of Parliament. How else might one explain the unsettling ending of "The Mask of Anarchy," which, without such a leap of faith in the efficacy of words, seems to represent the inability of opposition to generate anything other than verbal forms of resistance? In the poem's final stanzas, Shelley imagines what would happen if the wished-for assembly, convened in protest against Peterloo, were tragically to produce another, even larger Peterloo. Repetition of the massacre on that scale, the mysterious Shape assures its readers, would certainly provoke *the voice* of outrage:

> "And that slaughter to the Nation
> Shall steam up like inspiration,
> Eloquent, oracular;
> A Volcano heard afar.

> "And these words shall then become
> Like oppression's thundered doom
> Ringing through each heart and brain,
> Heard again—again—again—

> "Rise like lions after slumber . . ."
> (lines 360–68)

With this vision of efficacious martyrdom, the poem suggests that words will triumph over power by expanding the democratic voice until it becomes "oppression's thundered doom"—if not now, then eventually, inevitably. But Shelley never indicates how or why that triumph must occur; he never explains the causal links by which democratic representation reaches critical mass and suddenly, by some declarative fiat, puts to an end the realities of social domination. Indeed, by ending the poem with a vision of power yet again defeating resistance by brute force, he makes such radical change all the more difficult to imagine. When the resounding slogan returns for the last time, it does so with a certain uneasiness, and the ability of its inspirational words to enact the empowerment they promise seems nearly as unfounded as any of the "beautiful idealisms" one finds in *Prometheus Unbound*.[52]

---

[52] Shelley's belief in eventual triumph through symbolic action underscores one of the weak points of the parliamentary reform movement as a whole: its tendency to satisfy itself with symbolic victories. The enormous crowds created real concern for local and national authorities, but in fact they often became ends in themselves; as Calhoun puts it, "The reaffirmation of collective solidarity at such meetings served as a substitute for more concrete action as much as it stimulated it." *The Question of Class Struggle*, 88. Moreover,

As I have argued, "The Mask of Anarchy" demonstrates that poetic language, in order to be consequential, must lead to something beyond itself. Oddly, however, the "Popular Songs" as a whole never quite place the same demand on political expression; the apocalyptic transformation of the silenced into the speaking, or at least into the represented, tends to become something of an end in itself in these poems, as if the very practice of democratic representation, the widening exercise of political rights, were itself sufficiently liberating for those enabled to participate. By endowing the national assembly with such symbolic significance, Shelley drew on the assumptions of earlier liberal republicans and inevitably reproduced some of their limitations, something especially evident in the asymmetries that inform his idea of freedom. At times, looking to America as his model, Shelley approached the purest form of what Marx considered the political illusion, the conviction that political freedom is tantamount to freedom per se. In "A Philosophical View of Reform," an unfinished essay contemporary with the "Popular Songs," he plainly stated: "A sufficiently just measure is afforded of the degree to which a country is enslaved or free, by the consideration of the relative number of individuals who are admitted to the exercise of political rights."[53] The blind spot of this characteristically republican argument is perhaps most clearly displayed in a line about the United States in Paine's *Rights of Man:* "There, the poor are not oppressed, the rich are not privileged."[54] In Shelley, such an exaggeration of the freedom realized by "formal" democracy yields rather deep incongruities, for it collides with his unflinching observation of the economic injustices that are a structural feature of capitalism. A generation after Paine, with twenty-five years of further industrial development behind him, Shelley never shared his predecessor's belief that unregulated commerce was a

---

these demonstrations almost always accommodated themselves to the structures of power, taking place outside normal work hours, for instance, so as not to disrupt production. See Mark Harrison, *Crowds and History: Mass Phenomena in English Towns, 1790–1835* (Cambridge: Cambridge University Press, 1988), 130.

[53] Percy Bysshe Shelley, "A Philosophical View of Reform," in *Complete Works of Shelley,* ed. Ingpen and Peck, 7:23.

[54] Paine, *Rights of Man,* 167. Bryan Palmer summarizes the contradictions of the Jeffersonian "vision of classlessness" that Paine shared and that Shelley inherited as an idealized model of democracy in the United States: "Republicanism and its language were thus premised on an essential schizophrenia, in which the dominant personality of property grew in stature and power as the struggles of the eighteenth century gave way to the consolidations of the nineteenth, all the while nurturing, for its own purposes, the illusive personality of liberty and citizenship." *Descent into Discourse: The Reification of Language and the Writing of Social History* (Philadelphia: Temple University Press, 1990), 110–11. This schizophrenia is especially painful in Shelley; despite his sensitivity to the dynamics of economic exploitation, he remains surprisingly uncritical of republicanism's tendency to pursue only partial liberties in the name of total liberty.

harmonizing social influence, that "civil society" constituted a sphere of voluntary transaction free from coercive activities. When the long third section of "The Mask of Anarchy" takes up the question, "What art thou Freedom?" (line 209), Shelley suggests that poverty is indeed a systematic form of oppression and that genuine freedom requires not merely formal political rights but an end to economic domination as well: "For the labourer thou art bread, / And a comely table spread / From his daily labour come / In a neat and happy home. // Thou art clothes, and fire, and food / For the trampled multitude— / No—in countries that are free / Such starvation cannot be / As in England now we see" (lines 217–25). Those final lines would seem to mark a resounding indictment of Paine's attempt to consider freedom a political matter apart from glaring social inequities.

But exactly herein lies the disquieting asymmetry of these poems. This very passage that attends with such realism to the material needs of freedom begins with one of Shelley's most wishful assertions: "What art thou Freedom? O! could slaves / Answer from their living graves / This demand—tyrants would flee / Like a dream's dim imagery" (209–12). Here, the transformation from silence to speech, from death to life, which in these poems always means entry into political participation, ends oppression automatically, as if the dismantling of power on the terrain of political discourse were somehow a *generic* dismantling of domination itself. As in a leading radical tradition of the 1790s, power appears to be insubstantial, a mere language effect that evaporates the moment one brings to an end its monopoly over representation. Shelley's understanding of injustice is certainly more inclusive than that of earlier republicans, but his remedy remained surprisingly narrow, drawing on the very ideological source that fed the events of 1789: the belief, as François Furet puts it, "that there is no human misfortune not amenable to a political solution."[55] Thus despite one of the most remarkable analytical insights of the "Popular Songs"—that in England the fiscal-military state had rendered issues of political and economic power inextricable—Shelley typically subordinated economic to political reform.[56] In perhaps the most direct statement of these priorities, "A Philosophical View of Reform" contended that equality of property must be considered only the long-distance consequence of the political equality that is "our present business": "Equality in possessions must be the last result of the utmost refinements of civilization; it is one of the conditions of that

[55] François Furet, *Interpreting the French Revolution,* trans. Elborg Forster (Cambridge: Cambridge University Press, 1981), 25.

[56] That eighteenth-century English government developed into a powerful "fiscal-military state" is the favorite argument of John Brewer in *The Sinews of Power: War, Money, and the English State, 1688–1783* (New York: Knopf, 1989).

system of society, towards which with whatever hope of ultimate success, it is our duty to tend. . . . But our present business is with the difficult and unbending realities of actual life, and when we have drawn inspiration from the great object of our hopes it becomes us with patience and resolution to apply ourselves to accommodating our theories to immediate practice."[57] Beyond its expedient pragmatism—political equality is an objective attainable now, economic equality a mere theoretical possibility—this passage implies a certain faith in the work of democratic representation, a belief that, once inscribed within the discursive practices of politics, equality will progressively extend itself into the whole of social relations. As Tocqueville would argue, "That men should be eternally unequal among themselves in one respect and equal in others is inconceivable; they will therefore one day attain equality in all aspects." In Shelley's case, this assumption leads not so much to an outright contradiction between economic and political objectives as to an asymmetry regarding them, for while the poems tilt toward economic exploitation in describing the abuses of power, they tilt toward political change, toward representation, as their solution. The daily frustrations of the working-poor audience, which Shelley described with such agonizing immediacy in the poems, find their remedy deferred in "A Philosophical View of Reform" to a fantastic, socialist utopia—to the far goal of time, one might say—while the political freedom that bears some unspecified relation to those economic realities is endowed with a disproportionate urgency. The essay written for other intellectual reformers makes explicit what the poems had implicitly asked of their working-class audience: that they accept political empowerment for economic empowerment, in the belief that one will do the work of the other.

"The principle of politics," Marx once wrote, "is the will. The more one-sided, and thus the more perfect political intelligence is, the more it believes in the omnipotence of the will, the blinder it is to the natural and intellectual limits of the will, and thus the more incapable it is of discovering the sources of social evils."[58] Were one to couple the word *language* with *will* here, one would begin to approach the predicament of Shelley's democratic idealism, which, even as it acknowledges the economic evils that Marx felt bourgeois politics ignored, still finds in representative government and its linguistic empowerment a universal solvent. The "Popular Songs" imagine no needs beyond the formation of a genuinely representative assembly, for Shelley is sure that speaking

[57] Shelley, "A Philosophical View of Reform," in *Complete Works of Shelley*, ed. Ingpen and Peck, 7:43.

[58] Karl Marx, "Critical Remarks on the Article: 'The King of Prussia and Social Reform,'" in *Karl Marx: Selected Writings*, ed. David McLellan (Oxford: Oxford University Press, 1977), 125.

agents have everything necessary to alter their world, to make it conform to their own vital, collective interests. In this way, the utopianism of
Prometheus Unbound, act 4, is not so much the antithesis of Shelley's
political engagements as it is another way of representing them, for the
entire millennial scene is a single, sustained attempt to demonstrate that
linguistic acts are themselves capable of unlimited transformative effects. Song, in act 4, is the tool of a polyphonic omnipotent will that
empties all obstacles to freedom and fills the resulting void with the new
heaven and earth of its own apocalyptic imagining, of its own autogenic
voice:

> And our singing shall build,
> In the Void's loose field,
> A world for the Spirit of Wisdom to wield;
> We will take our plan
> From the new world of man
> And our work shall be called the Promethean
>
> . . . .
>
> We whirl, singing loud, round the gathering sphere
> Till the trees and the beasts, and the clouds appear
> From its chaos made calm by love, not fear—
>
> We encircle the Oceans and Mountains of Earth
> And the happy forms of its death and birth
> Change to the music of our sweet mirth.
>
> (4.153–58, 169–74)

"The more it believes in the omnipotence of the will, the blinder it is to
the natural and intellectual limits of the will"—so Marx said of *political*
not *poetic* intelligence. For Shelley, the two types intersect at the site of
language, converging in the eminently democratic conviction that if the
world consists of its representations, formed as it is through discourse,
then to participate in the acts of representation, to divest power of its
exclusive hold on such acts, is to experience the fullest measure of self-
determination. In and through language lies freedom.

Perhaps it is not surprising that Shelley's disembodied and highly
literary spirits, "singing . . . In the Void's loose field," should recall a
particular historical moment early in the French Revolution, the preparation of the July 14 Federation, the first anniversary of the fall of the
Bastille. According to Michelet, the digging of the Champs de Mars, an
enormous task that "converted a plain into a valley between two hills,"
was a work of populist transformation motored by the agency of song:

It was an extraordinary spectacle, to behold, both day and night, men of every class, and every age, even children, but all citizens . . . all handling the pickaxe, rolling barrows, or driving carts. Children walked in front, bearing torches; perambulating musicians played to enliven the workmen; and they themselves, whilst levelling the earth, continued still to chant their levelling song: "*Ah ça ira! ça ira! ça ira!* He that exalteth himself shall be abased!"

The song, the work, and the workmen, was one and the same thing.[59]

The climax of the revolution's early euphoria, the Federation became in Michelet's hands a mythic, foundational event that still speaks to the deepest desires of democratic politics: that the freedom of collective speech should be performative of its own content, that a leveling in words should be a leveling of the social landscape that voids the hierarchical influence of power. Michelet claimed that the Revolution's only real monument was empty space—literally a clearing, figuratively the negative mark left by democratic culture as it continuously enacts its task of emptying out power into language.[60] The torch-lit digging of the Champs de Mars anticipates in grand historical narrative what, as we saw in the last chapter, Claude Lefort has recently articulated as the ruling principle of democratic theory: "The locus of power is an empty place, it cannot be occupied—it is such that no individual and no group can be consubstantial with it."[61] In Shelley, we have already encountered such a figure of ideal negativity: Demogorgon, the subversive agent whose name Paul Foot translates literally to mean the "people-monster."[62]

> I see a mighty Darkness
> Filling the seat of power; and rays of gloom
> Dart round, as light from the meridian Sun,
> Ungazed upon and shapeless—neither limb
> Nor form—nor outline; yet we feel it is
> A living Spirit.

> (2.4.2–7)

[59] Jules Michelet, *History of the French Revolution*, trans. Charles Cocks, ed. Gordon Wright (Chicago: University of Chicago Press, 1967), 459. I thank Celeste Langan for pointing out to me the significance of Michelet in this context.

[60] On the second page of his preface, Michelet initiates this crucial democratic theme: "The Champs de Mars! This is the only monument that the Revolution has left. The Empire has its Column, and engrosses almost exclusively the arch of Triumph; royalty has its Louvre, its Hospital of Invalids; the feudal church of the twelfth century is still enthroned at Notre Dame: nay, the very Romans have their Imperial Ruins, the Thermae of the Caesars!

"And the Revolution has for her monument—empty space" (4).

[61] Claude Lefort, *Democracy and Political Theory*, trans. David Macey (Minneapolis: University of Minnesota Press, 1988), 17.

[62] Foot, *Red Shelley*, 196.

Demogorgon is the centrifugal political counterimage to concentrated, totalitarian authority, the decentered figure of democracy that nullifies the fixed, hierarchical power of the old regime. Limbless, his strength cannot be personified; it can never be made consubstantial with an individual, with the unifying, symbolic body of a monarch. In his revolutionary ascent, Demogorgon substitutes one linguistic formation for another; undoing the monologue of the throne, he fills the seat of power with all the indeterminate energy, the rich potentiality, of a democratic assembly. Shelley's image of the negative freedom that underlies the aesthetic is also his image of the negative freedom that underlies the political.

In *Prometheus Unbound,* as in the "Popular Songs," Shelley considered democratic revolution to be an essentially linguistic phenomenon. The legacy of his 1819—in which literary and political discourses diverged only to reveal a deeper symbiosis, only to become reflecting images of the same sort of liberation—remains firmly inscribed within the interpretations of Shelley today, especially in the deconstructive criticism that looks to Shelley's text as a model of freedom in and through language, a means of enacting democratic revolution yet again through the experience of reading and writing. Hogle writes, "We value or should value Shelley today . . . for how often he reveals and breaks open the rigid systems of self-assessment and social hierarchy that continue to restrict the potentials of men and women. . . . [H]e uncovers the deeper, more mobile logic that has been forgotten . . . and releases that movement into verbal activity so that our minds can be reoriented toward the personal freedom to change and the sense of equality among differences generated by truly relational thinking."[63] If this passage indicates the persistent utopianism of linguistic politics, the promise that language bears within itself the equality and the freedom from constraint we desire, it also reveals how democratic culture continues to transform—or deflect—matters of power and opposition, subordination and freedom, into matters exhausted by language. Democratic culture remains deeply embedded in an apocalyptic self-image; it is at once a Logos that overcomes all obstacles with its collective word-sword, and a messiah perhaps too content to dwell in a New Jerusalem of linguistic freedom.

[63] Hogle, *Shelley's Process,* 27.

APOCALYPSE AND GENDER:
MARY SHELLEY'S *LAST MAN*

> When the line is crossed, contagion is produced. This phenomenon has been located and attested. Witches spread on the surface of the globe "like caterpillars in our gardens," says an inquisitor. Young Greek girls hang themselves. Bitten women begin to dance the tarentella. The witches' madness is contagious and rapidly transmitted. It is an epidemic. . . . The illness is caught on contact, it heads for the surface. . . . The electricity is the identification which, circulating from hand to hand, cannot be imputed to any one female subject but to everyone: "sexual identity," "sexual community."
>
> —Catherine Clément, "The Guilty One"

In her essay "Gender Theory and the Yale School," Barbara Johnson recalls the response of some feminist practitioners of deconstruction to *Deconstruction and Criticism* (1979), the Yale school manifesto of sorts. The feminist writers envisioned a "companion volume" that would look at *Frankenstein* rather than "The Triumph of Life" and so demonstrate the value of deconstruction to feminist concerns. Almost as an afterthought, Johnson adds, "But perhaps it was not *Frankenstein* but rather *The Last Man,* Mary Shelley's grim depiction of the gradual extinction of humanity altogether, that would have made a fit counterpart to 'The Triumph of Life.' Percy Bysshe Shelley is entombed in both, along with a certain male fantasy of Romantic universality. The only universality that remains in Mary Shelley's last novel is the plague."[1] Johnson's hint at a critical project that never materialized is intriguing both for what it does and does not say. On the surface, "The Triumph of Life" and *The Last Man* would appear as similar as Johnson suggests they are antithetical; they are *both* powerfully skeptical, counterapocalyptic works that represent the inability of human beings to transcend their conditions. To argue their opposition implies that a novel by a woman undermines

---

[1] Barbara Johnson, *A World of Difference* (Baltimore: Johns Hopkins University Press, 1987), 33.

apocalyptic desires in a way different from a poem by a man. In what way is "The Triumph of Life" deeply subversive of traditional ideals and at the same time invested in the conventions of masculine and universalizing fantasy? Moreover, in what way does Mary Shelley avoid this same collusion?

Johnson's suggestion also provokes questions about method, about the relation between deconstructive practices and feminist practices. With nothing more than Johnson's hint, it is difficult to determine whether she meant the companion volume to be an extension or a critique of Yale school deconstruction or both. At the center of this problem lies the assessment of the all-male cast of *Deconstruction and Criticism*, a cast that very well might share with Percy Shelley a vestige of universalizing fantasy. After all, de Man, arguably the critic most significant to Johnson's own work, contributed an essay that crescendoes to a distinctly apocalyptic conclusion, a blowing of the trumpet one can hardly doubt is meant to represent finality of a kind: "*The Triumph of Life* warns us that nothing, whether deed, word, thought or text, ever happens in relation, positive or negative, to anything that precedes, follows or exists elsewhere, but only as a random event whose power, like the power of death, is due to the randomness of its occurrence."[2] To distill this masterly rhetoric to its basic assertion is to see, admittedly at great cost to the sentence's power, a skeletal absolutism: "nothing . . . ever happens in relation . . . to anything." This *is* a version of universality, even if negative universality, just as it is apocalyptic in Derrida's sense: it announces the truth—or the final limit to truth—and thus is "the end and the instance of the last judgment."[3] De Man does not encourage one to imagine a knowledge that could supersede this last judgment. Most important, his apocalyptic warning omits any awareness of sexual difference in its universality, despite the fact that it concludes a reading of a poem in which female figures play central, if cryptic, roles. De Man's interpretation works by objectifying these figures (the "Shape all light," for instance), by coercing them into definitive allegories of language, and thus repeats the unselfconscious, objectifying procedures of the poem itself. With much the same oversight, Shelley reveals his terrifying vision through the allegorization of two female "characters" who serve to collapse into identity various forces usually considered antithetical: light and darkness, life and death. In both cases, the way to a genderless knowledge—whether transcendental or blinding—is through a symbolic woman. When Mary Shelley published *The Last Man* in 1826, end-

[2] Paul de Man, "Shelley Disfigured," in *Deconstruction and Criticism*, by Harold Bloom, Paul de Man, Jacques Derrida, Geoffrey Hartman, and J. Hillis Miller (New York: Continuum, 1986), 69.

[3] Jacques Derrida, "Of an Apocalyptic Tone Recently Adopted in Philosophy," *Oxford Literary Review* 6 (1984): 24.

of-humanity fantasies were popular, and many functioned by an implicit antifeminism not unrelated to the simultaneous manipulation and effacement of gender that characterizes Percy Shelley's poem and its deconstructive reading. All of this is to say (in cursory fashion) that the project of Johnson and her colleagues, however it addressed these issues, might have significantly complicated our understanding of deconstruction, feminism, and romanticism.[4]

And yet the fact that the project was abandoned is in itself revealing. One could argue that the companion volume to *Deconstruction and Criticism* virtually has been written in the abundant feminist and deconstructive essays devoted to *Frankenstein* since 1980, essays that helped put Mary Shelley on the canonical map. *The Last Man*, meanwhile, remains merely an afterthought, an end-of-the-world novel relegated to passing critical gestures like Johnson's. The fixation on *Frankenstein* has reanimated Shelley, to be sure, but it has also, unintentionally, reinforced her "minor" status. With a few important exceptions, the emphasis on *Frankenstein* has made her a one-trick pony; literary critics don't take her as seriously as they generally profess. In this last chapter, I want to consider *The Last Man* as a work necessary not only to an understanding of Shelley but to any understanding of that central literary category, romantic apocalypse. It may not be Shelley's last novel, as Johnson mistakenly asserts, but it does mark a "last" of a different kind: an end to the very possibility of apocalypse. I have no reason to contest Anne Mellor's claim that *The Last Man* is "the first English example of what we might call apocalyptic or 'end-of-the-world' fiction."[5] And yet, the logic of the novel dictates that if it is the first apocalyptic novel it must also, in a sense, be

---

[4] The questions that I briefly raise here about de Man's version of deconstruction all have their source in the fact that his claims about language, ontology, and human action persistently disregard the significance of gender. Therefore, when viewed from a perspective concerned with sexual politics, his attempts to demystify the rhetoric of universalism in fact reinscribe the one universalist tendency he either cannot see or, worse, deems unimportant. No doubt I have done a great disservice in abstracting a core assertion out of de Man's climactic sentence in "Shelley Disfigured." He himself would probably point to "warns," the sentence's governing verb, and contend that, as a performative and not a constative, the sentence has little to do with a knowledge that could be called universalist. This is, however, to weigh "warns" rather heavily against the "nothing," "ever," "anything," and "only" that follow it. These words build a cumulative absolutism that finally eclipses the humbling power of the performative, leaving little room for consideration of the influence of gender (let alone any particular circumstances) on deeds, words, thoughts, and texts. De Man's theoretical speculation necessarily opens onto the very questions of sexual politics which its rhetoric precludes. To introduce a consideration of gender here is immediately to question both the statement's authority and the effect it is meant to have on a readership. In this chapter, for instance, I hope to show that the relation between the deeds of a woman who wrote novels and those of her husband who wrote poetry is anything but "random."

[5] Anne Mellor, *Mary Shelley: Her Life, Her Fiction, Her Monsters* (New York: Methuen, 1988), 148–49.

the last. Put simply, *The Last Man* dramatizes the incompatibility of the terms *apocalypse* and *novel*—unless, that is, *apocalypse* is so thoroughly revalued as to take on a different meaning, which is precisely what happens. This revaluation in turn places new demands on criticism of apocalyptic works. Mellor implies that we should *value* Shelley because she was the first English novelist of the apocalypse; the novel, however, by undermining the possibility of apocalypse, calls into question the critical ethos of originality.[6]

In its widest implication, Johnson's anecdote records the need felt by a rigorous reader to move from an insular deconstruction toward a socially engaged feminism, just as many feminists in the United States have been strengthening the conceptual basis of their project by making the opposite move toward a variety of French theories. Located within such landshifts, this chapter implicitly traces a development of feminist criticism (certainly not the only one), as if Shelley's feminist novel contained within its critique an overlay of various critical possibilities that finally push beyond anything we might speculate to be within the command of authorial intention. I begin with a deconstructive critique of the gender relations encoded in the popular "Last Man" poems written just before Shelley began her novel, poems written exclusively by men. I then discuss Shelley's desire, after her husband's death, to become the medium of his ideas, to write a novel worthy of him, to represent him by (as best she could) becoming him. When this desire reaches its limit of stifling self-contradiction, the novel gives way to an independent feminine force that liberates itself from the masculine altogether—the plague that literally ends "man."

This somewhat desperate liberation occurs in the novel only as the anguished reversal—in fact, nullification—of the patriarchal order, and were my reading to end here it would be limited to the anxious strategy of subversion Shelley herself worked out as she asserted her difference from her husband and his sometimes oppressive notions of literature. There is in *The Last Man*, however, an imagining of representation beyond the conventional categories of subjectivity and authorship—a shadowing forth of conditions which take one beyond the still humanist assumptions of individual experience and intentionality, be they grounded in the masculine or the feminine subject. In this way, my reading of this dystopian, counterapocalyptic novel locates in the text a

---

[6] In her chapter on *The Last Man*, Mellor makes sweeping claims in the name of originality: "*The Last Man* thus opens the way to twentieth-century existentialism and nihilism. . . ; [it] initiates the modern tradition of literary deconstruction. It is the first work to demonstrate that all cultural ideologies rest on nonreferential tropes. . . . But as the author of the first fictional example of nihilism . . ." and so on (169). If Shelley's novel is a "critique of Romantic ideology" (159), Mellor's criticism is not.

utopian inclination Shelley imagined but could not know, a utopian inclination that distantly anticipates the current work of various French feminist writers. To say that Shelley imagined what she could not know is neither to devalue her novel in favor of anachronistic theories nor to underestimate her ample intelligence; she knew a great deal. It is simply to say that for personal, social, and historical reasons, she, like anyone else, could experience and express more than she could fully conceptualize. The obscured utopianism of *The Last Man,* what I call (after Derrida) its articulation of a phase "beyond man and humanism," is one such element at the borders of Shelley's conscious control, but an element fairly accessible to a reader at a significant historical distance and a different ideological moment. The novel's utopian register loses some of the political immediacy of the more concrete feminist anger which accompanies it; it remains necessarily abstract ("theoretical") as it attempts to realize a discourse which did not, does not, and *cannot* as yet exist. The attempt in itself, however, points toward the limitations of all feminist protest grounded in a revised version of humanist subjectivity. It begins, and just begins, to make visible the line beyond which that protest, despite its real value now, cannot advance.

"Last Man" Poetry; or, The Last Man Who Would Not Leave

An odd permutation of the anxiety of influence haunts two passages written a century and a half apart. The first passage is by Harold Bloom; the second is from a ballad by Thomas Hood.

> In his diary, [Mann] wrote: "To be reminded that one is not alone in the world—always unpleasant," and then he added: "It is another version of Goethe's question: 'Do we then live if others live?'" . . . The matter is, alas, profound, as Mann well knew.[7]

> So there he hung, and there I stood
> The LAST MAN left alive,
> To have my own will of all the earth:
> Quoth I, now I shall thrive![8]

[7] Harold Bloom, *The Anxiety of Influence* (Oxford: Oxford University Press, 1973), 53.
[8] Thomas Hood, *Selected Poems of Thomas Hood,* ed. John Clubbe (Cambridge: Harvard University Press, 1970), 138–39.

The gallows humor of Hood's long-forgotten ballad almost seems to parody Bloom's critical posturing, despite the fact that it antedates Bloom's work. The two passages cross paths; with a touch of tragic seriousness ("alas," "profound"), Bloom recounts via Thomas Mann the frustrations of an ego that cannot achieve the transcendental autonomy it desires, while Hood's slapstick hangman is about to discover that the mind is not its own place, that solipsism is not nearly as sublime as, say, the paintings of Caspar David Friedrich make it out to be. Having killed his one surviving companion as only a *strong* poet might, the last man now cannot escape the burden of his isolated will and ego, the weight expressed in consecutive accents on the "I." Within forty lines, he ends the poem lamenting that no friend exists to "pull [his] legs," an act of kindness permitted the relatives of Newgate criminals that made as brief as possible the work of hanging.

Hood's satire may seem an apt response to Bloom's belated valoriza-tion of romantic egoism and its struggle to liberate the self into an apocalyptic space free of all material contingency and social relations (what Bloom calls "influence," or, after Milton, "the universe of death"), but in its time the poem responded to a specific formation of romanti-cism that concentrated the era's apocalyptic tendencies—the brood-ing representations of eschatological themes that appeared around the French Revolution and peaked with the several "Last Man" works writ-ten between 1823 and 1826. Hood's was probably not the first to parody the sublime nature of these apocalyptic visions; Shelley's novel appeared in February 1826 and if, as is likely the case, Hood's poem followed this publication, it seems conspicuously and remarkably unconcerned about influence.[9] Oddly enough, works that by thematic necessity took the form of monologues (visionary soliloquies) entered into dialogue with one another concerning the nature of intellect, imagination, and the teleology of freedom. Rather, Shelley's novel renders the genre dialogic, making the various works speak to one another, since, despite the petty rivalries among "Last Man" poets, the works that preceded hers tended to formulate themselves in surprisingly consistent and limiting ways. Bakhtin makes parody a constitutive feature of the novel. His descrip-tion of its relation to poetry is thus in many ways appropriate to the rela-tion between Shelley's prose *Last Man* and its verse contemporaries: the novel as parody introduces "a critique on the one-sided seriousness of the lofty direct word, the corrective of reality that is always richer, more fundamental and most importantly *too contradictory and heteroglot* to be fit

9 John Clubbe writes, "Hood was, in many ways, an imitative writer. Confronted with the romantic achievement, he adopted one of two courses, occasionally even in the same poem, both: he consciously imitated another poet's style, or he consciously parodied a romantic theme." Introduction to *Selected Poems of Thomas Hood*, 14–15.

into a high and straightforward genre."[10] Parodies such as Hood's poem (already declaring itself a hybrid, a "Verse Narrative") and Shelley's novel provided the grounds to subvert the exaggerated strain of apocalyptic idealism that increasingly came to characterize romanticism, even in its pessimistic "Last Man" phase. What Hood's relatively simple ballad could not express was the extent to which the novel, by its displaced representation of gender and discourse, undermined the very category of autonomous subjectivity that apocalyptic vision served to validate.

A number of studies have surveyed the "Last Man" theme and located Shelley's novel within the trend. Others have aligned it with the general pessimism of the genre, finding in a novel that details the annihilation of humanity by plague an appropriate vehicle for Shelley's rejection of the millennial inclinations of her parents and husband.[11] *The Last Man* is certainly counterapocalyptic in its denial of the mind's power to dictate its own transcendence, but I want to focus here on the novel's response to the particular kind of idealism represented in the "Last Man" poems. These works share a set of features that help to locate and specify Shelley's intervention in the discourse, a self-conscious intervention signaled almost automatically by the fact that a woman writes a first-person narrative of the last man and writes it in a prose work of three volumes. *The Last Man* seems at once deeply invested in Shelley's own experience *and* distanced, ironic, and moving toward parody in Bakhtin's wide-ranging use of the term. Shelley alters an exclusively masculine theme even as she imitates it and, in a way that only anachronistically could be considered intentional, approaches the feminist program of mimesis laid out by Luce Irigaray: "To play with mimesis is thus, for a woman, to try to recover the place of her exploitation by discourse, without allowing herself to be simply reduced to it. It means to resubmit herself— inasmuch as she is on the side of the 'perceptible,' of 'matter'—to 'ideas,' in particular to ideas about herself, that are elaborated in/by a masculine logic, but so as to make 'visible,' by an effect of playful repetition, what was supposed to remain invisible: the cover-up of a possible operation of the feminine in language."[12] This passage describes *The Last Man* with uncanny accuracy, with the one exception that Shelley could not "play"

[10] M. M. Bakhtin, *The Dialogic Imagination* (Austin: University of Texas Press, 1981), 55.

[11] The best of this kind of criticism is Lee Sterrenburg's essay, the title of which tells it all: "*The Last Man*: Anatomy of Failed Revolutions," *Nineteenth-Century Fiction* 33 (1978): 324–47. For a general survey of this apocalyptic literature in France and England, see A. J. Sambrook, "A Romantic Theme: The Last Man," *Forum for Modern Language Studies* 2 (1966): 25–33. In a more recent essay, Morton Paley details the ways in which *The Last Man* "denies the linkage of apocalypse and millennium that had previously been celebrated in some of the great works of the Romantic epoch, perhaps most fully in *Prometheus Unbound.*" *Keats-Shelley Review* 4 (1989): 7.

[12] Luce Irigaray, *This Sex Which Is Not One* (Ithaca: Cornell University Press, 1985), 76. Hereafter cited as *TS*.

in the term's sense of deliberate and liberating self-reflexiveness. When Shelley parodied she did so with self-conflicted anguish, and the operation of a suppressed feminine in her language produced plague rather than play.

The "Last Man" and Subjectivity

As a popular 1820s genre, "The Last Man" embodies a strange contradiction that allows it to secure the autonomy and self-generative capacity of consciousness at the moment it envisions the imminent annihilation of all consciousness. The typical scene invokes the sublime, with all its theatrical tendencies; in imagining the unimaginable—the very dissolution of the faculty of imagination—it stages fear in order to produce the effect of subsequent empowerment. As in the Kantian formulation, the vital powers are momentarily checked so that their quick recovery registers an increase in cognitive confidence. The degree to which this pattern is made explicit varies considerably in the poems, but all share the paradox of imagining an ending that reassuringly confirms the epistemological status quo. These are first and foremost lofty poems; as they depict panoramic landscapes of destruction and the defiance (though sometimes futile) of the mind to succumb, they assert, with less than tacit pride, the visionary powers and privileges of a poet able to see and represent the eschatological scene. When Beddoes, a friend of Mary Shelley's and an admirer of Percy Shelley's poetry, wrote in a letter that this was "a subject for Michael Angelo," he meant that it was a subject fit for a god, and in fact, Beddoes's last man transcends annihilation by willing his own apotheosis: "By heaven and hell, and all the fools between them, / I will not die, nor sleep, nor wink my eyes, / But think myself into a God."[13] The equation of divinity and cognition and the confident belief in the power of self-generation speak to a naive version of romanticism that runs contrary to and mitigates the despairing vision of the end.

The very phrase "vision of the end" helps to elucidate this paradox in works of less bravado than Beddoes's fragments. Without exception, the "Last Man" poems depend on a conventional hierarchy of subject and object that reduces heterogeneity to a more manageable and ultimately self-serving dualism. Inevitably the threatening, eschatological inversion of this hierarchy appears as the triumph of darkness over light: "The bright sun was extinguish'd" (Byron's "Darkness"); "The Sun him-

---

[13] Thomas Lovell Beddoes, *The Works of Thomas Lovell Beddoes,* ed. H. W. Donner (London: Oxford University Press, 1935), 600, 238. Hereafter cited as *TLB.*

self must die" (Thomas Campbell). As the sun goes out, so too disappears speech ("Earth's cities had no sound," Campbell), so that another version of the central opposition is that between silence and language. Without the enlightening agency of the sun, form loses its outline, dissolves into shadow ("All worldly shapes shall melt in gloom," Campbell), and leaves only an inarticulate material residue—"A lump of death—a chaos of hard clay" ("Darkness"), *adama* before the divine spark made it Adam.[14] In this formula, darkness becomes the encompassing trope that signals the end of culture, consciousness, and language—the end of the human. Yet how does one envision this end of vision? How does one make this darkness visible? In each of these poems sight remains the privileged epistemological mode, even as it did in Milton's prophetic blindness, confirming the integrity of the visionary ego. Byron's "Darkness" begins as all of these poems must: with self-possession, the intact ego from which the eschatological vision originates—"I had a dream." First appears the "I," then its power of possession: "I had," a movement that centers the entire poem on the self. Campbell takes the same pattern one step further when he replaces Byron's phrase with the near tautology, "I saw a vision in my sleep," and so stresses the agency of the eye/I and its generative, visionary power. The dying ego ("the last man") and the darkness that displaces its light apparently must share the sublime stage with the creative ego and its sight.[15]

These works, perhaps with the exception of Byron's, are not genuinely disturbing, and, in fact, seem to verge on unintentional self-parody. It is hard to take seriously the inflated rhetoric of Beddoes when he imagines not an end of consciousness but rather a cosmic extension of its self-sufficiency:

> I am an universe . . .
> And suns are launched, and planets wake within me . . .
> 'Round and around the curvous atmosphere
> Of my own real existence I revolve,
> Serene and starry with undying love.

[14] Byron, "Darkness," in *Byron*, ed. Jerome McGann (Oxford: Oxford University Press, 1986), 272–73. Thomas Campbell, "The Last Man," in *The Complete Poetical Works of Thomas Campbell* (Oxford: Oxford University Press, 1907), 232–34.

[15] The gratifying assertion of ego that is the implicit theme of these poems depends on the construction of a binary logic that seeks to escape from as it erases the threat of genuine dialectic, the engagement of other subjectivities. By eliminating the heterogeneity of the social altogether, by isolating the consciousness of the Last Man and setting it against a *merely* material and monolithic opposite (darkness), these poems stage the emergence of an absolute self in a way not unlike that which allows the triumph of Prometheus in Percy Shelley's play.

> I am, I have been, I shall be, O glory!
> An universe, a god, a living Ever.

(*TLB*, 252–53)

I, the trinity, the Logos, the Alpha and Omega. One realizes in reading these poems how deeply entrenched is the romantic ideology of the subject, taking on almost comically exaggerated proportions in a genre seemingly antithetical to its purposes. In poems the ostensible theme of which is the imminent erasure of subjectivity, these authors make little effort to efface themselves.

The nearly parodic, certainly contradictory element in the "Last Man" poems emerges into full absurdity with the debate on plagiarism that accompanied them. Byron published "Darkness" in 1816; Campbell followed with his "Last Man" in 1823; Beddoes gave up his pretensions to the theme in 1825, leaving a manuscript of Byronic fragments and vowing, "I will do the Last Man before I die" (*TLB*, 600). Controversy arose when a January 1825 article in the *Edinburgh Review* suggested that much of Campbell's best imagery had been lifted directly from Byron. In a long letter to the editor, an offended Campbell explained that Byron pilfered these ideas from him; they had discussed the theme of the last man in conversation as early as 1810. Campbell also contended that the only reason he undertook the theme in 1823 was that he had been informed that another poet, Beddoes, was about to undertake it: "I thought this hard! The conception of the Last Man had been mine fifteen years ago; even Lord Byron had spared the title to me: I therefore wrote my poem so called, and sent it to the press; for not one idea in which was I indebted to Lord Byron, or to any other person" (*TLB*, 752). This letter in turn prompted Beddoes's response in private correspondence: "I understand that Mr Thomas Campbell has in some newspaper, in a paltry refutation of some paltry charge of plagiarism regarding his paltry poem in the paltry Edinburgh, touched the egg of my last man" (*TLB*, 597). When Keats coined the phrase "egotistical sublime" in discussing Wordsworth, he probably did not realize that four years after his death a better characterization of the high romantic mode might be the "petty egotistical sublime." The *London Magazine* had something of the last word in this controversy when it pointed out that a novel, *The Last Man, or Omegarus and Syderia* had been published in 1806.

The issue, of course, is not that of sorting out chronological priority but the very status of originality and what it says about the idea of subjectivity operating in authors writing about the end of subjectivity. The explicit anxiety of influence in this incident suggests that for Campbell and Beddoes, at least in their literary production, it *was* unpleasant to be reminded that one is not alone in the world, as Bloom's Thomas Mann puts it. The concern for originality implies a number of assumptions about the self that make it virtually impossible to consider that self's eschatological dissolution, while it *already* assumes the self's apocalyptic freedom and integrity. The entire debate on priority and plagiarism, in other words, lampoons the very theme for which the poets competed. To value originality is to believe that one occupies the freedom of the origin; it is to believe that, outside of temporal difference, outside of history, one is self-constituted, whole, and that ideas emanate from and belong to a unitary presence free from the contamination of nonself in all of its forms. In this schema, words and ideas take on the character of metaphysical private property, devalued as they are circulated among others: "The conception of the Last Man had been *mine,*" Campbell states, and Beddoes regrets that Campbell "touched the egg of *my* last man" (my emphasis). The greatest threat to the self is that of debt, defining identity by a deficit relation to an other: "for not one idea . . . was I indebted." The tropes of property and debt are not gratuitous; given the evaluative criteria of literary England in 1825 (sincerity, spontaneity, authenticity), Campbell's reputation and hence his career to some extent depend on the validity of his claims to primacy. As much as any other poem, "The Last Man" secured Campbell's fame; the integrity of the self literally meant prestige and professional power. The plagiarism controversy thus foregrounds the investment of an 1820s poet in self-authorship and to some extent explains the background devices serving to sustain subjectivity in the "Last Man" poems. In the ethos of originality, the solipsism that is superficially the anguish of the last man figure, the death of whose consciousness is the death of *all* consciousness, paradoxically becomes a condition of inestimable value, the sign of genius, strength, and imaginative wealth.

The "Last Man" and Gender

"The opposition . . . mine/not mine (the valorization of the self-same)," writes Hélène Cixous, "organizes the opposition identity/difference."[16] Two elements characterize the three "Last Man" poems I have been discussing: a deep concern with self-possession and the tendency to dichotomize. The two are almost indistinguishable, as identity secures

[16] Hélène Cixous, "Sorties: Out and Out: Attacks/Ways Out/Forays," in Hélène Cixous, *The Newly Born Woman,* trans. Betsy Wing (Minneapolis: University of Minnesota Press, 1986), 80.

itself by declaring an opposite, precisely the initial moment of self-consciousness in Hegel's *Phenomenology*.[17] The "Last Man" confronts the absolute of darkness only to retain light at a deeper level. What remains to be shown is the masculine logic within which these two features are organized, a logic announced immediately by the genre's title, where "man" means "human." The masculine ideal of self-presence, universalized as identity itself, depends on a systematic hierarchy of metaphorical antitheses that subordinates the feminine to the masculine. When these poems bypass the annihilation of consciousness and round back upon their own creative agency, their capacity for self-generation, they do so *explicitly* at the expense of the feminine.

I will start with Byron, since "Darkness" almost entirely suppresses the role of gender until its stunning final line, where Byron assigns Darkness a feminine identity: "She was the universe." The impact of these closing words depends largely on the striking opposition they form to the poem's parallel opening: "I had a dream." The lines are clearly drawn: I/She, identity/otherness, subject/object—these pairs literally become the conceptual frame for all the poem's dichotomies (light/dark, life/death, consciousness/materiality, culture/nature). When dream is extinguished ("I had a dream"), only an inanimate universe remains ("She was the universe"). Or to put it another way, when the world is emptied of the ego, when the place vacated by the spirit of cognition hardens into a dense and undifferentiated material mass, only recalcitrant negativity is left: "The world was void . . . was a lump, / Seasonless, herbless, treeless, manless, lifeless— / A lump of death—a chaos of hard clay." The word "manless" in this series indicates the annihilation of *everyone* in this eschatological scene, of "man" the universal, the generic "he," and yet the residual negativity is not entirely inhuman, as it is personified, given gender. Byron imagines the end of *human* consciousness as a passage into the "inferior" materiality of the feminine. The precedence for this kind of eschatological misogyny goes back at least as far as Revelation, where the Whore of Babylon and her sensuous materialism represent the chief obstacle to transcendence, but a more direct influence is in the apocalyptic conclusion of Pope's *Dunciad,* which shares a number of features with Byron's vision:

> In vain, in vain,—the all-composing Hour
> Resistless falls: The Muse obeys the Pow'r.

[17] "Hegel isn't inventing things. What I mean is that the dialectic, its syllogistic system, the subject's going out into the other *in order to come back* to itself, this entire process, particularly described in the *Phenomenology of the Mind*, is, in fact, what is commonly at work in our everyday banality. Nothing is more frightening or more ordinary than Society's functioning the way it is laid out with the perfect smoothness of Hegelian machinery." Cixous, "Sorties," 78–79.

> She comes! she comes! the sable throne behold
> Of *Night* Primaeval, and of *Chaos* old!
>
> . . . .
>
> Nor *public* Flame, nor *private*, dares to shine;
> Nor *human* Spark is left, nor Glimpse *divine!*
> Lo! thy dread Empire, CHAOS! is restor'd;
> Light dies before thy uncreating word;
> Thy hand, great Anarch! lets the curtain fall;
> And Universal Darkness buries All.[18]

The human spark expires; the remainder is feminine; the implication that woman is outside the human and threatens the human is unmistakable. Pope's fear is that in the beginning was not the word, the rational logos, the linchpin of male identity, but a feminine language unanchored in the security of an origin (*Anarch:* without origin), a language that can only be approached in Pope's logic by the negative: "thy uncreating word."

The representation of gender that frames Byron's poem and structures its paired relations is a common denominator of the "Last Man" genre. Beddoes's 1837 notebook fragments included the following possibility: "Make Death a woman and enamored of Orion the last one" (*TLB*, 525–26). Even in poems where gender receives little attention, the same subordination of the feminine pertains. *Darkness, oblivion, eclipse,* the various terms of the world's end, are never personified in Campbell's "Last Man," for example, but the positive pole of *mind, language,* and *divinity* is so androcentric that the entire piece revels in a patriarchal self-satisfaction. The feminine is central to the poem; Campbell simply cannot name it as such. Of all the "Last Man" pieces, Campbell's is the most adamant in asserting the transcendental recovery of identity in the face of dissolution. The sun expires, but the protagonist knows that he will be gathered to the higher, immaterial light of the deity, male, of course: "This spirit shall return to Him / That gave its heavenly spark; / Yet think not, Sun, it shall be dim / When thou thyself are dark!" The poem's second line identifies the sun as masculine ("The Sun himself must die"), so that one can chart the entire progress of the poem as the passage of subjectivity from one masculine order to another that escapes the threatening intervention of the feminine. The point here is that Campbell's darkness is just as gender-identified as Byron's, but the insistence on the continuity of masculine ego is so violent that Campbell erases the very feminine presence without which his sublime

---

[18] Alexander Pope, *The Dunciad,* in *Poetry and Prose of Alexander Pope* (New York: Houghton Mifflin, 1969), 377–78.

vision of recuperation could not occur.[19] There is only one direct reference to the feminine in the poem, at the end of the first stanza.

> All worldly shapes shall melt in gloom,
>   The Sun himself must die,
> Before this mortal shall assume
>   Its Immortality!
> I saw a vision in my sleep
> That gave my spirit strength to sweep
>   Adown the gulf of Time!
> I saw the last of human mould
> That shall Creation's death behold.
>   As Adam saw *her* prime.

The specular logic of the masculine expands the stature of its subjectivity by constricting the feminine to the object ("Creation"). Vision and
light itself are definitively masculine, as the identification of the sun
confirms. By means of the poem's I/eye, the prophetic agent that sees
the future and records the vision in verse, Campbell links himself to
both the end and the origin, establishing the continuity of a universal,
transcendental male that sees: "I saw" / "[the last man] shall behold" /
"Adam saw." Campbell's poem begins where it ends, resisting temporality altogether, undisturbed in its transhistorical and distinctly masculine
subjectivity.

What happens when Shelley enters this manly genre and writes from
the position of that which is already excluded? *The Last Man* was begun
in desperate circumstances. Shelley found in the title figure an image of
her loneliness following the death of her husband and her return to
England from Italy. "The last man! Yes, I may well describe that solitary
being's feelings, feeling myself as the last relic of a beloved race, my
companions extinct before me."[20] Shelley unsexes the "solitary being" in
this journal entry, already suggesting some incompatibility between the
masculine hero and herself. She does, however, write *The Last Man* as a
first-person male narrative, and the novel employs much of the same
gender-based language common to the "Last Man" poems. The agent of
annihilation, the plague, for instance, is always personified as a feminine
force. More subtly, the novel's first paragraph reproduces a number of

---

[19] The role played by the feminine in Campbell's poem corresponds almost exactly to
the role Cixous sees for the feminine within patriarchal discourse as a whole: "Night to his
day—that has forever been the fantasy. Black to his white. Shut out of his system's space,
she is the repressed that ensures the system's functioning." "Sorties," 67.

[20] *Mary Shelley's Journal*, ed. Frederick Jones (Norman: University of Oklahoma Press,
1947), 193. Hereafter cited as *J*.

the maneuvers we have seen in Byron, Campbell, and Beddoes. Is their language of self and gender simply second nature?

> I am the native of a sea-surrounded nook, a cloud-enshadowed land, which, when the surface of the globe, with its shoreless ocean and trackless continents, presents itself to my mind, appears only as an inconsiderable speck in the immense whole; and yet, when balanced in the scale of mental power, far outweighed countries of larger extent and more numerous population. So true it is, that man's mind alone was the creator of all that was good or great to man, and that Nature herself was only his first minister.[21]

Organization by hierarchical opposition (mental expanse/geographical expanse); association of hierarchy with gender (Nature herself subordinated to man's mind); the confident assertion of an integral subjectivity that begins the novel with self-identification ("I am . . .")—all these elements suggest that Shelley has entered into the masculine discourse that constitutes the "Last Man" genre. Whether Shelley plays with mimesis or is reduced to the place of her exploitation in discourse, as Irigaray establishes the terms, is not easy to determine. With an author already marginalized by the very genre she chooses, perhaps the place to start is with the margins of her text, the introduction to the novel where in displaced form lies the gender relationship that speaks against the conventional "Last Man" wisdom.

"My Sibylline Leaves"

Lord Dillon wrote to Mary Shelley, "I should have thought of you—if I had only read you—that you were a sort of my Sybil, outpouringly enthusiastic, rather indiscreet, and even extravagant; but you are cool, quiet, and feminine to the last degree—I mean in delicacy of manner and expression. Explain this to me."[22] For Lord Dillon there can be no category of "feminine" prophecy. To be a Sibyl and to be properly feminine are assumed to be mutually exclusive. The assumption is inherent in the mythological derivation of the Sibyl's power, which origi-

---

[21] *The Last Man* (Lincoln: University of Nebraska Press, 1965), 5. Hereafter cited only by page reference.

[22] Lord Dillon, quoted by R. Glenn Grylls, *Mary Shelley: A Biography* (London: Oxford University Press, 1938), 211–12.

nates not within herself but in the male sun god. The Sibyl speaks at the expense of her autonomy as a woman. Apollo literally inspires her. Passing through the Sibyl, his breath transforms her into his medium, an event apparently not to her liking, one more like violation than privilege, and one that enacts a symbolic revenge on Apollo's part. The Sibyl becomes a prophetess only as she is subdued, broken even; she cannot simultaneously bear the divine word and be true to herself. In his letter, Dillon reproduces this view from the patriarchy. Imagine him, for instance, approaching Blake with this nonsequitur: "I should have thought of you as a modern-day biblical prophet, but I find instead that you are *masculine*."

If Dillon has the Cumaean Sibyl in mind when he speaks of Shelley, it is partly because she herself referred to *The Last Man* as "my Sibylline Leaves" and because the novel's elaborate introduction explains the unsettling vision to follow as the reworking of the ancient Sibyl's prophecies.[23] Outside the text proper, displaced to the margins of the introduction, the Sibyl bears within her history a trenchant representation of feminine voice and the violence done to it by masculine power. At the same time, she suggests the rage felt at this violence, for her prophecies, which comprise the narrative content of *The Last Man*, envision a furious return of the repressed, the annihilation of mankind by means of a "feminine" plague. Through the Sibyl Shelley locates an alternative line of prophecy, a feminine line, but, ironically, that inheritance says as much about debilitation as it does about empowerment.

The Sibyl's Story

The events of the introduction of *The Last Man* are relatively simple. Shelley (the first-person narrator) and a "matchless companion" (3)—obviously Percy—tour the subterranean cave of the Cumaean Sibyl. When their guides refuse to advance along a particularly forbidding passage, the Shelleys continue independently and in darkness, ascending after much difficulty to a dimly lit chamber. There, scattered on the floor, they find the leaves, "traced with written characters."

What appeared to us more astonishing, was that these writings were expressed in various languages: some unknown to my companion, ancient Chaldee, and Egyptian hieroglyphics, old as the pyramids. Stranger still,

[23] *Letters of Mary Wollstonecraft Shelley*, ed. Betty T. Bennett, 3 vols. (Baltimore: Johns Hopkins University Press, 1980), I. 508. Hereafter cited as *L*.

some were in modern dialects, English and Italian. We could make out little by the dim light, but they seemed to contain prophecies, detailed relations of events but lately passed. (3)

Gathering the leaves, they return to daylight and begin the task of study and transcription, a task the narrator continues after the death of her husband. Shelley concludes the introduction by apologizing for the finished product, having reduced the sublime fragments to a coherent narrative, but she also insists that "the main substance rests on the truths contained in these poetic rhapsodies, and the divine intuition which the Cumaean damsel obtained from heaven" (4).[24]

At least two significant contradictions mark this prefatory narrative. The first I can state plainly: the Cumaean Sibyl possessed none of the noble and sentimental innocence implied by the term *damsel*. Shelley's primary source for this introduction, book 6 of the *Aeneid*, describes the Sibyl as mad, monstrous, and frenetic, rendering the phrase "Cumaean damsel" incongruous to the point of deliberate absurdity. Second, and more subtle, the passage indicates a division in loyalties that might be put this way: although Shelley boldly designates her source in a woman's vision, she transcribes that vision only through the guidance and mediation of her husband. In a telling detail, not all the Sibyl's leaves are incorporated into the novel; Percy Shelley is said to have removed from the cave only those written in languages he could read. The novel, it turns out, is only a partial representation of the Sibyl's patchwork discourse, partial in both senses of the word; it is at once incomplete and biased. Mary Shelley tries to understand the Sibyl's vision *through* Percy's vision, as she thinks he would have wanted her to understand it. To translate the prophetic leaves through this mediation necessarily excludes something of the Sibyl's discourse. Despite his celebrated command of languages, Percy cannot understand the whole of her hybrid text. The Sibyl is remarkably heterogeneous, something Shelley might have recognized as one of her definitive traits when she reread the *Aeneid* in 1824: "The huge side of Euboean / Rock was hewn out as a cave, where a

---

[24] Very few readings of *The Last Man* have considered the importance of the Sibyl to the novel. In fact, most are surprisingly dismissive of it. Sterrenburg calls the introduction "an elaborate hoax . . . to explain how a confessional tale supposedly written in the year 2099 came to be published in 1826." "Anatomy of Failed Revolutions," 342. Mary Poovey considers the introduction Shelley's "most elaborate strategy of indirection," by which "she defers responsibility for the story." *The Proper Lady and the Woman Writer* (Chicago: University of Chicago Press, 1984), 157. Only Sandra Gilbert and Susan Gubar treat the introduction in detail, but they address it as a self-sufficient parable independent of the novel altogether.

hundred broad paths / Led on and a hundred doors whence as many voices, / The Sibyl's responses, roared forth."[25] Hundred-voiced, hyperbolically polyvocal, the Sibyl's oracles are to some extent beyond the poet-husband's grasp, leaving a portion of her story untranscribed in the fragments that remain upon the cavern floor. "Woman's desire," Irigaray suggests, "cannot be expected to speak the same language as man's" (*TS,* 25). What part of the Sibyl's story remains silent to the ears of the patriarchy?

Although *The Last Man* itself has received little critical attention, this introduction, because of its emphasis on the Sibyl, has become a celebrated, even archetypal, passage in a leading feminist interpretation. In the "Parables of the Cave" section that concludes the theoretical introduction to *The Madwoman in the Attic,* Sandra Gilbert and Susan Gubar see the Sibyl as a matriarch who represents the lost but recoverable language of woman's unmediated experience.

> The cave is a female space and it belonged to a female hierophant, the lost Sibyl, the prophetess who inscribed her "divine intuitions" on tender leaves and fragments of delicate bark. For Mary Shelley, therefore, it is intimately connected with both her own artistic authority and her own power of self-creation. A male poet or instructor may guide her to this place, but, as she herself realizes, she and she alone can effectively reconstruct the scattered truth of the Sibyl's leaves. . . . Mary Shelley portrays herself in this parable as figuratively the daughter of the vanished Sibyl, the primordial prophetess who mythically conceived all women artists.[26]

In this interpretation the prepatriarchal Sibyl is empowered and empowering. In order to convey that impression, however, the reading must twice minimize or efface altogether the fact of patriarchal media-

[25] Virgil, *Aeneid* 6.48–51, trans. L. R. Lind (Bloomington: Indiana University Press, 1962).

[26] Sandra Gilbert and Susan Gubar, *The Madwoman in the Attic* (New Haven: Yale University Press, 1979), 96–97. Gilbert and Gubar conclude this way: "This last parable is the story of the woman artist who enters the cavern of her own mind and finds there the scattered leaves not only of her own power but of the tradition which might have generated that power. The body of her precursor's art, and thus the body of her own art, lies in pieces around her, dismembered, dis-remembered, disintegrated. How can she remember it and become a member of it, join it and rejoin it, integrate it and in doing so achieve her own integrity, her own selfhood?" (98). As Toril Moi points out, the emphasis on wholeness here, the insistence on the integrity of both self and text, labors "under the traditional patriarchal aesthetic values of New Criticism." *Sexual/Textual Politics* (London: Methuen, 1985), 67. Just as Shelley's novel is mediated by her husband's knowledge (his actual aesthetics as well as his selection of the leaves in the fiction), so Gilbert and Gubar's interpretive act remains deeply and uncritically mediated.

tion—three times if you include the way the reading itself reproduces various assumptions of patriarchal aesthetics. The Sibyl's divine intuitions are not hers; neither does Shelley's reconstruction of the prophecies belong to her and her alone. Instead, the Sibyl's oracles serve precisely to introduce a culturally mediated image of woman's writing, one particularly pertinent to a novelist laboring under the shadow of a sometimes idolized husband-poet. Heterogeneous she may be, but the Sibyl does not voice the "different alphabet," the "different language," that Irigaray speculates belonged to a matriarchal civilization prior to the phallocentric rationalism of Western culture.[27]

A transitional figure between Greek and Roman empires—Cumae was the oldest Greek colony in Italy—the Sibyl appears at a crucial moment in the dissemination of Western patriarchy. Neither free nor empowered, the Sibyl's voice is that of a woman under patriarchy, a woman who must speak the masculine word despite the violence it does her, a circumstance made literal in Virgil's representation of her. As masculine discourse inscribes a vertical hierarchy in its dichotomies—heaven above earth, reason above madness, male above female—so the Sibyl's subterranean cavern is set beneath the Temple of Apollo, buried within the materiality of the body that Apollo subdues to order. Apollo masters the Sibyl from his position of superiority, rides her like a horse in Virgil's dominant trope: "So did Apollo / Shake reins upon her until she raved, and twist goads / Under her breast" (*Aeneid* 6.110–12). The violence Apollo uses against her body corresponds directly with her prophetic "ability": the Sibyl predicts the future only under the whip, and even then, the words are not her own but those of the power that enters her as an alien presence. "The priestess, not yet enduring Phoebus' huge frenzy, / Raged in her cave and tried to drive out of her breast / The great god. All the more did he weary her madly raving / Mouth, subdue her wild heart, and mold her with pressure" (6.86–89). Apollo breaks down her body's resistance in order to make her speak his mind. Few passages in literature more graphically display the desire for mastery inherent in the masculine representation of gender relations, the brutality by which the male seeks to command its other in the name of higher truths, and the additional violation of compelling the victim to speak a language

[27] Luce Irigaray writes, "One would have to dig down very deep indeed to discover beneath the traces of this civilization, of this history, the vestiges of a more archaic civilization that might give some clue to woman's sexuality. That extremely ancient civilization would undoubtedly have a different alphabet, a different language. . . . Woman's desire would not be expected to speak the same language as man's; woman's desire has doubtless been submerged by the logic that has dominated the West since the time of the Greeks." *TS*, 25.

antithetical to her interest.[28] The Sibyl's discourse, divided against itself, begins in pain.

Apollo's violence, of course, is not gratuitous. As allegory, the opening of *Aeneid* 6 is a scene of instruction; Aeneas must learn the severe virtues of authority necessary to found an empire. The Sibyl represents the twin threat to the masculine order of all that is designated feminine: the threat of bodies and passions to the rule of law and the danger of otherness to the rule of identity. At stake is the legitimacy of the masculine subject and the empire founded upon it, the legacy passed from Greece to Rome. Indivisible and lucid as the sun he embodies, Apollo is the god of ego and its language—poetry. His word carries the universalizing tendency of metaphor, the sometimes ruthless impulse to abstract identity out of difference. Once again, the masculine manifests itself in the conjunction between power and language, Apollo's arrows and his lyre.

Projecting and imposing a dream of identity each time it imagines the unity underlying disparate phenomena, metaphor organizes experience in reference to the self. In its logic, difference is superficial and similitude is truth, but always in reference to the effaced third term manipulating the tropes and benefiting by them. This hidden motivation is precisely what Irigaray brings to light when she says somewhat whimsically of analogy: "It's a little abstract. I don't quite understand 'alike.' Do you? Alike in whose eyes? in what terms? by what standard? with reference to what third?" (*TS*, 208). Elsewhere, she addresses the issue more formally: "Now, this domination of the philosophic logos stems in large part from its power to *reduce all others to the economy of the Same*. The teleologically constructive project it takes on is always also a project of diversion, deflection, reduction of the other in the Same. And, in its greatest generality perhaps, from its power to *eradicate the difference between the sexes* in systems that are self-representative of a 'masculine subject'" (*TS*, 74). In "molding [the Sibyl] by pressure," and in his association with the discourse of metaphor, Apollo acts and speaks so as to centralize and authorize his own subjectivity. "Fera corda domans fingitque premendo": fingo, fingere—to mold, but also to compose poetry. The imperial motive of identity, what Irigaray calls "the reduc-

---

[28] In his recent and wide-ranging study of abandoned women in poetry, Lawrence Lipking has looked to Virgil's Sibyl as an archetype of gender representation that has instances in the traditions of many patriarchal cultures. Although his emphasis is on the mastery that motivates the male poet rather than on the perspective of so many sibyls, his conclusions seem appropriate to Apollo: "The abandoned woman is nothing more than a male conceit, shaped by a fantasy of absolute domination. A man who uses a woman defines himself." *Abandoned Women and Poetic Tradition* (Chicago: University of Chicago Press, 1988), 134.

tion of the other in the Same," is the subject of Percy Shelley's "Song of Apollo," a piece Mary Shelley included in the collection of poems she edited a year after her husband's death, just prior to starting *The Last Man*. It is not clear whether Percy finds the sublimity of Apollo's ego appealing or appalling. The short lyrical monologue, devoted obsessively to the grammatical forms of the first person, culminates in a paean to possessive self-presence:

> I am the eye with which the Universe
>   Beholds itself, and knows it is divine.
> All harmony of instrument and verse,
>   All prophecy and medicine are mine;
> All light of art or nature—to my song
> Victory and praise, in its own right, belong.[29]

"I am the eye": no phrase, perhaps with the exception of Exodus's "I am that I am," better expresses the transcendental tautology of self-identity toward which the masculine subject aspires in its suppression of difference. This tautology then expands to cosmic significance when the ego equates itself with the totality of the universe, which it reduces in effect to its speculum.[30]

The Sibyl appears in this soliloquy of self-love only by exclusion and inference; Apollo assures us that, along with just about everything else, prophecy (and presumably the vehicle of prophecy) belongs to him. The Sibyl, however, does not belong to Apollo, despite the scene of coercion and ventriloquism. Never a particularly successful lover, Apollo's problems begin with sexual difference that cannot be reduced to his will; the Sibyl's problems begin, according to Ovid, when she refuses his seductions: "I scorned his gift and remained unwed."[31] If Apollo punishes the Sibyl by giving her immortality without perpetual youth, he also punishes her by "giving" her prophecy. Each time the Sibyl pronounces an oracle, Apollo enacts a violent ritual of possession that avenges her sexual reluctance. Underlying the Apollo/Sibyl myth, especially as it is portrayed in Virgil, one finds the fear of a feminine sexuality so self-sufficient that it cannot be represented and thus recovered by the logocentric reduction to identity.

Even on the most superficial level, the Sibyl is sexually charged; the

---

[29] P. B. Shelley, *Shelley's Poetry and Prose*, ed. Donald Reiman and Sharon Powers (New York: Norton, 1977), 368.

[30] The reduction of the cosmos to the eye's speculum is a constitutive necessity, not a by-product, of this image of self-construction. Already implicit in the tautology of self-identity is the fact of self-alienation: the "eye" cannot see itself without a mirroring universe.

[31] Ovid, *Metamorphoses*, trans. Mary M. Innes (New York: Penguin, 1955), 315.

damp darkness of her subterranean cave links her to the female body, and Virgil's description of her, focused almost exclusively on her physical being, makes her seem monstrous (*Aeneid* 6.54–57). More subtly, the text associates the Sibyl with Dido's destructive passion. Although they are in some ways opposite—Dido gives herself too completely and the Sibyl not at all—they both embody a feminine sexuality outside the jurisdiction of the male. Dido and Aeneas consummate their desire when, by chance, they take refuge from a storm in the same cave. Although their passion is barely recorded, almost unrepresented as if antithetical to language itself, it appears immediately in displaced form, in the elaborate and celebrated conceit Virgil employs to describe Rumor. Sexual licentiousness can only be represented as verbal licentiousness—and then only when personified as a distinctly feminine aberration that undermines the capacity of language to convey truth. Rumor is the signifier gone mad, become pure excess, as the disproportion between the trope and its narrative function implies. An uncontrollable feminine force, Rumor even prefigures the Sibyl in the fierce heterogeneity of her voice. "A frightful monster, huge, upon whose body / The feathers match in number watchful eyes / (A wondrous thing to say!) and match her tongues / And mouths and ears" (*Aeneid* 6.179–82).[32] Feminine sexuality becomes entangled with the decentered and polyvocal nature of a feminine discourse. Aeneas has been derailed by the pleasure of diffusion (sexual and linguistic), a pleasure directly subversive of his mission, his unitary focus of purpose, his telos: the securing of the patriarchal order. When Aeneas next arrives at a cave, it is by will and not by accident; there, Apollo, riding the Sibyl and compelling *her* hybrid voice to the order of *his* truth, instructs him in the necessary protocol of interaction between the sexes. Poised between Aeneas's sexual pleasure with Dido and the fulfillment of his cultural destiny, Apollo serves to demonstrate the cruelty one must be willing to inflict in order to command feminine desire.

On one of the gates leading into the Sibyl's chamber are sculpted images of the Minotaur and the labyrinth. This is not surprising, because Daedalus allegedly erected the Temple of Apollo after his aerial escape from Crete and his landing at Cumae. One of the panels, however, depicts in shorthand the fear of feminine sexuality that underlies Virgil's representation of the Sibyl: "Here the cruel love / Of the bull, the

[32] Interestingly enough, Shelley herself refers to Virgil's trope in the novel (215), explaining that all kinds of grotesque formations ("Gorgon and Centaur, dragon and iron-hoofed lion, vast sea-monster and gigantic hydra") result from the combination of fear and rumor. She recalls these specters, all of which associate hybridization and linguistic aberration, in order to introduce the new and distinctly feminine monster that overwhelms her novel—plague.

secret mating of Pasiphäe, / Their revolting offspring, the two-formed child Minotaur, / Was carven, memorial of unnatural lust" (*Aeneid* 6.26–29). Pasiphäe's deviance from the sanctioned norms of libidinal expression, taking sexual pleasure without the intervention of a man, bears within its consequences both the patriarchy's condemnation of her independent desires and the implicit danger that calls forth the strictest outrage. The mother of the Minotaur, Pasiphäe is also the daughter of Helios, the forerunner of Apollo; she therefore stands between the unitary identity the patriarchy projects for itself in the image of the sun and the dissolution of that identity into a deformed and monstrous hybrid, the dissolution of identity into "two-formed" difference. Masculine subjectivity passes into otherness through the unregulated sexual desires of women, whether in the form of Dido's excessive love, the Sibyl's decision *not* to yield, or, in the most extreme instance, Pasiphäe's "perversion."

The Sibyl's Story Revised

The Sibyl's story structures to some extent every aspect of *The Last Man*. It is the origin of the narrative. At times, drawing on the leaves she imagines Percy would have selected, Shelley rewrites the Sibyl's story as the sentimentalized mentor relation between poet-husband and novelist-wife, as the story of the "Cumaean damsel," the rhapsode who obtains her "divine intuition . . . from heaven." To a degree that should not be underestimated, Shelley has internalized Virgil's patriarchal lesson. Despite her self-declared intention to honor her husband, however, she cannot entirely efface either the Sibyl's palpable rage or its cause in the violent domination by Apollo. These elements surface indirectly in forms ranging from a marginal character, the Greek woman Evadne, to the feminine power so fiercely destructive that it literally ends culture and can be given no name other than PLAGUE. At the intersection between the sibylline paradigm and its altered appearance in the novel is the biographical text. A transparently autobiographical novel, *The Last Man* was conceived at a time when Shelley wavered between the trials and the always qualified attractions of feminine dependence within the patriarchy. The Sibyl/Apollo relationship gets recast as that of the central characters, Lionel and Adrian, a relationship which in turn reflects Shelley's anxieties about her dead husband.

In the two years between Percy Shelley's death and beginning *The Last Man*, Mary Shelley experienced all the pains of loneliness and none of the pleasures of independence. Almost from the moment her husband died, Shelley found her future directed by financial dealings in which she exercised little control. Byron managed the negotiations with Sir Timothy Shelley over an annuity that became the primary source of income for Shelley and her only remaining child, Percy Florence, and Shelley deferred to Byron's authority in this and other matters despite her reservations. To Jane Williams she wrote that all resistance would be detrimental to her prospects: "He would go with the reflection that I was self willed—whereas if I obey him he cannot find fault with the result" (*L*, 1.328). The real problem, however, was not Byron in Italy but Sir Timothy in England, who offered his assistance only if Shelley relinquished to him all responsibility for the education of Percy Florence. This meant, among other things, returning to England against her will. Without alternatives, she acquiesced. Even when she arrived in England under this agreement, Sir Timothy continued to exercise his financial leverage, always keeping his long-range intentions obscure and providing only a quarterly subsidy that he could easily withhold. In fact, he threatened to withhold the subsidy when her edition of Percy's poems came out in 1823. Embarrassed by the scandal associated with his son, Sir Timothy suppressed the publication, but only after more than half the copies had been sold. An accompanying collection of unpublished prose was never printed. A similar scene played itself out three years later when the father-in-law insisted that the Shelley name not appear on the title page of *The Last Man*. Thus the publication only included the phrase, "by the author of Frankenstein," a novel which had also appeared anonymously. When various reviews did mention Shelley by name, Sir Timothy yet again threatened to leave her without resources.

Perhaps even more revealing of her circumstances, however, was the obligation Shelley continued to feel to her husband after his death. Considering herself "a faint continuation of his being, . . . the revelation to the earth of what he was," and stating that his "spirit ever hovers over me" (*J*, 182, 187), Shelley played a willing Sibyl to Percy's Apollo. On her return to England, she devoted herself to publishing his work, to championing his genius through Adrian in *The Last Man*, and more generally to shaping her daily existence into the pattern she thought he would have desired. "I would fain know what to think of my desolate state; what you think I ought to do, what to think" (*J*, 181). In this case, Shelley *wished* to be molded by the divine male's pressure, and in his absence provided that pressure herself. Mary Poovey, who has written with great insight on this period of Shelley's life, suggests that "Percy had given Mary an image of herself that was compelling in many ways but in others was almost crippling. . . . [S]uch an ideal seemed not only unrealizable but frankly undesirable."[33] The governing motivations in Shelley's ob-

---

[33] Poovey, *The Proper Lady and the Woman Writer*, 152.

session with the dead seem to have been duty and guilt; the authority Percy exerted in their marriage survived his death. Shelley's most reliable pleasure at this time was the purpose she felt in honoring him, yet the word that recurs constantly in journals and letters is "task": "I shall commence my task, commemorate the virtues of the only creature worth loving or living for" (*J*, 181). Several letters and journal entries make it clear that Shelley's work was primarily driven by a vague but deeply felt sense of guilt: "not having been all I shd have been, I will at least bear my penance well & not making my S.— so happy as he deserved to be I will at least make him happy where he is now, if he can be conscious of my constancy & patience" (*L*, 1.366–67). The belief that she had somehow failed a superior presence—"I do not in any degree believe that his being was regulated by the same laws that govern the existence of us common mortals" (*L*, 1.512)—dictated her entire course of action in England, right up to the writing of *The Last Man*.

Shelley tried to reshape herself as her husband's mouthpiece. Under pressure, she tried to experience herself through her husband, and thus at an individual and partially deliberate level she reproduces a general and unconscious cultural phenomenon—the double-voicing of the feminine as it experiences itself through patriarchal mediation. This doubling becomes immediately apparent in Lionel Verney, narrator of *The Last Man* and Shelley's chief, though not exclusive, representative in the novel, the spokes*man* for this woman author. Lionel lives up to Adrian/Percy's standard as Shelley felt she had not; but to do so he must be transformed from a woman to a man. Although he announces himself with the secure subjectivity typical of the "Last Man" genre—"I am the native of a sea-surrounded nook"—Lionel is self-divided, both man and woman. Moreover, it is in his conversion by and to Adrian that Shelley rewrites the Sibyl's story to make it conform to the wishful version of her own relationship to her husband. All the Sibyl's rage disappears from the tale of Lionel's friendship with Adrian; in fact, this initial movement of the novel is ostensibly *about* the disarming of rage— how one learns to suppress it as one moves from the margins to the center of a culture. It is, in other words, about learning to speak Apollo's language while hiding the wound from oneself.

On first meeting Adrian, Lionel exhibits all the pent-up fury of the dispossessed. Face smeared with dirt, hair matted, clothes torn to rags, he holds in one hand birds stolen from Adrian's estate and in the other a knife still wet with blood. Just before Adrian's appearance, he stabs an estate warden who witnessed his act of transgression and tried to detain him. As Lionel himself concedes retrospectively, he is "lawless." Within moments of meeting Adrian, Lionel has been named fully for the first time in the novel; he conceives of his actions in terms of crime and guilt;

his rebellious spirit is tamed; and he has already experienced the change that will prompt him to emulate his new friend through intellectual study. The agent of assimilation, a law-bearer at times associated in the text with Moses (19, 23), Adrian provides Lionel with an acceptable identity, a legitimate subjectivity within the social order. Quite literally, he reforms him, inspiring and possessing him as Apollo does the Sibyl, only more gently, in a way that persuades him his socialization constitutes his humanity. "My plastic soul was remoulded by a master hand," Lionel states. "I now began to be human. I was admitted within that sacred boundary which divides the intellectual and moral nature of man from that which characterizes animals" (20). Lionel enters legitimacy (takes on a name) only as he ceases his "war against civilization" (12) and accepts not only its central terms but its governing forms of conceptualization: dichotomy and hierarchy, nature subordinated to culture, and the body (the animal) subordinated to "the intellectual and moral nature of man." Culture validates itself by means of its divisions, its sacred boundaries. Lionel becomes human, becomes a citizen, in other words, when he internalizes those divisions. And in doing so, he begins to think like a man, though as I will argue momentarily his transfiguration can never be complete. Something of the rage, just as some vestige of marginalization, remains; Lionel needs his society's vigilance to assure his cooperation: "Sometimes my lawless mood would return, my love of peril, my resistance to authority; but this was in [Adrian's] absence; under the mild sway of his dear eyes, I was obedient and good as a boy of five years old, who does his mother's bidding" (24). Lionel's progress looks like regression, almost infantilization, and Adrian's parental authority, despite its milder, "motherly" aspect, still serves the social hierarchy.

The taming of Lionel takes place through a steady process of abstraction, a form of violence directed at the body more subtle than that which Apollo inflicts on the Sibyl. Lionel's socialization amounts first to learning the value of abstract, universal principles that transcend social and material differences and then to conforming to the cultural patterns prescribed by those principles. Lionel becomes "human" as he disengages himself from his body; having once been "rough as the elements, and unlearned as the animals" (9), he now submits to the tutelage of a character celebrated for his nearly immaterial state. Adrian's soul, the narrator marvels, "appeared rather to inhabit his body than unite with it" (65). Despite Shelley's self-avowed weakness for poets of delicate health, it is difficult not to find implicit criticism in a phrase like "he was all mind" (18). Part of Lionel's internalization of his culture's dichotomous values appears in the odd reversal by which the lack of physical health becomes the sign of intellectual strength, a reversal that complements Shelley's own ascetic leanings at the time.

"I was an outcast and a vagabond, when Adrian gently threw over me the silver net of love and civilization" (189). To Lionel, ideological indoctrination and entrapment seem the necessary means of humanization, and the measure of his progress from margins to center appears when he in turn throws the net over another, catching Adrian's sister, Idris. Shelley carefully delineates the way in which Lionel's education shapes his subjectivity and forms the basis of his conception of sexual relations.

> I pored over the poetry of old times; I studied the metaphysics of Plato and Berkley. I read the histories of Greece and Rome, and of England's former periods, and I watched the movements of the lady of my heart. At night I could see her shadow on the walls of her apartment; by day I viewed her in her flower-garden, or riding in the park with her usual companions. Methought the charm would be broken if I were seen, but I heard the music of her voice and was happy. I gave to each heroine of whom I read, her beauty and matchless excellences—such was Antigone, . . . such was Miranda, . . . such Haidee. (55)

Having perceived Idris through the patriarchal formations of ideal womanhood and romantic love, Lionel becomes the cultural agent who assures that Idris will conform to the proper image. He secures their love by means of a conventional romance narrative, saving her from danger, taming her fears, and curing her bout of madness. When Idris appears at his door to escape her mother's malevolent designs, her disoriented appearance resembles nothing so much as Lionel's at the moment Adrian "saved" him. "With disordered dress, dishevelled hair, and aghast looks, she wrung her hands—the idea shot across me—is she also mad?" (61). It is not simply that Idris's madness threatens Lionel's new commonsense identity; it is that by curing her, by restoring her to composure, he modulates from a passive to an active role in stabilizing the cultural order. "With respect to the woman's madness," writes Shoshana Felman, "man's reason reacts by trying to *appropriate* it . . . to 'tame' in order to 'cure': such [is] the method used by masculine reason so as to *objectify* feminine madness."[34] Indeed, the signal that Lionel's assimilation by Adrian has succeeded is his capacity to re-form an other, to bring Idris back from disorientation to normative sanity. And this allows him to assume the power position within the ministructure of patriarchal stability—marriage. At this moment, Lionel becomes a husband. He protects Idris, soothes her raving, but in such a way that renders her dependent on his authority and reaffirms, by appropriating her madness, his new identity within the masculine order: "I comforted

---

[34] Shoshana Felman, "Women and Madness: The Critical Phallacy," *Diacritics* (Winter 1975): 7.

her as well as I might. Joy and exultation, were mine, to possess, and to save her" (63). From the joy of being possessed, Lionel advances to the pleasures of possessing.

Despite its apparent success, the centering of Lionel's subjectivity within the masculine order leaves an untransfigured remainder of his marginalization. In part, this appears in the odd incongruity whereby Lionel, as narrator, sits at the novel's center without ever being its central character—that is, until he becomes its only character. Lionel participates, but he reacts; he rarely initiates. He remains liminal—essentially an inside outsider. If in one respect he represents the dutiful and accepted student Shelley wished to be in relation to her husband and his circle, he also preserves the alienation she in fact felt. He remains a she. Of course, Lionel fares better than Victor Frankenstein's monster, who is always an outsider and can only listen in. Having been transformed from the monstrous and the feminine, Lionel has earned his place at the center of intellectual life. At Windsor, he tells us with implicit pride, the women "would ramble away together, and we remained to discuss the affairs of nations, and the philosophy of life" (65). But for Lionel, "to discuss" typically means listening to Adrian and Raymond discuss—and so his passive participation comes to reproduce Shelley's self-consciously feminine role in the famous discussions between Percy and Byron at Diodati. Anticipating the introduction to *Frankenstein* she wrote in 1831, Shelley was often preoccupied in 1824 with the memory of the voices of the male poets and her own silence in the Diodati conversations. "I have been accustomed, when hearing [Byron], to listen and to speak little; another voice, not mine, ever replied—a voice whose strings are broken. . . . [S]ince incapacity and timidity always prevented my mingling in the nightly conversations of Diodati, they were, as it were, entirely têtea-tête between my Shelley and Albè" (*J*, 184). Converted by Adrian and glad for it, Lionel never shares in all the privileges of power, particularly the privilege of voice. He remains, as the Sibyl was for Apollo, and as Shelley was for the poets, possessed by the words of others.

As Lionel learns to see through Adrian's eyes, and as Shelley tries desperately to see through her husband's, the paradigmatic domination of the Sibyl by Apollo comes to look like the necessary and admirable means of intellectual elevation: all that is barbarous, irrational and deformed ascends, through Apollo's possession, to its redemption in civilization. In such a revision, the Sibyl's story tells how differences succumb to universality, how culture assimilates its others until culture seems free of their weight altogether. "I thus began to be human." As Lionel transcends both his body and his fury, as he gravitates from outsider to insider, he reflects Irigaray's contention that masculine subjectivity defines itself most generally by attempting to eradicate the difference between the sexes. To become human, in other words, means to become a man. In this novel, however, the other is irrepressible, surfacing sporadically in a minor character who oddly intersects the narrative at crucial but scattered moments until, after her death, the difference she signifies monstrously expands, moves toward the center of the novel and the culture it describes, and finally consumes them both. Evadne, a Greek woman linked by Virgil to both the Sibyl and Dido, appears on the scene of each crime against the novel's masculine ideals and seems causally associated with both of its major tragedies. Evadne is the novel's unrepentant woman, the Sibyl as *she* might have represented herself.

Impossible to pin down, Evadne alters identity with a protean dexterity; when one considers all the forms she assumes in *The Last Man* along with her mythological associations, she becomes at various moments foreigner, traitor, homewrecker, sorceress, madwoman, patricide, obsessive lover, and prophetess. In all of her incarnations she is a sexual free agent, and no matter what role she plays she is always and irredeemably other. Twice she is mistaken for a man, once when anonymously submitting drawings for an architecture competition and once when dressing as a foot soldier. Gender divisions and the power distribution they serve seem to unravel in her presence. Evadne not only threatens the patriarchal order but in fact collapses it; susceptible to the witch's spell, she is, according to myth, capable of dismembering the father. In *The Last Man*, her power of dismemberment becomes more figurative than literal, though its impact on the narrative is irresistible. Her violence works by more subtle means than the knife. Often associated with excessive passion and delirium, Evadne is contagious; she produces madness even in enlightened Adrian when she rejects his love, succeeding in preserving her independence from the male where the Sibyl did not. If Evadne had been seduced by Adrian, she might have followed the same path of appropriation as Lionel. But just the opposite occurs: the agent of cultural power cannot possess her, loses his rational center, and slips into madness until, ironically, Lionel can nurse him to recovery.

But to describe her resistance to man's love and the madness such resistance causes is to describe only a part of Evadne; just as easily she can give herself up to love entirely, frighteningly—throwing herself, for instance, upon the burning body of her husband, Capaneus, in ancient legend. Chaste as the Sibyl wished to be or as violently passionate as Dido, Evadne remains unpredictable and beyond patriarchal assimilation. Her affair with Raymond not only brings down the simulacrum of the male's social power—the family and its ideal of monogamy—but it brings down the entire English government as well. His domestic life ruined, Raymond abandons the office of protectorship to pursue, rather desperately, personal glory on the battlefields of Greece and Turkey. He dies conquering a plague-ridden city; Perdita, his wife, commits suicide.

Evadne herself was married once; she was, we are briefly told, "the cause of her husband's utter ruin" (82), and thus the cause of his eventual suicide. Evadne leaves a trail of catastrophe. If these individual disasters seem small compared to the universal devastation effected by the plague, Evadne involves herself there as well. Is it possible that the plague issues forth from Evadne? Disguised as a Greek soldier, she follows the object of her insatiable desire, Raymond, into battle without his knowing it and incurs a fatal wound. By chance, Lionel discovers her just in time to hear her parting words: "Fire, and war, and plague, unite for thy destruction—O my Raymond, there is no safety for thee!" (131). It is impossible to determine whether these words amount to a lamentation, a warning, a prophecy, or a curse. Reporting them to Raymond, Lionel calls them "the ravings of a maniac" (134), but Raymond knows better the power of a discourse informed by vengeance, desire, and madness. Lionel may or may not be right to ridicule superstition, but Raymond's death by plague, as I will argue shortly, takes on a form particularly appropriate to a lover's revenge against phallic power. We never encounter the plague firsthand before Evadne speaks it; afterwards, we encounter nothing else. Whether or not it originates in her all-consuming desire, she is irrevocably associated with its power.

Lionel, thoroughly rationalized, describes Evadne in terms of the "too great energy of her passions" (83). After her Greek husband's suicide, Evadne returns to England and resumes the obsession with Raymond that proves to be so subversive to the novel's cultural order: "the tide of love ... deluged her soul with its tumultuous waves, and she gave herself up a prey to its uncontrollable power" (82). Evadne's overabundant desire makes it impossible for her to function within an order that demands sublimation from its citizens. Perhaps that is why Shelley chose her name from the list of those "whom harsh love destroyed with its cruel sorrow" (*Aeneid* 6.456), those whom Aeneas sees in the "Mourning Fields" when he tours the underworld with the Cumaean Sibyl. In one striking moment, the Sibyl, Pasiphäe, and Evadne all stand by silently as Aeneas feebly justifies his actions to an equally silent Dido. "Aeneas attempted to soothe / With these words the anger that blazed from her eyes and her soul" (*Aeneid* 6.479–80). The fury embodied in all four women cannot be assuaged; they would rather not speak than mouth the words that would reassure the male and confirm his telos.

The Sibyl's Story Expanded: The Structure of the Novel

The Sibyl's story, in all of its permutations, structures the novel as a whole; it organizes the hybrid voices of dominance and assimilation, exclusion and violence. Almost all the issues I have addressed thus far appear in the novel's first volume, where Lionel's assimilation by Adrian in the opening pages dictates the events and concerns that follow. Once Lionel has been given a proper identity, the volume proceeds to describe the cultural order he has entered—its gender relations and its local politics. From the perspective of the Sibyl, the dominant movement of volume 1 is the passage, by means of cultural agency, from margin to center, typically represented as the illegitimate made legitimate, the mad made sane, and the furious disarmed of their anger. Emerging out of this matrix, volume 2 reproduces the Apollo/Sibyl paradigm in its central action, only on the larger scale of international politics, where the imperial motive of masculine subjectivity gets translated into the violent Eurocentrism that justifies the Greek siege of Constantinople. Lionel accepts his socialization willingly and reads it according to the terms of his mentor. Islam resists European persuasion, though the terms of ethnic conversion are exactly those of Lionel's—the ascent from nature to culture, from body to spirit, from other to universally human. "He wished . . . to eradicate from Europe a power which, while every other nation advanced in civilization, stood still, a monument of antique barbarism" (127). "He" is Raymond, and it is important that the burden of cultural conversion now shifts to him from Adrian, since Shelley can be more openly critical of his brutal power without touching the dignity of her husband. Despite their many disagreements, however, Raymond and Adrian speak the same language; one enacts on the battlefield what the other valorizes in the intellectual sphere: the subjugation (or in Raymond's case, the annihilation) of the other in service of the prerogatives of Western cultural power. One could say that Raymond realizes what for Adrian remains innocently in ideas; Raymond exposes the connection between a certain understanding of identity and its lived practice. The means may be subject to debate, something Adrian learns after a disillusioning year as a soldier in Greece with Raymond, but both share the same end of extending "civilization," the telos that drove Aeneas in his cruelty.

When the novel's scene shifts from England to Constantinople and the domination of the Sibyl by Apollo escalates into the language of racial genocide, many of the contradictions and anxieties submerged in the first volume become manifest. Shelley can now confront directly and in the most frightening terms Apollo's ruthless assault on difference and at the same time expose the self-serving representation that permits him to undertake such an action. Adrian's indoctrination of Lionel into the ethos of Western patriarchy seems benevolent enough to Lionel, despite the dichotomizing impulse that already implies a violence of which both characters seem unaware. The European's perception of the Greco-

Turkish war as a struggle between light and darkness, civilization and barbarism, on the other hand, can disguise neither the viciousness of the Greek army nor the less than altruistic motives of European economic power. Shelley could not put the latter more baldly: "Their extensive commercial relations gave every European nation an interest in [Greek] success" (115). *The Last Man* is never particularly favorable to the Moslems; even when Shelley preaches sympathetic identification, she does so through the discourse of an ethnocentrism she herself cannot escape. But her open criticism of the Greek cause and its supporters undermines the language of hierarchy necessary to the European rationalization of domination. In Adrian's report upon returning to England from the front, any idealization of European motives swiftly collapses.

> "I shall not be suspected of being averse to the Greek cause; I know and feel its necessity; it is beyond every other a good cause. . . . But let us not deceive ourselves. The Turks are men; each fibre, each limb is as feeling as our own, and every spasm, be it mental or bodily, is as truly felt in a Turk's heart or brain, as in a Greek's. The last action at which I was present was the taking of ———. The Turks resisted to the last, the garrison perished on the ramparts, and we entered by assault. Every breathing creature within the walls was massacred. Think you, amidst the shrieks of violated innocence and helpless infancy, I did not feel in every nerve the cry of a fellow being? They were men and women, the sufferers, before they were Mahometans, and when they rise turbanless from the grave, in what except their good or evil actions will they be the better or worse than we? Two soldiers contended for a girl, whose rich dress and extreme beauty excited the brutal appetites of these wretches, who, perhaps good men among their families, were changed by the fury of the moment into incarnated evils. An old man, with a silver beard, decrepid and bald, he might be her grandfather, interposed to save her; the battle axe of one of them clove his skull." (116)

Shelley's sympathy cannot overcome her bias: the Moslems were human only before they became Moslems and they rise to a patently Christian version of transcendence only after they shed their cultural specificity (they rise "turbanless"). Still, the presupposed hierarchy between civilization and barbarism largely dissolves in this picture of shared brutality and suffering. I quote this passage in full, however, not to foreground the obvious contradiction between Greek savagery and Greek ideals, but to show how Shelley aligns this image of military coercion with the abuse of masculine sexual power. The atrocities of war constitute a conventional literary theme that does not touch Shelley closely. Describing these exceptional circumstances, she can represent indirectly what must remain silenced elsewhere: the violence done to women under peacetime conditions the patriarchy deems normative. Apollo's figurative rape of the Sibyl, the male possession of the other by force, becomes increasingly literalized in the passage as it advances toward the sexual assault of a Turkish girl by Greek soldiers. In a single moment, the patterns of sexual and racial domination merge, and Shelley continues to superimpose them more and more explicitly as the second volume moves toward the siege of Constantinople.

"When '*The* Repressed' of their culture and their society come back, it is an explosive return, which is *absolutely* shattering, staggering, overturning, with a force never let loose before."[35] The siege of Constantinople marks the thematic pivot in *The Last Man* from the forms of repression to the return of the repressed. If racial domination allows Shelley to say what she could not say about sexual domination, it also pressures her to imagine a stunning reversal of that domination. In a nearly transparent gender allegory that draws heavily on literary convention, Constantinople becomes feminine—"Our army looked on her as certain prey" (133)—and Raymond becomes the embodiment of the violent male ego, bent on transgression and appropriation of the sexual other— "pointing . . . his sword to the gates" and urging his soldiers to "force the gate; enter and possess" (139). Yet in this case, Raymond's desire to erect an everlasting monument to his fame, to plant the cross on St. Sophia, as he puts it, meets with a misfortune that subverts both martial and phallic power. Constantinople, Raymond finds, is plague-ridden and deserted. Unable to convince the fearful Greeks to enter the city they have stormed, Raymond proceeds alone and encounters the fate Evadne had prophesied: fire and plague. In a scene of gothic excess, he disappears amid explosions and flames that level the already depopulated city. Shelley's most revealing critique of male conquest, however, appears later, when Lionel enters the city to search for Raymond. After hours of futile and exhausting effort, he falls asleep and dreams Raymond's real destiny: "To my diseased fancy . . . my friend's shape, altered by a thousand distortions, expanded into a gigantic phantom, bearing on its brow the sign of pestilence. The growing shadow rose and rose, filling, and then seeming to endeavour to burst beyond, the adamantine vault that bent over, sustaining and enclosing the world. The night-mare became torture" (146). Plague, the feminine force that from this moment usurps the novel, possesses Raymond with all the appropriate fury of a venereal disease, or more accurately, of an irreversible tumescence. Through the plague, Raymond cannot escape a literal identification with the violent phallus; he becomes the victim of his own erection gone mad, his own sexual self-inflation pushed to its logical consequence, pushed to the point of explosion. In Shelley's sudden and perfect rever-

[35] Cixous, "Sorties," 95.

sal of domination (both racial and sexual), the impulse toward aggressive expansion ends in an annihilation too horrible for Lionel to envision ("with a strong effort I threw off sleep, and recalled reason" [146]). In gothic and visionary form, Raymond is the first plague victim encountered in the novel; the grotesque, parodic nature of his demise indicates a measure of revenge—the revenge of the violated other against the male's self-image.

Ironies more numerous than I can discuss here mark the plague's reversal and ultimate devastation of the patriarchal order. If economic self-interest informed the English representation of the Greeks as the bearers of civilization, the plague undermines commerce and renders its power concerns nil: "Bankers, merchants, and manufacturers . . . became bankrupt" (169–70); put simply, they lose their markets. The imperialist motive of extending trade through colonization becomes another target of the disease. "Even the source of colonies was dried up, for in New Holland, Van Dieman's Land, and the Cape of Good Hope, plague raged" (170). The repressed of the culture literally return when thousands of immigrants inundate Europe. For a period, England remains untouched, protected by the natural barrier between it and the continent, but the plague soon crosses the Channel. The English must flee their island as the Moslems fled Constantinople. The two cultures, dichotomized by the European mind as self and other, intellect and animal, become mirror images: "Hemmed in by [the ocean's] gulphs, we [the English] shall die like the famished inhabitants of a besieged town" (180). The point here is that the movements of the plague are directed against the specific forms of cultural hegemony established in the first half of *The Last Man*. When the plague explodes, introduced by Raymond's rape/siege of Constantinople, it appears with unanticipated violence. Only in the unrecorded leaves of the Sibyl's prophecies, which Percy Shelley could not read, and in the unrepentant madness of Evadne, which neither Raymond nor Adrian could contain, does one find even a suggestion of the annihilatory force that, once released, consumes all. Every event in the novel has its source in the Sibyl; every aspect of its tale emerges from her cavern of subjugation beneath Apollo's temple, whether she mouths the masculine justification of that arrangement or whether she finally allows her pain to speak.

Beyond Man and Humanism; or, The Last Man, at Last

Is an apocalyptic novel an oxymoron or, put another way, does this hybrid genre—at least in Mary Shelley's circumstances—consist of an ideological contradiction in terms, one that marks a limit to apocalyptic literature and in fact envisions, ironically, something like an end of apocalypse altogether? Genre, as writers from Bakhtin to Jameson argue, is deeply ideological, and historically, nothing could be more the case than with the Shelleys, where husband and wife abided by a gender division of literary labor that mirrored power relations in the culture at large. There is nothing intrinsically feminine about the novel, just as there is nothing intrinsically masculine about poetry, but as they were perceived and practiced in the early nineteenth century, these genres took on associations of gender and hierarchy.[36] Although such divisions were hardly absolute in England, they were for a variety of reasons definitive in the expatriate Shelley household, where Mary Shelley wrote fiction for the public and Percy Shelley verse. When, after her husband's death, Shelley began a novel about apocalypse, she not only entered a literary form traditionally associated with the sublimity of poetry but she subjected it to a discourse seemingly incompatible with it. Novelistic discourse infects apocalypse somewhat like the plague. In fact, *The Last Man* creates an association between disease and narrative language; the plague that consumes the second half of the novel can be seen as the novel's nullification of patriarchal literary privileges. The intersection of these imperatives gets expressed in a remarkable passage from *The Last Man:* "Once it was so; now is man lord of the creation? Look at him—ha! I see plague! She has invested his form, is incarnate in his flesh, has entwined herself with his being, and blinds his heaven-seeking eyes" (229–30). At this point in the novel, the plague has entered what used to be called "the human condition" and reversed its patriarchal dreams of transcendence, which can be taken to mean in various ways that difference now occupies the site of identity: the feminine has entered the masculine, matters of the body have entered man's self-image (his vision of himself, the platonic "form" he sees with "heaven-seeking eyes"), and the feminized language of the novel has entered that most masculine of literary genres, *his* form, the apocalypse. Does this horrific quotation

---

[36] Even in such a central work as *The Rise of the Novel* (Berkeley: University of California Press, 1957), Ian Watt can state of Jane Austen that "the feminine sensibility was in some ways better equipped to reveal the intricacies of personal relationships and was therefore at a real advantage in the realm of the novel" (298). This naturalization of the novel's femininity accompanied a dramatic increase in the production of domestic fiction by, for, and about women and, according to Nancy Armstrong, had little to do with women's sensibilities and much to do with historical and social changes. "It can hardly be accidental . . . that novels dealing primarily with sexual relations—with the vicissitudes of courtship and domestic life—should become a major literary genre at precisely the time in history when the work unit and the family unit could no longer be considered identical." "The Rise of Feminine Authority in the Novel," as her title puts it, functioned to naturalize the growing division between private and public life in capitalist society, to represent that division as if it were as natural as the division between the sexes was assumed to be. *Novel* 15 (1982): 129.

contain a subtext of pleasure, almost glee ("Ha! I see plague!"), so that the title of this dystopian novel might seem to harbor a utopian wish? The last man, good riddance! Frank Lentricchia has implied as much about *No Man's Land,* the title of Gilbert and Gubar's ongoing investigation into twentieth-century literature in English by women.[37]

This last point leads to a second question, one that complicates the first, since patriarchy in its various guises might not be as easily if spectacularly dispensed with as annihilation by plague suggests. If the novel does subvert apocalyptic discourse, rendering it vulnerable to a terminal illness, can we extend this subversion beyond the level of authorial intention, which the terms of the last paragraph imply? Toward the end of the previous section, I read the plague as a form of literary revenge, an allegory that enacts Shelley's indignation at the patriarchal formations of self, gender, and language. Such allegorizing is unavoidable to some extent, perhaps, and I believe it explains a great deal about the camouflaged resentment and symbolic violence that make the writing of this novel a covert and conflicted but ultimately deliberate feminist act. To *limit* my interpretation of the plague, however, to Shelley's revenge plot against patriarchy, an interpretation constrained by ideas of intentionality and individual genius, would threaten to restore naively apocalyptic assumptions to a novel that disables them. As discussed, the central irony of the visions of the end of consciousness in the "Last Man" poems is that they recuperate the security and the integrity of the patriarchal ego. To attempt to exhaust the feminist possibilities of Shelley's novel by recourse to the author herself is to risk repeating this critical gesture in a different key. In reading a novel that represents the end of the humanist subject, we would end by honoring Shelley's triumphant subjectivity. This contradiction is not debilitating; as I hope already to have demonstrated, Shelley's critique of the patriarchy is powerful and valuable in itself, and her resistance to the internalization of its values is moving. This author deserves to be honored. At the same time, however, I want to look past this type of feminist interpretation to argue that the very language of this novel, given the ideological valence of the genre in the early nineteenth century, begins to block any return to humanist configurations of the subject, configurations that to some degree simply relocate the essence of such subjectivity from "man" to "woman." Although Shelley writes this language, she does not command it; it writes her as much as she writes it. The chal-

---

[37] Gilbert and Gubar have denied Lentricchia's charges of essentialism and separatism. The overheated debate has been played out in the pages of *Critical Inquiry;* see especially Frank Lentricchia, "Patriarchy against Itself," *Critical Inquiry* 13 (1987): 775, and Sandra M. Gilbert and Susan Gubar, "The Man on the Dump versus the United Dames of America," *Critical Inquiry* 14 (1988): 389.

lenge is to account for that dimension of the novel's feminism which is not reducible in any simple way to authorial intention.

Novelistic Subversion

In the year before Shelley began *The Last Man,* she spent much of her time gathering her husband's unpublished poetry and prose for the volumes she hoped would secure his fame, the volumes Sir Timothy ultimately suppressed. In this process she edited the notebook manuscript that eventually became "A Defence of Poetry" and encountered a passage that at once implicitly disparages her work as a novelist and confirms what was becoming a widespread cultural norm.

> A poem is the very image of life expressed in its eternal truth. There is this difference between a story and a poem, that a story is a catalogue of detached facts, which have no other bond of connexion than time, place, circumstance, cause and effect; the other is the creation of actions according to the unchangeable forms of human nature, as existing in the mind of the creator, which is itself the image of all other minds. The one is partial, and applies only to a definite period of time, and a certain combination of events which can never again recur; the other is universal, and contains within itself the germ of a relation to whatever motives or actions have place in the possible varieties of human nature. . . . The story of particular facts is as a mirror which obscures and distorts that which should be beautiful: Poetry is a mirror which makes beautiful that which is distorted.[38]

This passage maps out a set of dichotomous terms that explicitly subordinate narrative to non-narrative poetic form: poetry is eternal, unchangeable, universal, a creation, truth, and related to wish fulfillment ("that which *should be* beautiful"); the story is temporally and spatially located, particular, a catalogue, distortion, and related to a reality principle ("that which *is* distorted"). Jay Clayton has reminded us that this judgment and the privileging of poetry that accompanies it were commonplace when Percy wrote "A Defence." For many romantic poets, he suggests, the very "sequence of a story often seems hostile to the freedom of the visionary imagination." Coleridge, to provide just one instance, feared that Southey would "rely too much on *story* and *event* in his poems, to the neglect of those *lofty imaginings,* that are peculiar to, and definitive of, the poet."[39] To return to "A Defence," although gender is

---

[38] *Shelley's Poetry and Prose,* 485.
[39] Jay Clayton, *Romantic Vision and the Novel* (Cambridge: Cambridge University Press, 1987), 12. In *Words and* The Word (Cambridge: Cambridge University Press, 1986),

effaced entirely from this conventional hierarchy of genres, the fact remains that in practice Percy wrote one way and his wife another; within their own relationship, this rivalry between discourses was underscored by sexual difference and an asymmetry of power. One need only remember the preface to the 1818 *Frankenstein,* in which Percy usurped his wife's voice, writing it as if he were she, to recognize that this genre competition could be painfully humbling for her: "I have thus endeavoured to preserve the truth of the elementary principles of human nature, while I have not scrupled to innovate upon their combinations. The *Iliad,* the tragic poetry of Greece,—Shakespeare, in the *Tempest* and *Midsummer Night's Dream,*—and most especially Milton, in *Paradise Lost,* conform to this rule; and the most humble novelist, who seeks to confer or receive amusement from his labours, may, without presumption, apply to prose fiction a license, or rather a rule, from the adoption of which so many exquisite combinations of human feeling have resulted in the highest specimens of poetry." Deference to the canon of Western male poets is not unusual for the author of "Adonais," but here Percy subordinates his wife's literary form to his own at the very moment he presumes to speak for her. "Prose fiction" succeeds to the extent that it suppresses its generic difference, conforms to standards set by "the highest specimens of poetry," and, as he later puts it in the same preface, avoids "the enervating effects of the novels of the present day," novels largely written by women.[40]

Two other suggestions in the passage from the "Defence" reinforce unspoken assumptions about gender, the first of which can be identified briefly. Percy defines narrative as body-centered and poetry as mind- or spirit-centered. Because narrative consists of events that occur locally in time and space, it functions like a body; free from such contingency, poetry is immaterial, existing "in the mind," and is thus associated with "truth." Truth is the privilege of a discourse distanced from the body, a high cultural truism Irigaray preserves but revalues when she writes, "Truth is necessary for those who are so distanced from their body that they have forgotten it" (*TS,* 214).

Finally, the passage registers a tension between two modes of discourse, between two signifying practices that emerge into contradistinc-

---

Stephen Prickett shows that in eighteenth-century England and Germany poetry rose even further in prestige as it became linked, by Bishop Lowth and his followers, to biblical prophecy. As early as 1704, John Dennis had called poetry the natural language of religion. Prickett's summary is historically accurate and revealing: "The Bible was, therefore, to be treated as belonging to a higher, more sublime order of discourse than prose: an inferior and late medium fit only for describing the mundane and practical world of everyday affairs" (40).

[40] Mary Shelley, *Frankenstein,* ed. James Rieger (Chicago: University of Chicago Press, 1974), 6–7.

tion with the competition between poetry and the novel at this particular historical juncture. Poetry functions by privileging identity over difference, by establishing a relation of similarity between things: poetry "contains within itself the germ of a relation to whatever motives or actions have place in the possible varieties of human nature," or, from the paragraph which precedes this one in the "Defence": the poet's "words unveil the permanent analogy of things." Because a universal common denominator underlies the appearances of difference, poetry is associated with the rhetorical mode of substitution, where one thing bears essential relation to all others and so can properly stand for them, or represent them: "the mind of the creator . . . is itself the image of all other minds." Poetry, for Percy Shelley, is metaphor, and metaphor is Apollo's discourse, the vehicle of the imperial and patriarchal ego that assumes its authority to represent others. Narrative, on the other hand, privileges difference over identity ("applies only to a definite period of time," "a certain combination . . . which can never again recur"); as such, it signifies by means of "combination" rather than substitution, relating various things not by their essential sameness, their collapsible or interchangeable quality, but by their local, even accidental, relations of time and space, a procedure which respects the integrity of their differences. Narrative, for Percy, consists of the inferior trope of metonymy. Only recently has criticism begun to question the sharp distinction he draws here between metaphor and metonymy. Indeed, it now appears that these tropes are best defined not scientifically, according to intrinsic principles, but culturally, according to value-laden descriptions propagated in documents like "A Defence." By the time he could divide discourse along metaphoric and metonymic lines, a set of assumptions regarding poetry and prose narrative was already firmly in place, assumptions that remain relatively unchanged straight through Jakobson's clinical studies of aphasia in our own century. If the distinction between tropes now appears to have little empirical validity, for the Shelleys it already possessed a powerful cultural validity.[41]

To position *The Last Man* within this differentiation of genre and discourse is not a simple matter, since Shelley simultaneously emulates and resists her husband's principles. Even when she writes her own introduction to *Frankenstein* in 1831, Shelley reproduces the hierarchy

[41] Some critics, like David Lodge, have continued to make a division of tropes the basis of a literary typology. See especially Part II of his *Modes of Modern Writing* (Chicago: University of Chicago Press, 1977). Others, like Maria Ruegg, have called the very opposition between metaphor and metonymy into question: "If Jacobson's attempt to analyze language in terms of a simple binary rhetoric leads to logical inconsistencies, it is, first of all, because he treats what are in fact very subtle, and often undecidable *differences* between metaphor and metonymy, in terms of an absolute opposition." "Metaphor and Metonymy: The Logic of Structuralist Rhetoric," *Glyph* 6 (1979): 147.

her husband assumed when he originally wrote the preface. In fact, she *praises* him for being *unable* to write a story: Percy, she claims, was "more apt to embody ideas and sentiments in the radiance of brilliant imagery, and in the music of the most melodious verse that adorns our language, than to invent the machinery of a story" (*Frankenstein*, 225). It is hardly surprising, then, to find Lionel Verney in *The Last Man* apologetically labeling his narrative "a catalogue." The ravages of the plague threaten to reduce his story to "a mere catalogue of losses" (301), a compiling of the dead who share no other bond of connection than the metonymic circumstance of being on earth at the wrong time. From the moment the disease appears the novel can be nothing more than a "journal of death" (192), a record of the material body's inescapable contingencies. The plague, in fact, exaggerates the very conditions of narrative outlined by Percy, grounding the novel in bodies that stubbornly resist any universalizing transcendence. In a letter written shortly after finishing *The Last Man,* Shelley expressed frustration at her inability to reconcile an apocalyptic novel with the claims of an aesthetic norm (her husband's norm) based on apocalyptic poetry: "The curiosity excited by the title frightens me, because of the disappointment that must of course follow. You can form no idea of the difficulty of the subject—the necessity of making the scene ⟨general⟩ universal to all mankind and of combining this with a particular interest which must constitute the novel—If I had at the commencement fore seen the excessive trouble & then (much worse) the state of imperfection in which partly for want of time I was obliged to leave it—I should never have had the courage to begin" (*L*, 1.510). The novel (both *The Last Man* in particular and the genre as Shelley understands it) consists of particular interests, or as Percy puts it, the novel is "partial," its interests determined by the untranscended location of particular people in particular circumstances, and nothing could be more the case than in a novel whose primary narrative agency is the plague. Her sense of the work's failure derives not simply from an internalization of feminine humility, then, but from a recognition that the plague, body-centered and limited to narrative expression, prevents the novel from achieving the level of disembodied generality prescribed by her husband's poetics. After the plague enters the novel, the narrative pace becomes feverish, paralleling the speed with which the last half of the book was written (the haste which led to its "state of imperfection").[42]

---

[42] In February 1825, approximately one year into writing *The Last Man*, Shelley was still researching material for the first volume, asking Sir John Hobhouse to procure her an observation seat in parliament so that she could render more accurately the novel's political debates. If she wrote the novel in sequence, and we have no reason to believe otherwise, it took her less than a year to write the last two volumes, both of which are given over almost entirely to the plague.

The plague, in other words, takes over the novel, working against any capitulation to proper aesthetics and making it impossible for Shelley to write a novel that reads like poetry. And by asserting the intractable priority of narrative, the plague undermines the basis of poetry's alleged superiority and its claim to transcendence.

The first time Lionel encounters an actual victim of the plague, the corpse bears the inscription that gradually becomes the signature of the disease: "This indeed was the plague. . . . rigid limbs, . . . distortion of his face . . . and the stony eyes lost to perception" (187). The last phrase is perhaps most typical, indicating that the plague operates by materialization, by repossessing the body as an untranscendable ground of existence. The eye, the faculty of vision central to the patriarchal and apocalyptic conception of the subject, the trope of an immaterial essence, consciousness, gets reduced to stone, so that the plague in this novel acts somewhat like the feminist rhetorical strategy Margaret Homans calls literalization: it strains to reduce an abstract metaphorical relation characteristic of the patriarchy (I/eye) to a more material component—here, a deadened, merely physiological eye. The description as a whole repeats this movement; it reduces the organic unity of the individual person to a field of component body parts. In many representations of the plague's work, Shelley lingers on a kind of rhetorical dismemberment, what we might call the body's revenge against consciousness-raising. When Lionel himself contracts the disease, he provides the only interior account of the symptoms, which manifest themselves as a disengaging, a separating out of the minute, individual parts of his body: "My eyes were bloodshot, starting from my head; every artery beat, methought, audibly, every muscle throbbed, each single nerve felt" (247). This anatomical splintering in turn has its correlative in the work of the sentence—which is itself rhetorically fragmented, disjointed, and staccato in effect—so that the plague, in one of the crucial features of the novel, constitutes form as well as content, as if it had a linguistic as well as a purely physical, pathological existence.

Almost from its introduction, the plague and the novel—or I should say, the plague and the language of the novel—become analogous, sometimes even indistinguishable. It is difficult to determine whether the novel represents the plague or the plague represents the novel. The disease reduces the individual to the body, but it also reduces language to the component parts of its body, enacting a recalcitrance of the signifier, what de Man calls "the prosaic materiality of the letter." This phrase appears in de Man's reading of Kant's third *Critique*, where he locates the moments in which Kant foregrounds a "nonteleological apprehension of nature," a concentration on scraps of the material world that cannot be gathered up in the cognitive processes on which aesthetic judgment depends. These moments, de Man then argues, correspond to a resistance in Kant's linguistic medium itself: "To the dismemberment of the body corresponds a dismemberment of language, as meaning-producing tropes are replaced by the fragmentation of sentences and propositions into discrete words, or the fragmentation of words into syllables or finally letters."[43] In *The Last Man*, the plague serves both processes of dismemberment, marking their intersection. From the moment it is first mentioned in the novel, the plague is so obsessively identified with words and, more specifically, with the material aspect of language that the two become virtually the same thing. "One word," states Lionel in the novel's first direct reference to the disease, "had alarmed her more than battles or sieges. . . . That word, as yet it was not more to her, was PLAGUE" (127). These sentences prepare us to associate the plague with a semantic unit, the word, but when that word finally appears at the end of the sequence, its unusual graphic representation, all capitals, calls attention instead to the form of the letters themselves, the material status of printed marks on a page which constitute the irreducible components of writing. Unlike any other word in the text, *plague* frequently appears in a form that brackets its graphic component, whether it is printed in capitals as above or in italics or set off in quotation marks. When the plague infects writing, language undergoes both materialization and dismemberment; language becomes print, with graphemes seeming to separate out like the single nerves of the plague victim, each taking on an independent existence that resists being totalized into organic units. When the British press first acknowledges that the plague has entered Europe, Lionel describes the effect in a startling passage: "Before it had been a rumour; but now in words uneraseable, in definite and undeniable print, the knowledge went forth. Its obscurity of situation [off the front page] rendered it the more conspicuous: the diminutive letters grew gigantic to the bewildered eye of fear: they seemed graven with a pen of iron, impressed by fire, woven in the clouds, stamped on the very front of the universe" (171). Dimunitive letters grow gigantic as the material basis of language (always visible but so often disregarded) becomes grotesquely and threateningly foregrounded. Again, Shelley's figurative language strains toward a literalization of the print medium. Printed marks, not words or sentences, are physically produced (engraved, impressed, woven, and stamped), they consist of material elements (iron, fire, and clouds), and in their dismembered state they possess an undeniable, unabstractable material body.[44]

---

[43] Paul de Man, "Phenomenality and Materiality in Kant," in *Hermeneutics: Questions and Prospects,* ed. Gary Shapiro and Alan Sica (Amherst: University of Massachusetts Press, 1984), 143–44.

[44] This dismemberment of language is fundamentally counterapocalyptic because it resists the illusion of wholeness that the projection of an ending allows. It demands in place

Touched by the plague, speech suffers similar results: "In answer to our eager questions, one word alone fell, as it were involuntarily, from his convulsed lips: *The Plague*"; a moment after this character has voiced his fear, Lionel reports that "these words were *syllabled* trembling by the iron man" (175; my emphasis). As the letter is to writing so the syllable is to dismembered speech. In *The Last Man*, words, in fact, syllables, become agents independent of human will; they emerge involuntarily, displacing consciousness in effect with language, with language *as* the plague. The plague-letter enters the person and the possibility of the individual subject who commands his or her discourse ceases, the events occurring simultaneously: "The man to whom I spoke, uttered the word 'plague,' and fell at my feet in convulsions; he also was infected" (292).

Such a reading of the plague, to go one step further, cannot be reduced in any simple way to Shelley's deliberate strategy, since to carry the novel's erasure of individual subjectivity to its logical conclusion means extending it to the author herself. *The Last Man*, in other words, anticipates the death of its own author. And by doing so, it resists any critical reading that implies a metaphysics of the self complicit in patriarchal culture. Toril Moi has recently taken some feminist criticism to task for uncritically reproducing certain humanist assumptions, primarily for relying "on the author as the transcendental signified of . . . her text."[45] Mary Jacobus, lamenting the tendency of some readings to assume "an unbroken continuity between 'life' and 'text,'" similarly argues that "feminist interpretations such as these have no option but to posit the woman author as the origin and her life as the primary locus of meaning."[46] In Mary Shelley's case, this is anything but a simple issue; her novels demand a feminist criticism that simultaneously makes her authorship central *and* begins to look past it. To minimize Shelley's importance—or to efface her from her novels altogether—is to repeat the patronizing critical gesture that doomed her to marginalization in the first place. Throughout her critical reception, Shelley has been dismissed precisely for *not* being the origin of her texts' meanings, for merely translating the ideas of others (men). "All Mrs. Shelley did," argues Mario Praz, "was to provide a passive reflection of some of the wild fantasies which, as it were, hung in the air about her."[47] Sylva

---

of that formalism the kind of disarticulation Irigaray has called for as part of the feminist project: "We need to proceed in such a way that linear reading is no longer possible: that is, the retroactive impact of the end of each word, utterance, or sentence upon its beginning must be taken into consideration in order to undo the power of its teleological effect" (*TS*, 80).

[45] Moi, *Sexual/Textual Politics*, 61–62.

[46] Mary Jacobus, "Is There a Woman in This Text?" *New Literary History* 14 (1982): 138.

[47] Mario Praz, *Romantic Agony*, trans. Angus Davidson (London: Oxford University Press, 1933), 114.

Norman writes that Shelley "was seeking all her life for subjects she could translate with no profound gestation into the required story."[48] Even the standard edition of *Frankenstein* places unusual emphasis on Percy's assistance in the novel's production; James Rieger defends his decision to print the 1818 version of the novel instead of Mary Shelley's later revision in part because he believes it includes more of Percy's influence. "In accepting final revisions as binding, an editor must also assume that there is a single author. What happens when there are two? Percy Bysshe Shelley worked on *Frankenstein* at every stage. . . . We know that he was more than an editor. Should we grant him the status of minor collaborator? Do we or do we not owe him a measure of 'final authority'?" (*Frankenstein*, xliv). One consequence of Rieger's affirmative answer to these questions is that he must print Shelley's 1831 introduction *after* the text of the novel, while Percy's preface remains in its original position, still able to mediate the reading that follows.[49] My point is that interpretations which locate the source of feminist resistance in Shelley's own literary strategies serve a necessary and immediate political function; they acknowledge that Shelley wrote independently and brilliantly in difficult circumstances, and thus they substantiate the very possibility of such action. At the same time, however, to restrict feminist criticism to an affirmation of authentic and individual subjectivity is to become, like the "Last Man" poets, more deeply entangled in the logic of plagiarism, turning language, the literary text, into the private property one must jealously guard in order to preserve a fantasia of individual authority and autonomy. One can and must redeem Shelley from implicit charges of plagiarism by defending her striking originality, but one must also do so by removing her altogether from terms like *originality* and *plagiarism,* by calling into question the values that sustain this policing function in the first place.

Apocalypse, Plague, and Narrative Contagion

To argue that *The Last Man* thematizes its own language in the form of the plague does not automatically free the text from humanist assumptions, even though the story of that freedom is literally the novel's utopian narrative content (the story of the end of "man"). As long as the plague's subversive work is confined to assumptions of intention, it is both feminist and still dependent on the patriarchal definition of the subject. An alternative reading might already seem implicit in the

---

[48] Sylva Norman, "Mary Wollstonecraft Shelley," in *Romantic Rebels*, ed. Kenneth Neill Cameron (Cambridge: Harvard University Press, 1973), 72.

[49] I owe these insights into the unintended implications of this edition of *Frankenstein* to Michael Cudahy.

plague's representation of the convergence of body and language, so that its self-reflexiveness displays the material rather than the cognitive or expressive status of language. This de Manian materialism of the signifier, however, plays Scylla to the Charybdis of feminist essentialism, and is in fact an essentialism of its own; it has the advantage of separating language from the command of individual subjectivity, but by reducing language to a body uninfluenced by ideology, a permanent, material ground removed from the conflicts of history, it records an impulse as suspiciously ahistorical as that which seeks to reduce language to the expression of an individual subject. Indeed, de Man's essay, "Phenomenality and Materiality in Kant," which declares that the "prosaic materiality of the letter" is "the bottom line" (or the body line) of language, explicitly sets out to subordinate ideology to materiality, the latter containing the former rather than the other way around. Objecting to a variety of body-centered critical theories, Fredric Jameson has recently cited as particularly troublesome the collapsing of "historical materialism" into the all-purpose term "materialism" with its suggestion of a "determinism by the body": "the drawback of the word 'materialism' is that it tends to suggest that only one form of dialectical reversal—the overthrow of idealism by materialism or a recall to matter—is at work."[50] In a slightly different register, "the prosaic materiality of the letter" is mistaken for the essence of a body without history, not print but an unproduced letter. In *The Last Man*, however, the plague does not merely represent a simple reversal of body and spirit, a recall to matter, just as it does not end with a reversal of the patriarchy that reintroduces the centered self in feminine disguise. Reducible to neither body nor subject, language in the novel, as it is thematized by the plague, represents a kind of discourse, a cultural practice deeply involved with the body, but concerned more with how it is represented than with any material reality beyond representation.

In a commonplace trope important to *The Last Man*, what matters is how the plague gets "communicated." When Percy Shelley describes a story as a "catalogue of detached facts, which have no other bond of connexion than time, place, circumstance, cause and effect," he understands metonymy to be the enabling condition of narrative, the verbal capacity to represent a horizontal sequence, to organize elements by their spatial and temporal contiguity. "Prose," says Jakobson in his important essay on metaphor and metonymy, "is forwarded essentially by contiguity."[51] In the context of *The Last Man*, he might as well have said "plague" instead of "prose." Narrative discourse moves by touch, by

---

[50] Fredric Jameson, "Architecture and the Critique of Ideology," in his *Ideologies of Theory* (Minneapolis: University of Minnesota Press, 1988), 2:42.

[51] Roman Jakobson, "Two Aspects of Language and Two Types of Aphasic Disturbances," in his *Fundamentals of Language* (The Hague: Mouton, 1975), 96.

contagion as it were; it "spreads." It can infect (or represent) only those things that come in contact, that share a border of "circumstance," a bond of time or space that defines relationship on the basis of accident, contingency, difference. In the governing logic of early nineteenth-century aesthetics, a logic that anticipates Jakobson himself, narrative remains inexorably local; the sum of its possible movements, as Percy argued, is contained within the field of accident, the grid of temporal and spatial contiguity; within narrative so defined there is no position that transcends this field, no essential or necessary relationship underlying the arbitrary proximity of different things that allows for the escape of a universal. In *The Last Man,* the plague violently maps such a narrative field; infecting everything human that it touches as it moves across the surface of the globe, the epidemic makes visible the extensive network of contiguous relationships until *that,* paradoxically, becomes the only condition one might call universal.

Artaud believed the plague was communicated by thought; he took the medical fact that not a single case recorded infection by contact to indicate the immaterial nature of the disease, its occurrence by phenomenological necessity.[52] By 1824, Shelley knew that "the plague was not what is commonly called contagious" (167); the novel consistently attributes fear of infection by contact to superstition. Just as often, however, it yields to that very superstition. As the novel progresses, it becomes impossible for Shelley, despite the evidence of science, to imagine the plague spreading by anything other than the contiguity that defines both contagion and narrative discourse: "Beside the yet warm corpse the mourner was stretched" (170). In one of the master tropes governing its representation, the plague becomes the hand that touches, whether this is expressed directly—the plague as the "palsying hand" (176)—or by extension through the metaphor of the hand-grasped weapon: victims "fell like ripe corn before the merciless sickle of the adversary"; there was no "guarding against the innumerable arrows of the plague" (161). This figural pattern is then complemented by numerous narrative episodes where touch in one form or another transmits the epidemic.

There are moments in *The Last Man,* particularly after the introduction of the plague, where the narrative seems a parodic exaggeration of Percy's description of a story, stringing along its events in a "catalogue of detached facts." In these passages narrative contiguity gets foregrounded to such an extent that the underlying assumptions regarding the metonymic base of novelistic discourse become absurdly visible. An

---

[52] "From all this emerges the spiritual physiognomy of a disease whose laws cannot be precisely defined and whose geographical origin it would be idiotic to attempt to determine." Antonin Artaud, *The Theatre and Its Double* (New York: Grove, 1958), 22.

excursion to London, for instance, becomes the occasion to discover the devastating effects of the plague but also to uncover the workings of narrative: "I had come to London" (201); "I was now in Holborn" (201); "We were set down at St. Bartholomew's" (202); "I rambled on. . . . [S]uddenly I found myself before Drury Lane Theater" (203); "I ran on at my utmost speed until I found myself I knew not how, close to Westminster Abbey" (205). The sensationalist nightmare of plague-ridden London indicates as much about form as it does about content; it exposes the dominance of contiguous relationship in representational discourse. Each of these phrases, at or near the beginning of a paragraph, marks the confinement of narrative movement to a local field of circumstance, to progress by contact. Immediately following this catalogue of disasters organized primarily by space (London), Lionel turns, in this relentlessly episodic novel, to a catalogue of disasters organized by time: "One day, it was the ninth of September, seemed devoted to every disaster" (207). In this grouping, one particular tale seems to confirm inescapably that the plague is contagious, and by implication, that it involves the principle of metonymic association itself. Having heard that the plague had reached her neighborhood, an elderly woman "barred her door, and closed her casement, refusing to communicate with any" (207). No contact, no plague: the woman, with a self-imposed quarantine that forbids even the exchange of words, is apparently deluded by superstition. One night, however, her regular foraging for provisions leads her to a cornfield, where she collapses with fatigue. By chance she finds herself lying next to a plague victim, still alive, and still able to bridge the remaining distance between them by touch:

> Her hand was seized with a convulsive violence that made the grasp feel like iron, the fingers like the keen teeth of a trap,—'At last you are come!' were the words given forth—but this exertion was the last effort of the dying—the joints relaxed, the figure fell prostrate, one low moan, the last, marked the moment of death. Morning broke; and the old woman saw the corpse, marked with the fatal disease, close to her; her wrist livid with the hold loosened by death. She felt struck by the plague. . . . [S]till she clung to life, and lamented her mischance with cries and hideous groans; while the swift advance of the disease shewed, what proved to be the fact, that she could not survive many hours. (208)

Within the logic of this novel, contagion has a reality beyond superstition; the plague, passed by the hand, is more faithful to the function of metonymic discourse than to the medical profile of disease. The novel simply cannot represent the plague without at the same time representing its own discursive practice. The only narrative relation between the

London episode and this tale of the old woman is their textual contiguity, but that in itself seems more to the point than an argument of arbitrary connection against it.

As the plague triumphs over "man," then, a type of discourse respecting the lateral and differential elements of representation begins to triumph over a host of patriarchal and humanist assumptions (presence, universality, transcendence, truth) erected on the vertical dimension of language (substitution, metaphor, semantics). In the nineteenth century generally, and in Shelley's household in particular, that horizontal discourse was understood to be prose fiction, a genre culturally marked and subordinated as feminine. When *The Last Man* hyperbolically foregrounds its narrative discourse, when it makes its narrative progress indistinguishable from the progress of the plague itself, and most important, when it invariably personifies the plague as a feminine force, it anticipates an end to both patriarchal and generic hierarchies. The novelistic plague is a distinctly feminine monster. If this novel imagines the end of apocalypse, the end of the Logos with its economy of the same and the beginning of a discourse constituted by difference—by social, historical, and sexual contingencies—it does so not simply as an intentional act but by the ideological valences of genre itself. As a utopian agent latent within the culturally constructed form of the novel, the plague enacts an erasure of individual patriarchal identity and its displacement by a discourse of difference. The plague forces us to take the implications of the "feminine" novel seriously, forces us to see it as the harbinger of an alternative linguistic practice, and beyond that, as an imperfect allegory of social relations that do not yet exist. In this sense, the plague is purely utopian—a wishful negation of the patriarchal powers that be and, at the same time, a searching attempt to represent that which might supersede our given culture.

When the plague passes violently beyond man and humanism, the result cannot but look monstrous. The as yet unnamable can emerge "only under the species of the non-species, in the formless, mute, infant, and terrifying form of monstrosity."[53] This apocalyptic conclusion to an essay by Derrida seems a pertinent gloss on a novel that imagines the end of man, the end of his dream of apocalypse, and in so doing imagines the emergence of a heterogeneous discourse at once frightening, de-forming, and perhaps distantly empowering. In terms of gender, monstrosity might simply be the patriarchy's word for those threatening values projected onto metonymy, not the least of which is the opening up of language to the competing claims of differently located speakers.

[53] Jacques Derrida, "Structure, Sign and Play in the Discourse of the Human Sciences," in *Writing and Difference* (Chicago: University of Chicago Press, 1978), 293.

Perhaps this, rather than an inclination toward biological essentialism, accounts for the implicit valorization of metonymy in some French feminist writing, especially in Irigaray, where touch and contiguity continuously mark the intersection of sexual difference and difference in writing: "Woman 'touches herself' all the time, . . . for her genitals are formed of two lips in continuous contact. Thus within herself she is already two" (*TS*, 24)—or—"What she says is never identical with anything, moreover; rather, it is contiguous. *It touches (upon)*" (*TS*, 29). Monstrous to the patriarchy and its metaphors, metonymy seems to preclude the possibility of a monologic, self-authorizing discourse by localizing language, embedding it within context. Urging a shift from metaphorical to metonymic rhetoric in feminist discourse, Domna Stanton has contended that "the metonymic process would favor more concrete, contextual inscriptions of differences within/among women. Because of its association with contiguity . . . it exposes specific cultural values, prejudices and limitations."[54] Even Jakobson, in his quasi-scientific studies, observes a dialogic principle within metonymic discourse, something he saw in the verbal disabilities of aphasics but, ironically, something that also faintly shadows forth an enabling image of discursive health:

> For aphasics of the first type (selection deficiency), the context is the indispensable and decisive factor. When presented with scraps of words or sentences, such a patient readily completes them. His speech is merely reactive: he easily carries on conversation, but has difficulties in starting a dialogue; he is able to reply to a real or imaginary addresser when he is, or imagines himself to be, the addressee of the message. It is particularly hard for him to perform, or even to understand, such a closed discourse as the monologue. The more his utterances are dependent on the context, the better he copes with his verbal task. He feels unable to utter a sentence which responds neither to the cue of his interlocuter nor to the actual situation. The sentence "it rains" cannot be produced unless the utterer sees that it is actually raining.[55]

The decentered subject and her metonymic language proceed relationally or not at all; she cannot generate words that function as a sign of self-possession, autonomy, and individual authority; instead, she enters

[54] Domna Stanton's essay effectively critiques the use of the maternal metaphor in the writings of French feminists. She does, however, seem to overlook how Irigaray's use of tropes often enacts precisely the displacement from metaphor to metonymy for which Stanton herself calls. "Difference on Trial: A Critique of the Maternal Metaphor in Cixous, Irigaray, and Kristeva," in *The Poetics of Gender*, ed. Nancy K. Miller (New York: Columbia University Press, 1986), 175.

[55] Jakobson, "Two Aspects of Language," 77–78.

a discursive field already shot through by the ideological significations of others equally contextualized. Metonymic discourse, then, can serve as an emblem that revalues what in Western culture has so often been disparaged as the feminine multiplicity of voices. It marks the triumphant return of John's Babylon, Virgil's Rumor.

On a more immediate level, to reverse the hierarchy of cultural values inscribed within the distinction between metaphor and metonymy is to reveal more clearly the construction of Shelley's marginalization, since one can infer her lack of originality only out of a defensive stake in metaphor and its dream of an autonomous, universalizing subject. In the 1831 introduction to *Frankenstein*, an articulation of the conflicted assumptions that inform her writing, Shelley struggles with the idea of originality and at times strains past it toward a valorization of metonymy. Feminist critics have often and justly pointed to Shelley's aggressive defense of her integrity, her lack of debt—"I certainly did not owe the suggestion of one incident, nor scarcely of one train of feeling, to my husband" (*Frankenstein*, 229)—but this intellectual territorialism indicates the deepest influence of romantic ideology. I would turn instead to a contradictory passage. Just before her description of the Percy-Byron conversations that provided the subject for her novel, Shelley outlines the principles of a metonymic discourse and its mosaic subject that render a concern with originality insignificant: "Every thing must have a beginning, to speak in Sanchean phrase; and that beginning must be linked to something that went before. The Hindoos give the world an elephant to support it, but they make the elephant stand upon a tortoise. Invention, it must be humbly admitted, does not consist in creating out of void, but out of chaos; the materials must, in the first place, be afforded: it can give form to dark, shapeless substances, but cannot bring into being the substance itself" (*Frankenstein*, 226). One recalls Jakobson's patient for whom original words and autonomous subjectivity simply do not exist: "It is particularly hard for him to perform, or even to understand, such a closed discourse as the monologue. The more his utterances are dependent on the context, the better he copes with his verbal task."[56]

The Last Man ends, appropriately, with a reversal of the hopes that conclude Percy Shelley's most apocalyptic poem, "Adonais." While Percy,

[56] Writing on *Frankenstein*, Margaret Homans has suggested that we see Shelley's passivity, her lack of originality, her tendency to listen, as a deliberate and dialogic strategy: "It is part of the subtlety of her strategy to disguise her criticism of such works as a passive transcription, to appear to be a docile wife and 'devout listener' to the conversations of important men. Indeed, central to her critical method is the practice of acting out docilely what these men tell her they want from her, to show them the consequences of their desires." *Bearing the Word* (Chicago: University of Chicago Press, 1986), 116.

in an unabashedly autobiographical moment, wavers over the sublime terror of commitment to literary transcendence, the beckoning of the abode of the eternals, Lionel Verney sets sail, Homer and Shakespeare ironically in hand, hopelessly in search of a community that no longer exists. Literary eternity, it seems, has its limits. At this point, the plague has ended, but it has done its work, for "man" is no longer possible, fated to end with the death of Lionel himself. Now only discourse is possible; in the literal terms of the novel, Lionel's death leaves only the metonymic text he has written; narrative itself displaces the "human." This inverted apotheosis receives remarkable expression, aptly enough for an end-of-the-world novel, in the text's final sentence: "Thus around the shores of deserted earth, while the sun is high, and the moon waxes or wanes, angels, the spirits of the dead, and the ever-open eye of the Supreme, will behold the tiny bark, freighted with Verney—the LAST MAN" (p. 342). Lionel, the last vestige of atomized subjectivity, enters into the plague's order of metonymic signification; as his name is displaced by the capitals in the appositional designation, the LAST MAN, he gets written into the graphic status that has been the special province of the PLAGUE. Lionel dies into language, not into the canon as Adonais did but into the metonymy of the letter and its field of difference. The plague as a disease may end fifty pages before this novel's last word, but the PLAGUE as a discursive practice, a feminist practice, outlives the last man.

I began this section by asking whether Mary Shelley's apocalyptic novel is an oxymoron. Historically, metonymy and its expression in narrative were defined in terms so antithetical to the aestheticizing function of apocalypse, to the idea of a literary form that could displace and so terminate history, that the two cannot easily coexist in the same text. As I argued at the beginning of this book, the Book of Revelation can be read to imply a linguistic allegory whereby the promiscuity of tongues gets reduced to the unity of the Logos, a coercive transformation encoded in the defeat of the Whore of Babylon by the forces of Christ, the Word. Linguistic and sexual containment in this text are simultaneous; the feminine gets suppressed only to be recuperated in terms acceptable to the son/husband, only as it is reconstituted within the confines of the patriarchal marriage. Babylon must become the undeviating bride in white linen, Jerusalem. The silencing of the feminine voice, the silencing of the very possibility of linguistic heterogeneity, becomes the preliminary symbolic act necessary for language to transcend history, for words to enter the immaterial and universal condition of the New Jerusalem. The very possibility of interpretation, in fact, depends on this confrontation: for the text to become transparent the Whore must be understood and identified, removed from the contamination of "MYSTERY" or indeterminacy and brought into the sphere of monologic (or monogamous) meaning:

> Then one of the seven angels who had the seven bowls came and said to me, "Come, I will show you the judgment of the great harlot who is seated upon many waters."

> And I saw the woman, drunk with the blood of the saints and with the blood of the martyrs of Jesus.
> When I saw her I marveled greatly. But the angel said to me, "Why marvel? I will tell you the mystery of the woman, and of the beast with seven heads and ten horns that carries her. . . ."

> And he said to me, "The waters that you saw, where the harlot is seated, are peoples and multitudes and nations and tongues."
>   (Revelation 17:1, 6–7, 15)

The angel tells John how to read like a man—with confidence. One will remember that this passage, especially as it goes on to identify the Whore with Rome, played a central if not the central role in establishing a method of exegesis for Renaissance commentators. It reassured them that Revelation is a self-interpreting text, that because it provides its own hermeneutical key, the act of interpretation could become entirely intrinsic to the text, independent of contaminating, external influences, the merely relative contingencies of living in the world. In this way, the reading act reproduces the textual form; they are perfectly analogous: both, in a sense, end history and the linguistic limitations associated with it. Here is the fantasy of interpretation as the text's unmediated substitute, its double, its ideal metaphor. Is it surprising that Joseph Mede developed his influential method of apocalyptic criticism on the model of metaphor itself, proposing that we read the text's structure as a non-narrative series of substitutions, what he called synchronisms, whereby one textual event or series merely repeats another in analogous form? The suppression of temporality (history) that is the explicit end of the Apocalypse, which in turn is inseparable from the suppression of alternative voices concentrated in the image of the feminine, belongs to the linguistic order of metaphor. And this privileging of the association of apocalypse and metaphor has had a long life beyond Mede's theology, reflecting the depth of aesthetic assumptions and desires it encodes. Narrative is anathema to apocalypse: "Then I heard another voice from heaven saying, 'Come out of her, my people, lest you take part in her sins, lest you share in her *plagues*" (18:4).

In rewriting the Book of Revelation, *The Last Man* makes it impossible to remain free from contamination, free from the plagues of Babylon. The novel's distinctly feminine protagonist—the plague itself—thus marks the persistence of all that the Book of Revelation seeks to end apocalyptically: historical, sexual, and linguistic differences. But beyond its reversal of the patriarchal content of apocalypse, *The Last Man* assures that the literary *form* of apocalypse must remain a matter of ideological conflict, not a vehicle for the claim to transcend such conflict. By subjecting apocalypse to the requirements of narrative, and by exaggerating the effects of that generic difference, the novel indicates that literary form is itself a sign of historical content. In other words, it exposes the pretense of a privileged mode of apocalyptic representation, of a literary form that might transcend history, for all modes of representation have rivals; they are all inscribed by cultural circumstances that are never free of conflict. *The Last Man* tells us that even the voice from the place beyond history speaks the ideological words of a discourse within history. The very existence of an apocalyptic novel within romanticism reminds us that apocalypse is a site of struggle, not a position of strength from which one can authorize an end to conflict. This realization may not bear the subversive force that the plague possesses in the world of the novel; it may not be the catalyst of dramatic change. It merely suggests that the apocalyptic voice cannot be used to foreclose on the possibility of change. In this way, it participates fully in that romantic activity of still indeterminate consequences—unbuilding Jerusalem.

INDEX

Library of Congress Cataloging-in-Publication Data

Goldsmith, Steven, 1959–
    Unbuilding Jerusalem : apocalypse and romantic representation / Steven Goldsmith.
        p. cm.
    Includes bibliographical references and index.
    ISBN 0-8014-2717-7 (alk. paper). — ISBN 0-8014-9999-2 (pbk. : alk. paper)
    1. English literature—19th century—History and criticism.   2. English literature—
18th century—History and criticism.   3. Apocalyptic literature—History and criticism.
4. End of the world in literature.   5. Romanticism—Great Britain.   6. Prophecies in
literature.   7. Mimesis in literature.   8. Bible in literature.
I. Title.
PR468.A66G65   1993
820.9'38—dc20   92-27066